PAUL AND THE RESURRECTED BODY

EMORY STUDIES IN EARLY CHRISTIANITY

Vernon K. Robbins, General Editor
David B. Gowler, General Editor
Bart B. Bruehler, Associate Editor
Robert H. von Thaden Jr., Associate Editor
Juan Hernández Jr.
Susan E. Hylen
Brigitte Kahl
Mikeal C. Parsons
Russell B. Sisson
Shively T. J. Smith
Elaine M. Wainwright

Number 22

PAUL AND THE RESURRECTED BODY
Social Identity and Ethical Practice

Matt O'Reilly

SBL PRESS

Atlanta

Copyright © 2020 by Matt O'Reilly

Publication of this volume was made possible by the generous support of the Pierce Program in Religion of Oxford College of Emory University.

The editors of this series express their sincere gratitude to David E. Orton and Deo Publishing for publication of this series 2009–2013.

All rights reserved. No part of this work may be reproduced or transmitted in any form or by any means, electronic or mechanical, including photocopying and recording, or by means of any information storage or retrieval system, except as may be expressly permitted by the 1976 Copyright Act or in writing from the publisher. Requests for permission should be addressed in writing to the Rights and Permissions Office, SBL Press, 825 Houston Mill Road, Atlanta, GA 30329 USA.

Library of Congress Cataloging-in-Publication Data

Names: O'Reilly, Matt, Dr., author.
Title: Paul and the resurrected body : social identity and ethical practice / Matt O'Reilly.
Description: Atlanta : SBL Press, 2020. | Includes bibliographical references and index.
Identifiers: LCCN 2019059624 (print) | LCCN 2019059625 (ebook) | ISBN 9781628372762 (paperback) | ISBN 9780884144410 (hardback) | ISBN 9780884144427 (ebook)
Subjects: LCSH: Bible. Epistles of Paul—Socio-rhetorical criticism. | Resurrection—Biblical teaching. | Human body—Biblical teaching. | Identity (Psychology)—Biblical teaching
Classification: LCC BS2655.R35 O74 2020 (print) | LCC BS2655.R35 (ebook) | DDC 236/.8—dc23
LC record available at https://lccn.loc.gov/2019059624
LC ebook record available at https://lccn.loc.gov/2019059625

Cover design is an adaptation by Bernard Madden of Rick A. Robbins, Mixed Media (19" x 24" pen and ink on paper, 1981). Cover design used by permission of Deo Publishing.

Contents

Acknowledgments vii
Abbreviations ix

1. Questions, Context, and Method 1
   1.1. Speaking of Bodies   1
   1.2. The Body and the Future in the Greco-Roman World   4
   1.3. The Body in Pauline Scholarship   16
   1.4. The Body and the Future in Pauline Scholarship   24
   1.5. Methodological Considerations   30
   1.6. The Contribution of This Study   40

2. Embracing Resurrection: The Corinthian Correspondence 43
   2.1. First Corinthians   43
   2.2. Second Corinthians   109
   2.3. Conclusion   127

3. From Mortal Body to Redeemed Body: The Letter to
   the Romans 129
   3.1. Intragroup Conflict in Rome   130
   3.2. Romans as Deliberative Rhetoric   132
   3.3. Resurrection and the Rhetoric of Interrogation   134
   3.4. Resurrection, the Spirit, and the Hope of Creation   149
   3.5. Bodily Resurrection as Future Social Identity   157
   3.6. Table Fellowship as Bodily Practice   165
   3.7. Conclusion   169

4. Resurrection or Destruction? The Letter to the Philippians 171
   4.1. The Rhetorical Situation in Philippi   171
   4.2. Rhetoric and Social Identity   174

	4.3. The Deliberative Rhetoric of Philippians	175
	4.4. Bodily Resurrection in Philippians	178
	4.5. Future Social Identity and the Rhetoric of Contrast	183
	4.6. Bodies, Identity, and the Rhetoric of Example	191
	4.7. Conclusion	207
5.	The Body and the Future in the Letters of Paul	209
	5.1. Bodily Resurrection in Social Perspective	209
	5.2. Resurrection and the Rhetoric of Reconciliation	212
	5.3. Resurrection and the Suffering Body	213
	5.4. The Body and the Question of Perseverance	214
	5.5. Resurrection and Present Transformation	215
	5.6. Conclusion	216

Bibliography 217

Ancient Sources Index 237

Modern Authors Index 247

Acknowledgments

This book would not have been completed without contributions from a variety of people. First and foremost, I am unspeakably grateful to my wife, Naomi O'Reilly, for graciously encouraging and supporting me throughout the duration of this project. She self-sacrificially carried more than her share of family responsibilities during the many, many hours that I was engaged in research and writing. Without her steadfast encouragement and commitment, this book would not have reached publication. I dedicate it with love to her.

Words cannot adequately express my gratitude to Andrew T. Lincoln for his outstanding support of this project. He was always attentive both to the big picture and to the smallest detail. Without his guidance, this book would not have taken its present shape. I am likewise indebted to Ben Witherington for his support. His input was of inestimable value. He has been a mentor to me for more than a decade, and I cannot express the extent of my appreciation for the many kindnesses he has extended.

Philip Esler and Stephen Barton also gave the manuscript a thorough reading and offered incisive feedback that helped to strengthen it for publication. Though I do not know their names, I am indebted to the anonymous reviewers who read the manuscript and recommended it for publication. Their feedback was encouraging and, once again, served to buttress the overall argument. I offer my thanks to others who sacrificed time and energy to read portions of this study and provide useful comment. They include Gary Cockerill, Dean Flemming, and Carl Sweatman. I am also indebted to the members of the Saint Peter Fellowship of the Center for Pastor Theologians who read and offered constructive feedback on several chapters at a number of our fellowship gatherings. Others were kind to engage in conversation on various aspects of my research along the way including Adrian Long, Michael Halcomb, and Fredrick Long. Through the duration of this project, Jay Arnold encouraged me to pursue excellence in my research and challenged me to continually clarify and refine my thinking and writing. For his friendship and encouragement, I am exceedingly grateful.

It would have been altogether impossible to conduct this study without the cutting-edge research support provided by the excellent staff of the Information Commons and the B. L. Fisher Library at Asbury Theological Seminary. They are to be commended. I am grateful to the many members of my family who offered their encouragement and support. I am also grateful to the people of the churches I served during the research and writing of this book for allowing me to devote necessary time to study while also serving as their pastor.

The team at SBL Press is to be commended for the professionalism with which they have executed the publication of this volume. In his role as series editor, Vernon Robbins has wisely guided me through the process of preparing the book for publication. Nicole L. Tilford lent her judicious editorial eye to the manuscript and advanced it toward publication with grace and efficiency. Heather McMurray has been diligent and professional in her work on sales and marketing. I am deeply grateful to all of them. The shortcomings that remain are, of course, my responsibility.

Abbreviations

Primary Sources
1 En.	1 Enoch
2 Bar.	2 Baruch
3 Bar.	3 Baruch
Abr.	Philo, *De Abrahamo*
A.J.	Josephus, *Antiquitates judaicae*
Apoc. Mos.	Apocalypse of Moses
Apoc. Sedr.	Apocalypse of Sedrach
b.	Babylonian Talmud
B.J.	Josephus, *Bellum judaicum*
Cael.	Aristotle, *De caelo*
Con.	Demosthenes, *In Cononem*
Crat.	Plato, *Cratulus*
De an.	Aristotle, *De anima*
De or.	Cicero, *De oratore*
Det.	Philo, *Quod deterius potiori insidari soleat*
Diatr.	Epictetus, *Diatribai* (*Dissertationes*)
Ebr.	Philo, *De ebrietate*
Ep.	Demosthenes, *Epistulae*; Seneca (the Younger), *Epistulae morales*
Fug.	Philo, *De fuga et inventione*
Gen. Rab.	Genesis Rabbah
Gorg.	Plato, *Gorgias*
Her.	Philo, *Quis rerum divinarum heres sit*
Inst.	Quintilian, *Institutio oratoria*
Inv.	Cicero, *De invention rhetorica*
Jub.	Jubilees
Men.	Lucian, *Menippus* (*Necyomantia*)
Migr.	Philo, *De migratione Abrahami*
Nat.	Pliny the Elder, *Naturalis historia*

Nat. d.	Cicero, *De natura deorum*
[*Neaer.*]	Demosthenes, [*In Neaeram*]
Od.	Homer, *Odyssea*
Opif.	Philo, *De opificio mundi*
Orat.	Dio Chrysostom, *De virtue* (*Or. 8*)
Part. or.	Cicero, *Partitiones oratoriae*
Phaed.	Plato, *Phaedo*
Phaedr.	Plato, *Phaedrus*
Prog.	*Progymnasmata*
Ps.-Phoc.	Pseudo-Phocylides
Pss. Sol.	Psalms of Solomon
Rep.	Cicero, *De republica*
Resp.	Plato, *Respublica*
Rhet.	Aristotle, *Rhetorica*
Rhet. Her.	Rhetorica ad Herennium
Rom.	Plutarch, *Romulus*
Sanh.	Sanhedrin
Sen.	Cicero, *De senectute*
Spec.	Philo, *De specialibus legibus*
T. Ab.	Testament of Abraham
T. Benj.	Testament of Benjamin
T. Jud.	Testament of Judah
T. Levi	Testament of Levi
T. Mos.	Testament of Moses
Tg. Ps.-J.	Targum Pseudo-Jonathan
Vit. phil.	Diogenes Laertius, *Vitae philosophorum*

Secondary Sources

AB	Anchor Bible
AGJU	Arbeiten zur Geschichte des antiken Judentums und des Urchristentums
ANTC	Abingdon New Testament Commentaries
A(Y)BRL	Anchor (Yale) Bible Reference Library
BECNT	Baker Exegetical Commentary on the New Testament
BETL	Bibliotheca Ephemeridum Theologicarum Lovaniensium
BFT	Biblical Foundations in Theology
BHT	Beiträge zur historischen Theologie
Bib	*Biblica*

BNTC	Black's New Testament Commentaries
BT	*The Bible Translator*
CBQ	*Catholic Biblical Quarterly*
CurBR	*Currents in Biblical Research*
ConBNT	Coniectanea Biblica: New Testament Series
ECL	Early Christianity and Its Literature
EJSP	*European Journal of Social Psychology*
EKKNT	Evangelisch-katholischer Kommentar zum Neuen Testament
ERSP	*European Review of Social Psychology*
ESV	English Standard Version
FRLANT	Forschungen zur Religion und Literatur des Alten und Neuen Testaments
GBS	Guides to Biblical Scholarship
GNS	Good News Studies
GTA	Göttinger theologischer Arbeiten
HCSB	Holman Christian Standard Bible
HSS	Harvard Semitic Studies
HTA	Historisch Theologische Auslegung
HTR	*Harvard Theological Review*
ICC	International Critical Commentary
Int	*Interpretation*
JAAR	*Journal of the American Academy of Religion*
JBL	*Journal of Biblical Literature*
JETS	*Journal of the Evangelical Theological Society*
JSNT	*Journal for the Study of the New Testament*
JSNTSup	Journal for the Study of the New Testament Supplement Series
JSPL	*Journal for the Study of Paul and His Letters*
KEK	Kritisch-exegetischer Kommentar über das Neue Testament (Meyer-Kommentar)
KJV	King James Version
KNT	Kommentar zum Neuen Testament
LCL	Loeb Classical Library
LEC	Library of Early Christianity
LNTS	Library of New Testament Studies
NAC	New American Commentary
NASB	New American Standard Bible
NBBC	New Beacon Bible Commentary

NCB	New Century Bible
NewDocs	Horsley, G. H. R., et al., eds. *New Documents Illustrating Early Christianity*. North Ryde, NSW: The Ancient History Documentary Research Centre, Macquarie University, 1981–.
NIB	Keck, Leander E. *The New Interpreter's Bible*. Nashville: Abingdon, 1994–2004.
NICNT	New International Commentary on the New Testament
NIGTC	New International Greek Testament Commentary
NIV	New International Version
NIVAC	New International Version Application Commentary
NovT	*Novum Testamentum*
NovTSup	Supplements to Novum Testamentum
NRSV	New Revised Standard Version
NTAbh	Neutestamentliche Abhandlungen
NTL	New Testament Library
NTOA	Novum Testamentum et Orbis Antiquus
NTS	*New Testament Studies*
OTP	Charlesworth, James H., ed. *The Old Testament Pseudipigrapha*. 2 vols. ABRL. New York: Doubleday, 1983–1985.
RSV	Revised Standard Version
SBT	Studies in Biblical Theology
SNTSMS	Society for New Testament Studies Monograph Series
SP	Sacra Pagina
TGl	*Theologie und Glaube*
Tusc.	Cicero, *Tusculanae disputationes*
TynBul	*Tyndale Bulletin*
WBC	Word Biblical Commentary
WUNT	Wissenschaftliche Untersuchungen zum Neuen Testament
ZBK	Zürcher Bibelkommentare
ZNW	*Zeitschrift für die neutestamentliche Wissenschaft und die Kunde der älteren Kirche*

1
Questions, Context, and Method

1.1. Speaking of Bodies

Questions about the nature of human bodies have been before us from antiquity to the present.[1] Advances in science, medicine, and related fields shed constant light on our understanding of the body, its composition, and its processes. Each discovery raises new questions that impact attitudes toward the body, whether religious, theological, or philosophical. We have wrestled with what it means to experience bodily life for centuries, and the apostle Paul is among those whose influence cannot be overstated. His importance is due not only to the widespread translation and circulation of the New Testament, but also to the frequency with which he discussed the body. One seasoned scholar has even remarked: "I cannot think of anybody in antiquity who spoke so much about the body as Paul did."[2] To be sure, it would be difficult to overstate Paul's impact on Western attitudes toward the body, and his influence is related to the integration of anthropology with a range of theological questions. From Christ to the church, the Spirit to soteriology, eschatology to ethics, Paul's attitude

---

1. See, e.g., Peter Brown, *The Body and Society: Men, Women, and Sexual Renunciation in Early Christianity*, Lectures on the History of Religions 13 (New York: Columbia University Press, 1988); Dale B. Martin, *The Corinthian Body* (New Haven: Yale University Press, 1995), 3–37; James I. Porter, ed., *Constructions of the Classical Body*, Body in Theory (Ann Arbor: University of Michigan Press, 1999); Dag Øistein Endsjø, *Greek Resurrection Beliefs and the Success of Early Christianity* (New York: Palgrave Macmillan, 2009); David H. Kelsey, *Eccentric Existence: A Theological Anthropology*, 2 vols. (Louisville: Westminster John Knox, 2009); David H. Nikkel, *Radical Embodiment* (Eugene, OR: Pickwick, 2010).

2. This quote is attributed to Wayne Meeks by Troels Engberg-Pedersen, *Cosmology and Self in the Apostle Paul: The Material Spirit* (New York: Oxford University Press, 2010), 3.

toward the body is vital to his overall theology, and any effort to deal with any area will require attention to his vision of embodied life. One scholar has even gone so far as to suggest—famously, if not convincingly—that "Paul's theology can best be treated as his doctrine of man."[3] While Paul's theology can hardly be reduced to anthropology, few would deny that his anthropology is vital to his theological thinking. We would naturally think a prominent Pauline topic—like the body—with such far-reaching implications would garner extensive scholarly attention. Nevertheless, as Colleen Shantz observes, "When we consider the whole picture of what is produced in Pauline scholarship, even though more and more exceptions are appearing, it is the body that tends to remain absent or partial."[4]

Given the importance of Paul's attitude toward the body and the need for further attention to the topic, this book aims to answer three questions: (1) How do Paul's expectations about the future resurrection of the body relate to his expectations for believers' use of their bodies in the present? (2) What attitudes toward the body and the future in the world of Paul and his hearers may have shaped or influenced his own understanding of this relationship? (3) In the major passages under review, how do the social setting and Paul's pastoral and persuasive purposes shed light on his articulation of the relationship between bodily practice and bodily resurrection? To answer these questions, I will offer a close reading of those texts in the undisputed letters in which language about the present use of the body (primarily σῶμα and synonyms) appears in a context dealing with the future resurrection of the body: 1 Cor 6:12–20; 15:12–58; 2 Cor 4:7–5:10; Rom 6:1–23; 8:9–25; Phil 3:12–4:1.[5] Taking them chronologically also puts us in a position to consider the possibility of development in Paul's thought.

These questions raise the further question of how to speak of human bodies. Advances in neuroscience and related fields increasingly provide materialist accounts for experiences historically attributed to the soul (e.g., will, emotion). Some now reject the existence of a nonphysical

---

3. Rudolf Bultmann, *Theology of the New Testament*, 2 vols., trans. Kendrich Grobel (New York: Scribner, 1951–1955), 1:191.

4. Colleen Shantz, *Paul in Ecstasy: The Neurobiology of the Apostle's Life and Thought* (New York: Cambridge University Press, 2009), 3.

5. While Paul does not explicitly articulate his expectations of the recipients in terms of σῶμα in 1 Cor 15:12–58, it is included as context for the discussion of future bodily resurrection and bodily practice in 1 Cor 6:12–20.

1. Questions, Context, and Method

soul altogether and argue that it is inaccurate to speak of human beings as having both physical body and nonphysical soul.[6] If correct, it seems inappropriate to speak of human beings as *having* a body for that implies the existence of another nonbodily part. It could even imply that the body is a nonessential extension controlled by that essential nonphysical component. The rejection of the soul is, of course, a major shift in thinking that cuts against the religious beliefs of billions of people, not only today but throughout history.[7] And this scientifically grounded denial has not gone unchallenged by philosophers and theologians, though they do not necessarily relegate the body to nonessential status. One particularly significant critique comes from John Cooper, who argues for what he calls "wholistic dualism." This view says human beings are composed of body and soul, which are two discrete yet equally essential parts. He thus avoids the criticism of relegating the body to nonessential status and maintains the necessity of a nonphysical soul.[8]

Given the range of views, is it appropriate to say that humans *have* bodies? Or is it better to speak of *being* bodies? David Kelsey has considered this question in detail and suggests the answer is not found in choosing one option or the other. Instead, he argues that to be human is both "to be and to have a living body."[9] Reflecting at length on Job's description of his birth in Job 10, Kelsey suggests that human life should be thought of as the result of the process of coming to birth. To be born a

---

6. See, e.g., Patricia Smith Churchland, *Neurophilosophy: Toward a Unified Science of the Mind-Brain* (Cambridge: MIT Press, 1986); Francis H. Crick, *The Astonishing Hypothesis: The Scientific Search for the Soul* (New York: Simon & Schuster, 1994); Patricia Smith Churchland, *Brain-Wise: Studies in Neurophilosophy* (Cambridge: MIT Press, 2002); Joel B. Green, ed., *What about the Soul? Neuroscience and Christian Anthropology* (Nashville: Abingdon, 2004); Nancey Murphy, *Bodies and Souls, or Spirited Bodies?* (Cambridge: Cambridge University Press, 2006); Joel B. Green, *Body, Soul, and Human Life: The Nature of Humanity in the Bible*, Studies in Theological Interpretation (Grand Rapids: Baker, 2008); David Cave and Rebecca Sachs Norris, eds., *Religion and the Body: Modern Science and the Construction of Religious Meaning*, Studies in the History of Religions 138 (Leiden: Brill, 2012).

7. Green, *Body, Soul, and Human Life*, 17–21.

8. John W. Cooper, *Body, Soul, and Life Everlasting: Biblical Anthropology and the Monism-Dualism Debate* (Grand Rapids: Eerdmans, 1989). Cf. J. P. Moreland and Scott B. Rae, *Body and Soul: Human Nature and the Crisis in Ethics* (Downers Grove, IL: InterVarsity Press, 2000).

9. Kelsey, *Eccentric Existence*, 242.

human being is to be born a living human body. Our experience of life is inseparable from bodily life and cannot be understood apart from the way that living bodies relate to their proximate contexts. There is no way to think about human life without reference to embodiment. The living body is essential to human being.[10] This does not, however, exclude other legitimate ways of speaking about the body. Kelsey appeals to our capacity for responsibility to suggest that being a living body involves self-regulation that makes the body an object for which human beings are accountable. This creates a subtle distinction between the person and the body. He is careful to insist that this distinction does not imply either separation or dichotomy between the person and the living body, though it does establish legitimate grounds for speaking of human beings as *having* living bodies.[11] We will find that Paul's language resembles Kelsey's approach. The apostle undoubtedly sees the body as essential to full human existence, yet he also speaks of the body as something for which believers are responsible. It is an object of their control.[12] Thus, as we consider the shape of Paul's thought, we'll also adopt Kelsey's both/and approach for speaking of bodies.

1.2. The Body and the Future in the Greco-Roman World

1.2.1. Greek and Roman Sources

Attitudes toward the body among Jewish and non-Jewish sources in the Greco-Roman period were many and varied.[13] One challenge that arises out of this diversity is deciding the extent to which the various views were

---

10. Kelsey, *Eccentric Existence*, 242–50.
11. Kelsey, *Eccentric Existence*, 270–80.
12. Paul's account of his visionary experience in 2 Cor 12:2–4 seems to further suggest that he can conceive of human existence and experience apart from the body.
13. In the past, scholarship on ancient attitudes toward the body and the future was cast in terms of a sharp dichotomy between, on the one hand, Hellenistic dualism concerned with the immortality of the soul and, on the other, holistic Jewish attitudes that focused on the resurrection of the body; see, for example, Oscar Cullmann, *Immortality of the Soul or Resurrection of the Dead?* (London: Epworth, 1958). There is now increasing agreement that this dichotomy fails to account for the range of views evidenced in both Jewish and non-Jewish sources; indeed, there is good reason to take the Judaism of Paul's day as part of or even an expression of ancient Hellenism rather than something to be read over against it. For this approach, see the essays in Troels

known or held in the first century. Applied to the letters of Paul, the questions are whether and how much each perspective was known by Paul and his hearers and to what extent they may have been influenced by the range of views current in their day. These issues will be worked out in the detailed exegesis to come; for now, it is sufficient to note the difficulties. I begin with a consideration of the non-Jewish Greco-Roman sources and then turn to the Jewish sources, being careful not to press the distinction too strongly. All these works found their home in the Hellenistic culture of the Greco-Roman world. The principal Greco-Roman accounts of embodied life in relation to the future come in Plato, Aristotle, the Epicureans, and the Stoics. If these attitudes were placed on a spectrum, Platonic dualism would be at one end with Epicurean materialism at the other. Aristotle and the Stoics fall in between.[14]

Plato's dualism is consistent and well-known (Plato, *Phaed.* 80–83; *Phaedr.* 245c–247c; *Meno* 81a–e). In his view, human beings are composed of two parts, the body being the more base and burdensome part subject to decay and dissolution. In contrast, the soul is immortal, akin to the divine, and thought to be the more noble and pure part of a person. The soul, for Plato, is subdivided into three hierarchical parts or levels, the lowest of which was most closely connected to the body. At death, the soul departs the body to which it was joined, a union, we should remember, not willingly undertaken.[15] Plato's understanding of the body in relation to the future is set forth in the *Phaedo*. The dialogue is set in the prison of Socrates, who takes a positive attitude toward the prospect of his death. He sees his body as a hindrance to the soul in its quest for truth and wisdom. The passions and desires of the body distract from thought and reason. He understands the soul to be a slave to the body. Its chief need is to be set free (66a–67a). Socrates thus faces death in hope that he will "attain fully to that which has been my chief object in my past life," namely, the purification which consists in separating soul from body (67b [Fowler]). The true philosopher is one who takes a hostile stance toward the body in order to achieve the soul's liberation (67e–68a).

Engberg-Pedersen, ed., *Paul beyond the Judaism/Hellenism Divide* (Louisville: Westminster John Knox, 2001).

14. See A. A. Long, *Stoic Studies* (Cambridge: Cambridge University Press, 1996), 225.

15. For Greek inscriptions that illustrate the ascent of the soul after its release from the body at death, see *NewDocs* 1.103; 3.11; 4.6, 8, 10, 29; 9.8.

In contrast, if the soul was consumed by the interests of the body during life, then the soul would be punished by union with another body corresponding to the practices of the previous life. Socrates explains, "those who have indulged in gluttony and violence and drunkenness, and have taken no pains to avoid them, are likely to pass into the bodies of asses and other beasts of that sort" (81e–82a [Fowler]). The key to the soul's liberation from corporeality was the pursuit of the social and civic virtues of moderation and justice (82a–b). To attain that future liberated state, a person must resist and master bodily desire. That is the true love of wisdom (82b–c). Thus, in Platonic perspective, the character of one's present embodied life has a great deal to do with the desirability, or lack thereof, of one's future and postmortem existence. For the wise and virtuous, death was to be desired because it meant freedom from bondage to corporeality.[16]

In stark contrast to Plato, the Epicureans rejected the view that the soul survives the death of the body; instead, death was considered the natural end of a person's life.[17] Against Plato's vision of a future in which the soul was freed from corporeality and joined to the divine, the Epicureans insisted that the universe and everything in it was material, composed of atoms. This included the gods.[18] Matter was uncreated and eternal; it could change, but it could not be destroyed. In Epicurus's materialistic cosmology, the body housed the soul, which was itself viewed as a material entity: "we must recognize generally that the soul is a corporeal thing, composed of fine particles" (Diogenes Laertius, *Vit. phil.* 10.63 [Hicks]). For Epicurus, life consisted in the union of body and soul. That union provides

---

16. For the desirability of death in Platonism, see N. T. Wright, *The Resurrection of the Son of God* (Minneapolis: Fortress, 2003), 49. For the suggestion that Platonism carried limited influence in the first century, see Martin, *Corinthian Body*, 15.

17. The idea that death is the end of a person's existence can be traced back to Democritus (ca. 460–370 BCE). For Epicurus's philosophy, see Diogenes Laertius, *Vit. phil.* 10. For a survey of ancient critiques of Epicureanism, see Karl O. Sandnes, *Belly and Body in the Pauline Epistles*, SNTSMS 120 (Cambridge: Cambridge University Press, 2002), 65–78. Cf. John Gaskin, *The Epicurean Philosophers*, Everyman Library (London: Dent, 1995). For the significance of Epicureanism in the first century, see Peter G. Bolt, "Life, Death, and the Afterlife in the Greco-Roman World," in *Life in the Face of Death: The Resurrection Message of the New Testament*, ed. Richard N. Longenecker (Grand Rapids: Eerdmans, 1998), 67–68.

18. For Epicurus's understanding of the gods, see A. J. Festugière, *Epicurus and His Gods*, trans. C. W. Chilton (Cambridge: Harvard University Press, 1956).

sensation and consciousness. Also in contrast to Plato, the soul did not survive the death of the body, "when the whole frame is broken up, the soul is scattered and has no longer the same powers as before, nor the same motions; hence it does not possess sentience either" (Diogenes Laertius, *Vit. phil.* 10.65 [Hicks]). The death of the body means the disintegration of the soul. Given their rejection of any postmortem state, the Epicureans had no reason to suppose one's behavior in life had any bearing on the future state; death is simply the end of a person's existence. Thus, the future carried no promise of reward nor threat of punishment.[19] Without concern for a future life after death, the Epicureans turned their attention to attaining a happy life in the present which was to be gained by pursuing pleasure and avoiding pain. This pursuit of pleasure, however, should not be confused with modern notions of gratuitous and excessive hedonism. For Epicurus and many who adopted his philosophy, happiness was not a matter of self-indulgence. Instead, happiness came through attaining virtue and living wisely.[20] It is noteworthy that despite the contrasting perspectives between Plato and the Epicureans with regard to the future of the body, both still insisted on the importance of cultivating virtue during life.

Aristotle's view of the soul-body relationship bears some similarity to the Epicurean perspective, though we must not overlook the distinctions between them. Like the Epicureans, Aristotle rejected the view of his teacher Plato that the soul survived the death of the body. In Aristotle's view, the soul actualizes and shapes the matter of the body; indeed, the soul is the cause of the body and that which empowers it for movement (*De an.* 412a; 415b). The soul is form; the body matter. And while he can distinguish between body and soul, he also sees unity between them: "So one need no more ask whether the wax and the imprint it receives are one, or in general whether the matter of each thing is the same as that of which it is the matter; for admitting that the terms unity and being are used in many senses, the paramount sense is actuality" (412b [Hett]). Actualization is thus an expression of unity. While the soul is not a body, it does require one (414a). Aristotle saw additional evidence that the soul required a body in that all functions of the soul (e.g., emotion, gentleness, shame, fear, joy) affect the body. "In most cases," he observed, "it seems that none of the affections, whether active or passive, can exist apart from

---

19. Gaskin, *Epicurean Philosophers*, xxxiv.
20. Gaskin, *Epicurean Philosophers*, xl–xli.

the body" (403a [Hett]). Shame causes the body to blush; fear causes the hairs on the neck to stand upright. Even small and obscure provocations result in bodily movement (403a). He could find no function of the soul that was peculiar to it, which led him to conclude that it was inseparable from the body.

Aristotle also rejected the Platonic view that a single soul could be attached to any number of bodies (407b). He believed that the distinctive form of soul is suitable to a single body. Thus, there is no body without a soul and no soul without a body. Distinct from the Epicureans, Aristotle left open the possibility that some element of the intellect might survive death, but his view that the death of the body is also the end of the soul left little room for thought of an afterlife in his philosophy.

This leaves Stoicism as the fourth major philosophical perspective on embodied life current in the Greco-Roman world of Paul and his hearers. This philosophical school remained highly significant into the first century and, as we shall see below, has played an important role in recent scholarship on Paul's attitude toward the body. Stoic anthropology was complex and can be distinguished from other ancient accounts of bodiliness in a variety of ways.[21] In the Stoic view, all existence was thought of in terms of corporeality. The complexity of the Stoic conception of bodiliness shows up in their understanding of the corporeal *spiritus* or πνεῦμα, the substance which gave the entire cosmos its coherence. The universe was seen as animate rational substance and the human soul as a fragment of it (Diogenes Laertius, *Vit. phil.* 7.143; cf. Cicero, *Nat. d.* 2.115-116). The Stoics distinguished between body and soul, but body and soul were composed of matter, the body of a heavier sort and the soul of a lighter and more refined sort. Thus, the soul was understood in corporeal terms. If Plato thought the soul was antithetical to the body, the Stoics thought it was a finer sort of body.[22] This materialism they had in common with Epicurus.[23] The heavier matter of the present body was seen in dim light when compared to the soul. As Cicero remarks, "the soul is celestial, brought

---

21. Key figures in Stoicism are Epictetus, Seneca, and Cicero. For an extended discussion of the complexity of Stoic attitudes toward the body, see the chapter "Soul and Body in Stoicism" in Long, *Stoic Studies*, 224-49. Cf. Michelle V. Lee, *Paul, the Stoics, and the Body of Christ*, SNTSMS 137 (Cambridge: Cambridge University Press, 2006), 40-58.

22. To paraphrase Martin, *Corinthian Body*, 11.

23. Long, *Stoic Studies*, 226.

down from its most exalted home and buried, as it were in earth, a place uncongenial to its divine and eternal nature" (*Sen.* 77 [Falconer]). The soul thus precedes present bodily life and, as Cicero sees it, survives the death of the body: "I, for my part, could never be persuaded that souls, which lived while they were in human bodies, perished when they left those bodies" (80 [Falconer]). He saw the departure of the soul from the more base body as purification and freedom from defilement (80). To further distinguish the Stoics from Plato, they did not consider the postmortem existence of the soul as personal survival of death but instead as an impersonal union of the soul with the divine through the agency of πνεῦμα. We should also observe that, while Plato may have affirmed the immortality of the soul, that idea is not to be attributed to the Stoic notion of the soul's postmortem existence because there is no indication that the individual soul in any way survives the great conflagration in which "nothing will remain but fire," which is divine living being (Cicero, *Nat. d.* 2.118). After this event, a new world is created and an ordered universe emerges.

One observation to be made in light of the preceding survey of the principal Greco-Roman philosophies is that, despite their many differences, none envision a return from death to some form of resurrected and embodied life as the ultimate future state for human beings, though that is not to say return to bodily life was unheard of in that world.[24] Pliny knew stories of people returning from the dead, though he took them to be cases in which death was diagnosed early (Pliny, *Nat.* 7.51–52). The myths contain examples of temporary restoration to embodied life that was then followed by another experience of death.[25] The peculiarity of these examples illustrates the point that a return to embodied life would be thought irregular at best and undesirable at worst by a significant majority in the first century of the common era. As we shall see, many Jewish sources from the Hellenistic period stand in contrast by holding out hope for the resurrection of the body, though the extent to which these sources stand in continuity or discontinuity one to another is a matter of ongoing debate.

---

24. See further M. David Litwa, *Iesus Deus: The Early Christian Depiction of Jesus as a Mediterranean God* (Minneapolis: Fortress, 2014), 156–68.

25. Bolt, "Life, Death, and the Afterlife in the Greco-Roman World," 73; cf. Endsjø, *Greek Resurrection Beliefs*, 47–52. Endsjø also argues that instances where mortal human beings are transformed into gods who have immortal flesh parallel Christian understandings of resurrection (54–64). Notably, those instances are not considered paradigmatic for human afterlife in general.

1.2.2. Hellenistic Jewish Sources

Before looking at the various attitudes toward the relationship between resurrection and present embodied life in the Jewish sources, two related observations should be made. First, Jewish beliefs in the postbiblical period found their home in the larger Hellenistic context of the Mediterranean world; thus, the perspectives we find expressed in these sources should be interpreted as a part of their Hellenistic cultural context rather than over and against it. Keeping this in mind will help us avoid the common pitfall of too strongly emphasizing any dichotomy between Greek perspectives on the one hand and Jewish perspectives on the other. Second, the attitudes toward the body and the future that we find in the Jewish sources should not be conflated to suggest that there was a single Jewish view.[26] As we shall see, attitudes toward embodied life and its ultimate future varied among the sources, and this diversity must be kept in mind as we prepare to consider the relevant material in the letters of Paul.[27]

As with the Greek and Roman sources discussed above, the Jewish sources in our period exhibit a variety of perspectives on what might be expected after death and how those expectations relate to embodied life in the present. Unlike the major Greco-Roman philosophies, however, many of the Jewish writers held out hope for some sort of resurrection of the body. Given my interest in Paul's understanding of the relationship between bodily resurrection and bodily practice, I will limit the following discussion to texts that also envision a form of resurrection to new embodied life, though there were other schools of thought that either rejected the resurrection of the body outright or anticipated some alternative expe-

---

26. See E. P. Sanders, *Judaism: Practice and Belief, 63 BCE–66 CE* (Philadelphia: Trinity Press International, 1992).

27. For Jewish expectations with regard to resurrection and life after death, see, e.g., A. J. Avery-Peck and J. Neusner, eds., *Death, Life-after-Death, Resurrection and the World-to-Come in the Judaisms of Antiquity*, part 4 of *Judaism in Late Antiquity* (Leiden: Brill, 2000); R. H. Charles, *A Critical History of the Doctrine of a Future Life in Israel, in Judaism, and in Christianity*, 2nd ed. (London: Black, 1913); Émile Puech, *La Croyance des Esséniens en la Vie Future. Immortalité, Résurrection, Vie Éternalle? Histoire d'une Croyance dans le Judaïsme Ancien*, 2 vols. (Paris: Lecoffre, 1993); Simcha P. Raphael, *Jewish Views of the Afterlife* (Northvale, NJ: Aronson, 1994); Wright, *Resurrection*; George W. E. Nickelsburg, *Resurrection, Immortality, and Eternal Life in Intertestamental Judaism and Early Christianity* (Cambridge: Harvard University Press, 2006).

rience of life after death.[28] In the following discussion we will see two common and recurring strands of thought with regard to the relationship between resurrection and embodied life: (1) resurrection as vindication in the context of persecution or oppression and (2) resurrection as reward for piety.[29] This distinction should not be pressed too firmly, of course, as if every text could be easily sorted into one category or the other; some texts reveal an interest in both. Nevertheless, the distinction can be made and will aid us in understanding the richness of the relationship between resurrection and bodily practice. The clearest canonical text that refers unambiguously to a future resurrection of the body and one that figured significantly in the postbiblical period is Dan 12:1–3, 13.[30] The literary form is that of an apocalyptic vision, and the context is that of persecution.[31] Michael, the angelic messenger, says that,

---

28. There are, of course, a variety of Jewish sources that do not reflect belief in bodily resurrection. According to second-hand primary sources, the Sadducees denied resurrection altogether; for descriptions of their views, see Mark 12:18 and parr.; Acts 23:7–9; Josephus, *B.J.* 2.165; *A.J.* 18.16; b. Sanh. 90b. Cf. N. T. Wright, *The New Testament and the People of God* (Minneapolis: Fortress, 1992), 211–13; Wright, *Resurrection*, 131–40. Other Jewish writers exhibit a belief in the disembodied immortality of the soul: Ps.-Phoc. 105–115; T. Ab. 20.14–15; 1 En. 103.3–8; 4 Macc 18:23. For Philo's Platonic understanding of the body and the future, see *Ebr.* 26; *Migr.* 2; *Det.* 22; *Opif.* 46; *Spec.* 1.295; 4.24; *Heres* 68–70, 276.

29. Nickelsburg (*Resurrection*, 211–18) identifies these two strands in three distinct forms: (1) the story of the righteous man and the Isaianic exaltation, (2) the judgment scene, and (3) two-ways theology. The first and second forms are generally found in contexts of oppression or persecution while the third form is generally found in contexts dealing with reward.

30. See John J. Collins, *Daniel: A Commentary on the Book of Daniel*, Hermeneia (Minneapolis: Fortress, 1993), 391; Wright, *Resurrection*, 109. Other texts that speak less clearly of resurrection include Isa 26:14, 29 and Hos 6:2. Resurrection language appears in Ezek 37, but it refers to national reconstitution rather than individual hope for a postmortem resurrection of the body.

31. The precise dating of Daniel is a matter of debate. Most scholars take it to have been written after the persecutions of the Maccabean period, though others argue for an earlier date in the sixth century BCE. For the later date, see John E. Goldingay, *Daniel*, WBC 30 (Dallas: Word, 1989), 326–27; Collins, *Daniel*, 23–24; James D. Newsome, *The Hebrew Prophets* (Atlanta: John Knox, 1984), 220–23; André LaCoque, *Daniel in His Time* (Columbia: University of South Carolina Press, 1988), 7–8. For the earlier date, see Stephen R. Miller, *Daniel*, NAC 18 (Nashville: B&H, 1994), 21–43; Tremper Longman, *Daniel*, NIVAC (Grand Rapids: Zondervan, 1999).

> Many of those who sleep in the dust of the earth shall awake, some to everlasting life, and some to shame and everlasting contempt. Those who are wise shall shine like the brightness of the sky, and those who lead many to righteousness, like the stars forever. (12:2-3 NRSV)[32]

Resurrection is here understood to be the final element in a two-stage postmortem sequence. Those who have died are said to "sleep in the dust of the earth" for an undefined period of time before being raised to new life. No comment is made on the nature of this sleep or whether the dead are, in any sense, conscious.[33] The focus is on the future hope for resurrection, which is here envisioned as something that happens to both the righteous and the unrighteous as a prelude to divine judgment. Those consigned to shame and contempt are the persecutors of the faithful, while the righteous martyrs are raised that they might shine like stars. Some have seen here a belief in astral immortality.[34] Wright argues alternatively that this is a way of saying that the righteous wise will be given positions of authority over the earth. He concludes, "They will be raised to a state of glory in the world for which the best parallel or comparison is the status of stars, moon and sun within the created order."[35] Either way the function of resurrection is the same; the dead are raised in order that they might be judged, that the persecutors might be recompensed for their crimes and the martyrs vindicated.[36] It is important to note that resurrection is not here itself the vindication of the martyrs; rather, it is the

---

32. Biblical and apocryphal translations are my own unless otherwise indicated. Translations of texts from the Pseudepigrapha are from James H. Charlesworth, ed., *The Old Testament Pseudepigrapha*, 2 vols., ABRL (New York: Doubleday, 1983–1985). Translations of *progymnasmata* texts are from George A. Kennedy, ed., *Progymnasmata: Greek Textbooks of Prose and Composition*, WGRW (Atlanta: Society of Biblical Literature, 2003). All other ancient translations are from the LCL.

33. Wright observes that "the passage uses the *metaphor* of sleep and waking to denote the *concrete event* of resurrection" (*Resurrection*, 109, emphasis original).

34. Martin Hengel, *Judaism and Hellenism: Studies in Their Encounter in Palestine during the Early Hellenistic Period* (London: SCM, 1974), 196; Pheme Perkins, *Resurrection: New Testament Witness and Contemporary Reflection* (London: Geoffrey Chapman, 1984), 38; Shaye J. D. Cohen, *From the Maccabees to the Mishnah*, LEC 7 (Philadelphia: Westminter, 1987), 91; Martin, *Corinthian Body*, 118.

35. Wright, *Resurrection*, 113.

36. J. R. Daniel Kirk, *Unlocking Romans: Resurrection and the Justification of God* (Grand Rapids: Eerdmans, 2008), 17.

means by which both the good and the evil are delivered to judgment.[37] Resurrection thus provides hope for justice and functions to sustain those who suffer unjustly with the hope that God will, at some future point, put the world to rights.

The connection between resurrection and vindication is also present in the account of the martyrs in 2 Macc 7. The narrative describes the efforts of Antiochus Epiphanes to force seven Jewish brothers to eat pork, thus disobeying their laws. One brother responds on behalf of the others declaring their readiness to die rather than transgress (7:2). The outraged Antiochus then tortures each of the brothers in turn who, though tortured and threatened with death, respond by expressing fidelity to and hope in their God. The specific language of bodily suffering is relevant for the present study; for example, after being scalped, the second brother is asked, "Will you eat rather than have your body punished limb by limb?" (7:7 NRSV). In response to this injustice, he declares his hope for resurrection: "you dismiss us from this present life, but the King of the universe will raise us up to an everlasting renewal of life, because we have died for his laws" (7:9 NRSV). In this brother's thinking, martyrdom for the sake of God's laws effects resurrection. The bodily nature of this resurrection hope is plain in the words of the third brother, who put forth his hands to the torturer declaring, "I got these from Heaven, and because of his laws I disdain them, and from him I hope to get them back again" (7:11 NRSV). The fourth brother likewise shares the hope expressed by the others: "One cannot but choose to die at the hands of men and to cherish the hope that God gives of being raised by him again" (7:14 NRSV). In each instance, when faced with the injustice of being punished for faithfulness to the laws of their God, the brothers respond with hope for resurrection. Their bodies that were gruesomely taken apart by their torturers will be put together again by the mercy of the creator God (cf. 7:23). Unlike Dan 12, resurrection itself is here the martyrs' vindication, for they assure Antiochus that he will have no part in the resurrection to life (7:14). In this narrative context, then, resurrection relates to life in the present by motivating faithfulness and perseverance in the face of persecution. Resurrection functions to rectify the gross acts of injustice committed against the bodies of the faithful martyrs. The evil actions of

---

37. Nickelsburg, *Resurrection*, 33.

their persecutors will be overturned at the resurrection when their bodies are put together once again.

Hope for future life after a period of death also appears in the composite work known as 1 Enoch. In the portion of the book known as the Similitudes (1 En. 37–71), there is the expectation of a day in which "Sheol will return all the deposits which she had received" (51.1 [trans. E. Isaac, *OTP* 1:36). As in Daniel, resurrection is seen as the means by which a person is delivered to judgment; the righteous are subsequently chosen from among the larger group of the risen ones to receive salvation and glory (51.2–5). Both reward and vindication are in view in the larger context. The notion of reward is present in that the elect one is said to sit in judgment of people's deeds (5.3), and sinners are later warned of impending judgment (38.1–6). "Those who have committed sin" will have no place in the transformed creation (45.5), but the holy ones will receive glory and honor (50.1–5). That persecution is also in view is clear in that the holy ones are spoken of as righteous ones whose blood was shed. They are to hope, though, for the day when judgment is executed, when their prayers are heard, and their blood is "admitted before the Lord of the Spirits" (47.4). The final section of 1 Enoch, composed of chapters 91–107, begins with a warning of judgment in which the readers are exhorted to "walk in righteousness" even in the face of oppression (91.1–9). Unlike the Similitudes, the only ones to be raised from the dead are the righteous and wise; sinners will be destroyed (91.10–11). The literary function of the description of judgment is revealed at the end of the chapter, "Now listen to me, my children, and walk in the way of righteousness, and do not walk in the way of wickedness, for all those who walk in the ways of injustice shall perish" (91.19). The hope of resurrection, together with the threat of divine punishment, serves to undergird the instruction to live a pious and righteous life (see 102.4; 103.4; 104.1–4; 108.11–15).

Another major apocalyptic work that contributes to our understanding of Jewish attitudes toward resurrection around the time of the New Testament is 4 Ezra, which is a series of visions about the destruction and rebuilding of Jerusalem after the crisis of 70 CE. Fourth Ezra is marked by what may be called a strong body-soul dualism, though this does not result in a negative attitude toward the body.[38] After the death of the body, the

---

38. Michael E. Stone, *Features of the Eschatology of IV Ezra*, HSS 35 (Atlanta: Scholars, 1989), 143–47.

souls of the righteous are kept in chambers while the souls of the wicked are consigned to wander in torment (7.79, 85, 95).[39] As in Daniel and the Similitudes, resurrection precedes judgment and is the means by which the dead come to face judgment (7.32–37; 14.35). The wicked receive recompense for their evil deeds while the righteous are rewarded for keeping the commandments (7.32–37; cf. 7.90). Resurrection thus serves to check unrighteous behavior and motivate a pious life.[40]

Resurrection also functions to promote piety in book 4 of the Sibylline Oracles. God is said to "raise up mortals again as they were before" in order to then preside over them in judgment (4.179–180 [J. J. Collins, *OTP* 1:389]). Sinners and the impious will be covered by the earth and consigned to Tartarus and Gehenna while the pious "will live on earth again when God gives spirit and life and favor" (4.185). Vindication of the righteous against persecution may be in view as well. The account of resurrection and judgment is preceded by a recounting of the rise of Rome (4.102–114) and the destruction of Jerusalem (4.115–130). This may suggest that judgment includes recompense for those who have perpetrated evil acts against God's people, though caution is warranted because the focus of the judgment account at the end of book 4 is on reward for piety rather than vindication for injustice received in the body.

The book of 2 Baruch deals also with judgment after the destruction of Jerusalem in 70 CE. For Baruch, the death of the righteous and the happiness of sinners undermines the importance of avoiding evil and pursuing righteousness (14.2–4). Even more problematic is that this state of affairs undermines the very glory of God (21.21–23; cf. 76.2).[41] Resurrection serves to vindicate God's glory by properly exalting the righteous and punishing the wicked and thus putting things in right order. It is promised to those who "sleep in hope" of the Anointed One that they will rise and experience joy while the souls of the wicked are to be tormented (30.1–5).

We may say then that while not all Jews of the period believed in bodily resurrection, many certainly did, and they had very rich language to describe this hope. They also reflect very specific attitudes toward the relationship between future resurrection and embodied life in the present. Those attitudes centered especially on two distinct, though often overlap-

---

39. Notably, 4 Ezra 7.32 says that the souls of the dead are in chambers without distinguishing between the righteous and the wicked. See Stone, *Features*, 144.

40. See Pss. Sol. 3.11–12. where resurrection functions in a similar way.

41. See further Kirk, *Unlocking Romans*, 22.

ping, focal points. First, the hope for resurrection is the hope that injustice done in the present will one day be made right, not least with regard to pagan oppression as experienced in persecution even to the point of martyrdom. Some texts, like 2 Maccabees, only envision a resurrection of the righteous, and in these texts their resurrection is their vindication. Others, like Daniel and 4 Ezra, reflect an expectation that both the righteous and the wicked will be raised; in these cases resurrection functions as the means by which they are delivered to divine judgment, an event in which the evil receive the due punishment for their evil deeds and the righteous experience blessing. Second, the promise of resurrection as reward functions to motivate righteous behavior in present bodily life while the threat of future punishment works to restrain sin. Vindication and reward are the chief ways that the relationship between resurrection and bodily practice were worked out in the literature of the Second Temple period.[42]

The Hellenistic period gives evidence for a range of attitudes toward the body and the future in both the Jewish and non-Jewish sources. To varying degrees, these perspectives informed Paul's own thinking and the attitudes of his hearers toward the body and bodily practice. This rich background must be kept in mind as we proceed to look at the Pauline material and the way it has been handled in contemporary scholarship.

1.3. The Body in Pauline Scholarship

Scholarly discussion of Paul's attitude toward the body has centered around his use of σῶμα, which is the apostle's most common descriptor for embodied human life.[43] Prior to the twentieth century, the study of Pauline

---

42. Resurrection language appears elsewhere in the literature and even functions in various other ways that are not as focused on the relationship between resurrection in the future and behavior in the present. The preceding survey has focused on texts that inform the body-future dynamic, since that relationship is at the center of the present study. For resurrection elsewhere in the period, see Apoc. Mos. 13.3–5; 41.1–3; 43.2–3; T. Mos. 10.1–10; T. Levi 18.3; T. Jud. 25.4; T. Zeb. 10.1–3; T. Benj. 10.6–9. Beyond vindication and righteous behavior, Kirk argues that resurrection also functions with regard to the corporate vindication of Israel and the restoration of the cosmos (*Unlocking Romans*, 14–32). Cf. Jon D. Levenson, *Resurrection and the Restoration of Israel: The Ultimate Victory of the God of Life* (New Haven: Yale University Press, 2006).

43. Paul's somatic language falls broadly into two categories: (1) anthropological usage with regard to the human body and (2) ecclesiological usage with regard to the body of Christ. These categories are certainly related, but given the focus of this study

anthropology focused largely on whether human beings are dichotomous, consisting of body and soul, or trichotomous, consisting of body, soul, and spirit.[44] But with the publication of Rudolf Bultmann's *Theology of the New Testament*, the focus of the discussion moved to whether Paul's anthropology was characterized by essential unity (or monism). Bultmann's anthropological monism can be summarized with his now well-known dictum, "Man does not *have* a *soma*, he is a *soma*."[45] By this he meant that Paul understood σῶμα to be constitutive of human existence; that is, σῶμα is the term that describes a human being as an indivisible whole. Bultmann did not see σῶμα as "something that outwardly clings to a man's real *self* (to his soul, for instance), but belongs to its very essence."[46] Thus, σῶμα refers to the whole person rather than a distinct material substance in contrast to a noncorporeal part that might be called the soul. "*Man*," he says, "*his person as a whole*, can be denoted by *soma*."[47] Bultmann's rejection of dichotomous (body-soul) and trichotomous (body-soul-spirit) anthropologies marked a paradigm shift in the study of New Testament anthropology in general and Pauline anthropology in particular.[48] His holistic approach to Paul's anthropology has been widely influential and followed by others, though sometimes with varying degrees of nuance.[49]

---

the present survey of scholarship will be limited to anthropological usage. For Paul's understanding of the body of Christ as an ecclesial term, see, e.g., Ernst Käsemann, *Leib und Leib Christi* (Tübingen: Mohr, 1933); Robert H. Gundry, *Sōma in Biblical Theology: With Emphasis on Pauline Anthropology*, SNTSMS 29 (Cambridge: Cambridge University Press, 1976), 223–44; Jerome H. Neyrey, *Paul, in Other Words: A Cultural Reading of His Letters* (Louisville: Westminster John Knox, 1990), 137–40; James D. G. Dunn, *The Theology of Paul the Apostle* (Grand Rapids: Eerdmans, 1998), 533–64; Lee, *Paul, the Stoics, and the Body of Christ*, 105–52; Yung Suk Kim, *Christ's Body in Corinth: The Politics of Metaphor*, Paul in Critical Contexts (Minneapolis: Fortress, 2008).

44. See the survey of views by J. K. Chamblin, "Psychology," in *Dictionary of Paul and His Letters*, ed. Gerald F. Hawthorne and Ralph P. Martin (Downers Grove, IL: InterVarsity Press, 1993), 765–75. Cf. Green, *Body, Soul, and Human Life*, 5 n. 12.

45. Bultmann, *Theology of the New Testament*, 1:194, emphasis original.

46. Bultmann, *Theology of the New Testament*, 1:194.

47. Bultmann, *Theology of the New Testament*, 1:195, emphasis original.

48. Green, *Body, Soul, and Human Life*, 5 n. 12.

49. John A. T. Robinson, *The Body: A Study in Pauline Theology*, SBT 5 (Colorado Springs: Bimillenial, 1952); David Stacey, *The Pauline View of Man in Relation to Its Judaic and Hellenistic Background* (London: Macmillan, 1956); M. E. Dahl, *The Resurrection of the Body* (London: SCM, 1962); H. M. Shires, *The Eschatology of Paul*

The most comprehensive critique of Bultmann's holistic interpretation of Pauline anthropology comes from Robert H. Gundry in his book *Sōma in Biblical Theology*.[50] Conducting an extensive study of extrabiblical and biblical usage, he argued that Paul, in line with the Judaism of his day, maintained a holistic anthropological dualism. That is, essential humanness is composed of two parts: the physical body and the nonphysical soul (or spirit). Neither of these two parts in isolation constitutes a fully human being. Instead, to have a whole human being, one must have both parts. Paul, Gundry concluded, typically used σῶμα to refer to the physical body as a component part of a human being, though he did concede that the apostle occasionally used σῶμα to refer to the whole person.

More recent scholarship on Paul's use of σῶμα has moved beyond questions of human composition to wrestle with a variety of other issues. Given the methodological approach of this study (see below), Jerome Neyrey's application of insights drawn from the social sciences to Paul's somatic language in 1 Corinthians is particularly important.[51] Neyrey applies a model developed by Mary Douglas that identifies the human body as a symbol of the social body; like the human body, the social body is marked by boundaries, margins, and internal structure. Thus, attitudes toward the physical body shed light on one's perception of a corresponding social body, and expectations with regard to the social body provide insight into one's attitude toward the physical body.[52] Douglas later developed this hypothesis by arguing that a group in which there is strong pressure to conform to specific norms for behavior will correspond to the attitude that the body is a bounded system, the boundaries of which are highly guarded and controlled. In contrast, where there is little pressure from the group to control the bodily behavior of the individual, Douglas expected to find the corresponding perception of the social body as generally unbounded.[53] Neyrey's application of Douglas's work

---

in *Light of Modern Scholarship* (Philadelphia: Westminster, 1966); Green, *Body, Soul, and Human Life*.

50. Gundry, *Sōma*. Cf. Ernst Käsemann, *Perspectives on Paul*, trans. M. Kohl (Philadelphia: Fortress, 1971), 20–21; Cooper, *Body*; Moreland and Rae, *Body and Soul*.

51. Neyrey, *Paul, in Other Words*, 102–46.

52. Neyrey, *Paul, in Other Words*, 104–14. Cf. Mary Douglas, *Purity and Danger: An Analysis of Concept of Pollution and Taboo* (repr. New York: Routledge, 2009), 114–15.

53. Mary Douglas, *Natural Symbols*, 2nd ed. (repr. New York: Routledge, 2010), 72–79.

1. Questions, Context, and Method

to 1 Corinthians led him to conclude that two different attitudes toward the body were present in Corinth, that of Paul and that of his opponents. Paul's own attitude toward the body is marked by a high degree of control which corresponds to his view of the social body as having strong boundaries, formality, structure, smoothness, and ritual. Alternatively, Paul's opponents perceive the body as marked by a low degree of control. This corresponds to their perception of the social body as being characterized by minimal group pressure, informality, and little structure. This approach sheds light on the situation in Corinth by explaining the conflict in terms of contrasting attitudes toward the body.[54]

The eschatological dimension of Paul's thought does not always figure significantly in Neyrey's analysis of the major passages from 1 Corinthians under review in the present study (6:12–20; 15:50–58). While the physical nature of the resurrection body is accounted for in his analysis of 1 Cor 15, no consideration is given to the future resurrection of the body in the discussion of 6:12–20, a passage in which hope for future bodily resurrection is articulated in the midst of Paul's insistence that the Corinthians abstain from illicit sexual activity.[55] One goal of this study is to broaden the discussion by exploring more fully the body-future relationship in 1 Corinthians and in Paul's other undisputed letters in order to further clarify his perception of bodily behavior in the social context as it relates to future bodily resurrection.[56]

Dale B. Martin has also produced a substantial study of Paul's language of the body in 1 Corinthians. He argues that "the theological differences reflected in 1 Corinthians all resulted from conflicts between various groups in the local church rooted in different ideological constructions of the body."[57] Martin takes ancient constructions of the body as a window into these contrasting somatic ideologies. Like Neyrey, Martin sees the Corinthian church as divided in two factions separated by their respective attitudes toward the body. He also agrees with Neyrey and Douglas that the physical body and the social body serve as models that correlate with one another. Martin identifies one group, which he calls the *weak* and which he views as the likely majority, as perceiving the body to be highly

---

54. Neyrey, *Paul, in Other Words*, 116–17.
55. Neyrey, *Paul, in Other Words*, 118–19, 140–43.
56. Neyrey identifies this as a fruitful avenue for further research (*Paul, in Other Words*, 145).
57. Martin, *Corinthian Body*, xv.

porous and liable to pollution. The second group, called the *strong* and seen by Martin as the likely minority, emphasized the hierarchical structure of the body and were less concerned with pollution. Here he disagrees with Neyrey, who sees a focus on structure and hierarchy associated with elevated concern for boundaries and guarding against pollution.[58] Martin argues that the attitude of the strong toward the body correlates with higher socioeconomic status. The strong would have had increased access to education, which was the means by which their ideology of the body would have been shaped. In contrast, the majority weak (and Paul) had a lower socioeconomic status and thus had less access to education, which correlates with their unenlightened concern with somatic boundaries and pollution. Martin argues that the conflicts addressed in 1 Corinthians were rooted in the differing attitudes toward the body between the strong and the weak, between those of higher socioeconomic status and those of lower socioeconomic status.[59] In light of this overarching conflict, Paul's body language in 1 Corinthians functions to undermine the community's power structure by challenging the hierarchical attitude of the strong.[60]

With regard to the future resurrection of the body, Martin sees Paul responding primarily to the objections of the strong who, he thinks, would have likely rejected Paul's teaching on the resurrection as simply the resuscitation of a corpse. The question posed by the strong has to do with the nature of the resurrection body: "How are the dead raised? With what sort of body do they come?" (1 Cor 15:35).[61] In Martin's view, Paul's description of the resurrection body as a pneumatic body (σῶμα πνευματικόν, 1 Cor 15:44) should be understood in terms of Greek philosophy in which πνεῦμα referred not to a nonphysical or immaterial reality but to the light or airy matter of which celestial entities were thought to be composed. Martin concludes that Paul has redefined the resurrection of the body in terms taken from Greek philosophy with a view to resolving the dispute between himself and the strong by making use of terminology they would have found acceptable.

Like Martin, Troels Engberg-Pedersen argues both that Paul understood πνεῦμα as a material substance and that the material is the light airy

---

58. Neyrey, *Paul, in Other Words*, 133.
59. Martin, *Corinthian Body*, xv.
60. Martin, *Corinthian Body*, 248. Cf. Neyrey, *Paul, in Other Words*, 133–36.
61. Martin, *Corinthian Body*, 125.

stuff of which the celestial bodies are composed.⁶² He insists bodiliness pervades Paul's thought and is intrinsic to everything Paul says with regard to those who are in Christ.⁶³ His starting point for understanding Paul's attitude toward the body is the σῶμα πνευματικόν in 1 Cor 15:44, which he interprets in terms of Stoic philosophy in which, as we saw above, the πνεῦμα was considered to be a material or bodily substance.⁶⁴ Engberg-Pedersen maintains throughout that Stoic philosophy is the proper framework for interpreting Paul; he claims explicitly that Paul's "basic, philosophical reference point was materialistic and monistic Stoicism."⁶⁵ From this perspective, believers are literally infused with the material πνεῦμα, which then functions instrumentally to transform fleshly (or psychic) bodies into pneumatic bodies, and cognitively to reveal the wisdom of God to believers.⁶⁶ As the infusion proceeds, believers are increasingly transformed from the lower fleshly body to a higher and purer pneumatic body as the material love of God is physically poured into their hearts. This transformation comes to a climax at the resurrection when the bodies of believers are transformed into fully pneumatic bodies.

Engberg-Pedersen relates his understanding of the material πνεῦμα to bodily practice by applying his model to Paul's missionary activity and letter writing. With regard to Paul's preaching as an initial missionary contact, Engberg-Pedersen proposes that Paul understands his proclamation of the gospel to actually convey the physical πνεῦμα to his hearers, who receive the πνεῦμα into their bodies through their ears as they hear Paul's speech.⁶⁷ The reception of the πνεῦμα enables them to respond with faith to what they have heard. Paul's missionary activity of proclamation is thus conceived of as a distinctly bodily practice because it conveys the physical πνεῦμα. With regard to Paul's letter writing, Engberg-Pedersen argues that Paul sees his letters acting as a substitute for the spoken word. As substitutes, the letters were thought by Paul to function in a way similar to his personal proclamation. As with speech, the letters themselves transmit the material πνεῦμα to the letter recipients. Paul thus aimed to influence the

---

62. Engberg-Pedersen, *Cosmology and Self*, passim.
63. Engberg-Pedersen, *Cosmology and Self*, 3.
64. See Troels Engberg-Pedersen, *Paul and the Stoics* (Louisville: Westminster John Knox, 2000).
65. Engberg-Pedersen, *Cosmology and Self*, 4.
66. Engberg-Pedersen, *Cosmology and Self*, 62.
67. Engberg-Pedersen, *Cosmology and Self*, 194–98.

recipients of his letters by means of the transmission of the πνεῦμα. Again, the physical nature of the πνεῦμα transmitted by the letters makes Paul's letter writing a distinctly bodily practice.

Taking a somewhat different approach, Karl Sandnes has explored Paul's attitude toward the body through the lens of belly worship; he argues that in the Greco-Roman world the language of belly worship was a common indictment against persons whose bodily practice demonstrated that they were ruled by their desires. Through an extensive investigation of ancient physiognomics, moral philosophy, banquet descriptions, and Jewish-Hellenistic sources, he has shown that excessive eating, drinking, and copulation were ordinarily critiqued in terms of belly-devotion.[68] The evidence is so far-reaching that Sandnes argues for a belly-topos in the writings of ancient philosophers. In addition, that this topos was appropriated by the Jewish philosopher Philo suggests that it was widely known and recognized.[69] From a political perspective, belly worshipers were considered unfit for public service; those consumed with satisfying their bodily desires for food, drink, and sex were considered to be devoted to serving their own ends and pleasures, which meant they were not fit to serve the polis.[70] In contrast to belly devotees, athletes exemplified mastery of the body through perseverance in hard work to achieve long-term goals.[71] Drawing on his analysis of belly-worship, Sandnes argues that Paul's belly sayings (Phil 3:19; 1 Cor 6:12-20; Rom 16:18) are appropriations of this topos to warn his recipients against self-indulgence, not least with regard to illicit sexual activity. As those who have been joined to Christ, they are not to offer their bodies to the indulgent pleasure of self-satisfaction; rather, they are to offer their bodies in worship to God.[72]

The final work that we will consider in this section is that of Lorenzo Scornaienchi, who has produced a significant philological study that analyzes Paul's use of σάρξ and σῶμα in light of their Greco-Roman background and in contrast to one another.[73] He argues that the terms were

---

68. Sandnes, *Belly and Body*, 24–107.
69. Sandnes, *Belly and Body*, 108–32.
70. Sandnes, *Belly and Body*, 42–45, 47–52, 67–71.
71. Sandnes, *Belly and Body*, 267.
72. Sandnes, *Belly and Body*, 269–74.
73. Lorenzo Scornaienchi, *Sarx und Soma bei Paulus: Der Mensch zwischen Destruktivität und Konstruktivität*, NTOA 67 (Göttingen: Vandenhoeck & Ruprecht, 2008).

basically synonymous in Classical Greek usage, referring in general to the body and its members, with σῶμα also used sometimes with reference to a corpse. While both terms were basically neutral in Greco-Roman usage, Paul consistently attributes a more active and negative role to σάρξ, which is tied to the present evil age and stands as the destructive power behind sin.[74] In contrast, "σῶμα, in Paul, thus means the person as an inactive, externally determined being."[75] As the inactive or passive aspect of human being, σῶμα needs to be liberated from the destructive power of σάρξ in order for a person to live a constructive life of freedom in service to Christ. This movement of σῶμα from the power of σάρξ to freedom is effected by the power of the Holy Spirit. Scornaienchi sees the work of the Spirit as manifest in three ways that are relevant to the relationship between bodily resurrection and bodily practice. He sees the present constructive work of the Spirit as that which (1) points forward to the eschatological resurrection of the body, (2) incorporates people into the ecclesiological community, and (3) empowers an ethic marked by worship of God and service to others.[76] So, resurrection relates to practice in that the ethics of the worshiping community proleptically anticipate the resurrection of the body.

This review of scholarship with regard to Paul's use of σῶμα demonstrates, at the very least, that no small amount of attention has been given to the topic, and the reader may legitimately question why yet another study is warranted. I offer two points in response. First, despite the variety of approaches to Paul's somatic language throughout his letters, social-scientific readings have typically focused more narrowly on the Corinthian correspondence, and then primarily on 1 Corinthians. There is good reason for this; more than any other of the letters, the Corinthian epistles reveal a great deal of information about the social context of Pauline Christianity and thus lend themselves to social-scientific analysis. This focus, however, leaves open the need for further work to compare and correlate the findings of social-scientific readings of Paul's body language in the Corinthian letters with his other letters. Second, when social-scientific readings of Paul's somatic language have been done, eschatology in general and bodily resurrection in particular have not been sufficiently considered. The nature of my own social-scientific approach will be further developed below; for

---

74. Scornaienchi, *Sarx und Soma bei Paulus*, 288–97.
75. Scornaienchi, *Sarx und Soma bei Paulus*, 353, my translation.
76. Scornaienchi, *Sarx und Soma bei Paulus*, 234–79, 353.

now, suffice it to say that further scholarship is needed to consider how Paul's eschatology impacted the social life of the churches and how his social and ethical expectations may have related to his beliefs about the future in general and the resurrection in particular. In dialogue with the works outlined above, I will endeavor to shed fresh light on Paul's understanding of embodied life by taking up the questions once again and coming at them with a view to the social dynamics of Paul's hope for resurrection.

1.4. The Body and the Future in Pauline Scholarship

Modern scholarship on Pauline eschatology has seen three dominant approaches to interpreting the apostle's view of the future and his expectations for the believer's use of the body in light of those expectations.

1.4.1. Futurist Eschatology

A century has now passed since scholars began to give significantly increased attention to the eschatological dimension of Paul's thought. Albert Schweitzer is sometimes credited with first bringing this element of Paul's theology to a place of prominence in the critical study of the apostle's letters,[77] though Geerhardus Vos was engaged in significant work in Pauline eschatology at approximately the same time.[78] Schweitzer's two major works on Paul, *Paul and His Interpreters* and *The Mysticism of Paul the Apostle*, were attempts to correct earlier arguments that Paul was the first step in the Hellenization of early Christianity.[79] Schweitzer argued instead that Paul's letters were characterized by Jewish apocalyptic eschatology, which asserted: (1) that the crucified and resurrected Jesus was the Messiah and (2) that the return of Jesus was imminent.[80] For Schweitzer, Paul's theology was shaped by the failure of the messianic kingdom to arrive with the suffering, death, and resurrection of Jesus. If the beginning of the king-

---

77. C. Marvin Pate, *The End of the Age Has Come: The Theology of Paul* (Grand Rapids: Zondervan, 1995), 31.

78. Geerhardus Vos, *The Pauline Eschatology* (Princeton: Princeton University Press, 1930).

79. Albert Schweitzer, *Paul and His Interpreters* (repr. Macmillan, 1951); Schweitzer, *The Mysticism of Paul the Apostle*, trans. William Montgomery (London: Black, 1931).

80. Schweitzer, *Paul and His Interpreters*, 238.

dom was to be marked by the resurrection, and if Jesus had been raised, then why had other events associated with the inauguration of the messianic age not come to be (e.g., resurrection of the righteous, judgment)? That the kingdom was not inaugurated during the life of Jesus caused a shift in early Christianity in general, and in its Pauline expressions in particular, to a focus on eschatology and the future, though imminent, arrival of the kingdom.[81] But this temporal separation between the resurrection of Jesus and the advent of other eschatological events posed a problem: how were believers who continued in their natural existence to be in union with Jesus in his resurrected and glorified state?[82] Schweitzer argued that Paul's common description of believers as "in Christ" described the apostle's theology of mystical union with Christ or "being-in-Christ."[83] For Schweitzer, understanding Paul's mystical doctrine of being-in-Christ was the key to unlocking his theology as a whole. Through this mystical union with Christ, the believer transcends the present world. According to Schweitzer, "The fundamental thought of Pauline mysticism runs thus: I am in Christ; in Him I know myself as a being who is raised above this sensuous, sinful, and transient world and already belongs to the transcendent; in Him I am assured of resurrection; in Him I am a Child of God."[84] The mystical union with Christ is, from baptism onward, a constant experience of dying and rising again that comes to characterize the whole of life.[85]

With Schweitzer's emphasis on the present participation of the believer in the death and resurrection of Christ, it is important to note his assertion that the believer is mystically united with Christ in a kingdom that is not yet inaugurated. Schweitzer's view of the kingdom is that it is a thoroughly future reality. As we shall soon see, this is a key detail that distinguishes his interpretation of Paul from the "realized eschatology" of C. H. Dodd and the "already/not yet" eschatology of later interpreters. For Schweitzer, the kingdom has not yet come to be and remains a fully eschatological expectation. He insists that, "Inasmuch as believers have died and risen with Christ, and possess the Spirit, they are already partakers of the Kingdom of God, although they will not be made manifest as such *until the Kingdom*

---

81. Schweitzer, *Mysticism*, 52.
82. Schweitzer, *Mysticism*, 110–11.
83. Schweitzer, *Mysticism*, 3.
84. Schweitzer, *Mysticism*, 3.
85. Schweitzer, *Mysticism*, 17.

begins."[86] Mysteriously, the believer's union with Christ is a participation in a kingdom that is yet to be inaugurated.

Schweitzer's approach to Paul's Christ-mysticism had implications for his view of ethics in general and the believer's use of the body in particular. Schweitzer understood the believer's mystical union with Christ to be a proleptic participation in the resurrection of Christ. That is, the believer shares with Christ "the resurrection mode of existence before the resurrection has begun for the remainder of the dead."[87] Therefore, mystical union with Christ means that dying and rising with Christ constantly characterizes the believer's present bodily experience despite the continuance of present natural existence.[88] Since the believer's mystical union with Christ is considered a physical or corporeal union, certain uses of the body could destroy the believer's union with Christ. Engaging in sexual immorality, submitting to circumcision, or eating meat sacrificed to idols and thus establishing union with demons could all jeopardize and bring an end to the believer's mystical union with Christ.[89] Continued union with Christ and the future realization of that union in the resurrection of the body at the parousia depended on bodily conduct appropriate to being in Christ.

1.4.2. Realized Eschatology

In contrast to Schweitzer's futuristic eschatology, Dodd argued that the letters of Paul are characterized by "realized eschatology."[90] Dodd argued that, for Paul, the eschatological messianic community was fully realized in the church as a community of those who are the presence of Christ on earth.[91] Christ did not merely give the Spirit; the presence of the Spirit is the presence of Christ in the community. That which is true of Christ is realized in the church: "If Christ has died to this world, so have the members of His body; if He has risen into newness of life, so have they; if He being risen from the dead, dieth no more, neither do they; if God has

---

86. Schweitzer, *Mysticism*, 120, emphasis added.
87. Schweitzer, *Mysticism*, 109–10.
88. Schweitzer, *Mysticism*, 110.
89. Schweitzer, *Mysticism*, 128–29.
90. C. H. Dodd, *The Apostolic Preaching and Its Developments* (repr. Grand Rapids: Baker, 1980), 65.
91. Dodd, *Apostolic Preaching and Its Developments*, 62.

glorified Him, He has also glorified them."[92] Thus, on Dodd's reading, no future coming of the kingdom remains to be expected. The full realization of the eschaton has taken place in the Spirit-filled messianic community.

Dodd also believed that such a realized eschatology established a stronger foundation for ethics than was possible in a futuristic eschatology. An emphasis on the future, as in Schweitzer, devalued the present and undermined "the finer and more humane aspects of morality."[93] Alternatively, realized eschatology is the "foundation for a strong, positive, and constructive social ethic."[94] That Christ's presence is realized in the church necessitates an attitude of love toward those in whom Christ dwells. Love is thus the greatest gift of the Spirit and the chief characteristic of the eschatological community realized in the church.

1.4.3. Already/Not Yet Eschatology

A third approach attempts to combine the strengths of Schweitzer's futuristic eschatology and Dodd's realized eschatology by identifying a tension in Paul's thinking between that which has already been realized and that which has not. Oscar Cullmann is credited with first advancing this already/not yet scheme, though it has since gained widespread acceptance among Pauline scholars.[95] He recognized that Paul's letters, like other

---

92. Dodd, *Apostolic Preaching and Its Developments*, 62–63.

93. Dodd, *Apostolic Preaching and Its Developments*, 64; C. H. Dodd, *New Testament Studies* (New York: Scribners, 1954), 109–13.

94. Dodd, *Apostolic Preaching and its Developments*, 64.

95. Oscar Cullmann, *Christ and Time: The Primitive Christian Conception of Time and History*, trans. Floyd V. Filson (London: SCM, 1951). While Cullmann is often credited with first arguing this position, the already/not yet scheme was anticipated by Vos in *Pauline Eschatology*. For others who have read Paul's eschatology through the already/not yet lens, see W. G. Kümmel, *Promise and Fulfillment: The Eschatological Message of Jesus* (Naperville, IL: Allenson, 1957); Käsemann, *Perspectives on Paul*, 60–78; Herman Ridderbos, *Paul: An Outline of His Theology*, trans. John Richard Dewitt (Grand Rapids: Eerdmans, 1975); Richard B. Gaffin, *Resurrection and Redemption: A Study in Paul's Soteriology* (Peabody, MA: Hendrickson, 1978); J. Christiaan Beker, *Paul the Apostle: The Triumph of God in Life and Thought* (Philadelphia: Fortress, 1980); Andrew Lincoln, *Paradise Now and Not Yet: Studies in the Role of the Heavenly Dimension in Paul's Thought with Special Reference to His Eschatology*, SNTSMS 43 (Cambridge: Cambridge University Press, 1981); John Ziesler, *Pauline Christianity*, rev ed., Oxford Bible Series (Oxford: Oxford University Press, 1983); Dale C. Allison, *The End of the Ages Has Come: An Early Interpretation of the Passion and Resurrection*

Second Temple literature, are characterized by a division of time into two ages, namely the present age and the age to come. For Paul, the age to come (or the messianic age) was inaugurated with the death and resurrection of Jesus Christ. However, many events associated with the coming of the messianic age did not come to pass (e.g., judgment of the wicked, resurrection of the righteous). Thus, Paul saw the age to come as having been inaugurated in the Christ event prior to the end of the present evil age. Paul and his contemporaries saw themselves as living in the period of time in which the messianic age had *already* been inaugurated even though it had *not yet* been brought to its consummation.

When considered from this already/not yet perspective, Paul's concern for bodily practice is often viewed in terms of the ethics of the new age, inaugurated though not yet consummated, being brought to bear on the lives of believers even as the present age continues. This eschatological perspective sheds light on various elements of Paul's thought. From a Christological perspective, the believer's solidarity with the resurrected Christ is the basis for her ongoing sanctification as the future life of resurrection is worked out in the believer's present life. Union with Christ means freedom from the life of sin and the present, though paradoxical, experience of the life of the age to come.[96] From a pneumatological perspective, the Holy Spirit is seen as the agent who applies the life of the age

---

of Jesus (Philadelphia: Fortress, 1985); Wolfgang Schrage, *The Ethics of the New Testament*, trans. D. E. Green (Philadelphia: Fortress, 1988), 181–86; Judith M. Gundry Volf, *Paul and Perseverance: Staying in and Falling Away* (Louisville: Westminster John Knox, 1990); J. Paul Sampley, *Walking between the Times: Paul's Moral Reasoning* (Minneapolis: Fortress, 1991); Ben Witherington, *Jesus, Paul, and the End of the World: A Comparative Study in New Testament Eschatology* (Downers Grove, IL: InterVarsity Press, 1992); Gordon D. Fee, *God's Empowering Presence: The Holy Spirit in the Letters of Paul* (Peabody, MA: Hendrickson, 1994); Pate, *The End of the Age Has Come: The Theology of Paul*; Richard B. Hays, *The Moral Vision of the New Testament: Community, Cross, New Creation: A Contemporary Introduction to New Testament Ethics* (San Francisco: Harper Collins, 1996); Dunn, *Theology of Paul*; Calvin Roetzel, *Paul: The Man and the Myth*, Studies on Personalities of the New Testament (Minneapolis: Fortress, 1999); Wright, *Resurrection*, 252, 272–75; Richard B. Hays, *The Conversion of the Imagination: Paul as Interpreter of Israel's Scripture* (Grand Rapids: Eerdmans, 2005); Kirk, *Unlocking Romans*; Rodney Reeves, *Spirituality according to Paul: Imitating the Apostle of Christ* (Downers Grove, IL: InterVarsity Press, 2011); N. T. Wright, *Paul and the Faithfulness of God* (Minneapolis: Fortress, 2013).

96. See, e.g., Sampley, *Walking*, 18–19; Gaffin, *Resurrection and Redemption*, 33–60; Schrage, *Ethics of the New Testament*, 181–86; Wright, *Resurrection*, 253.

to come in the present and empowers the believer to live a mature Christian life, a life in which she is under no compulsion to sin.[97]

A growing subset of scholars among those who adopt the already/not yet approach advocate what has come to be known as an apocalyptic reading of the apostle.[98] Apocalyptic readings tend to emphasize the discontinuity between the two ages.[99] The old age is marked by the rule of

---

97. Fee, *God's Empowering Presence*, 803–25.

98. The beginnings of the apocalyptic appraoch to Paul are often traced back to Ernst Käsemann, *New Testament Questions of Today* (Philadelphia: Fortress, 1969), 102. For what is commonly considered the first comprehensive articulation of an apocalyptic approach to Paul, see Beker, *Paul the Apostle*. For others who take an apocalyptic approach to Paul, see Leander E. Keck, "Paul and Apocalyptic Theology," *Int* 38 (1984): 229–41; Martinus C. de Boer, *The Defeat of Death: Apocalyptic Eschatology in 1 Corinthians 15 and Romans 5*, JSNTSup 22 (Sheffield: JSOT Press, 1988); Charles B. Cousar, *A Theology of the Cross: The Death of Jesus in the Pauline Letters*, Overtures to Biblical Theology 24 (Minneapolis: Fortress, 1990); Alexandra Brown, *The Cross and Human Transformation: Paul's Apocalyptic Word in 1 Corinthians* (Minneapolis: Fortress, 1995); J. Louis Martyn, *Theological Issues in the Letters of Paul* (Nashville: Abingdon, 1997); Beverly Roberts Gaventa, *Our Mother Saint Paul* (Louisville: Westminster John Knox, 2007); Michael J. Gorman, *Inhabiting the Cruciform God: Kenosis, Justification, and Theosis in Paul's Narrative Soteriology* (Grand Rapids: Eerdmans, 2009); Douglas A. Campbell, *The Deliverance of God: An Apocalyptic Rereading of Justification in Paul* (Grand Rapids: Eerdmans, 2009). For a critical evaluation of apocalyptic approaches to Paul, see R. Barry Matlock, *Unveiling the Apocalyptic Paul: Paul's Interpreters and the Rhetoric of Criticism*, JSNTSupp 127 (Sheffield: Sheffield Academic, 1996).

99. The language of *apocalyptic* has been used in the study of the New Testament in four distinguishable ways: (1) apocalypticism as a social ideology, (2) apocalypse as a literary genre, (3) apocalyptic imagery as the various motifs associated with apocalypticism and found in the apocalypses in the early Jewish and Christian sources, and (4) apocalyptic eschatology as a set of ideas often emphasizing the transcendence and sovereignty of God and radical discontinuity between the present and God's future. This final option reflects the use of the term with regard to Paul. For apocalyptic in early Judaism and Christianity, see, e.g., D. S. Russell, *The Method and Message of Jewish Apocalyptic* (Philadelphia: Fortress, 1964); Käsemann, *New Testament Questions of Today*, 108–37; Paul D. Hanson, *The Dawn of Apocalyptic* (Philadelphia: Fortress, 1975); Christopher Rowland, *The Open Heaven: A Study of Apocalyptic in Judaism and Early Christianity* (London: SPCK, 1982); Wright, *New Testament and the People of God*, 280–338; David E. Aune, "Apocalypticism," in *Dictionary of Paul and His Letters*, ed. Gerald F. Hawthorne and Ralph P. Martin (Downers Grove, IL: InterVarsity Press, 1993); John J. Collins, *The Apocalyptic Imagination: An Introduction to Jewish Apocalyptic Literature*, Biblical Resource Series (Grand Rapids: Eerdmans,

oppressive powers to which human beings are enslaved and from which human beings need to be liberated (Gal 4:3–5). The Christ event marks the inbreaking of the new age, which is also the decisive victory that liberates those who are in Christ from the bondage of the powers that rule in the old age. The discontinuity between the ages provides a way of mapping Paul's flesh and Spirit language. As a power that holds human beings in bondage, the flesh is associated with the old age and is subject to corruption, decay, and death.[100] Through their identification with Christ, believers are transferred to life in the Spirit, leaving the bondage of the flesh behind. It is here that an apocalyptic ethic emerges. Paul expects believers to live in a way that accords with their liberated state rather than returning to the manner of life that is characterized by the regulations of the old age. Thus, apocalyptic interpreters of Paul aim to shed light on the apostle's eschatology and ethics by interpreting these themes with a view to the discontinuity between the ages. Much more could be said to describe the nuances of the various apocalyptic readings of Paul, and we will engage some elements of those readings in the chapters to follow. For now, it will suffice to say that the decisive inauguration of the new age figures significantly in Paul's attitude toward the believer's use of the body, and the insights of those who argue for an apocalyptic reading of Paul will inform my own discussion of the texts under consideration.

1.5. Methodological Considerations

Sociorhetorical interpretation was first introduced to biblical studies by Vernon K. Robbins in 1984 with the publication of *Jesus the Teacher: A Socio-rhetorical Interpretation of Mark*.[101] Robbins aimed to provide researchers with a hermeneutical framework that gives detailed attention

---

1998); Richard Bauckham, "Apocalypses," in *The Complexities of Second Temple Judaism*, vol. 1 of *Justification and Variegated Nomism*, ed. D. A. Carson, Peter T. O'Brien, and Mark A. Seifrid (Grand Rapids: Baker, 2001), 1:136–87.

100. While the flesh is a power that enslaves humanity, it should not be identified with the cosmic powers, though the cosmic powers might be said to exercise power through the flesh. See Keck, "Paul and Apocalyptic Theology," 238.

101. Vernon K. Robbins, *Jesus the Teacher: A Socio-rhetorical Interpretation of Mark* (repr. Minneapolis: Fortress, 2009); Robbins later set forth his methodology in two handbooks: *Exploring the Texture of Texts: A Guide to Socio-rhetorical Interpretation* (Valley Forge, PA: Trinity Press International, 1996); *The Tapestry of Early Christian Discourse: Rhetoric, Society, and Ideology* (New York: Routledge, 1996).

1. Questions, Context, and Method   31

not only to the text of the New Testament itself but also to the interpreter's own ideology, presuppositions, and perspectives. In order to accomplish this goal, he drew on elements of modern linguistic theory, the social sciences, and rhetorical studies. His approach requires reading and rereading the text through the different lenses of a variety of interpretive strategies, or textures, as he calls them, which are often kept separate.[102] The intended result is a rich reading of the text that is sensitive to the details of the text and the larger frameworks of meaning that shape the beliefs of author and interpreter.

Following Robbins's initial introduction of sociorhetorical criticism to the study of the New Testament, Ben Witherington adopted the term to describe a somewhat different approach. Where Robbins's methodology draws on modern rhetorical and linguistic categories in addition to ancient rhetorical arrangement and strategy, Witherington's use of the sociorhetorical method focuses primarily on the historical categories by analyzing the New Testament documents against the background of ancient Greco-Roman rhetorical practice common during the New Testament period. His work has been characterized by questions as to whether the New Testament authors adopted and utilized Greco-Roman rhetorical convention and how their persuasive efforts might have been understood within their first-century Hellenistic social setting.[103] He has, at times, drawn on modern social-scientific theory in his interpretation of the New Testament. For the most part, Witherington's published writings have focused more on social history than the application of modern sociological concepts to the biblical text.[104] Given these divergent approaches to sociorhetorical criticism, it is necessary to define precisely what is meant by the sociorhetorical approach of this study.

---

102. Robbins proposes five textures: (1) inner texture, (2) intertexture, (3) social and cultural texture, (4) ideological texture, and (5) sacred texture (*Exploring the Texture of Texts*, 2–4). Cf. Robbins, *Tapestry of Early Christian Discourse*, 37–40.

103. Ben Witherington, *New Testament Rhetoric: An Introductory Guide to the Art of Persuasion in and of the New Testament* (Eugene, OR: Cascade, 2009). Cf. Witherington's sociorhetorical commentaries on all of the New Testament documents.

104. Witherington did, however, make use of group-grid analysis in his *Conflict and Community in Corinth: A Socio-rhetorical Commentary on 1 and 2 Corinthians* (Grand Rapids: Eerdmans, 1995). As will be further explained below, the present study will also draw on modern social-scientific studies where they shed light on the historical questions.

1.5.1. Social-Scientific Criticism

The central concern of this study is Paul's attitude toward the relationship between bodily resurrection and bodily practice. The mention of bodies immediately raises questions that are sociological in nature. Embodied existence is central to the social dimension of every person's life. The body is the means by which we all engage society in general and specific groups and people in particular.[105] In 1934, Marcel Mauss argued that all knowledge of how to behave with the body is learned from society, even if such knowledge and its corresponding behavior varies from society to society.[106] That is to say, adults do not behave in purely natural ways but in habits acquired by means of cultural immersion.[107] Despite the critique of Douglas that Mauss creates a false dichotomy between nature and culture, the central point stands: the (natural) way human beings use their bodies is necessarily conditioned by their social context.[108] In light of this point, Douglas advanced the hypothesis that "bodily control is an expression of social control."[109] This hypothesis comes as part of her argument that (1) the use of the body will be coordinated to achieve consonance with other means of expression and that (2) social controls limit the ways the body might be used as a medium of expression.[110] If the means of expression are to be coordinated, then bodily behavior and social control will coordinate with ideology. Thus, if correlations between bodily and social controls are identified, it creates a basis for studying coordinate attitudes toward ideology in general and theology in particular.[111] Since the issue is correlation rather than causation, the relationships need not necessarily work in only one direction, from bodily controls to theology, for example. The correlations might begin with the theological attitudes that shed light on

---

105. Dunn, *Theology of Paul*, 61.
106. Marcel Mauss, "Techniques of the Body," *Economy and Society* 2 (1973): 70–76. This essay was originally delivered as a lecture on May 17, 1934, at a meeting of the Société de Psychologie.
107. Mauss, "Techniques of the Body," 73–74.
108. Douglas, *Natural Symbols*, 76. Cf. John H. Elliot, *What Is Social-Scientific Criticism?*, GBS (Minneapolis: Fortress, 1993), 36–37; Bruce J. Malina, *The New Testament World: Insights from Cultural Anthropology*, 3rd ed. (Louisville: Westminster John Knox, 2001), 7–9.
109. Douglas, *Natural Symbols*, 78.
110. Douglas, *Natural Symbols*, 74–79.
111. Douglas, *Natural Symbols*, 78.

corresponding attitudes toward the body. The key insight is that any hope of motivating new bodily practices requires corresponding social forms and social influence.

These sociological considerations carry potential for shedding light on Paul's understanding of the relationship between bodily resurrection and bodily practice. In what sense is future bodily resurrection a social phenomenon? Does Paul's understanding of the eschatological resurrection of the body correspond to his expectations for the way believers relate to one another and to the world through their bodies? How might Paul's eschatological ideology reinforce, adapt, or challenge the social world of his hearers? Questions like these provide opportunity for further insight and a more holistic understanding of the relationship between Paul's eschatological ideology of bodily resurrection, social identity and control, and somatic behavior in the Pauline communities.

One potentially fruitful avenue for considering the social dynamics of Paul's attitude toward the body comes from the field of social psychology. Social identity theory (SIT) was initially developed by Henri Tajfel and is defined as "that *part* of an individual's self-concept which derives from his knowledge of his membership of a social group (or groups) together with the value and emotional significance attached to that membership."[112] Tajfel recognized that the way individuals view themselves is shaped in part by their membership in social groups.[113] He articulated three aspects of group membership: (1) a cognitive aspect comprised by the awareness that one belongs to a group, (2) an evaluative aspect involving the positive or negative value attached to group membership, and (3) an emotional aspect involving sentiment toward members of one's own group and others in relation to the group.[114] Tajfel was particularly interested in how

---

112. Henri Tajfel, "Social Categorization, Social Identity and Social Comparison," in *Differentiation between Social Groups: Studies in the Social Psychology of Intergroup Relations*, ed. Henri Tajfel, European Monographs in Social Psychology (London: Academic, 1978), 63, emphasis original. For the use of SIT to interpret the New Testament, see J. Brian Tucker and Coleman A. Baker, eds., *T&T Clark Handbook to Social Identity in the New Testament* (London: Bloomsbury T&T Clark, 2014).

113. Henri Tajfel, "Introduction," in *Social Identity and Intergroup Relations: Studies in the Social Psychology of Intergroup Relations*, ed. Henri Tajfel, European Monographs in Social Psychology (Cambridge: Cambridge University Press, 1982), 2.

114. Henri Tajfel, "Interindividual Behavior and Intergroup Behavior," in *Differentiations between Social Groups: Studies in the Social Psychology of Intergroup Rela-

groups form and relate to one another, especially in terms of positive differentiation.[115]

Tajfel's work was largely focused on intergroup relations and had little to say with regard to intragroup processes.[116] In an effort to move beyond the limits of SIT, John C. Turner, a student of Tajfel, developed what is known as self-categorization theory (SCT) and published it together with a group of other researchers.[117] SCT is distinguished from SIT in that self-categorization "is focused on the explanation not of a specific kind of group behavior but of how individuals are able to act as a group at all."[118] Turner was thus interested in questions of how individuals become a group, how they define themselves as a group, and how they behave as a group.[119] The theory suggests that individuals coalesce into a group through a process of self-categorization, which involves "cognitive groupings of oneself and some class of stimuli as the same ... in contrast to some other class of stimuli."[120] That is, when two or more people perceive that they bear some similarity that distinguishes them from others, they constitute a group. This is aided by the process of depersonalization, which "refers to the process of 'self-stereotyping' whereby people come to perceive themselves more as the interchangeable exemplars of a social category than as unique personalities defined by their individual differences from others."[121] It is important to understand that an individual will have multiple social categories, and those categories exist at different and variable levels of importance.[122] This brings us to the concept of salience, which "refers to the conditions under which some specific group membership becomes cognitively prepotent in self-perception to act as the immediate influence

---

tions, ed. Henri Tajfel, European Monographs in Social Psychology (London: Academic, 1978), 28–29.

115. See further the discussion of Tajfel's work in Philip F. Esler, "An Outline of Social Identity Theory," in Tucker and Baker, *T&T Clark Handbook to Social Identity in the New Testament*, 13–22.

116. Esler, "An Outline of Social Identity Theory," 22.

117. John C. Turner et al., *Rediscovering the Social Group: A Self-Categorization Theory* (Oxford: Blackwell, 1987).

118. Turner et al., *Rediscovering the Social Group*, 42.

119. Turner et al., *Rediscovering the Social Group*, 1.

120. Turner et al., *Rediscovering the Social Group*, 44.

121. Turner et al., *Rediscovering the Social Group*, 50.

122. Michael A. Hogg and Dominic Abrams, *Social Identifications: A Social Psychology of Intergroup Relations and Group Processes* (New York: Routledge, 1988), 19.

on perception and behavior." Identity salience depends on context and can be affected by a variety of circumstances.[123] Whichever identity is active at the moment is said to be salient.[124]

Our interest in the social function of hope for future bodily resurrection raises the question of how embodiment relates to the formation and maintenance of social identity over time. But as Susan Condor has observed, the role of time in relation to group identity has not been the subject of extensive discussion among social identity theorists.[125] One theorist who has attempted to deal with the temporal processes in group identity is Marco Cinnirella, who turns to the concept of possible selves developed by Hazel Markus and Paula Nurius. According to Markus and Nurius, possible selves refer to a person's beliefs about the self in the past and what the self might become in the future. Such beliefs about the self are particularly important for two reasons: (1) "they function as incentives for future behavior," and (2) "they provide an evaluative and interpretive context for the current view of self."[126] Individuals attempt to achieve positively valued possible selves and avoid other more negatively valued possible selves.[127] This means that possible selves help to explain past behavior and allow new behavior to be interpreted and evaluated in terms of the probability that it will result in the desired future self. Cinnirella identifies as a weakness, however, the failure of the possible selves tradition to adequately deal with the dynamic between individual and group, and he argues that possible social identity, which is the self's perception of present or future group memberships, should be numbered among other possible selves.[128] That is to say, one possible self is the self as a member of this or that group. Focused on the dynamic between individual and

---

123. Hogg and Abrams, *Social Identifications*, 25.

124. While SIT and SCT are distinct theories, the latter is a development of the former, and they are often referred to simply as social identity theory, a practice I will follow in subsequent chapters.

125. Susan Condor, "Social Identity and Time," in *Social Groups and Identities: Developing the Legacy of Henri Tajfel*, ed. P. Robinson (Oxford: Butterworth Heinemann, 1996), 285–315; cf. Philip F. Esler, *Conflict and Identity in Romans: The Social Setting of Paul's Letter* (Minneapolis: Fortress, 2003), 22.

126. Hazel Markus and Paula Nurius, "Possible Selves," *American Psychologist* 41.9 (1986): 955.

127. Marco Cinnirella, "Exploring Temporal Aspects of Social Identity: The Concept of Possible Social Identities," *EJSP* 28 (1998): 229.

128. Cinnirella, "Exploring Temporal Aspects of Social Identity," 230.

group processes, Cinnirella hypothesizes that "ingroup members are concerned to persuade both other ingroupers *and also outgroupers*, to endorse the desired possible social identities of the ingroup i.e. [sic] to accept positively evaluated 'visions' of what might happen to the ingroup in the future, or alternatively, positively evaluated constructions of the ingroup's history."[129] Additionally, he argues that ingroup members craft narratives, which he calls "life stories," that give coherence to the past, present, and desired future of the group. These "life stories" undergird the social identity of the group and have the potential to persuade members of the group to adopt a particular desired future group identity.[130]

One other theory that will prove useful in our study is the Common Ingroup Identity Model developed by Samuel L. Gaertner and John F. Dovidio.[131] Each of the Pauline letters under review in this study involves conflict. The theory considers potential avenues for reducing bias between competing groups in order to foster intergroup cooperation. Gaertner and Dovidio argue that the perception of social categories and group boundaries are significant factors in achieving that goal. Antagonism between groups can be reduced more effectively if the embattled group members can come to see one another as members of the same category. Recategorization thus involves encouraging "the members of both groups to regard themselves as belonging to a common, superordinate group—*one group* that is inclusive of both memberships."[132] This can happen through a variety of means including, but not limited to, highlighting common superordinate group memberships, introducing new factors like shared goals, and introducing shared benefits. The process of recategorization is more likely to be effective if individuals are not required to abandon their previously held group identities. Rather, it is possible for them to "maintain a 'dual' representation in which both superordinate and original group identities are salient simultaneously."[133] The question for us as this study proceeds is whether and to what extent Paul's hope for resurrection

---

129. Cinnirella, "Exploring Temporal Aspects of Social Identity," 235, emphasis original.

130. Cinnirella, "Exploring Temporal Aspects of Social Identity," 235–36.

131. Samuel L. Gaertner and John F. Dovidio, *Reducing Intergroup Bias: The Common Ingroup Identity Model*, Essays in Social Psychology (New York: Routledge, 2000).

132. Gaertner and Dovidio, *Reducing Intergroup Bias*, 33.

133. Gaertner and Dovidio, *Reducing Intergroup Bias*, 3.

and attitude toward embodiment function in conflict settings to facilitate recategorization into a single superordinate group.

Interpreters of ancient texts must always be cautious to avoid imposing theories that are themselves foreign to the world in which the text was originally composed, and the letters of Paul are no exception. Three observations will help us to guard against this danger. First, Douglas argues that the body is universally seen as a symbol of society, even if the specific elements of that relationship vary from culture to culture. The danger is not in suggesting correlation between body, society, and ideology; the danger is presupposing that the correlations are the same as in another culture, that of the interpreter for example. Second, in order to sufficiently distinguish between the culture of the Pauline communities and alternative cultures, careful attention will be given to the social world of first century Christianity.[134] This balance of social theory with early Christian social history will serve to protect us from the temptation to press the data to fit a theory.[135] Third, the temptation to manipulate the textual data to accommodate the theory is also mitigated by considering the extent to which the data may run contrary to the theory. When that happens, it does not necessarily mean the theory is unhelpful. Rather, it prompts us to consider why the text and theory do not align.

---

134. Wayne A Meeks, *The First Urban Christians: The Social World of the Apostle Paul*, 2nd ed. (New Haven: Yale University Press, 1983); John E. Stambaugh and David L. Balch, *The New Testament in Its Social Environment*, LEC 2 (Philadelphia: Westminster, 1986).

135. There is debate as to whether and to what extent social-scientific criticism of the New Testament must be conducted on the basis of accepted models established by social scientists. For the view that models must form the basis for social-scientific interpretation, see Bruce J. Malina, "Social-Scientific Methods in Historical Jesus Research," in *The Social Setting of Jesus and the Gospels*, ed. Wolfgang Stegemann, Bruce J. Malina, and Gerd Theissen (Minneapolis: Fortress, 2002), 3. For the view that social-scientific criticism need not necessarily proceed on the basis of models and that "there is no sustainable distinction to be drawn between what is 'social-science' and what is 'social history,'" see David G. Horrell, "Whither Social-Scientific Approaches to New Testament Interpretation? Reflections on Contested Methodologies and the Future," in *After the First Urban Christians: The Social-Scientific Study of Pauline Christianity Twenty-Five Years Later*, ed. Todd D. Still and David G. Horrell (New York: T&T Clark, 2009), 6–20, esp. 17. For a detailed analysis of Horrell's argument, see Matthew P. O'Reilly, "Review of *After the First Urban Christians*, Todd D. Still and David G. Horrell (eds.)," *Reviews in Religion and Theology* 19.3 (2012): 369–72.

1.5.2. Rhetorical Criticism

Paul's letters in general, and his discussion of the body in particular, have a persuasive agenda. He wrote to convince his recipients to use their bodies in a way consistent with his articulated expectations. Since Paul's letters are persuasive documents from the Greco-Roman period, and in order to investigate how Paul's persuasive purposes shed light on his understanding of the relationship between the use of the body and his eschatological expectations, the future resurrection of the body not least, the major passages under review will be read in light of ancient Greco-Roman rhetorical convention.

Hans Dieter Betz's commentary on Galatians is considered the landmark study that opened the door for rhetorical criticism of the Pauline epistles, and since Betz's work, numerous rhetorical analyses of Paul's letters have been produced.[136] As the discipline of rhetorical criticism developed, two distinct schools of thought have emerged. The first takes rhetorical criticism to be an historical-critical method and aims to classify texts according to classical Greco-Roman rhetorical convention.[137] With regard to the study of Paul, historical rhetorical critics consider whether and how the apostle's letters conform to or deviate from customary practices in the first century with regard to the invention, arrangement, and style of speeches and letters. Primary sources for this historical endeavor are the standard ancient rhetorical handbooks, speeches, and persuasive letters. The second school of thought is known as New Rhetoric, and while advocates sometimes make use of classical rhetorical sources and categories, New Rhetoric looks also to modern language theory and epistemology to evaluate the rhetorical force of biblical texts.[138] Where historical rhetorical criticism classifies texts according to ancient categories that could have been familiar to the biblical authors and their first readers, New Rhetoric

---

136. Hans Dieter Betz, *Galatians: A Commentary on Paul's Letter to the Churches in Galatia*, Hermeneia (Philadelphia: Fortress, 1979). Cf. Betz, *2 Corinthians 8 and 9: A Commentary on Two Administrative Letters of the Apostle Paul*, Hermeneia (Philadelphia: Fortress, 1985).

137. George A. Kennedy, *New Testament Interpretation through Rhetorical Criticism* (Chapel Hill: University of North Carolina Press, 1984); Witherington, *New Testament Rhetoric*. Cf. Duane F. Watson, *The Rhetoric of the New Testament: A Bibliographic Survey* (Blandford Forum: Deo, 2006), esp. 18–53, 121–72.

138. Chaïm Perelman and L. Olbrechts-Tyteca, *The New Rhetoric: A Treatise on Argumentation*, trans. John Wilkinson and Purcell Weaver (repr. Notre Dame, IN: University of Notre Dame Press, 2008).

incorporates modern categories unknown to the first-century authors of the New Testament. This is not to say that one school of rhetorical criticism is to be preferred over the other. It is to say that, given the different uses of the rhetorical critical label, clarity as to which sort of rhetorical critical analysis is being conducted is essential.

The present study will draw primarily on the historical rhetorical methods developed by proponents of the first school of thought, though insights from New Rhetoric will be included where they shed light on the historical questions driving this investigation. As an historical study, the rhetorical critical methodology will be employed to consider Paul's discussion of the relationship between bodily practice and bodily resurrection in light of the rhetorical categories common in the first century Roman Empire, not least with regard to Paul's efforts to persuade his hearers to use their bodies in particular ways that accord with his expectations. Paul's discussion of the relationship between bodily resurrection and bodily practice will be analyzed as it relates to the rhetorical species of each letter, its place within the overall arrangement of material in classical rhetorical divisions, and the manner in which it contributes to the argumentative strategy and persuasive aims of each individual letter.

It must be said that this historical rhetorical method has not come without critics, often from within the larger discipline of New Testament historical criticism.[139] For example, concern has been expressed over the use of oratorical convention to analyze written letters. This criticism often comes from advocates of epistolary criticism and claims that the analysis of written texts should not be conducted on the basis of oratorical convention.[140] Epistolary critics point to ancient theorists who differentiate between the written word and speechmaking to substantiate the point that rhetorical convention is out of place in the analysis of Paul's written letters.[141] Three points can be raised in response. First, evidence exists that

---

139. What follows draws heavily on Peter Lampe, "Rhetorical Analysis of Pauline Texts-Quo Vadit? Methodological Reflections," in *Paul and Rhetoric*, ed. J. Paul Sampley and Peter Lampe (New York: T&T Clark, 2010), 3–21, esp. 10–17.

140. See the discussion in Lampe, "Rhetorical Analysis of Pauline Texts," 12–17. For ancient epistolary theory see Stanley K. Stowers, *Letter Writing in Greco-Roman Antiquity*, LEC 5 (Philadelphia: Westminster, 1986); John L. White, *Light from Ancient Letters* (Philadelphia: Fortress, 1986).

141. Stanley E. Porter and Bryan R. Dyer, "Oral Texts? A Reassessment of the Oral and Rhetorical Nature of Paul's Letters in Light of Recent Studies," *JETS* 55 (2012): 335–36.

rhetorical convention was sometimes integrated into the writing of letters in the ancient world. Speech structures have been identified in ancient letters, not least in letters that fall within the deliberative species.[142] Second, Paul's epistles do not function as mere letters; they were delivered as speeches upon their arrival at the recipient churches. This means that the letters were almost certainly composed with a view to their oral presentation for a specific rhetorical situation. Therefore, even though Paul's letters have typical epistolary features, their openings and closings for example, they cannot be said to have no oral component, and their analysis on the basis of oral rhetorical convention should not be ruled out.[143] Third, while Paul's letters do adopt (and adapt) some features of Greco-Roman letters, they also depart in significant ways from ancient epistolary convention. As a result, the comparison of Paul's letters to other ancient letters may yield limited insight.[144] In light of these considerations, rhetorical criticism should be seen to be of enduring value because it provides a legitimate approach for analyzing the persuasive nature of the Pauline epistles that complements epistolary analysis.[145]

1.6. The Contribution of This Study

Past approaches to the body-future dynamic in Paul's letters have made use of theological, anthropological, and ideological approaches. When a social-scientific perspective is utilized, the focus is often on 1 Corinthians, with less attention to the other undisputed letters. No definitive consensus has emerged with regard to the social function of Paul's attitude toward the body, and there is a need to open up more generally the social nature

---

142. Margaret M. Mitchell, *Paul and the Rhetoric of Reconciliation: An Exegetical Investigation of the Language and Composition of 1 Corinthians* (Louisville: Westminster John Knox, 1993), 20–23; Lampe, "Rhetorical Analysis of Pauline Texts," 14.

143. Witherington, *New Testament Rhetoric*, 1–5.

144. Witherington, *New Testament Rhetoric*, 5.

145. The question of whether Paul had a formal rhetorical education is also matter of scholarly debate. For a survey of the debate, see Ryan S. Schellenberg, *Rethinking Paul's Rhetorical Education: Comparative Rhetoric and 2 Corinthians 10–13*, ECL 10 (Atlanta: Society of Biblical Literature, 2013), 17–56. In my view, the question of Paul's education is less important than the question of whether his letters give evidence that he was familiar with the canons of Greco-Roman rhetoric. As this study proceeds, it will be clear that I join those in arguing that the apostle was not only familiar with but also employed the standard persuasive tools of his day.

of future bodily resurrection in Paul's thought. Work remains to be done on the social function of resurrection in Paul's thought, not least with regard to the way beliefs about the resurrection may have related to early Christian practice on the one hand and Paul's persuasive ambitions on the other. The questions under investigation in this study, therefore, aim to shed further light on Paul's attitude toward the relationship between the resurrection of the body and bodily practice, with particular reference to his social and rhetorical purposes.

In light of these needs, chapter 2 will offer a close reading of the designated texts in the Corinthian correspondence. As the discussion proceeds, special attention will be given to the social nature of Paul's hope for future bodily resurrection. I argue that in 1 Cor 15:12–58 future bodily resurrection functions in Cinnirella's terms as a "future social identity." That is to say, for Paul, the future self is the self as a member of the resurrected group. We will then consider that future social identity as it relates to Paul's expectations for the use of the body with regard to sexual practices (1 Cor 6:12–20) and in situations that involve suffering (2 Cor 4:7–5:10). Chapter 3 will focus on the relationship between the body and the future in Rom 6 and 8. We will find that Paul sees believers as free from the power of sin by virtue of their union with Christ in his death, which anticipates union with Christ in his resurrection. This freedom gives believers the ability to resist sin and embody holiness as a means of showing continuity between the present life and the future resurrection of the body. I argue that Paul's theology of the body functions as a framework for interpreting the conflict over table fellowship in Rom 14 and 15, and that bringing bodies together at the table is itself a practice that stands in continuity with the hope for resurrection. Chapter 4 takes us to Philippians, which is occasioned in part by conflict among the recipients and suffering imposed on them by outsiders. I argue again that future bodily resurrection functions as a future social identity and that Paul portrays the group's history in a way that constructs a coherent diachronic representation. Paul's account of the future identity facilitates ingroup distinctiveness which has potential to mitigate existing faction and strengthen the recipients to stand firm in the face of persecution. The study will conclude with a final chapter that integrates the overall findings and points to potential avenues for further research.

It is well known that Paul's attitude toward the body and the hope of resurrection have been the object of significant scholarly focus. My hope is that the contribution of this project will be seen in terms of framing old problems with a fresh methodological approach. The desired result is a more well-rounded understanding of Paul's attitude toward bodily resurrection and its function in relation to the use of the body, particularly in terms of the social and persuasive dynamics of that relationship and its role in forming and maintaining group identity among early groups of Christ-followers. As the argument develops, it will become increasingly clear that future bodily resurrection functions as one marker of group identity that carries significant implications for the shared life of the community. For Paul, belief in resurrection defines the people of God.

2

Embracing Resurrection:
The Corinthian Correspondence

We begin this investigation of Paul's understanding of bodily resurrection in relation to bodily practice with his letters to Corinth. This is advantageous in that no other letter in the Pauline corpus deals more extensively with Paul's attitude toward the body and the resurrection of the body than 1 Corinthians.[1] Our study of 1 Corinthians begins with an analysis of the social and rhetorical situation that formed the background of the concerns addressed in the letter. We will then consider the apostle's attitude toward bodily practice in relation to bodily resurrection in 1 Cor 15:12–58 and 6:12–20. That relationship is more clearly in view in 6:12–20, but 1 Cor 15:12–58 shows concern for the relationship between ethics and resurrection, and it provides essential context for our reading of 6:12–20. It may seem counterintuitive to begin with material from the end of the letter; however, 1 Cor 15 is Paul's lengthiest extant discussion of bodily resurrection and provides a natural place for initial data gathering. As the discussion proceeds, we will consider the rhetorical structure and aims of Paul's argument and how it relates to questions of identity that arise from the exegesis of the major passages under consideration.

2.1. First Corinthians

2.1.1. Social and Rhetorical Situation

As one of the earliest interpreters to read Paul's letters through the lens of Greco-Roman rhetorical categories, Wilhelm Wuellner argued that 1 Corinthians was an example of epideictic rhetoric. His study was focused

---

1. See Neyrey, *Paul, in Other Words*, 114–15.

particularly on digressions in the letter (1:19–3:21; 9:1–10:13; 13:1–13), which functioned to strengthen the recipients' affirmation of shared values.[2] As interest in rhetorical criticism increased, Wuellner's view became increasingly questioned. Without providing an extended analysis, George A. Kennedy suggested that 1 Corinthians was "largely deliberative," though some passages could be considered judicial.[3] Michael Bünker has argued that 1:10–4:21 and the whole of chapter 15 should be classified as judicial rhetoric intended to change the minds of high status members of the Corinthian congregation.[4] Elisabeth Schüssler Fiorenza sees elements of judicial and deliberative rhetoric in the letter. She takes chapters 1–4 to be judicial apology and chapters 5–14 to be a deliberative appeal for unity on a range of matters (cf. 1 Cor 1:10).[5] Of particular importance is the extensive study by Margaret M. Mitchell, who argues that 1 Corinthians is a unified composition exhibiting the characteristics of deliberative rhetoric, including (1) a future time frame, (2) appeal to advantage, (3) use of examples often calling for imitation, and (4) a focus on factionalism and concord.[6] I agree with Mitchell that the letter as a whole is intended to persuade the recipients to overcome divisions and cultivate unity among themselves.[7]

After the epistolary prescript in 1:1–3, we find an *exordium* in which Paul builds good will by expressing his gratitude to God for the Corinthians (1:4–9). The *propositio* follows in 1:10 and sets forth the major deliberative

---

2. Wilhelm Wuellner, "Greek Rhetoric and Pauline Argumentation," in *Early Christian Literature and the Classical Tradition: In Honorem Robert M. Grant*, ed. William R. Schoedel and Robert L. Wilken (Paris: Beauchesne, 1979), 177–88, esp. 184–85.

3. Kennedy, *New Testament Interpretation*, 87.

4. Michael Bünker, *Briefformular und rhetorische Disposition im 1. Korintherbrief*, GTA 28 (Göttingen: Vandenhoek & Ruprecht, 1984), 48–76.

5. Elisabeth Schüssler Fiorenza, "Rhetorical Situation and Historical Reconstruction in 1 Corinthians," *NTS* 33 (1987): 386–403, esp. 390–93.

6. Mitchell, *Rhetoric of Reconciliation*, 20–64; for others who take 1 Corinthians as deliberative in nature, see Witherington, *Conflict and Community*, 75–77; Martin, *Corinthian Body*, 38–39; Insawn Saw, *Paul's Rhetoric in 1 Corinthians 15: An Analysis Utilizing the Theories of Classical Rhetoric* (Lewiston, NY: Mellen, 1995), 183–93; Craig S. Keener, *1–2 Corinthians*, New Cambridge Bible Commentary (New York: Cambridge University Press, 2005), 23–24. I would add that the overall deliberative character of the letter does not rule out the use of other rhetorical genres to support the overall deliberative aims of the letter (e.g., the epideictic quality of 1 Cor 13).

7. Mitchell, *Rhetoric of Reconciliation*, 17.

appeal of the letter in which Paul urges the recipients to resist division and remain united. This is followed by a brief *narratio* in which Paul explains how he came to know of the factions in Corinth and reminds the recipients of his purpose in coming there in the first place (1:11–17). Most of the letter should be classified as the *probatio* (1:18–16:12), in which Paul deals first with divisions over apostolic leadership (1:18–4:21) and then with questions on a variety of topics, such as sexual immorality, lawsuits among believers, marriage, singleness, idol meat, matters relating to worship, bodily resurrection, and the collection (5:1–16:12). The letter then concludes with a *peroratio* in 16:13–14 and final greetings in 16:19–24.[8]

Given that the letter is an extended appeal for unity, we need to consider the social makeup and the question of factions among the Corinthians. The data suggests some amount of ethnic diversity among the Corinthian Christ-followers. Paul's negative use of ἔθνος in 1 Cor 12:2 suggests a predominantly gentile composition (cf. 6:10–11; 8:7). Nevertheless, there is evidence of a Jewish presence. Paul reports that he baptized Crispus, who was a leader in the synagogue according to Acts 18:8 (1 Cor 1:14). Acts also indicates that Paul met Aquila in Corinth (18:2), and the influence of Apollos may suggest a Jewish presence among the Corinthian believers (Acts 18:24; 19:1). Fee adds that many of the issues addressed in the letter suggest the audience is mostly gentile, for example, seeking judgments from gentile authorities (6:1–11), debating the right to go to prostitutes (6:12–20), arguing over attendance at temple feasts (8:1–10:22).[9] All of these suggest difficulty in assimilating former pagans into the fellowship of Christ-followers. At the very least, a Jewish minority in Corinth cannot be denied, even if the composition of the Corinthian ἐκκλησία was largely gentile.[10]

Early twentieth-century scholars tended to view the early Christian communities as populated primarily from the lower social classes.[11] How-

---

8. With regard to the arrangement of the argument, I am in general agreement with Witherington and with Mitchell allowing for some modification; see Witherington, *Conflict and Community*, 75–76; Mitchell, *Rhetoric of Reconciliation*, 184–86.

9. Gordon D. Fee, *The First Epistle to the Corinthians*, NICNT (Grand Rapids: Eerdmans, 1987), 4.

10. Fee, *First Epistle*, 4; cf. David G. Horrell, *The Social Ethos of the Corinthian Correspondence: Interests and Ideology from 1 Corinthians to 1 Clement* (Edinburgh: T&T Clark, 1996), 91–92.

11. See, e.g., A. Deissmann, *Light from the Ancient East: The New Testament Illus-*

ever, a "new consensus" has emerged in which the social status of the early Christ-followers is considered to be more diverse.[12] Space does not permit a full analysis of the social composition of the Christ-followers of Corinth, but it will be helpful to point to a few key pieces of data that illustrate the diversity of the group.[13] In 1 Cor 1:26, Paul remarks, "not many of you were wise according to the flesh, not many were powerful, not many were of noble birth." The implication is that if "not many" among the Corinthians were wise, powerful, and of noble birth, then at least some of them were. A significant majority would have been from the lower classes; nevertheless, it appears there were some higher status members also.[14] Paul's instructions on the Lord's Supper (1 Cor 11:17–22) suggest that some of the recipients were people of means; he chides those who apparently have the means to indulge themselves while τοὺς μὴ ἔχοντας are disgraced (11:22). Paul also mentions the "household (οἶκος) of Stephanus" (1 Cor 1:16). Theissen argues that οἶκος would have included not only family members but slaves and servants also, which would suggest enough wealth to maintain such a household.[15] Paul tells the Romans that Gaius served as a host to him and to ὅλης τῆς ἐκκλησίας (Rom 16:23). As Horrell notes, having a group meet in one's house says little about that person's status; however, if multiple smaller fellowships gathered at times and Gaius acted as a host, then he would have likely occupied a more sizable home.[16] Paul also sends greetings from a city official named Erastus, who is described as ὁ οἰκονόμος τῆς πόλεως (Rom 16:23). The same name appears on an inscription, likely from the first century CE, which reads,

> [praenomen nomen] Erastus pro aedilit[at]e s. p. stravit
> Erastus in return for aedileship laid [the pavement] at his own expense.[17]

---

trated by Recently Discovered Texts of the Greco-Roman World (London: Hodder & Stoughton, 1927), 143–45, 250–51, 385.

12. Horrell, *Social Ethos*, 92–101, esp. 93 n. 177.

13. For the social composition of the Corinthian ἐκκλησία, see Gerd Theissen, *The Social Setting of Pauline Christianity: Essays on Corinth*, trans. John H. Schütz (Eugene, OR: Wipf & Stock, 2004), 69–120; cf. Meeks, *The First Urban Christians*, 51–73.

14. Witherington notes that the influence of these few powerful persons would have been out of proportion to their numbers (*Conflict and Community*, 22).

15. Theissen, *Social Setting*, 85–87.

16. Horrell, *Social Ethos*, 96.

17. J. H. Kent, *The Inscriptions, 1926–1950*, vol. 8.3 of *Corinth: Results of Excavations Conducted by the American School of Classical Studies at Athen*, (Princeton, NJ: America School of Classical Studies at Athens, 1966), 99–100, no. 232.

2. Embracing Resurrection

There is no way to know with certainty whether the Erastus mentioned by Paul is the one named in the inscription, though the uncommon name increases the probability that this is the same person.[18] Theissen argues that οἰκονόμος in Rom 16:23 refers to the office of *quaestor* and that Erastus later achieved the position of *aedile*.[19] A. D. Clarke suggests alternatively that Paul's use of οἰκονόμος may be equivalent to *aedile*.[20] Whichever the case, if the Erastus known to Paul is the one referred to in the inscription, it indicates that a person of elite status and significant wealth was part of the Corinthian ἐκκλησία.

It was to this apparently diverse congregation that Paul wrote urging the recipients both to maintain unity (τὸ αὐτὸ λέγητε πάντες) and to avoid divisions (μὴ ᾖ ἐν ὑμῖν σχίσματα, 1 Cor 1:10). Paul had received reports that quarrels or strife (ἔρις) had arisen among them (1 Cor 1:11). He elaborates by associating the divisions with specific persons: Paul, Apollos, Cephas, and Christ (1:12). Many proposals have been made attempting to account for Paul's use of these four names.[21] A number of interpreters agree that Paul is writing to deal with factionalism. The precise nature of those factions, however, is a matter of continued debate. L. L. Welborn sees the factions as focused on differing political allegiances.[22] Mitchell argues that Welborn goes beyond the evidence, insisting instead that Paul's use of names in 1 Cor 1:12 only shows that the factions depend upon a leader.[23] Witherington rightly stresses that Paul's use of political terminology

---

18. A. D. Clarke, "Another Corinthian Erastus Inscription," *TynBul* 42 (1991): 146–51; cf. Clarke, *Secular and Christian Leadership in Corinth: A Socio-historical and Exegetical Study of 1 Corinthians 1–6*, AGJU 18 (Leiden: Brill, 1993), 46–56; Timothy A. Brookins, "The (In)frequency of the Name 'Erastus' in Antiquity: A Literary, Papyrological, and Epigraphical Catalog," *NTS* 59 (2013): 496–516.

19. Theissen, *Social Setting*, 75–83; cf. John K. Goodrich, "Erastus, *Quaestor* of Corinth: The Administrative Rank of ὁ οἰκονόμος τῆς πόλεως (Rom 16.23) in an Achaean Colony," *NTS* 56 (2010): 90–115; Goodrich, "Erastus of Corinth (Romans 16.23): Responding to Recent Proposals on his Rank, Status, and Faith," *NTS* 57 (2011): 583–93.

20. Clarke, *Secular and Christian Leadership*, 49–56.

21. For a thorough survey of debate over "The Four So-Called Groups," see Anthony C. Thiselton, *The First Epistle to the Corinthians*, NIGTC (Grand Rapids: Eerdmans, 2000), 123–33.

22. L. L. Welborn, "On the Discord in Corinth: 1 Corinthians 1–4 and Ancient Politics," *JBL* 106 (1987): 83–113; cf. Welborn, *Politics and Rhetoric in the Corinthian Epistles* (Macon, GA: Mercer University Press, 1997), 7.

23. Mitchell, *Rhetoric of Reconciliation*, 84.

does not mean the dividing issue is politics. Paul draws on rhetorical convention to deal with ecclesial issues. Witherington thus sees the problem as one of allegiance to different apostolic teachers and proposes that the factions have formed as a result of zeal for oratory on the part of some Corinthians.[24] Neyrey draws on social anthropology to suggest that the factions depend on differing attitudes toward control of the body. On one side are those who insist on highly regulated and tight control over the body; on the other are those with more relaxed attitudes resulting in more liberal social ethics.[25] Martin also interprets the conflicts evident in 1 Corinthians through the lens of attitudes towards the body. He argues that all of the theological disputes in 1 Corinthians were the result of contrasting ideologies of the body. In Martin's view, the lower-status majority of the Corinthians perceived the body as highly permeable and easily threatened by pollutants. A higher-status minority of their number emphasized the hierarchical arrangement of the human body without showing much interest in boundaries or pollutants. Martin sees Paul aligned with those who see the body as permeable and vulnerable.[26] The ideological polarity that Martin sees has come under criticism; it is unclear that boundaries and hierarchy are mutually exclusive perspectives.[27] Alistair Scott May notes that Paul seems to draw on both in his understandings of spiritual gifts and the relationship between the sexes.[28] It is thus unlikely that distinct ideologies can be confidently assigned to each of the parties.[29] It may even be the case that Paul is speaking hyperbolically and that the four names in 1 Cor 1:12 may not represent four neat divisions.[30]

J. Brian Tucker takes a somewhat different approach to the apparent problem of divisions in 1 Cor 1:10 by arguing that Paul is primarily concerned with the recipients' "understanding and definition of groups within the Christ-movement."[31] The problem is the absence of a salient "in

---

24. Witherington, *Conflict and Community*, 100–101.

25. Neyrey, *Paul, in Other Words*, 102–46.

26. Martin, *Corinthian Body*, xv.

27. Alistair Scott May, *'The Body for the Lord': Sex and Identity in 1 Corinthians 5–7*, JSNTSup 278 (London: T&T Clark, 2004), 8.

28. May, *'The Body for the Lord,'* 8.

29. Richard B. Hays, *First Corinthians*, Interpretation (Louisville: Westminster John Knox, 1997).

30. Keener, *1–2 Corinthians*, 24.

31. J. Brian Tucker, *You Belong to Christ: Paul and the Formation of Social Identity in 1 Corinthians 1–4* (Eugene, OR: Pickwick, 2010), 153.

Christ" social identity.[32] Tucker argues that some of the Corinthians continued to identify with their Roman identity instead of their "in Christ" identity, which contributed to the problems Paul addresses in the letter.[33] Paul's call for unity among the various groups in 1 Cor 1:10–12 points to disparate social identities among the recipients. What is needed among the Corinthians is recategorization so that their "in Christ" identity is at the top of their social identity hierarchy.[34]

Scholarly debate over the Corinthian parties is unlikely to be resolved anytime soon. What is generally agreed upon is the presence of some factionalism among the Corinthian believers. First Corinthians was written in part with a view to resolving their conflict and avoiding further fracturing of the community. Given our interest in the persuasive and social function of Paul's resurrection language, the following analysis of the major passages will pay close attention to the role of that language with regard to its social impact and Paul's rhetorical aims. What is the potential of Paul's attitude toward future bodily resurrection to impact the way the recipients think of themselves as members of a group of Christ-followers? How do those matters relate to the way the recipients use their bodies?

2.1.2. Bodily Resurrection in 1 Corinthians 15

The primary passage in which Paul articulates his expectation for use of the body in relation to future bodily resurrection is 1 Cor 6:12–20, though his mention of the believer's future resurrection in that passage is brief (see 6:14b). The apostle has far more to say about the hope for resurrection in 1 Cor 15:12–58, and a detailed analysis of that passage is necessary to provide context for reading the material in chapter 6. To be clear, Paul does address the matter of behavior in 1 Cor 15:29–34 and 15:58, but he does not do so with explicitly somatic language as he does in the other major passages under review in this study. Even though Paul's expectations are not articulated using the σῶμα word group, I will argue that standards of bodily practice are implicit in the way ethical expectations are expressed in chapter 15.

A variety of reconstructions have been proposed as background to the problems addressed in 1 Cor 15. And while some views have been more widely defended than others, no clear consensus has emerged with regard

---

32. Tucker, *You Belong to Christ*, 153.
33. Tucker, *You Belong to Christ*, 35.
34. Tucker, *You Belong to Christ*, 153–54.

to the specific nature of resurrection denial by some of the Corinthians. The proposals are usually grouped into three major categories that have each been nuanced in various ways by different interpreters: (1) denial of future resurrection, (2) denial of bodily afterlife, and (3) denial of any kind of afterlife.[35]

The first approach argues that the Corinthians had an over-realized eschatology which led them to believe they had already received the full benefits of salvation.[36] In this view, it is the *futurity* of the resurrection that is rejected. Proponents often point to 1 Cor 4:8 as evidence of this attitude among the recipients: "already you are filled, already you are rich, without us you reign" (ἤδη κεκορεσμένοι ἐστέ, ἤδη ἐπλουτήσατε, χωρὶς ἡμῶν ἐβασιλεύσατε). This view also seems to account for sections of chapter 15 that emphasize the futurity of the resurrection (e.g., 15:22-23). Nevertheless, several difficulties arise on this view. Paul does not say specifically in 1 Cor 15 that any of the recipients thought they were already raised from the dead, and it is unclear that 1 Cor 4:8 should

---

35. Thiselton, *First Epistle*, 1172-75; cf. Matthew R. Malcolm, *Paul and the Rhetoric of Reversal in 1 Corinthians: The Impact of Paul's Gospel on His Macro-rhetoric*, SNTSMS 155 (Cambridge: Cambridge University Press, 2013), 236-50; Paul J. Brown, *Bodily Resurrection and Ethics in 1 Corinthians 15: Connecting Faith and Morality in the Context of Greco-Roman Mythology*, WUNT 2/360 (Tübingen: Mohr Siebeck, 2014), 68-79.

36. C. K. Barrett, *Commentary on the First Epistle to the Corinthians*, BNTC (London: Black, 1971), 347-48; cf. Anthony C. Thiselton, "Realized Eschatology at Corinth," *NTS* 24 (1978): 510-26; Fee, *First Epistle*, 716; Wolfgang Schrage, *Der erste Brief an die Korinther*, 4 vols., EKKNT 7.1-4 (Zürich: Benziger, 1991-2001), 4:111-19; J. Paul Sampley, "The First Letter to the Corinthians: Introduction, Commentary, and Reflections," *NIB* 10:980-81; Christopher M. Tuckett, "The Corinthians Who Say 'There Is No Resurrection of the Dead' (1 Cor 15,12)," in *The Corinthian Correspondence*, ed. Reinmund Bieringer, BETL 125 (Leuven: Leuven University Press, 1996), 247-75; Thiselton, *First Epistle*, 1173-76. Lincoln understands Corinthian over-realized eschatology in terms of the presence and blessings of the kingdom, though not in terms of a resurrection having already taken place. The recipients deny resurrection because they think they already have the fullness of the kingdom and there is nothing left for which to wait; see his *Paradise*, 33-37. Witherington defends the realized eschatology approach, but he articulates it in terms of a "present imperial eschatology" (*Conflict and Community*, 295-98, here 298); cf. J. Brian Tucker, *"Remain in Your Calling": Paul and the Continuation of Social Identities in 1 Corinthians* (Eugene, OR: Pickwick, 2011), 186-226.

govern the interpretation of chapter 15.[37] In fact, arguments have been made that 4:8 is not actually about eschatology but rather suggests elements of social status-seeking.[38]

The second major proposal for identifying the problem behind 1 Cor 15 suggests that some of the recipients rejected bodily resurrection because they did not believe in postmortem embodied life. Instead, they may have affirmed the immortality of the soul or some other form of disembodied afterlife.[39] If some of the Corinthians saw the body as a prison for the soul, then it makes sense for them to deny future bodily resurrection on the grounds that it would be nonsensical, undesirable, or perhaps even impossible. Others may have reacted against the concept of *bodily* resurrection because they thought it referred to the raising of decaying corpses.[40] This approach seems to make sense of the questions raised in 15:35, "How are the dead raised? With what sort of body do they come?" The emphasis on future embodiment in 1 Cor 15:44 could also be read as an argument for postmortem *embodied* afterlife: "It is sown a natural body, it is raised a pneumatic *body*. If there is a natural body, there is also a pneumatic *body*" (emphasis added). Evidence for belief in postmortem disembodied existence can be found in some Second Temple Jewish texts (Wis 3:1–4; 9:15; Jub. 23.31; 1 En. 103.2–3; Philo, *Abr.* 258). But if such a view were present among the Corinthian Christ-followers, it would have been more likely to come through Greco-Roman philosophy (Plutarch, *Rom.* 28.7–8; Seneca, *Ep.* 65.16).

Like the first approach, this view comes with difficulties. Belief in the immortality of the soul was one of many understandings of the afterlife attested in the first century, but there is also evidence that it was not a widely

---

37. Brown, *Bodily Resurrection*, 69. Lincoln's understanding of Corinthian over-realized eschatology avoids the first problem but not the second (*Paradise*, 36–37).

38. James D. G. Dunn, *1 Corinthians*, T&T Clark Study Series (London: T&T Clark, 2003), 44, 110; cf. David E. Garland, *1 Corinthians*, BECNT (Grand Rapids: Baker, 2003), 138–39; Eckhard J. Schnabel, *Der erste Brief des Paulus an die Korinther*, HTA (Wuppertal: Brockhaus, 2006), 246.

39. F. F. Bruce, *1 and 2 Corinthians*, NCB (Grand Rapids: Eerdmans, 1971), 144; Martin, *Corinthian Body*, 106; cf. Hays, *First Corinthians*, 252–53; de Boer, *Defeat of Death*, 103–4; Garland, *1 Corinthians*, 699–701; Wright, *Resurrection*, 330–31; Schnabel, *Korinther*, 911–12; Kenneth E. Bailey, *Paul through Mediterranean Eyes: Cultural Studies in 1 Corinthians* (Downers Grove, IL: IVP Academic, 2011), 464.

40. Martin, *Corinthian Body*, 130.

held view.[41] Additionally, Wolfgang Schrage argues that the intensity of Paul's argument throughout 1 Cor 15, which emphasizes the relationship between the resurrection of Jesus and the future resurrection of believers, suggests that the problem involved more than mistaken notions about the nature of life after death.[42] Bodily resurrection is the focal point of faith and hope because it marks the victory of God. The problem is that the Corinthians have not understood what the resurrection of Jesus reveals about the nature of God: "Just as all is nothing without love (13,1–3), so also all is nothing without the resurrection of Jesus and the resurrection of the dead (15,12–19)."[43] Resurrection is indispensable because it constitutes the beginning of God's new world. Paul's goal is not merely better teaching about the afterlife; he writes that they may know God as the one who gives life to dead bodies and invades the old world with the new. Another problem arises when the ethical material in 1 Cor 15:32–34 is taken into consideration. Paul J. Brown asks, "How does an immortality of the soul encourage one to live a life of dissipation?"[44] Plato taught that those who indulge in gluttony and other bodily desires would likely enter into beastly bodies after the death of the human body while those who resisted these desires would have their souls liberated from the body (*Phaed.* 81e–83b).[45]

A third major proposal is defended by a group of scholars who argue that some of the Corinthians deny the afterlife altogether.[46] Proponents interpret Paul's rhetoric as an argument against Epicurean influence that viewed the death of the body as the end of individual existence and advocated the pursuit of pleasure and the avoidance of pain. This approach attempts to reckon with Paul's understanding of the relationship between resurrection and ethics in 1 Cor 15:32–34. As Karl O. Sandnes remarks, "To

---

41. Richard A. Lattimore, *Themes in Greek and Latin Epitaphs* (Urbana: University of Illinois Press, 1942), 342; cf. Martin, *Corinthian Body*, 11–15; Brown, *Bodily Resurrection*, 74.

42. Wolfgang Schrage, *Studien zur Theologie im 1. Korintherbrief* (Neukirchen-Vluyn: Neukirchener Verlag, 2007), 206–8.

43. Schrage, *Studien zur Theologie*, 207, my translation.

44. Brown, *Bodily Resurrection*, 74.

45. See further Brown, *Bodily Resurrection*, 74.

46. Thomas Schmeller, *Paulus und die "Diatribe": Eine vergleichende Stilinterpretation*, NTAbh 19 (Münster: Aschendorff, 1987), 381–85; cf. August Strobel, *Der erste Brief an die Korinther*, ZBK NT 6.1 (Zürich: Theologischer Verlag Zürich, 1989), 243; Johan S. Vos, "Argumentation und Situation in 1 Kor. 15," *NovT* 41 (1999): 313–33; Sandnes, *Belly and Body*, 181–87.

Paul's ancient readers, 1 Cor. 15:32 is very likely a critique of the morality associated with the loaded table. According to Paul, this morality and its call for immediate satisfaction militates against the faith of the resurrection."[47] The presence of Epicureans among the Corinthian Christ-followers runs into some difficulty, however, given the substantive differences between Epicureanism and Christianity. Brown points out that Epicurean materialist cosmology cannot be reconciled with what we find in early Christianity.[48] He adds that the Epicurean principle of avoiding pain is difficult to reconcile with the Christian expectation of persecution and tribulation.[49]

All three major approaches endeavor to shed light on various aspects of 1 Cor 15. Nevertheless, they all raise further questions, and they share the common difficulty of explaining the apparent disconnect among some of the recipients between Jesus's bodily resurrection in the past and the possibility of their own bodily resurrection in the future. In the first instance, it is unclear why some of the recipients would think of Jesus's resurrection in material terms but their own resurrection metaphorically as having already happened. In the second, it is hard to see how they understood Jesus's bodily resurrection as the basis for their own disembodied immortality. In the third, if Jesus experienced new postmortem life, why should some of the Corinthians think there is no afterlife at all? In the end, none of the approaches outlined above offer a thoroughly satisfactory reconstruction of the background to 1 Cor 15.[50]

Brown has recently made a fourth proposal that aims to account for the problem of how some of the Corinthians could affirm the resurrection of Jesus and still deny the possibility that they too will be raised. He argues that the Corinthians were more likely influenced by popular level understandings of Greco-Roman mythology than by the views of various philosophical schools.[51] Roman religion depended heavily on Greek mythology—Homer and Hesiod not least—and was known by

---

47. Sandnes, *Belly and Body*, 185.
48. Brown, *Bodily Resurrection*, 77.
49. Brown, *Bodily Resurrection*, 77.
50. See Malcolm, *Reversal*, 249–50.
51. Brown, *Bodily Resurrection*, 81–83. Cf. Endsjø, *Greek Resurrection Beliefs*, 12–15; Dieter Zeller, *Der erste Brief an die Korinther*, KEK (Göttingen: Vandenhoeck & Ruprecht, 2010). Zeller remarks, "Die korinthischen Zweifler wären also nicht von hochphilosophishcen Vorurteilen motiviert gewesen, sondern von der *heidnischen Durchschnittsmentalität*" (458, emphasis original).

rich and poor, educated and uneducated.[52] Brown's proposal is that some of the Corinthians incorporated aspects of Greco-Roman mythology into their eschatology, which led them to deny future bodily resurrection. According to Brown, an eschatology shaped by Greek myths is marked by three key features. First, it involves a pessimistic outlook on the fate of the ordinary dead: "The Homeric literary evidence suggests that almost all mortals die with little or no hope of any afterlife other than a shadowy existence in Hades."[53] Inscriptional evidence suggests that this sort of postmortem pessimism remained widespread in the first century.[54] Second, an eschatology influenced by Greek mythology is characterized by the notion that heroes enjoyed a positive experience of the afterlife due to their nobility or achievements.[55] Third, Greek mythology divorced ethics from the afterlife. Roman veneration of the gods was largely focused on obtaining blessings in life, not after death. Ordinary people were thought to enter the shadowy existence of Hades regardless of the moral quality of their lives, and the heroes could enjoy a favorable afterlife even if they behaved immorally.[56]

If we read 1 Cor 15 with this background as a lens, then a plausible scenario comes into focus. If most ordinary people in the Greco-Roman world thought of their own postmortem destiny in terms of a gloomy existence as shades in Hades, then it makes sense that they would deny their own future bodily resurrection. It is possible that these same people thought of Jesus in a way similar to the Greek heroes. He was known for performing miracles, and he was the son of a deity and a mortal woman; he had been raised from the dead to an immortal bodily existence. If they saw Jesus in heroic terms, it is plausible that those who deny their own resurrection could affirm the resurrection of Jesus.[57] Roman religion was characterized by this sort of dichotomy. Further, if the Corinthians were influenced by the Greco-Roman separation of ethics and religion, then

---

52. Brown, *Bodily Resurrection*, 83–84; cf. Luke Timothy Johnson, *Among the Gentiles: Greco-Roman Religion and Christianity*, AYBRL (New Haven: Yale University Press, 2009), 35.

53. Brown, *Bodily Resurrection*, 85. See, e.g., Homer, *Od.* 11.204–222; cf. Plato, *Phaed.* 69e–70a.

54. Brown, *Bodily Resurrection*, 86–89; cf. Wright, *Resurrection*, 39.

55. Brown, *Bodily Resurrection*, 89–90.

56. Brown, *Bodily Resurrection*, 94–97.

57. Brown, *Bodily Resurrection*, 94.

it explains why Paul sets forth ethical expectations that accord with his eschatological vision.[58] Those two things were not typically associated in the popular religion of the Roman Empire. Brown's proposal is strengthened by its detailed attention to a range of primary source material.[59] Moreover, it provides a plausible and coherent scenario for the apparent dislocation among the recipients between belief in Jesus's resurrection but not their own.

Anthony C. Thiselton is right when he says that we lack the evidence to adopt one reconstruction with certainty and disregard the others altogether.[60] But this is not so significant a problem as it might initially seem given A. Erickson's insight that one

> problem with many reconstructions is the assumption that Paul correctly represents the Corinthian opinions.... Seen as rhetorical argumentation, the assumption that Paul is so "accurate" and "truthful" in his use of sources that he gives an unbiased account is naïve. In a rhetorical argumentation, the biased representation of opponent opinions is the rule.[61]

With that warning in mind, our interest in the rhetorical and social functions of the text prompt us to consider not only reconstructions of possible problems the text addresses but also the way those problems are portrayed by Paul. We need to recognize that the way Paul portrays the rhetorical situation is itself a part of his persuasive strategy. The way he characterizes different groups and their views contributes to the social impact of the argument and the text's potential to create social pressure and perhaps effect social change. This is not to say that he is deceptively describing a situation that does not exist. If Paul's rhetoric is to be effective, it would be unwise to so distort the views of those he aims to persuade that they become biased against him.[62] The point is that, while we will keep in mind possible attitudes that might have been embraced by the recipients, we will

---

58. Brown, *Bodily Resurrection*, 97.
59. Brown, *Bodily Resurrection*, 28–56.
60. Thiselton, *First Epistle*, 1176.
61. A. Eriksson, *Traditions as Rhetorical Proof: Pauline Argumentation in 1 Corinthians*, ConBNT 29 (Stockholm: Almqvist & Wiksell, 1998), 237.
62. See Malcolm: "an intentional misrepresentation of his opponents would surely not advantage his persuasion" (*Reversal*, 232).

also pay close attention to the way Paul depicts the situation and consider how his account may contribute to the function of the text.[63]

What, then, is the rhetorical strategy of 1 Cor 15? How will Paul persuade the recipients to embrace the hope of future bodily resurrection and behave accordingly? Deliberative rhetoric is the natural choice for that double task, and chapter 15 exhibits the characteristics of that genre as described above.[64] That Paul is attempting to persuade the recipients of the hope for bodily resurrection and how they should behave given that eschatological perspective gives the chapter its future orientation.[65] To the extent that the Corinthians disagree on the matter of a future resurrection (15:12), the chapter is concerned with overcoming factionalism and encouraging concord. Deliberative rhetoric is often concerned with persuading the hearer to adopt an expedient course of action and avoid what is harmful (Aristotle, *Rhet.* 1.3.5; cf. Quintilian, *Inst.* 3.8.35). Paul is interested to show the recipients that continued denial of future resurrection has detrimental consequences (1 Cor 15:13-19), and in verses 50-53 he points to the advantages of incorruptibility and immortality. The resurrection of Jesus in 1 Cor 15:1-3 functions in part as an historical example, and later Paul points to the examples of a seed and to the various glories of the heavenly bodies (15:37-41).[66] That gives us a sense of the deliberative elements in 1 Cor 15. As our discussion proceeds, the deliberative tone will become further apparent.

First Corinthians 15 stands on its own as a rhetorical unit.[67] The chapter begins with a *narratio* (vv. 1-11) that recounts how the gospel came to the Corinthians and the events of Jesus's death, resurrection, and appearance to a significant number of eyewitnesses. According to Aristotle, a narra-

---

63. See further D. L. Stamps, "Rethinking the Rhetorical Situation: The Entextualization of the Situation in New Testament Epistles," in *Rhetoric and the New Testament: Essays from the 1992 Heidelberg Conference*, ed. Stanley E. Porter and Thomas H. Olbricht (Sheffield Academic, 1993), 193-210.

64. Duane F. Watson, "Paul's Rhetorical Strategy in 1 Corinthians 15," in *Rhetoric and the New Testament: Essays from the 1992 Heidelberg Conference*, ed. Stanley E. Porter and Thomas H. Olbricht (Sheffield: Sheffield Academic, 1993), 233-34; cf. Saw, *Paul's Rhetoric*, 193-98; Witherington, *Conflict and Community*, 291-92.

65. Saw, *Paul's Rhetoric*, 195-96.

66. Saw, *Paul's Rhetoric*, 196-98.

67. Burton L. Mack, *Rhetoric and the New Testament*, GBS (Minneapolis: Fortress, 1990), 56-59; cf. Watson, "Paul's Rhetorical Strategy," 248-49; Witherington, *Conflict and Community*, 292.

tion is rare in deliberative speeches because it is impossible to narrate the future. When a narration does appear in a deliberative speech, it speaks of the past in order that "the hearers may take better counsel about the future" (*Rhet.* 3.16.11). Paul begins by reminding the recipients of the events surrounding the resurrection of Jesus because it stands as shared belief from which he can argue for the future resurrection of believers. The *narratio* is followed by a *refutatio* in 15:12–19.[68] It might seem strange to place a refutation near the beginning of the argument. Quintilian, however, notes that some occasions require beginning with the refutation, and he indicates that flexibility is allowed as appropriate for the speech (*Inst.* 5.13.53–58). The *refutatio* in 15:12–19 reflects the strategy set out in the *progymnasmata*, which instruct students to articulate the false claim before proceeding to explain the problems with it (Aphthonius, *Prog.* 5). The false claim that Paul argues against is ἀνάστασις νεκρῶν οὐκ ἔστιν, which is set forth in 15:12 and attributed to "some" (τινες) of the recipients. The preliminary exercises suggested a number of strategies for refuting false claims, which included showing that it was unclear, unbelievable, impossible, illogical, inconsistent, inappropriate, or inexpedient (Aphthonius, *Prog.* 5; cf. Hermogenes, *Prog.* 5). Paul argues that it is inconsistent to affirm the resurrection of Jesus and deny the resurrection of believers (15:13). He suggests that it is illogical to deny bodily resurrection and affirm the resurrection of Jesus (15:16).[69] He also argues on the basis of the disadvantage of remaining in sin and becoming objects of pity (15:18–19). The *propositio* comes in 15:20 with the statement that the resurrected Christ is "first fruits of those who have fallen asleep."[70] Paul is not aiming to prove the resurrection of Christ, but to prove the future resurrection of believers as an inference from the fact of the resurrection of Christ. This is followed by an argument for future bodily resurrection based on the relationship between Adam and Christ (vv. 21–28) and the relationship between various present bodily practices and the hope for resurrection (vv. 29–34). Paul then responds to questions about the nature of the resurrection body (vv. 35–49) before bringing the argument to a conclusion with a narrative recapitulation, a citation of Scripture, an expression of gratitude, and an exhortation.[71]

---

68. Thiselton, *First Epistle*, 1177.
69. See Witherington, *Conflict and Community*, 303.
70. Mack, *Rhetoric and the New Testament*, 56.
71. Mack, *Rhetoric and the New Testament*, 57; cf. Witherington, *Conflict and Community*, 292.

2.1.2.1. Consequences of Denying the Resurrection (15:12–19)

The question of the believer's future bodily resurrection is first introduced in 15:12. The mention comes in Paul's description of resurrection denial by some of the Corinthians, "how can some among you say that there is no resurrection of the dead?" (πῶς λέγουσιν ἐν ὑμῖν τινες ὅτι ἀνάστασις νεκρῶν οὐκ ἔστιν;). That the problem of resurrection denial is limited to a subgroup of the larger community is evident in Paul's use of τινες, which singles out "some" or "certain ones." These specific people are located "among you" (ἐν ὑμῖν), which is to say they are one faction within the larger group.[72] Since resurrection denial is only attributed to "some," we may conclude that the others affirm future bodily resurrection. Gordon D. Fee suggests that the "some" in 15:12 are to be identified with the "some" (τινες) of 1 Cor 4:18 and elsewhere.[73] Caution is warranted, however, as we recall that the Corinthian factionalism is portrayed in different ways at different points in the letter. In 1 Cor 1:12, Paul portrays the factions in terms of their association with three different apostles and with Christ. In 4:18, some are arrogant and others, presumably, are not. In 1 Cor 15:12, we find one group that denies future bodily resurrection, and one that affirms it. The point is that Paul portrays the situation in various ways as the letter proceeds; we need to reckon with the possibility that the factions in Corinth did not divide neatly along party lines. Different subgroups may have agreed on some matters while disagreeing on others. This does not mean that Paul is deceptive or misrepresents the situation; it simply means that the situation is complex and multifaceted. Based on the evidence of 1 Cor 15:12, we can say that Paul portrays the sociorhetorical setting in terms of two subgroups within the larger group of Corinthian Christ-followers. One group denies the future resurrection of the body; the other appears to affirm it. Paul's aim is to convince the former group of their error and persuade them to believe in the resurrection of their bodies.

When this situation is viewed through the lens of social identity, a few other observations can be made. First, the two subgroups are differentiated by their view of the body's place in the future. One group denies that the body has any part in life after death; the other affirms postmortem embodied life. As Philip F. Esler remarks, "The foundational concept is that of

---

72. Mitchell, *Rhetoric of Reconciliation*, 176–77; cf. Garland, *1 Corinthians*, 697–98; Brown, *Bodily Resurrection*, 140.

73. Fee, *First Epistle*, 740.

difference as constituting identity, since something only *is* to the extent that it is distinguished from something else."⁷⁴ That the Corinthians could be divided into identifiable groups based on their attitudes toward the nature of postmortem existence fits comfortably in their Greco-Roman milieu where, "in philosophical circles, words about life in the face of death (as well as words about the possibility of an afterlife) distinguished one group from another and therefore *contributed to group self-definition*."⁷⁵ As we saw in chapter 1, the Epicurean view of death as the end of a person's existence distinguished it from the Stoic view that the material soul ascended to higher levels of the universe. More significantly, 1 Cor 15:12 is not the only place in the New Testament where the attitude toward resurrection defines a group boundary. In Mark 12:18, the Sadducees are described in terms of resurrection denial. And in Acts 23:8, resurrection denial is one of several beliefs said to distinguish Sadducees from Pharisees who affirm resurrection.⁷⁶ That some of the Corinthians rejected future bodily resurrection while others affirmed it distinguishes them from one another and suggests that it constitutes an aspect of their social identity.⁷⁷ The extended attention that Paul devotes to the matter also suggests that future bodily resurrection is an important component of Paul's understanding of Christian identity. Second, the fact that this group distinction is oriented toward the future and involves a dispute over the destiny of the group raises questions about the relationship between social identity and time. It is here that Cinnirella's approach has potential to shed light on the situation. If those who embrace future bodily resurrection understand it as something that happens to the group *as a group*, then future bodily resurrection may be described as a future possible social identity. To put it another way, if those recipients who embrace the hope for bodily resurrection desire to be

---

74. Esler, *Conflict*, 19.

75. Stephen C. Barton, "Eschatology and Emotions in Early Christianity," *JBL* 130 (2011): 83, emphasis original.

76. See further Claudia Setzer, "Resurrection of the Dead as Symbol and Strategy," *JAAR* 69.4 (2001): 65–101; cf. Setzer, *Resurrection of the Body in Early Judaism and Early Christianity: Doctrine, Community, and Self-Definition* (Leiden: Brill, 2004), 21–36.

77. For the function of resurrection in the formation of early Christian social identity after Paul, see Outi Lehtipuu, *Debates over the Resurrection of the Dead: Constructing Early Christian Identity*, Oxford Early Christian Studies (Oxford: Oxford University Press, 2015). Lehtipuu is particularly interested in how different beliefs about resurrection distinguished different groups from one another.

members of the group of resurrected people, then resurrection is a possible social identity.[78] The social component of resurrection will be explored in more detail below. It is enough at this point to note the presence of these dynamics in the way Paul portrays the conflict in 1 Cor 15.

The concept that is denied by some is ἀνάστασις νεκρῶν (15:12). Martin argues that νεκροί would have been understood by educated members of the Corinthian community as referring specifically to corpses, and he cites a number of ancient sources that reflect this sense.[79] Taken this way, some of the Corinthians may have denied the resurrection because they were put off by the notion of decaying corpses being resuscitated. Thiselton notes, however, that the LXX would have been the Scriptures used by the Corinthian Christ-followers, and there the term does not always refer to a dead body; sometimes it means "the dead" without referring specifically to a corpse.[80] In my judgement, it is best to recognize that there were a variety of possible reasons that some Corinthians had difficulty with the notion of future bodily resurrection. Several options were discussed above, including the possibility that heroes (in contrast to average people) might enjoy embodied immortality, and there is no need to rehearse the details here. The attempt to single out one reason to the exclusion of others is in danger of neglecting the complex matrix of ideas that would have been found in Corinth in the first century. Put differently, the Corinthians may have had any number of reasons to suppose something like future bodily resurrection would not happen.[81]

That Paul portrays the situation only in terms of resurrection denial and not in terms of the timing of the resurrection does present a problem for those who take the view that some of the Corinthians had an over-realized eschatology. If Paul were dealing with a group of people who believed they had already experienced the resurrection, we might expect him to portray them as denying a specifically future resurrection. As Johan S. Vos observes, "It is striking then that Paul nowhere emphasizes the futuristic aspect."[82] He goes on to suggest that if the question was one of timing, we

---

78. Cinnirella, "Exploring Temporal Aspects," 227–48, esp. 29–31.
79. Martin, *Corinthian Body*, 122–23. See, e.g., Lucian, *Men.* 17, 18. Cf. Fee: "'The dead' refers not simply to people who have died, but also to their dead bodies" (*First Epistle*, 776).
80. Thiselton, *First Epistle*, 1217. See, e.g., Ps 87:5, 11.
81. See Wright, *Resurrection*, 330.
82. Vos, "Argumentation," 323, my translation.

might expect Paul to argue that the resurrection is not now but later.[83] But Paul does not depict the denial itself in terms of temporality. He simply asserts that some of the Corinthians deny the fact of the resurrection of believers.[84] This suggests that the timing of the resurrection was not under dispute. The point is granted that if the Corinthians deny *the fact* of bodily resurrection, they also implicitly deny the *futurity* of it. The question, however, has to do with their primary objection, and Paul's portrayal of the denial does not suggest that the timing of the resurrection is at issue.

After naming the false position of those who deny the resurrection, Paul proceeds to refute that position in 15:13–19 by setting forth multiple unacceptable consequences of it. As Insawn Saw notes, the argument follows a form identified by Quintilian that "argues that because one thing is not, another thing is not."[85] Paul assumes a logical connection between the resurrection of Jesus in the past and that of believers in the future: "Now if there is no resurrection of the dead, neither has Christ been raised" (εἰ δὲ ἀνάστασις νεκρῶν οὐκ ἔστιν, οὐδὲ Χριστὸς ἐγήγερται, 15:13).[86] There is no indication in 1 Corinthians that the recipients denied the resurrection of Jesus. The problem seems to be their failure to make the connection between Jesus's resurrection and their own. So, for the sake of argument, Paul assumes the truth of their view in order to demonstrate its disastrous results.[87] According to Quintilian, a conventional approach in deliberative rhetoric involved "pointing out some frightening consequences of taking the opposite course" from what the orator has argued or will argue (*Inst.* 3.8.38–41). The strategy is to set forth an unacceptable yet logical inference of his opponents' opinion with the aim of persuading them to abandon

---

83. Vos, "Argumentation," 323. Cf. de Boer: "Paul is not combatting the slogan 'resurrection has already occurred,' but the slogan 'there is no (bodily) resurrection of the (physically) dead'" (*Defeat of Death*, 111).

84. So Witherington: "The group he is countering believes that 'there is *no* resurrection (v. 12), not that 'there is *no longer* any resurrection'" (*Conflict and Community*, 301, emphasis original). Cf. Martin: "It is much simpler to assume, as Paul's arguments against them indicate, that what they found objectionable about Paul's teaching was not the *future* aspect of the resurrection but that it was to be a *bodily* resurrection" (*Corinthian Body*, 106, emphasis original).

85. Saw, *Paul's Rhetoric*, 233. See Quintilian, *Inst.* 5.8.7.

86. Paul's assumption anticipates the coming argument in 15:20–28 for a logical connection between the resurrection of Christ and the resurrection of believers.

87. See Daniel B. Wallace, *Greek Grammar Beyond the Basics: An Exegetical Syntax of the New Testament* (Grand Rapids: Zondervan, 1996), 690–91.

it.⁸⁸ The protasis in 15:13 restates exactly the position of the deniers of the resurrection as set forth in verse 12, and if that condition were true, Paul reasons that Christ has not been raised. If the recipients deny bodily resurrection in principle, then they implicitly deny the bodily resurrection of Jesus.⁸⁹ In 15:14, Paul uses the apodosis from the previous verse as the hypothetically assumed condition in order to demonstrate further problematic implications: "And if Christ has not been raised, then our preaching is in vain, and your faith is in vain" (εἰ δὲ Χριστὸς οὐκ ἐγήγερται, κενὸν ἄρα [καὶ] τὸ κήρυγμα ἡμῶν, κενὴ καὶ ἡ πίστις ὑμῶν, 15:14). It is unclear whether the notion of Paul's preaching being emptied refers to the content of his proclamation (see 15:3–5) or to the futility of preaching given that its historical basis has been lost.⁹⁰ In either case, Paul is convinced that a denial of future bodily resurrection renders his ministry ineffective. This highlights the significance of the resurrection in Paul's thinking. The believer's bodily resurrection is not a doctrine of secondary importance. For Paul, it is essential and nonnegotiable. Denial of bodily resurrection constitutes a denial of the gospel.⁹¹ If there is no future resurrection of believers, then his ministry is worthless.

To make matters worse, Paul insists his ministry is not only emptied of significance, it is also deceptive. If the fact of Jesus's resurrection is untrue, then Paul's proclamation of it is also untrue (15:15).⁹² The word ψευδόμαρτυς is used by Paul only here (cf. Matt 26:60). It is language drawn from the judicial sphere in Demosthenes and other Greek authors.⁹³ Paul uses it to amplify the disadvantage of denying the resurrection by depicting the apostles as perjured witnesses.⁹⁴ ψευδομάρτυρες τοῦ θεοῦ is best taken as an objective genitive indicating that the deceptive testimony is about God.⁹⁵ This fits the context in that Paul is about to say: ὅτι ἐμαρτυρήσαμεν κατὰ τοῦ θεοῦ (15:15). ὅτι introduces information that substantiates the charge. That God is the object of Paul's perjured testimony is clarified by

---

88. Witherington, *Conflict and Community*, 303.

89. See Thiselton: "An *a priori* denial of the possibility of resurrection thereby *logically excludes* the resurrection of Christ" (*First Epistle*, 1217, emphasis original).

90. Fee, *First Epistle*, 742.

91. Fee, *First Epistle*, 743.

92. Fee, *First Epistle*, 742.

93. Raymond F. Collins, *First Corinthians*, SP (Collegeville, MN: Liturgical, 1999), 544. See Demosthenes, *Con.* 31; [*Neaer.*] 6.

94. Collins, *First Corinthians*, 544; cf. Garland, *1 Corinthians*, 702.

95. Thiselton, *First Epistle*, 1219; cf. Garland, *1 Corinthians*, 702.

2. Embracing Resurrection

the κατά plus genitive construction ("against God").[96] The point should not be missed: if the recipients are correct that there is no resurrection, then Paul argues that he has ultimately set himself against God by saying that God raised Jesus from the dead. He goes on to reiterate the content of that alleged false testimony, ὅτι ἤγειρεν τὸν Χριστόν (15:15). He then concludes verse 15 by continuing to assume the truth of the Corinthian error, reminding them that their error entails a denial of Christ's resurrection, "who was not raised, since, as they say, the dead are not raised" (ὃν οὐκ ἤγειρεν εἴπερ ἄρα νεκροὶ οὐκ ἐγείρονται). Barrett notes that "as they say" is a classical use of ἄρα.[97] By repeating the Corinthian error at this point in the argument, Paul again amplifies the point that it is the recipients' wrongheaded idea that has led to the absurd conclusion that Paul has misrepresented God.[98]

The *refutatio* comes to a conclusion with a demonstration that the negative consequences are not limited to Paul but extend to the Corinthians also. Two problems are in view. First, given that Christ has not been raised, Paul says, "your faith is worthless, and you are still in your sins" (ματαία ἡ πίστις ὑμῶν, ἔτι ἐστὲ ἐν ταῖς ἁμαρτίαις ὑμῶν, 15:17). The logic is that if Christ is not raised, then he is still dead. If he is dead, then he is powerless to save you from sin and is not a worthy object of faith. Additionally, if Paul's preaching is worthless, as he has argued, then their faith is also worthless, since his preaching led to the recipients' experience of faith.[99] Second, if the Corinthians who deny the resurrection are right, "then those who have gone to sleep are lost" (ἄρα καὶ οἱ κοιμηθέντες ἐν Χριστῷ ἀπώλοντο, 15:18). Sleep was a common metaphor for death among early Christ-followers, and οἱ κοιμηθέντες here refers to the dead.[100] Paul's use of ἐν Χριστῷ will be developed in the next phase of the argument in contrast to being "in Adam" (1 Cor 15:22).[101] Since this is a continuation of what Paul just said in verse 14, that they are ἐν Χριστῷ means they had faith in Christ when they died.[102] To say that they "are lost" again

---

96. Thiselton, *First Epistle*, 1219.
97. Barrett, *First Epistle*, 348; Thiselton, *First Epistle*, 1219.
98. See Saw, *Paul's Rhetoric*, 234.
99. Fee, *First Epistle*, 742.
100. Thiselton, *First Epistle*, 1220. See, e.g., Matt 27:52; Acts 7:60; 1 Thess 4:13; 2 Pet 3:4.
101. Brown, *Bodily Resurrection*, 143.
102. For the uses of ἐν Χριστῷ, see Dunn, *Theology of Paul*, 397–99.

amplifies the seriousness of denying the resurrection. He is asserting that believers who have been joined to Christ have no hope of rescue if the recipients' denial of the resurrection is true. Whether the Corinthians saw the afterlife in terms of the immortality of the soul or something else, Paul "would not classify non-bodily survival of death as 'salvation', presumably since it would mean that one was not rescued, 'saved', from death itself, the irreversible corruption and destruction of the good, god-given human body."[103] For Paul, without future bodily resurrection, there is no salvation.

This also sheds light on Paul's attitude toward the human body. First, it is the body that is the object of God's saving work. God's gracious rescue of human beings is the rescue of the body. Apart from embodiment, there is no future hope for believers. That hope is, of course, for *transformed* embodied life, as we will see below. Nevertheless, Christian hope is hope for embodied life, and there is no hope that is not ultimately realized in bodily experience. Second, all this suggests that Paul sees the body as a point of continuity between the present and the future. And given that the body is essential to Christian existence over time, it also suggests that the body plays a role in Christian identity. That role will become clearer as the exegesis of 1 Cor 15 proceeds.

The negative implications of resurrection denial are summarized in 15:19 by saying, "If in this life we have hoped in Christ, and only that, then we are of all people most to be pitied" (εἰ ἐν τῇ ζωῇ ταύτῃ ἐν Χριστῷ ἠλπικότες ἐσμὲν μόνον, ἐλεεινότεροι πάντων ἀνθρώπων ἐσμέν). The syntactical function of μόνος is debatable, but it should probably be taken to modify the entire protasis.[104] Given there is no hope for bodily resurrection, and all the problems that entails, the only thing left is present hope in Christ. But without the resurrection, that hope amounts to nothing. What is particularly important is that this final sentence of the *refutatio* is not merely another negative consequence in the list Paul has drawn up. It summarizes and emphasizes the cumulative force of all the negative consequences inferred from denying the future resurrection of the body.[105] If Christ has not been raised, if the apostolic preaching is worthless, if faith is in vain, if the apostles are deceivers, if believers are still in their sins, and

---

103. Wright, *Resurrection*, 332–33.

104. Barrett, *First Epistle*, 348; cf. Thiselton, *First Epistle*, 1221; Garland, *1 Corinthians*, 702–3.

105. Thiselton, *First Epistle*, 1222.

if the dead in Christ have no hope, then then those who hope in Christ are the most to be pitied.

According to Quintilian, appeal to emotion is particularly important in deliberative rhetoric (*Inst.* 3.8.12), and amplification of the sort we have seen in 1 Cor 15:12–19 was recommended in the handbooks as useful for producing an emotional response that favored the orator's proposition, whether a negative response to its denial or a positive response to its affirmation (Cicero, *Part. or.* 15.53; cf. 8.27). Strong emotions have great power to persuade or dissuade. The increasing intensity of Paul's argument climaxing with the realization that believers are in a pitiable state would have been likely to evoke a variety of emotions among the hearers. The suggestion that their faith is in vain might evoke sadness. That their denial makes Paul a liar has potential to make them feel pity for him. His insistence that their dead are lost might elicit a renewed experience of grief. The claim that they are still in their sins could produce an experience of fear. If Paul's *refutatio* is able to associate negative emotions with denial of future bodily resurrection, it increases the likelihood that his upcoming argument for the resurrection of believers will be persuasive.

Emotional dynamics are a significant component of the social function of verses 12–19. Cinnirella suggests that individuals tend to avoid "negatively evaluated (i.e. feared) possible selves."[106] If future bodily resurrection is indeed a desired possible social identity, then we might expect Paul to offer a negative evaluation of alternative visions of the future that call the desired identity into question. The variety of negative emotions that he attempted to arouse in the recipients in verses 12–19 would have carried potential to motivate the deniers of the resurrection to distance themselves from that view of the future. Their emotional experience of the text would have been an integral component in the recipients' appraisal of their own view and their judgment of Paul's argument.[107] Additionally, by placing this emotionally charged passage (vv. 12–19) near the beginning of the argument means the rest of the argument will be heard in light of the affective impact of the *refutatio*.

Given our interest in the body, it is also worth highlighting that emotions are bodily experiences. The sciences have taught us that human

---

106. Cinnirella, "Exploring Temporal Aspects," 229.

107. Mark Johnson, *The Meaning of the Body: Aesthetics of Human Understanding* (Chicago: University of Chicago Press, 2007), 61. See also the discussion of emotions as a form of judgment in Barton, "Eschatology and Emotions," 575–76.

emotions are the result of complex neural, chemical, and physiological processes.[108] Drawing on the social sciences, Stephen C. Barton suggests that attention to emotions as a bodily experience has potential to increase our understanding of early Christian anthropology and morality: "Attention to the emotions is one way of putting the body back into belief."[109] He goes on to suggest that attention to the emotions may shed light on "the impact of emotions on how relations are conceived *between bodies—* whether between individual persons, or within the body politic."[110] In the case of 1 Cor 15:12–19, Paul's attitude toward bodily resurrection, and the emotionally charged language he attached to it, had potential to impact a variety of relationships. Paul's insistence that denying the resurrection emptied faith of its value might have resulted in a fresh evaluation on the part of the recipients of their relationship to Christ. Paul's relationship to the recipients is also in view. If they found his evaluation of denying the resurrection persuasive, it would cultivate reconciliation among the recipients. It would have brought their bodies together and cultivated unity in the body politic. If, however, his emotionally charged rhetoric evoked anger instead of pity, then it could have been counterproductive, and the Corinthians might have become further entrenched in their divisions.

Another aspect involves the relationship of the recipients to the dead. Their practice of baptizing on behalf of the dead (see 1 Cor 15:29) suggests a continuing perceived relationship between the recipients and those who have died, and that relationship was apparently expressed in terms of a bodily practice (i.e., baptism). How might the emotional impact of Paul's argument that the dead are lost (15:18) have affected the recipients' perception of their relationship to the dead? How might it have affected their understanding of the bodily practice of baptism? The point here is that the bodily experience of emotions has the potential to significantly impact the recipients on multiple levels. The bodily experience of emotion also has potential to shape belief. The emotions evoked in 1 Cor 15:12–19 are part of the recipients' deliberative process. And if they are persuaded to embrace Paul's vision of future bodily resurrection, it will be due, in part, to their emotional experience. Emotion thus plays an essential role

---

108. For a summary of current emotion research in the sciences, see Johnson, *Meaning*, 61–65.
109. Barton, "Eschatology and Emotions," 579.
110. Barton, "Eschatology and Emotions," 580, emphasis original.

2. Embracing Resurrection

in shaping their system of beliefs and the way they understand themselves both as individuals and as members of the group.

2.1.2.2. Christ as First Fruits (1 Cor 15:20–28)

If 1 Cor 15:12-19 articulated the consequences of denying the future resurrection of the body, then verses 20-28 argue for the connection between Christ's resurrection and the resurrection of believers.[111] As indicated above, verse 20 contains the *propositio* of the argument that runs through the whole of chapter 15, namely, that Christ is "the first fruits of those who sleep" (ἀπαρχὴ τῶν κεκοιμημένων). To be clear, Paul is not here arguing for the resurrection of Christ. Instead, having established the resurrection of Christ in 15:1-11, he is now arguing that Christ's bodily resurrection means that believers will also be raised bodily from the dead.[112] The connection between Christ's resurrection and the resurrection of Christ-followers is expressed through the image of "first fruits" (ἀπαρχή). The concept of first fruits is drawn from the Old Testament, where it refers to the initial harvest that is set apart for God (cf. Rom 8:23; 11:16). As Fee notes, however, the point here is not primarily the idea of consecration.[113] Paul uses the image to illustrate how the resurrection of Christ relates to the resurrection of believers both in terms of temporality and representation.[114]

With regard to temporality, the idea is similar to that of a down payment that ensures or guarantees that the full payment will be made.[115] Paul clarifies this aspect of Christ as "first fruits" in 15:23, "But each one in his own order: Christ the first fruits, then, at the time of his coming, those who belong to Christ" (Ἕκαστος δὲ ἐν τῷ ἰδίῳ τάγματι· ἀπαρχὴ Χριστός, ἔπειτα οἱ τοῦ Χριστοῦ ἐν τῇ παρουσίᾳ αὐτοῦ). τάγμα indicates temporal order with the sequence of events defined by ἔπειτα in 15:23

---

111. Brown, *Bodily Resurrection*, 141.
112. Watson, "Paul's Rhetorical Strategy," 240–41.
113. Fee, *First Epistle*, 748–49.
114. Joost Hollemann, *Resurrection and Parousia: A Traditio-Historical Study of Paul's Eschatology in 1 Cor 15*, NovTSup 84 (Leiden: Brill, 1996), 49–50. Cf. Philipp Bachmann's comment that ἀπαρχή here involves "a causal, and not merely temporal, relationship between the resurrection of Christ and the rest" (*Der erste Brief des Paulus an die Korinther*, KNT 7 [Leipzig: Deichert, 1910], 444, my translation).
115. Fee, *First Epistle*, 749. Thiselton notes that the meaning parallels Paul's use of ἀρραβών in 2 Cor 1:22 and 5:5 with regard to the Holy Spirit (*First Epistle*, 1224).

and εἶτα in 15:24. Christ was raised first, and since he is the first fruits, his resurrection will be followed by the resurrection of those who belong to Christ. This, of course, is a future event, but the fact that Paul talks about the resurrection of those who belong to Christ as a future event does not mean that he is arguing against the view that it has already happened. We must remember that his comments about the timing of the resurrection come in the context of an argument about the relationship between Christ's resurrection and the resurrection of those who belong to Christ. Paul's point here is that the resurrection of Jesus inaugurates a series of events that necessarily leads to the resurrection of believers.

The resurrection of believers at the time of the parousia is followed by "the end, when he will yield the kingdom to the God and Father" (τὸ τέλος, ὅταν παραδιδῷ τὴν βασιλείαν τῷ θεῷ καὶ πατρί, 15:24). Paul thus sets out a series of three events: the resurrection of Christ, the resurrection of those in Christ, and the end.[116] ὅταν with the present subjunctive leaves the timing of the end (or consummation) unspecified.[117] This yielding of the kingdom to God the Father comes with the ultimate destruction of "every ruler and every authority and power" (καταργήσῃ πᾶσαν ἀρχὴν καὶ πᾶσαν ἐξουσίαν καὶ δύναμιν, 15:24). Witherington argues that Paul is here combatting Roman imperial eschatology in which "the emperor was portrayed as not only divine but also as 'father of the fatherland' (*pater patriae*)."[118] David E. Garland also sees Paul subverting Roman ideology with his use of παρουσία in verse 23, which is a term the Corinthians would have associated with an imperial visit.[119] This point is especially helpful in pointing to the ways that Christ-followers in Corinth may have experienced the challenge of and need for reassessing their civic identity in relation to their "in Christ" identity.[120] While drawing attention to these overtones is certainly helpful, imperial propaganda does not exhaust Paul's meaning here.[121] Paul must also have in mind supernatural or cosmic powers, which is demonstrated by his inclusion of "death" among the powers to be defeated (15:26).[122] He envisions the final defeat of all powers, whether natural or

---

116. Brown, *Bodily Resurrection*, 147.
117. Thiselton, *First Epistle*, 1231.
118. Witherington, *Conflict and Community*, 305; Tucker, "Remain," 221–26.
119. Garland, *1 Corinthians*, 708; cf. Setzer, *Resurrection*, 61.
120. Tucker, "Remain," 225.
121. Thiselton, *First Epistle*, 1232.
122. Brown, *Bodily Resurrection*, 147 n. 36.

cosmic, that stand in opposition to God.¹²³ The only one of these powers that Paul actually names is death, which serves to remind us that a key point in the overall argument involves the resurrection of believers as the defeat of death.¹²⁴

The concept of representation is developed in verses 21–22 through an analogy between Adam and Christ. The causal link between the proposition in verse 20 and the double parallel between the two representative figures in verses 21–22 is strengthened with the use of two conjunctions: ἐπειδὴ γὰρ (21). The first parallel involves the common humanity of Adam and Christ; both are ἄνθρωποι (v. 21). As human beings, they both function as representative heads for other human beings. This is communicated through the ἐν τῷ formula used with both Adam and Christ. To be "in Adam" is to be in corporate solidarity with him. As representative head, Adam is the agent that brings death into the world (v. 21) with the result that all human beings die (ἐν τῷ Ἀδὰμ πάντες ἀποθνῄσκουσιν, v. 22). Christ also functions as a representative head, but he is different in that his death was followed by his resurrection (v. 21), which guarantees the future bodily resurrection of those who belong to him.¹²⁵ What is true of him will also be true of them, namely, their bodies will be raised.

Paul's understanding of death, and thus of Adam's representative role, is developed further in verses 25–28. The significance of death is not merely *the fact* that all human beings die. That is certainly true, but it does not tell the whole story. Death (ὁ θάνατος) is also portrayed as a cosmic power which Christ must and will defeat (15:26). Paul alludes to Ps 110:1 in 1 Cor 15:25 in order to locate the defeat of the powers in the context of the reign of Christ: "For he must reign until he has put all enemies under his feet" (δεῖ γὰρ αὐτὸν βασιλεύειν ἄχρι οὗ θῇ πάντας τοὺς ἐχθροὺς ὑπὸ τοὺς πόδας αὐτοῦ). δεῖ points to the conviction that God's providential outworking of his purposes will not ultimately be hindered by any opposing force.¹²⁶ One problem that arises with the allusion to the psalm has to do with the subject of the aorist subjunctive θῇ. Is it God?¹²⁷ Or is it

---

123. See Thiselton, *First Epistle*, 1232.
124. Wright, *Resurrection*, 336.
125. de Boer, *Defeat of Death*, 111.
126. See Hans Conzelmann, *1 Corinthians: A Commentary*, Hermeneia (Philadephia: Fortress, 1975), 272; Thiselton, *First Epistle*, 1233.
127. For this view, see Barrett, *First Epistle*, 358.

Christ?[128] Two key pieces of evidence suggest it is the latter. First, Christ is the subject of the previous statement ("he must reign") and is naturally carried forward to the verb in question.[129] Second, Paul is here explaining his statement in the previous verse about Christ's destruction of every ruler.[130] If Christ is the one who overcomes the powers, it makes the most sense if he is also the one who subjects them to himself. Paul goes on to quote Ps 8:6 in 1 Cor 15:27 to show how Christ as a human being has come into his place of authority. As Thiselton observes, Ps 8:5–8 recounts the God-given vocation of humankind to have authority over creation.[131] By interpreting this psalm Christologically, Paul is making the point that Christ as ἄνθρωπος fulfills God's intention for humanity by defeating the cosmic forces that oppose God's people and God's purposes in creation.[132] The contrast between Adam as ἄνθρωπος and Christ as ἄνθρωπος suggests that Christ succeeded where Adam failed. Instead of faithfully overseeing the world that God had entrusted to him, Adam unleashed the power of death into God's good creation. Christ has come to overthrow that power. Paul's point is that the resurrection of Christ guarantees that he will fully and finally defeat death.

While Paul does not explicitly use the language of "this age" and "the age to come" in the immediate context, he does use it elsewhere in the letter. Those who think they are wise by the standards of "this age" (τῷ αἰῶνι τούτω) are fooling themselves (1 Cor 3:18). In 1 Cor 10:11, Paul says that he and the recipients are those "to whom the ends of the ages [τὰ τέλη τῶν αἰώνων] has come." Of particular importance is 1 Cor 2:6–8, where Paul contrasts the "wisdom of this age" (σοφίαν δὲ οὐ τοῦ αἰῶνος τούτου), which is the wisdom of "the rulers of this age" (τῶν ἀρχόντων τοῦ αἰῶνος τούτου), with the wisdom of God. That Paul thinks in terms of a series of ages is evident in 2:7, where he writes of God's action to predetermine his wisdom "before the ages" (πρὸ τῶν αἰώνων). The failure of the "rulers of this age" (τῶν ἀρχόντων τοῦ αἰῶνος τούτου) to understand God's wisdom correlates with their action to crucify Jesus (2:8). The ἄρχοντες responsible for Christ's death in 2:6–8 are presumably numbered among the ἀρχαί that are being subjected to the resurrected Christ in 15:24. The argument

---

128. For this view, see Fee, *First Epistle*, 755–56.
129. Fee, *First Epistle*, 755.
130. Fee, *First Epistle*, 755.
131. Thiselton, *First Epistle*, 1235.
132. Wright, *Resurrection*, 334–35.

of 1 Cor 15:20–28 as a whole makes sense against the background of the two-age scheme. This age is associated with the Adamic unleashing of death into the world, but the death and resurrection of Christ mean that age is coming to its end as every cosmic power is subjected to Christ in anticipation of the consummation of the age to come. The period of waiting between the resurrection of Christ and the final defeat of death is explained by the overlap of the ages and Paul's already/not yet eschatology. The resurrection of Christ is an eschatological event that has already taken place, and it guarantees the resurrection of believers which has not. Christ's resurrection also proleptically ensures the final overthrow of death, even though that enemy has not yet been fully defeated. Christ already reigns in the present, and yet the final destruction of the cosmic powers awaits.

What must not be missed is that the ultimate defeat of death does not happen until the bodies of believers are raised. This is what the Corinthians who deny the resurrection have failed to see. The resurrection of Christ as an event in the past is not the climax of God's saving work. As long as God's people are subject to death and remain in the grave, then death still exercises its power, even if it is defeated in an anticipatory way by the resurrection of Christ. This is why Paul has so little patience with any notion of salvation that does not incorporate resurrected human bodies. The dead bodies of believers reveal the reality that Christ has not yet fully defeated the last enemy, and yet the certainty of that coming defeat is sure. Those who belong to Christ will be raised from the dead as the full and final manifestation of Christ's triumph over death.

I suggested above that future bodily resurrection might function as a possible social identity in 1 Corinthians. This suggestion was based on the knowledge that differentiation is central to identity and on the observation that attitudes towards postmortem embodiment distinguished one Corinthian subgroup from another. We are now in a position to consider the question further. How does the hope for future bodily resurrection relate to the group identity in 1 Cor 15? To answer the question, we need to consider whether and to what extent individual hope for resurrection was tied to group membership. That Paul thinks of resurrection in terms of the social body can be inferred from his argument that resurrection comes through participation "in Christ." Paul thinks of the world largely in terms of two groups: those "in Adam" and those "in Christ." These two terms constitute social identities that define Christ-followers against outsiders. Outsiders are "in Adam," who is associated with the reign of death. In fact, human beings are subject to death precisely because they are a part of the "in Adam" group.[133] Movement from death to hope for resurrection life happens as one moves from one group to the other. Christ defeats death with his resurrection and shares it with "those who belong to him" (οἱ τοῦ Χριστοῦ, 15:23). The resurrection of Christ as first fruits thus necessitates the resurrection of believers. This prompts Martin to say, "Christian bodies have no integral individuality about them. Due to their existence 'in Christ,' they *must* experience the resurrection."[134] For Paul, future bodily resurrection cannot be had on an individual basis, and it is a necessary outcome for group members. That is not to ignore the point that Paul envisions individual bodies being raised; it is only to say that those individuals are raised as part of a group, not apart from it. The future self is the self as a member of the group that shares in Christ's resurrection.

2.1.2.3. Implications for Bodily Practice (15:29–34)

Several features of 1 Cor 15:29–34 have been particularly puzzling for interpreters of Paul. Hans Conzelmann calls it "one of the most hotly disputed passages in the epistle."[135] Despite the difficulties, these verses reveal that Paul is not only interested in correcting the eschatology of those who deny the hope of resurrection, he is also interested in correcting their behavior.[136] Paul does not speak of that behavior with the specific language of σῶμα in verses 29–34; nevertheless, three topics he raises suggest that bodily practices are implied: (1) baptism for the dead, (2) facing danger with the possibility of death, and (3) indulging in food and drink. While Paul's precise meaning is unclear, the function of these sayings in the text can still be discerned.[137] In the first two instances, Paul sees the practice as inconsistent with belief in resurrection. In the third, he sees the practice as consistent with denial of the resurrection. We will take each in turn.

What Paul means by "those who are baptized on behalf of the dead" (οἱ βαπτιζόμενοι ὑπὲρ τῶν νεκρῶν, 15:29) has been the subject of numer-

---

133. Martin, *Corinthian Body*, 132.
134. Martin, *Corinthian Body*, 131.
135. Conzelmann, *1 Corinthians*, 275.
136. Brown, *Bodily Resurrection*, 150.
137. So Garland: "The gist of his argument is clear, but its specifics are not" (*1 Corinthians*, 716); cf. Sandnes, *Belly and Body*, 182.

2. Embracing Resurrection

ous proposals, with none finding broad scholarly support.[138] The many and varied nuances of each proposal can be organized into three general groups.[139] First is the view of most scholars that Paul is referring to some sort of vicarious baptism on behalf of dead people.[140] Those that take this approach see it as the most natural way to read Paul's Greek. Those that object tend to do so on the basis of theological difficulties that arise with the notion of proxy baptism. Second are those who understand Paul to be referring to the regular Christian practice of baptism.[141] In this view, τῶν νεκρῶν is metaphorical for the spiritual deadness of baptismal candidates. Or it could refer to the fact that the physical body is bound to mortality. This view was widely held in the early church and is attractive because it avoids the theological problems associated with vicarious baptism. A third view takes the preposition ὑπέρ to mean not "on behalf of" but "for the sake of."[142] Taken this way, baptism is received as an appeal or means of accomplishing postmortem reunion with believing community members.

Whatever view is taken, what is important for our purposes is that Paul here seems to assume a connection between the ritual of baptism for the dead and the future resurrection of the body. The connection is made in 15:29 with two rhetorical questions designed to reveal the inconsistency between the Corinthians' belief and practice: "Now in that case, what will those baptized on behalf of the dead do? If the dead are not raised at all, why are people being baptized on their behalf?" (Ἐπεὶ τί ποιήσουσιν οἱ βαπτιζόμενοι ὑπὲρ τῶν νεκρῶν; εἰ ὅλως νεκροὶ οὐκ ἐγείρονται, τί καὶ βαπτίζονται ὑπὲρ αὐτῶν;) Paul here assumes the truth that there is

---

138. See the table of possible interpretations in Joel R. White, "Recent Challenges to the *communis opinio* on 1 Corinthians 15:29," *CurBR* 10 (2012): 382.

139. I am here drawing on the survey in Garland, *1 Corinthians*, 716–19; cf. the detailed excurses in Thiselton, *First Epistle*, 1242–49.

140. Conzelmann, *1 Corinthians*, 275; cf. Fee, *First Epistle*, 763–67; Hays, *First Corinthians*, 267; Dunn, *Theology of Paul*, 449; Collins, *First Corinthians*, 556–59; Schrage, *Der erste Brief*, 4.239; Witherington, *Conflict and Community*, 294; Pheme Perkins, *First Corinthians*, Paideia Commentaries on the New Testament (Grand Rapids: Baker, 2012), 185.

141. Charles H. Talbert, *Reading Corinthians: A Literary and Theological Commentary on 1 and 2 Corinthians* (New York: Crossroad, 1987), 123–29; cf. Garland, *1 Corinthians*, 717–19; Schnabel, *Korinther*, 944; Roy E. Ciampa and Brian S. Rosner, *The First Letter to the Corinthians*, Pillar New Testament Commentary (Grand Rapids: Eerdmans, 2010), 784–85.

142. Thiselton, *First Epistle*, 1248–49.

no resurrection in order to call into question the actual practices of the recipients. The questions reveal that he sees a clear correlation between the practice of baptism for the dead and the expectation of bodily resurrection, to the extent that the nonexistence of future bodily resurrection makes nonsense of the practice of baptism for the dead. For Paul, then, belief in bodily resurrection is prerequisite to the practice. Of particular interest for the purposes of this study is that the ritual of baptism in this context involves the practice of putting water on a human body in a way that correlates with the future resurrection of the body. At the very least, we can say that continuity between the ritual and the resurrection depends on the fact that both involve human bodies. This may shed light on Paul's understanding of the relationship between bodily resurrection and ritual as bodily practice: if there is no resurrection of the body, then there is no point in doing things to the body that correlate with the resurrection. In this instance, Paul's expectations for bodily life in the present stand in continuity with his expectation for bodily resurrection in the future. What one does in the body now should correlate with the bodily life to come.

Paul turns next to the topic of risking personal danger and even death in order to further demonstrate correlation between present behavior and future bodily resurrection. In 15:30, he asks, "And why are we putting ourselves in danger every hour?" (Τί καὶ ἡμεῖς κινδυνεύομεν πᾶσαν ὥραν;). The continuing and consistent nature of the danger is emphasized with the present tense of κινδυνεύω in combination with πᾶσαν ὥραν. This is the only time Paul uses κινδυνεύω, which in the LXX usually carries the sense of life-threatening danger.[143] Eckhard J. Schnabel sees here an allusion to the opposition that Paul's message provoked. He points out that πᾶσαν ὥραν is hyberbolic but adds that it highlights the offensive nature of Paul's gospel: "He proclaimed a message that questioned many of the religious convictions and practices that governed the everyday life of gentiles and Jews in ancient times."[144] Schnabel perceives a manifestation of Paul's awareness that he could face charges and penalties at any time in either Jewish or pagan courts.[145] I agree that Paul has in mind the suffering that resulted from his preaching, though I would add that other dangers are likely in view also. The next verse draws further attention to the perpetual and significant danger that Paul faced: "I stand face-to-face with death on a daily

---

143. Brown, *Bodily Resurrection*, 161–62. See, e.g., Eccl 10:9; Jonah 1:4; Dan 1:10.
144. Schnabel, *Korinther*, 945, my translation.
145. Schnabel, *Korinther*, 945.

basis" (καθ' ἡμέραν ἀποθνῄσκω, v. 31). The catalog of sufferings in 2 Cor 11:26–27 describes a range of dangers including the authorities, bandits, and the natural elements. ἀποθνῄσκω is probably inclusive of the various types of danger he has encountered in service to Christ, which further suggests that by ἀποθνῄσκω Paul also likely intends his willing identification with the sufferings of Christ.[146]

Two aspects of this danger point to the relationship between present embodiment and future bodily resurrection. First, Schnabel suggests that Paul endures personal danger because his gospel is for the whole person as an embodied person and thus anticipates the resurrection of the whole person as an embodied person:

> This perilous life would be bleak if there were no coming resurrection of the dead.... Because the gospel is about the whole person, Paul speaks with his whole life for the people who must hear the gospel, and therefore he argues for the (bodily) resurrection of the whole person.[147]

Paul expects his gospel to impact the bodily life of his recipients, which stands in continuity with his hope that their bodies will be raised. Second, Paul is willing to "stand face-to-face with death every day" because he himself expects to be raised from the dead. As an argument for the relationship between behavior and bodily resurrection, the logic should be clear. He is willing to risk his bodily life because, even if he dies, his future bodily life is guaranteed. Paul only faces danger to his body because he believed it would be returned to him at the resurrection. Once again, the way believers use their bodies is implied. If there is no future resurrection of the body, there is no reason to put his body in harm's way. For Paul, the use of the body in the present correlates with what he believes about the resurrection.[148]

Verse 32 initially appears to be about the risk of bodily harm by wild animals, but several points mitigate against a literal interpretation: "If, according to human thinking, I fought with wild beasts in Ephesus, what

---

146. Thiselton, *First Epistle*, 1250; Garland, *1 Corinthians*, 719. Cf. 2 Cor 4:10; Phil 3:10–11.

147. Schnabel, *Korinther*, 945–46, my translation.

148. See Wright: "What matters is once more the *continuity* which Paul sees between the present life and the resurrection life, and the fact that the future life thus gives meaning to what would otherwise be meaningless" (*Resurrection*, 339, emphasis original).

benefit is it to me?" (εἰ κατὰ ἄνθρωπον ἐθηριομάχησα ἐν Ἐφέσῳ, τί μοι τὸ ὄφελος; v. 32.) Most interpreters take Paul's use of θηριομαχέω figuratively.[149] Nowhere else does he mention fighting literal beasts in the arena. Sandnes points out that ancient philosophy often portrayed human desires as beasts which must be fought, and that the language taken from the arena became a common way of depicting the struggle against the passions.[150] Questions could easily be raised as to whether Paul was talking about fighting passion and desire.[151] He will mention later in 1 Cor 16:8–9 his experience of opposition in Ephesus, and the "wild beasts" mentioned in 15:32 may be a description of those who proved troublesome to him while there.[152] If bodily harm is in view here, it is human opponents, not wild animals. Again, for Paul, without the hope of resurrection, there is no benefit in this type of self-sacrifice.

Having pointed to behaviors that stand in continuity with the hope for resurrection, Paul proceeds in 15:32b to describe those bodily practices that correlate with a denial of the future bodily resurrection: "If the dead are not raised, let us eat and let us drink, for tomorrow we die" (εἰ νεκροὶ οὐκ ἐγείρονται, φάγωμεν καὶ πίωμεν, αὔριον γὰρ ἀποθνῄσκομεν). Paul's earlier description of his self-sacrifice stands in contrast with self-indulgence that sounds hedonistic in nature. As in 15:29b, the protasis assumes the truth of the opponent's position for the sake of argument. The apodosis is a quote from Isa 22:13, but it also reflects critiques of Epicureanism contemporary with Paul.[153] And whatever Paul meant by "wild beasts," he was there also using language that was employed to combat hedonistic indulgence in the passions. Sandnes has shown that critiques of eating and drinking were used on a widespread basis in the ancient world to oppose a lifestyle characterized by overindulgence and a lack of self-control with regard to food and sex.[154] We cannot conclude from this alone that some of the Corinthians are actually engaging in these self-indulgent practices. The hortatory subjunctives simply indicate that Paul sees this as the logical

---

149. Abraham J. Malherbe, "The Beasts at Ephesus," *JBL* 87 (1968): 71–80; cf. Fee, *First Epistle*, 770; Collins, *First Corinthians*, 557; Thiselton, *First Epistle*, 1252; Sandnes, *Belly and Body*, 183.

150. Sandnes, *Belly and Body*, 183. See, e.g., Dio Chrysostom, *Orat.* 8:20–25.

151. Sandnes, *Belly and Body*, 184.

152. See Garland, *1 Corinthians*, 721; Sandnes, *Belly and Body*, 184.

153. Fee, *First Epistle*, 722.

154. Sandnes, *Belly and Body*, passim.

behavior that follows from a rejection of bodily resurrection. Once again, Paul has shown the link between future resurrection and bodily practice. If there is no hope for bodily redemption after death, then there is no reason to use the body for anything other than self-indulgence in the present.

The imperative "Do not be led astray" (μὴ πλανᾶσθε, 15:33) is followed by a quote from Menander's now lost *Thais*: φθείρουσιν ἤθη χρηστὰ ὁμιλίαι κακαί (*Thais* frag. 218).[155] The sense can be captured by saying, "Bad associations corrupt good lifestyles." Paul could be warning one faction about associating with another faction within the congregation (e.g., the resurrection deniers) or another outside group.[156] It may be that Paul is warning the congregation as a whole about the influence of those who deny the resurrection. He has been arguing since 15:29 that one's view of the future correlates with the manner of one's living, and he may be worried that those who deny the resurrection will influence the behavior of the rest of the congregation. This is followed by two further imperatives in 15:34: "Be right and sober-minded and stop sinning" (ἐκνήψατε δικαίως καὶ μὴ ἁμαρτάνετε), and a warning about the danger that "some [τινες] have no knowledge of God." If τινες here refers back to its use in 15:12, then it strengthens the possibility that the "bad associations" described in the previous verse are those who deny the resurrection.[157] If so, their lack of knowledge would involve ignorance of God's power to raise the dead.[158] The section concludes with a striking statement from Paul: "I say this to your shame" (πρὸς ἐντροπὴν ὑμῖν λαλῶ, 15:34). This stinging rebuke highlights the seriousness of the situation for Paul. He is willing to shame the recipients publicly in order to persuade them to forsake their detrimental beliefs.

Throughout 15:29-34, Paul draws connections between present behavior and future bodily resurrection. In each case, his comments about present behavior imply bodily practices like baptism, bodily danger to the point of death, and eating and drinking. What is clear is Paul's conviction that believers should live in a way that stands in continuity with the future resurrection. Sandnes puts it this way: "Believers are therefore expected to live with a view towards the resurrection of the

---

155. For a survey of the strengths and weaknesses of various translations, see Thiselton, *First Epistle*, 1254–55.
156. Thiselton, *First Epistle*, 1254–55.
157. Wright, *Resurrection*, 340.
158. Thiselton, *First Epistle*, 1256.

body."[159] If there is no resurrection of the body, the body can be used for self-indulgence. However, given that God will indeed raise the dead in Christ, then the body should be used in the present in a way that correlates with that hope.

One benefit of thinking in terms of future possible identities is that it provides a context for interpreting behavior. Individuals tend to behave in ways that are perceived to help them achieve a desired future identity.[160] This provides a framework for considering the ethical sections of 1 Cor 15. I have argued that Paul's behavioral expectations for the recipients corresponded to his hope for future bodily resurrection. He wants them to act in ways that stand in continuity with future bodily resurrection. If his rhetoric is successful in bringing future bodily resurrection to the top of their identity hierarchy, then it increases the likelihood that the recipients will begin to behave in a way that they believe will help them achieve that future identity. Paul himself is willing to risk death because he is a member of the group that will be raised from the dead. In the same way, he wants the recipients to stop sinning (15:34) because their behavior is incongruous with the hope for resurrection. We cannot say with certainty what their sin is. Nevertheless, if Paul successfully shows that their sin is out of step with their future possible identity, and if he can persuade them to embrace that future possible identity, then they are more likely to bring their behavior into alignment with Paul's expectations.

2.1.2.4. The Nature of the Resurrection Body (15:35–49)

Paul argued for the connection between the resurrection of Christ and the future resurrection of believers in 15:20–28. In verses 35–49, he takes up questions related to the nature of resurrected bodies. The questions are raised by an imaginary interlocutor: "How are the dead raised? With what sort of body do they come? (πῶς ἐγείρονται οἱ νεκροί; ποίῳ δὲ σώματι ἔρχονται; 15:35.) This is the first time σῶμα has appeared in 1 Cor 15. Up until now the *bodily* nature of the resurrection has been implied; here it becomes explicit.[161] It could be said that Paul has been arguing *the fact* of the resurrection; now he is explaining *the nature* of it. The questions

---

159. Sandnes, *Belly and Body*, 186.
160. Cinnirella, "Exploring Temporal Aspects," 243.
161. Brown, *Bodily Resurrection*, 179.

are obviously related, though a slight distinction can be discerned. The first seems to raise the question of agency? What sort of power raises the dead? The second question gets at the substance of the resurrection body. What type of body is it? What is it like?[162] The second question also invites the recipients to consider the possibility that there are different types of bodies.[163] The concerns of both questions are addressed in the section that follows, though the bulk of Paul's attention goes to the second inquiry. His particularly strong response—"Fool!"—was a common insult used by orators against their opponents.[164] For Paul, it functions to embarrass his opponents and undermine the intellectual rigor of their objections to bodily resurrection.[165]

The apostle turns to the agricultural world to draw an analogy between bodily resurrection and the growth of a plant from a seed that has been planted: as a planted seed dies only to grow into a plant, so also God can raise dead bodies to new life (see John 12:24). The point of similarity is that both resurrection and new plant life involve transformation. The analogy suggests that resurrection involves both continuity and discontinuity with the present body. This is an important point if the Corinthian opposition was thinking solely in terms of continuity between present and the future. If they thought that resurrection meant present dead and decaying bodies being raised in that form, then Paul's analogy functions to correct the misunderstanding by explaining the transformation between present and future. The present body and the resurrection body are continuous in a way similar to a seed and the plant that grows from it; the one emerges from the other, but this does not preclude transformation and new life. Paul is also eager to emphasize that the extent of the discontinuity is surprising and unexpected. This emerges from 15:37, "That which you sow is not the *body* that will come to be" (καὶ ὃ σπείρεις, οὐ τὸ σῶμα τὸ γενησόμενον σπείρεις, emphasis added). This claim reiterates the reality of discontinuity and transformation while continuing to emphasize that the future body is indeed *a body*. What begins as "naked

---

162. Wright, *Resurrection*, 342–43.
163. Lincoln, *Paradise*, 38.
164. Keener, *1–2 Corinthians*, 130. See, e.g., Epictetus, *Diatr.* 2.16.13; 3.13.17; 3.22.85. For further examples, see the extensive lists in Craig S. Keener, *The Gospel of Matthew: A Socio-rhetorical Commentary* (Grand Rapids: Eerdmans, 2009), 185, 526.
165. Mark T. Finney, *Honour and Conflict in the Ancient World: 1 Corinthians in Its Greco-Roman Setting*, LNTS 460 (London: Bloomsbury, 2012), 212–13.

seed" (γυμνὸν κόκκον) becomes a stalk of wheat. Likewise, there are two modes of bodily existence: one before death and the other after the resurrection.[166]

Verse 38 gives a succinct yet clear answer to the first question before continuing to explain the type of body that is to be raised: "But God gives it a body just as he willed, and to each of the seeds its own body" (ὁ δὲ θεὸς δίδωσιν αὐτῷ σῶμα καθὼς ἠθέλησεν, καὶ ἑκάστῳ τῶν σπερμάτων ἴδιον σῶμα). The emphatic placement of ὁ δὲ θεός at the beginning of the sentence highlights the agency of God in the giving of bodies. This is followed by a striking shift in verb tense. The present tense highlights the continuing process of giving various bodies which is a function of God's past determination to do so as depicted by the aorist. Thiselton locates this determination with the divine decree in creation to continuously fill the earth with life.[167] Paul is, of course, still talking about seeds, but it is clear that what he says applies to human bodies also. By what power are new bodies given? How will they be raised? This verse indicates that it is a function of God's own power and resonates with the rebuke in 15:34, "For some of you have no knowledge of God." Those who deny the resurrection raise the question of agency because they are ignorant of God's power to raise the dead. The God who made the world has the power to give new bodies to the dead. Paul would have them learn that the creator God gives bodies as he sees fit, whether to plants or people, and he does it according to the pleasure of his will.[168] It should be further noted that somatic continuity before death and after the resurrection is not here depicted primarily as a principle of anthropology. To be human is to be embodied, but human beings do not have the power to create, redeem, or resurrect their bodies. For Paul, all of that is a function of the Creator's will. Whether present or future, human bodies are gifts from God.

Verses 39–41 describe several different types of flesh and bodies. The strategy for answering the question regarding what sort of body the dead will receive entails demonstrating that there are a variety of bodies. These verses also substantiate the claim of 15:37 that the future body is substantially different than the present body or, for that matter, a corpse. Paul identifies four different kinds of flesh: human, animal, bird, fish. σάρξ has

---

166. See Fee, *First Epistle*, 781–82.

167. Thiselton, *First Epistle*, 1264. The reference in v. 37 to γυμνὸν κόκκον may also be an allusion to the creation story (Brown, *Bodily Resurrection*, 182).

168. Finney, *Honour*, 213.

a range of meanings in Paul.[169] It should not here be taken in the negative sense of human life in opposition to God (see Rom 8:5–8, 13). Instead, the point is to locate the diversity of fleshly types in the created order itself. It is implicit that these varied substances are given by the power of the sovereign Creator. They are expressions of his vast and imaginative creativity. If God can give different types of flesh, can he not also bring a new kind of body out of the one that has died?[170]

This line of thinking is further developed in 15:40 with the shift from σάρξ to σῶμα. Paul points out that there are different kinds of bodies (σώματα) with different kinds of glory (δόξα). The range of σώματα include heavenly bodies (σώματα ἐπουράνια) and earthly bodies (σώματα ἐπίγεια).[171] The difference between these earthly bodies and heavenly bodies is articulated in terms of their various glories: "the glory of the heavenly is one thing, the glory of the earthly is something else" (ἀλλ' ἑτέρα μὲν ἡ τῶν ἐπουρανίων δόξα, ἑτέρα δὲ ἡ τῶν ἐπιγείων). The glory of the heavenly bodies is then further subdivided to account for the distinct glories of the sun, moon, and stars. There is precedent in the Greco-Roman world for referring to these celestial objects as σώματα (see, e.g., Aristotle, *Cael.* 2.8). If Paul can draw on concepts that might have been familiar to the recipients to substantiate his argument that bodies exist in significant variety, then they are more likely to consider his position. δόξα probably has the sense of radiance or splendor (cf. Sir 43:1–10). But the point here is not to explain the resurrection of the body in terms of astral immortality.[172] Rather, there are two keys to take away. First, Paul is eager to make the point that there is a diversity of heavenly σώματα that differ from one another in a variety of ways that are right and proper. As Andrew Lincoln put it, "there is no type of life for which God has not found appropriate glory," including that of the resurrection, as Paul will argue.[173] Second, Paul has introduced an important distinction between earthly bodies and heavenly bodies that he

---

169. See Robert Jewett, *Paul's Anthropological Terms: A Study of Their Use in Conflict Settings* (Leiden: Brill, 1971), 49–166.

170. Thiselton, *First Epistle*, 1267.

171. For the debate over the meaning of σώματα ἐπουράνια, see Thiselton, *First Epistle*, 1268–69.

172. Martin remarks, "One cannot help being impressed by how similar Paul's arguments are to the assumptions underwriting 'astral soul' theory in popular philosophy" (*Corinthian Body*, 126); cf. Endsjø, *Greek Resurrection Bodies*, 145. I follow the alternative account in Finney, *Honour*, 214.

173. Lincoln, *Paradise*, 39.

will develop in verses 42–49. This distinction is central in Paul's argument for the difference between the corpse that is buried in the ground and the body that will be raised at the parousia.[174]

Verse 42 begins a sustained answer to the second question raised by the interlocutor regarding the type of body with which the dead will be raised (see 15:35). The answer begins with a series of four binary antitheses initially introduced by, "So also is the resurrection of the dead" (Οὕτως καὶ ἡ ἀνάστασις τῶν νεκρῶν). οὕτως indicates that Paul is drawing on what he has said thus far in order to substantiate what he is about to say. The four contrasting statements read:

15:42b	σπείρεται ἐν φθορᾷ,	ἐγείρεται ἐν ἀφθαρσίᾳ·
15:43a	σπείρεται ἐν ἀτιμίᾳ,	ἐγείρεται ἐν δόξῃ·
15:43b	σπείρεται ἐν ἀσθενείᾳ,	ἐγείρεται ἐν δυνάμει·
15:44a	σπείρεται σῶμα ψυχικόν,	ἐγείρεται σῶμα πνευματικόν.

The importance of the sowing metaphor is now on full display. Like the seed that grows into a plant, the body that is sown is strikingly different from the one that is raised. The body that is sown is described in terms of corruption, dishonor, and weakness; the body that is raised in terms of incorruptibility, glory, and power. To be clear, the body that is sown should not be taken merely as a reference to a dead body, though that is not excluded. Each characteristic of the body that is sown applies to all bodies that have not been raised, whether living or dead. In this way, the series of contrasts thus highlights differences between the present body and the resurrection body.[175] The first contrast is particularly important if the deniers of the resurrection misunderstood bodily resurrection as the raising of a rotting corpse. Wright captures the significance well: "The fundamental leap of imagination that Paul is asking the puzzled Corinthian to make is to a body which cannot and will not decay or die: something permanent, established, not transient or temporary."[176] φθορά carries the sense of subjection to decay. Paul wants them to begin imagining a body that is free from decay, one that is blossoming with incorruptible life. Mark T. Finney recognizes

---

174. Finney, *Honour*, 214.

175. See Lincoln: "The series of antithetic characteristics sets the pre-eschatological state of the body over against the eschatological" (*Paradise*, 39–40).

176. Wright, *Resurrection*, 347.

that Paul's language would have been heard through the honor-shame framework of the Greco-Roman world.[177] By describing the resurrection body with the language of glory (δόξα), Paul associates it with the most important and highly valued concept in the ancient world. δόξα does not here mean radiance or splendor.[178] Jewish texts regularly described the eschatological state of the righteous in terms of glory, and Paul is likely to be working with similar ideas.[179] The extent to which the recipients were influenced by Jewish notions of eschatological glory is questionable; they would have undoubtedly understood Paul's use of ἀτιμία and δόξα in light of their culturally conditioned desire for honor. δύναμις is wrapped together in that matrix of concepts. Paul's ever so brief hint in 6:1–3 that the people of God would be granted the role of judging the world may shed light on what sort of power he has in mind. Given these associations, the resurrection body was likely to have been heard in terms of status elevation.[180] Contextualizing bodily resurrection in light of significant cultural values, even if those values are taken up and transformed in Christ, carries significant persuasive appeal and is a smart rhetorical strategy.

Interpretation of the terms presented in the fourth and final contrast—σῶμα ψυχικόν and σῶμα πνευματικόν—is significantly more complex and will require more detailed attention. Scholarly debate over the meaning of σῶμα πνευματικόν falls largely into two categories. The first takes σῶμα πνευματικόν to mean a body *composed* of πνεῦμα while the second interprets it to mean a body *characterized* or *animated* by πνεῦμα.[181] The first approach has been argued most forcefully by Dale

---

177. Finney, *Honour*, 214–15.
178. Lincoln, *Paradise*, 39; cf. Fee, *First Epistle*, 785.
179. Fee, *First Epistle*, 785. See Dan 12:3; 1 En. 62.15; 105.11–12; 2 Bar. 51.10.
180. Wright, *Resurrection*, 347–48.
181. Robin Scroggs has argued that σῶμα πνευματικόν refers to a "non-corporeal" body, but his argument has not been found generally persuasive. Nonphysical life-after-death is unlikely to have been objectionable to the Corinthians, and it is difficult to see why Paul would have needed to write 1 Cor 15 at all if he believed in a noncorporeal postmortem existence; see Scroggs, "Paul and the Eschatological Body," in *Theology and Ethics in Paul and His Interpreters: Essays in Honor of Victor Paul Furnish*, ed. Eugene H. Lovering and Jerry L. Sumney (Nashville: Abingdon, 1996), 14–29. More recently, Endsjø has argued that σῶμα πνευματικόν refers to a fleshless and immaterial body (*Greek Resurrection Beliefs*, 143), but he neglects to consider the corporeal implications of Paul's somatic language in this context.

Martin and Engberg-Pedersen.[182] This approach reads Paul against the background of philosophical schools, Stoicism in particular, which understood πνεῦμα to be a physical substance, though it was considered less dense and lighter than other substances. The stars and other heavenly bodies were thought to be composed of this airy material. Martin argues that Paul believed the human body to be composed of three substances: σάρξ, ψυχή, and πνεῦμα. "The resurrected body," he goes on to say, "will shed the first two of these entities—like so much detritus—and retain the third, a stuff of thinner, higher nature."[183] Such bodies were considered to be at the top of ancient hierarchical cosmologies. Martin argues that Paul is drawing on that sort of cosmology to argue that resurrected bodies are not raised corpses but are instead bodies composed of a physical substance that ancient persons believed could be immortal.[184]

The view that Paul sees the resurrection body as composed by πνεῦμα faces several difficulties. One problem that arises with this view is that the first three pairs in the series of contrasts in 1 Cor 15:42–44 do not address the matter of composition.[185] ἀφθαρσία, δόξα, and δύναμις are not substances. Why should we take πνεῦμα to denote a substance of composition when none of the preceding terms is used that way? Second, while some Corinthians may have encountered or even embraced the notion of a material spirit, the evidence that Paul held such a view is lacking.[186] Third, while πνεῦμα is used regularly in Stoic physics, one important difference between that philosophical school and Paul is illustrated in that the Stoic sources do not use πνεῦμα with regard to people.[187] Fourth, Thiselton and others point to the noteworthy, though not definitive, evidence that adjectives ending in -ινος usually denote composition, while those that end in -ικος usually denote characteristics or modes of being.[188]

---

182. Martin, *Corinthian Body*, 105–29; Engberg-Pedersen, *Cosmology and Self*, 26–31.

183. Martin, *Corinthian Body*, 128.

184. Martin, *Corinthian Body*, 128; cf. Engberg-Pedersen, *Cosmology and Self*, 28.

185. Thiselton, *First Epistle*, 1276.

186. See the extensive analysis by Volker Rabens, *The Holy Spirit and Ethics in Paul: Transformation and Empowering for Religious-Ethical Life*, WUNT 283 (Tübingen: Mohr Siebeck, 2010), 86–120.

187. John M. G. Barclay, *Pauline Churches and Diaspora Jews* (Grand Rapids: Eerdmans, 2016), 211.

188. Thiselton, *First Epistle*, 1276–77; cf. Wright, *Resurrection*, 351–52.

2. Embracing Resurrection

The second approach is more likely: σῶμα πνευματικόν refers to a human body that is somehow animated or characterized by the Spirit.[189] Paul introduced the key contrasting terms in 1 Cor 2:14-15:

> But the psychical person [ψυχικὸς ἄνθρωπος] does not receive the things of the Spirit of God [τοῦ πνεύματος τοῦ θεοῦ]; for they are nonsense to him, and he is unable to know them because they are spiritually [πνευματικῶς] discerned. But the spiritual person [ὁ πνευματικός] discerns all things.

These verses come in a context in which Paul is contrasting the wisdom of the present age with the wisdom of God. For Paul, a person is only able to understand the wisdom of God through the agency of the Spirit; the substantival use of πνευματικός here refers to those who have God's Spirit to instruct them in the wisdom of God. In contrast, the ψυχικός person functions exclusively on a human level.[190] As a result, that person is fundamentally unable to understand what the one who has the Spirit is able to understand. It should be observed that Paul is not using either term anthropologically in order to say something about the parts of which human beings are composed; instead, the terms describe a person in relation to the Holy Spirit.[191] Particularly important for our reading of 1 Cor 15 is the eschatological context of the ψυχικός/πνευματικός contrast in chapter 2. The ψυχικός person is associated with "this age" (2:6). In contrast, the Spirit has already begun to reveal what is to come to those who have the Spirit and, as a result, belong to the new aeon (2:9). Thus, as Lincoln argues, Paul's ψυχικός/πνευματικός "distinction is no longer merely describing an anthropological dualism but takes its force from his eschatological perspective."[192]

I argued above that Paul's Adam/Christ contrast indicates that 1 Cor 15 should be read in light of the apostle's already/not yet eschatology. That

---

189. Barrett, *First Epistle*, 372; cf. Gundry, *Sōma*, 165-66; Lincoln, *Paradise*, 41-42; Witherington, *Conflict and Community*, 308-9; Collins, *First Corinthians*, 567; Thiselton, *First Epistle*, 1278-81; Garland, *1 Corinthians*, 734; Wright, *Resurrection*, 352; Finney, *Honour*, 216.

190. Thiselton, *First Epistle*, 269-70.

191. See Barclay: "πνευματικός is not in origin an anthropological but an eschatological term: it describes people not through analysis of their human constitution, but in relation to their new status as graced by the Spirit of God" (*Pauline Churches*, 208-9).

192. Lincoln, *Paradise*, 41.

ψυχικός and πνευματικός in 1 Cor 15:44 should be interpreted in light of the same already/not yet eschatological perspective is confirmed in 15:45, where Paul associates ψυχή with Adam and πνεῦμα with Christ as the last Adam. The σῶμα ψυχικόν, then, is an ordinary human body that is subject to frailty and weakness. It is a body that lives and dies in the present age. The σῶμα πνευματικόν, however, is a physical human body that has been enlivened, transformed, and is continually characterized by the Spirit for life in the age to come. Unlike the first three contrasting pairs which focused only on the discontinuity between what is sown and what is reaped (15:42b–43), this final pair holds together both continuity and discontinuity. Both are σώματα and should be understood as physical human bodies. Nevertheless, resurrection means that body undergoes a dramatic transformation such that the character of the body that is sown is altogether different when it is raised. This develops Paul's answer to both questions raised at in 15:35. The resurrection body is raised by the agency of God's own Holy Spirit to be the sort of body characterized by incorruptibility, glory, power, and the life of the Spirit.

Paul's pneumatic language is also significant in the way it relates bodily resurrection to group identity. John M. G. Barclay has argued that πνεῦμα and the adjective πνευματικός that derives from it were used in an altogether distinctive way by the early Christians.[193] Outside of Judaism, the use of πνεῦμα to describe the presence of a deity would have been strange to most Greek speakers.[194] Barclay notes that in non-Jewish Greek πνευματικος often meant "gaseous" or "windy." It could refer to vapors within the body, though it was "never used in relation to some higher dimension of existence."[195] In stark contrast, the term was used by early Christ-followers in relation to the eschatological giving of the Spirit, which was considered to be a new situation unlike any before. The use of the term to describe early Christianity was, therefore, "self-consciously new" in so far as it was distinct from broader cultural usage.[196] The use of πνεῦμα and cognates also functioned to define Christ-followers in contrast to outsiders. In-group members were πνευματικοί; out-groupers were differentiated in binary terms with labels like ψυχικοί (1 Cor 2:14; cf. 15:44, 46) and

---

193. Barclay, *Pauline Churches*, 208–12.
194. Terence Paige, "Who Believes in 'Spirit'? Πνεῦμα in Pagan Usage and Implications for Gentile Christian Mission," *HTR* 95 (2002): 417–36, esp. 434.
195. Barclay, *Pauline Churches*, 210–11.
196. Barclay, *Pauline Churches*, 209.

σαρκινοί/σαρκικοί (1 Cor 3:1–3). Pneumatic language thus functioned as a significant tool for interpreting and defining social reality and social distinctions.[197] In 1 Cor 15, that deeply social language is taken up to describe the resurrection of the body. The adjective πνευματικός is used to describe the resurrection body in terms of a body enlivened by the Spirit (15:44). The term is then associated with Christ as the second man who is characterized by heavenly existence (15:47), and, as representative head, he shares that heavenly and pneumatic life with the group that he represents (15:48). The point is that Paul has taken a key term used to describe the early Christian social group and intertwined it with his hope for future bodily resurrection through participation in Christ. As spiritual people, group members will receive spiritual bodies.

The next stage of the argument further clarifies the nature of the resurrection body by associating it specifically with the resurrected Jesus. In order to do this Paul returns to the Adam-Christ contrast by quoting Gen 2:7 with some modification:

καὶ ἐγένετο ὁ   ἄνθρωπος   εἰς ψυχὴν ζῶσαν (Gen 2:7 LXX)
ἐγένετο ὁ πρῶτος ἄνθρωπος Ἀδάμ   εἰς ψυχὴν ζῶσαν (1 Cor 15:45)

By adapting Gen 2:7 to include πρῶτος and Ἀδάμ, Paul reintroduces the contrast between Adam and Christ, whom he now calls "the last Adam" (ὁ ἔσχατος Ἀδάμ, 15:45). The two are not only contrasted in terms of temporal sequence, they are also distinguished in terms of ψυχή and πνεῦμα: Adam is a "living being" (ψυχὴν ζῶσαν), but Christ is a "life-giving spirit" (πνεῦμα ζῳοποιοῦν). Adam is associated with ψυχή, which here seems to carry a more neutral sense than it did in 1 Cor 2:14–15 since Adam is portrayed prior to his transgression followed by the entrance of death.[198] Nevertheless, he has been associated with the reign of death in chapter 15, and that association must be taken into account. Adam as ψυχή represents humanity in a state of frailty, and through him death came to hold sway over those he represents. Against the power of death introduced by the first Adam, Christ as the last Adam is a "life-giving spirit." What Paul means by πνεῦμα ζῳοποιοῦν is a matter of debate. Does he intend the recipients to think of the Holy Spirit? Is he somehow conflating the work of Christ

---

197. Barclay, *Pauline Churches*, 210.
198. See Lincoln, *Paradise*, 42–43.

and the Spirit? Or is he simply referring to Christ as "*a* life-giving spirit" distinct from "*the* life-giving Spirit"? James D. G. Dunn suggests that the work of Christ and the Spirit are here intertwined to some degree.[199] Fee suggests the latter option is the case.[200] What must not be missed is that Adam is associated with ψυχή, but Christ with πνεῦμα.

Just as important to *what* Paul means by "life-giving spirit" is *why* he chose to put it this way. First, Adam and Christ are both portrayed in their representative roles. Adam represents the bodily life associated with the old age and the power of death. That death is the enemy of human life is a point made explicitly in 1 Cor 15:26, and it will be made again in 15:54–55. As "life-giving spirit," Christ deals the decisive blow against death and thus opens the possibility for those who are "in Adam" to escape the tyranny of death. The first Adam introduced death; the last Adam gives life to the dead.[201] As the life-giving πνεῦμα who is also the first fruits, the life he gives comes in the form of pneumatic bodies, like his own, at the resurrection. Second, the language of "life-giving spirit" resonates with the creation narrative that Paul is citing. It suggests that the creator God is now at work through Christ to bring about a new creation. The God who gave life in the first place is now at work to give it again, this time through Jesus and his resurrection.[202]

This leaves us with the contrast between earthly (χοϊκός) and heavenly (οὐρανός) that runs through 15:47–49. Before introducing that contrast, Paul associates the protological man with τὸ ψυχικόν and the eschatological man with τὸ πνευματικόν (15:46). He then says that the first man, Adam, is "from the earth, that is earthly" (ἐκ γῆς χοϊκός), while the second man, Christ, is "from heaven" (ἐξ οὐρανοῦ, v. 47). A comparison is then drawn between "the earthly one" (ὁ χοϊκός) and "those who are earthly" (οἱ χοϊκοί) in contrast to "the heavenly one" (ὁ ἐπουράνιος) and "those who are heavenly" (οἱ ἐπουράνιοι, v. 48). One problem that arises in translating and interpreting these verses is the lack of verbs. Some interpreters supply "to come" in verse 47, which suggests that location or perhaps origin is in view.[203] Another option takes Paul to be referring both to location and

---

199. Dunn, *Theology of Paul*, 263–64.
200. Gordon D. Fee, *Pauline Christology: An Exegetical-Theological Study* (Peabody, MA: Hendrickson, 2007), 118.
201. Brown, *Bodily Resurrection*, 210.
202. See Wright, *Resurrection*, 353–54.
203. Barrett, *First Epistle*, 375; Garland, *1 Corinthians*, 736–37.

2. Embracing Resurrection 89

to the material of which the earthly and heavenly bodies are composed.²⁰⁴ Paul has just associated Adam with ψυχικός and Christ with πνευματικός (46), which, as I argued above, do not refer to composition. Given that the discussion is framed in terms of those two animating powers of the relative bodies, origin is unlikely to be what Paul has in mind. Lincoln argues for a qualitative interpretation that focuses on the character of Christ's human life after his resurrection. In this way, Christ "is the model for the new eschatological humanity."²⁰⁵ Paul's earthly/heavenly contrast in these verses should be read in light of his eschatological perspective. Earthly existence corresponds to the old age, and heavenly existence corresponds to the new age that is inaugurated by the resurrection of Christ. This interpretation is confirmed in verse 48 where the representative roles of "the earthly one" and "the heavenly one" in relation to "those who are earthly" and "those who are heavenly" are in view, respectively. This verse rules out the possibility that earthly and heavenly refer to origin. What sense would it make to say that believers come from heaven?²⁰⁶ Paul's point is that the character of the representative head is shared with those they represent.²⁰⁷ The character of Adam's bodily life was corruptible, weak, and earthly. Those represented by Adam participate in those frailties. Christ's pneumatic resurrection body is incorruptible, glorious, powerful, and heavenly. And those who are "in Christ" can look forward to participating in those qualities that characterize his bodily life. Again, all of this makes sense against the background of Paul's already/not yet eschatology. Believers already belong to Christ, but their full experience of pneumatic and heavenly embodiment awaits the resurrection at the parousia.

Paul again alludes to the creation narrative by introducing εἰκών language into the contrast between the earthly and the heavenly. Before we consider that language, there is a textual discrepancy that bears significantly on the interpretation of 15:49. Both NA²⁸ and UBS⁵ choose the future indicative φορέσομεν over the subjunctive φορέσωμεν despite the weighty manuscript evidence for the latter. The more difficult subjunctive is supported by 𝔓⁴⁶ ℵ A C D F G K L P Ψ. The indicative is attested by B and some miniscules. The choice of the indicative in UBS⁵ is carried over from UBS⁴. Bruce M. Metzger explained the judgment of the edito-

---

204. Martin, *Corinthian Body*, 132, 276 n. 82.
205. Lincoln, *Paradise*, 45–46; cf. Brown, *Bodily Resurrection*, 215–16.
206. See Lincoln, *Paradise*, 46.
207. Brown, *Bodily Resurrection*, 216–17.

rial committee in the earlier edition by saying: "Exegetical considerations (i.e., the context is didactic, not hortatory) led the Committee to prefer the future indicative, despite its rather slender external support."[208] In my judgment, however, the internal evidence could be understood differently. The context is certainly full of didactic material. Nevertheless, as I have argued, Paul also has ethical concerns in mind as he writes 1 Cor 15 (see 2.1.2.3. above). Given that the first half of chapter 15 concluded with hortatory material (15:33–34), perhaps we should not be surprised to find the second half of the chapter also turns to hortatory concerns as the argument begins to draw to a close. The rhetorical lens utilized in this study brings the point into even clearer focus. Paul's deliberative rhetoric is oriented toward changing both the beliefs and behaviors of the recipients, and the *peroratio* that restates that double aim will begin in the very next verse. If Paul is going to highlight ethical implications from his teaching before transitioning to the next section that will summarize the whole argument, this is the place to do it. Even though he has been largely focused on didactic concerns, the subjunctive could be understood to amplify the contrast between the earthly and heavenly by introducing an exhortation.[209] The additional point has been made that the subjunctive helpfully portrays the eschatological tension present in Paul's argument. He would have the recipients live in a way that anticipates the future full attainment of "the image of the heavenly one" at the resurrection.[210] Together these reasons suggest that the internal evidence is not so decisive as to outweigh the manuscript evidence. Thus, the verse can be translated in a way that resonates with the earlier ethical material in chapter 15: "And just as we have borne the image of the earthly one, so let us also bear the image of the heavenly one" (καὶ καθὼς ἐφορέσαμεν τὴν εἰκόνα τοῦ χοϊκοῦ, φορέσωμεν καὶ τὴν εἰκόνα τοῦ ἐπουρανίου, 15:49).

In the Greco-Roman world εἰκών, or the Latin *imago*, referred to a portrait or statue that might have been used in a variety of ways.[211] Among those uses were honorifics and funerary statues that made statements about social status, benefaction, and sometimes afterlife destiny. Paul J. Brown argues that Paul's Corinthian audience might have understood his

---

208. Bruce M. Metzger, *A Textual Commentary on the Greek New Testament*, 2nd ed. (New York: United Bible Societies, 1994).

209. See Watson, "Paul's Rhetorical Strategy," 246.

210. Lincoln, *Paradise*, 50–51.

211. Brown, *Bodily Resurrection*, 218–19.

εἰκών language to have ethical implications because these sorts of statues were erected to portray the benefactors as virtuous persons whose examples should be followed.[212] One of the main functions of the inscriptions on such honorific statuary was to exhort others to emulate the person being honored.[213] They promoted the sort of behavior that was considered essential for the common good.[214] In 1 Cor 15:49, the εἰκών of the heavenly one refers to the resurrection body, but Paul's use of εἰκών may have carried ethical implications for his hearers. They may have understood this language to be portraying Christ as an example whose behavior they should emulate. A full experience of the heavenly and pneumatic body awaits; nevertheless, Paul used language to suggest that their behavior in the present should stand in continuity with that of the resurrected Christ, the one who already has a heavenly body.[215]

To summarize, the argument that runs through 1 Cor 15:35–49 answers the double question of how the body will be raised and what sort of body it will be. The answer to the first question is that it will be raised by the power and agency of the creator God. Throughout this passage Paul alludes to the creation narrative in Genesis to suggest that the God who made human bodies in the first place can make them anew at the resurrection. Paul's answer to the second question depends on the creative power of God also. As creator, God has made a variety of fleshes and a variety of bodies. Each of those bodies has its own appropriate glory. Included in this range of bodies are not only ordinary human bodies but human bodies enlivened and characterized by the Spirit. To illustrate the difference between ordinary bodies and pneumatic bodies, Paul draws on the image of a seed that is sown and sprouts into a very different looking plant. The image is useful in that there is continuity between the seed and the plant, the one comes from the other. But there is also rather dramatic discontinuity; that which is raised far outshines that which was sown. Paul draws on these various images to show what sort of body the resurrection body will be. He envisions a body set free from all the ordinary weaknesses common to human life. It will be incorruptible, glorious, powerful, and animated by the Spirit of God. If some of the Corinthians rejected the notion of bodily resurrection because they were imagining corpses being raised, Paul has

---

212. Brown, *Bodily Resurrection*, 218.
213. Brown, *Bodily Resurrection*, 219.
214. Brown, *Bodily Resurrection*, 218–19.
215. See Lincoln, *Paradise*, 51.

shown them an alternative vision of glorious bodies transformed by the power of God.

2.1.2.5. Recapitulation and Final Appeal (15:50–58)

The *peroratio* of verses 50–58 performs two major functions. It recapitulates the argument that somatic transformation at the resurrection is essential and certain, and it does so in a way that evokes a positive emotional response to the appeal Paul will make (see Aristotle, *Rhet.* 3.19; *Rhet. Her.* 2.30.47).[216] Paul begins 15:50, "Now this is what I say" (Τοῦτο δέ φημι), which signals the beginning of a new textual unit in which he will reiterate and amplify what he has argued already.[217] He then says that "flesh [σάρξ] and blood [αἷμα] are not able to inherit the kingdom of God, neither can what is corruptible [φθορά] inherit what is incorruptible [ἀφθαρσία]." The use of parallelism suggests that σάρξ and αἷμα should be understood in relation to φθορά, which was first in the series of contrasts beginning in 15:42b.[218] Paul is not suggesting that physical bodies cannot inherit the kingdom; instead, his point is that ordinary human bodies in a state of corruptibility cannot inherit the kingdom.[219] They need to be transformed into pneumatic bodies free from corruptibility, which is the point Paul makes in the next verse.

Beginning in 15:51, Paul takes on the role of a narrator telling the story of future resurrection, "Look, I will tell you a mystery." He then begins to utilize the first-person plural which draws author and audience together in the story he is telling. Paul recognizes that some will be alive at the parousia, "not all will sleep" (v. 51). Nevertheless, he asserts in the same verse, "we will all be changed." πάντες δὲ ἀλλαγησόμεθα is a brief summary of what Paul has been arguing throughout the chapter, namely, that resurrection entails somatic transformation. The importance of this short summary is illustrated when it is repeated in the next verse: ἡμεῖς ἀλλαγησόμεθα (v. 52). The divine passive reminds the hearer that God is

---

216. See Mack, *Rhetoric and the New Testament*, 57; Saw, *Paul's Rhetoric*, 238.
217. Collins, *First Corinthians*, 573–74.
218. Witherington, *Conflict and Community*, 310.
219. Wright, *Resurrection*, 359. In contrast, Endsjø takes this verse to mean Paul believed in a noncorporeal fleshless resurrection. He recognizes that Paul associates flesh with corruptibility but fails to see that this does not mean Paul anticipates a nonphysical future existence (*Greek Resurrection Beliefs*, 142–47).

the agent whose power accomplishes the resurrection, and the notion of change resonates with Paul's extensive earlier argument that ordinary bodies need to be transformed into new sorts of bodies. The timing of this change is when the "last trumpet" heralds the parousia (cf. 1 Thess 4:16); at that time the dead will gain incorruptibility (cf. the adjective ἄφθαρτος used here to the noun ἀφθαρσία in 15:42). That resurrection entails movement from corruptibility to incorruptibility has been argued already. Now that transformation is amplified in 15:53 by the parallel movement from mortality (θνητός) to immortality (ἀθανασία).

Verses 55–57 recapitulate the earlier argument with regard to the defeat of death (15:24–26) by portraying that event as the fulfillment of two eschatological passages from the Old Testament. Paul cites Isa 25:8 and follows that with a slightly modified quote from Hos 13:14.[220] The defeat of death as enemy happens as human beings take on immortality.[221] From a rhetorical perspective, the recurring language of victorious triumph over death has potential to arouse an exuberant emotional response.[222] The jubilant tone continues with a celebration of victory in 15:57 before concluding the chapter with an exhortation: "Therefore, my beloved brothers and sisters, be steadfast, immovable, always excelling in the work of the Lord, knowing that your work in the Lord is not empty [κενός]" (15:58). ὥστε indicates that the coming imperative is grounded in what has come before, and it adds weight to the argument that Paul sees his discourse on the future resurrection of the body as having concrete ethical implications.[223] κενός recalls Paul's reasoning that resurrection denial means the recipients' faith is empty or vain (15:14). Given, however, the certainty of future bodily resurrection, energy expended "in Christ" is not empty or wasted. Resurrection means that behavior matters. This closing exhortation highlights the point that Paul is not only intent on persuading the recipients to believe in resurrection; he also wants them to adopt certain ethical behaviors. He expects their ethics to stand in continuity with the hope for future bodily resurrection, their behavior to embody the group's future identity.

---

220. The Isaiah quotation is more closely aligned with the Hebrew text, while the Hosea citation modifies the LXX.
221. Brown, *Bodily Resurrection*, 225.
222. See Saw, *Paul's Rhetoric*, 238.
223. Brown, *Bodily Resurrection*, 227.

This raises the question of how bodily resurrection as a future social identity might function to motivate behavioral transformation in the present. According to Cinnirella, individuals tend to embrace positively valued future social identities. When a possible identity is embraced, individuals are increasingly motivated to behave in such a way as to attain that future identity.[224] Throughout the main arguments of 15:20–28, 35–49, and the conclusion of 50–58, Paul portrayed future bodily resurrection in a particularly favorable light. Resurrection itself is participation in the victory of Christ over the enemy of death. It is freedom from corruptibility, dishonor, and weakness. It is entrance into incorruptibility, glory, and power. We noted above that these terms would have been heard by the Corinthians within the framework of the Greco-Roman system of honor and shame, in which nothing was valued more highly than honor, and nothing was avoided more fervently than shame. Resurrection is a way of escaping the frailty of an ordinary body and receiving the glory and power of a body brought to life and sustained by God's own Spirit. Another positive portrayal of bodily resurrection comes with the "heavenly" language in 15:47–49. That positive evaluation of future bodily resurrection is then summarized and amplified for emotional response in 15:50–57, where Paul again highlights incorruptibility, immortality, and victory over death. This favorable evaluation of resurrection as a future possible identity ought to heighten its desirability. If the recipients are drawn to Paul's positive evaluation, the likelihood increases that they will begin to behave in a way that coheres with that future social identity.

I argued above that the *refutatio* in 15:12–19 carried potential to arouse fiercely negative emotions with Paul's argument that resurrection denial overturns the whole of the Christian faith. Now that we have the full weight of the positive evaluation in front of us, we are in a better position to see the force of Paul's negative evaluation of resurrection denial. For Paul, bodily resurrection is a central tenet of the Christian faith, and its rejection is detrimental. It undermines the apostolic preaching, leaves believers in their sin, and makes faith a matter of futility. The gospel stands or falls with resurrection of the body. Taken through the lens of SIT, resurrection denial involves rejecting a defining marker of the group's future identity. It is a renunciation of that which is necessitated by membership "in Christ" and a denial of the future pneumatic embodiment that is

---

224. Cinnirella, "Exploring Temporal Aspects," 229.

promised to those who are spiritual. To reject future bodily resurrection is to define oneself outside the boundaries of the group, thus jeopardizing one's participation in the victory of Christ over death.

Additionally, if one subgroup of Corinthians is defined by its belief in future bodily resurrection while another subgroup rejects that belief, it calls the group's future identity into question and poses a threat to the overall unity of the group. The indispensability of future bodily resurrection means there is no middle ground. As Mitchell observed, "Paul cannot easily conciliate between the two sides because the problem, as he understands it, is proper adherence to the gospel."[225] The *refutatio* functions to challenge the legitimacy of the alternative identity with a view to neutralizing the threat.[226] The strength of Paul's negative evaluation sheds light on the high threat level he perceived. If his rhetoric is effective, it will forge a salient future identity with potential to help mitigate factionalism and cultivate cohesion, thus neutralizing the threat to the group.

Throughout this section I have argued that three dynamics in the text of 1 Cor 15:12–58 provide evidence to support interpreting future bodily resurrection as a future possible social identity: (1) belief in future bodily resurrection differentiated one subgroup from another; (2) future bodily resurrection is only realized through participation in the "in Christ" group; and (3) future bodily resurrection is expressed in pneumatic language, which was a key linguistic tool that distinguished early Christ-followers from other groups. The cumulative force of the argument clears the way for a fourth observation: the very fact that resurrection involves bodies reinforces the social dynamic of future bodily resurrection. Embodiment is an inherently social phenomenon.[227] The body enables and facilitates human relationships. It is the means by which an individual relates to her community. The senses through which we experience the world are contained within our bodies. Chris Shilling observes that the body is vital to human agency: "It is our bodies which allow us to act, to intervene in, and to alter the flow of daily life."[228] He goes on to insist that any adequate theory of human agency must take the body into account.[229] The human

---

225. Mitchell, *Rhetoric of Reconciliation*, 288.
226. Cinnirella, "Exploring Temporal Aspects," 240.
227. See Dunn, *Theology of Paul*, 59–61.
228. Chris Shilling, *The Body and Social Theory*, Theory, Culture and Society, 2nd ed. (London: Sage, 2003), 8; cf. Kelsey, *Eccentric Existence*, 248–49.
229. Shilling, *The Body and Social Theory*, 8.

capacities for language and cognition are embodied phenomena; thus, our ability to communicate with others and our perceptions of ourselves in relation to others are part of our embodied identity.

The inherently social nature of embodiment illumines a distinction between future bodily resurrection and disembodied postmortem existence. Platonic dualism saw the body as a burden from which the soul needed to be free. If social experience is bound up with embodiment, it is difficult to imagine a social dimension to Plato's view of the afterlife. And while Stoicism understood the soul to be corporeal in nature, the postmortem existence of the soul involved its impersonal absorption into the divine πνεῦμα. Even with Stoic materialism, there is no sense of postmortem personal or social identity. Paul's vision of resurrected bodies thus implies a social dimension that is quite distinct from those alternatives.

All of this invites reflection on the social dynamics of raised bodies, especially in light of Paul's insistence that the present body is both continuous and discontinuous with the resurrected body. To what extent might future bodily resurrection entail a transformed social experience? We have been attentive throughout to the role of emotion in Paul's reasoning, and taking the question from that angle provides further opportunity for reflection. We saw that Paul's argument against resurrection denial depended to some extent on its ability to evoke fear and perhaps a renewed sense of grief upon the realization that the Corinthians' fellow believers who have died are without hope apart from future bodily resurrection. But how is grief experienced after the transformation entailed in future bodily resurrection? To what extent would an individual experience grief in a social context where death is no more and bodies are immortal?

That personal agency is an implication of embodiment also raises questions about the nature of human freedom in a postresurrection social context. Kelsey puts the question this way,

> Given that prior to their resurrection personal bodies exhibit the power to enact ... orientations to their proximate contexts that are contrary to their basic personal identities as one elect by God for eschatological glory, should we affirm that having been transformed by their resurrection they continue to have this power?[230]

---

230. Kelsey, *Eccentric Existence*, 558–59.

Would a resurrected body as agent have the freedom to behave in a way that is contrary to its identity? This question brings us back to the relationship between bodily resurrection and bodily practice. Might a resurrected body be able to "enact practices" that run counter to its identity?[231] And questions of agency raise questions of accountability. In what sense might those who have been raised from the dead be accountable for their behavior to one another and to the community as a whole? And if bodily practices matter in the present as a way of embodying the future identity, what sort of practices might be appropriate postresurrection when the future identity has been realized? Questions like these emerge from our SIT approach and underscore that, for Paul, future redemption is not merely a matter of individual salvation. It is the redemption of a community of bodies "in Christ" through the Spirit together with one another.

2.1.3. Bodily Resurrection and Practice in 1 Cor 6:12–20

The next passage under consideration is replete with interest in bodily practice. Paul touches on appropriate use of food and the stomach (6:13), the body and sexual immorality (6:14), prostitution and bodies in relation to Christ (6:15), sins against the body (6:18), and glorifying God in the body (6:20). Planted in the midst of those concerns is a brief expression of hope for future bodily resurrection (6:14b). The passage comes in a section of the letter that runs from 5:1–6:20. Issues of group identity arise throughout the larger section, not least with regard to group boundaries. In 5:1–13, Paul deals with sexual immorality and instructs the recipients to discontinue fellowship with community members who engage in those and other problematic practices (5:11). In 6:1–11, he instructs the recipients to handle disputes within the boundaries of the group rather than going to outsiders for judgment. So the context is characterized by questions related to social identity and expectations for bodily practice.

Interpretive problems arise with the opening words of 6:12, "All things are permissible for me" (πάντα μοι ἔξεστιν). Most scholars take this to be a slogan used by some of the recipients to justify some forms of behavior.[232] Despite the certainty on the part of some interpreters, others question the

---

231. Kelsey, *Eccentric Existence*, 559.
232. Barrett, *First Epistle*, 144; cf. Conzelmann, *1 Corinthians*, 1975; Jerome Murphy-O'Connor, "Corinthian Slogans in 1 Cor. 6:12–20," *CBQ* 40 (1978): 390–96; Fee, *First Epistle*, 251; Mitchell, *Rhetoric of Reconciliation*, 118; Witherington, *Conflict and*

likelihood that Paul is quoting the Corinthians.²³³ The worry is sometimes expressed that many who take this as a quote do not clearly show how they come to that conclusion.²³⁴ Garland goes further by making a detailed case for why it is unlikely that Paul is quoting the Corinthians.²³⁵ Also concerned with the quest for Corinthian slogans, Brian J. Dodd argues that Paul is affirming Christian freedom but placing limits on it with the qualifier: "not all things are beneficial" (6:12).²³⁶ The shorter πάντα ἔξεστιν appears in 1 Cor 10:23 with the same qualification and is applied to the matter of what foods believers may be permitted to eat. Paul there embraces a freedom-within-limits approach to food. The suggestion has been made that some recipients have misused Paul's teaching with regard to food by applying it to sexual ethics.²³⁷ Or, perhaps, Paul sees the potential for that sort of misuse of his earlier teaching and here uses it to introduce his comments on sexual immorality, in order to remind the recipients of the limits on the principle.²³⁸

Whether it is his own or the recipients, Paul repeats the maxim a second time but now qualifies it by saying, "but I will not be lorded over by anything" (ἀλλ' οὐκ ἐγὼ ἐξουσιασθήσομαι ὑπό τινος, 6:12). He is preparing to argue for the lordship of Christ over the bodies of believers, and that sex with a πόρνη violates that lordship. For Paul, sexual union involves authority over the partner, as is evident in 1 Cor 7:3-4. The difference is that a marriage is a relationship in which it is appropriate to yield one's body to the authority of the spouse. Outside of marriage, sexual union still involves submitting one's body to another authority, but that mastery is inappropriate. It is likely that ἐξουσιάζω in 6:12 anticipates the upcoming argument regarding sex with a πόρνη and introduces the potential of being mastered by an immoral sexual desire or an illicit sexual partner. That is

---

Community, 167; Hays, *First Corinthians*, 102; Collins, *First Corinthians*, 243; Schrage, *Der erste Brief*, 2:17; Thiselton, *First Epistle*, 461.

233. Schnabel suggests that the phrase "is probably not a Corinthian slogan but a maxim with which Paul describes the behavior of Corinthian Christians" (*Korinther*, 333, my translation).

234. Roger L. Omanson, "Acknowledging Paul's Quotations," *BT* 43.2 (1992): 201; cf. May, *Body*, 100.

235. Garland, *1 Corinthians*, 225-29.

236. Brian J. Dodd, *Paul's Paradigmatic 'I': Personal Example as Literary Strategy*, JSNTSup 177 (Sheffield: Sheffield Academic, 1999), 55.

237. Sandnes, *Belly and Body*, 195-96.

238. See May, *Body*, 102.

2. Embracing Resurrection

to say, in this context, the alternative authority could be πορνεία or it could be the πόρνη.[239]

While some caution was in order with regard to whether 6:12 contains a Corinthian quote, it is indeed likely that 6:13a–b reflects the views of the recipients and could even be a reformulated slogan.[240]

6:13a τὰ βρώματα τῇ κοιλίᾳ καὶ ἡ κοιλία τοῖς βρώμασιν,
6:13b ὁ δὲ θεὸς καὶ ταύτην καὶ ταῦτα καταργήσει.
6:13c τὸ δὲ σῶμα οὐ τῇ πορνείᾳ ἀλλὰ τῷ κυρίῳ, καὶ ὁ κύριος τῷ σώματι·

The most significant piece of evidence that 6:13a–b is a summary of the perspective of the recipients is that it reflects a different attitude toward the body and the future than that held by Paul. The view reflected in 6:13a–b is that some bodily functions and appetites are inconsequential or insignificant because the stomach (as an organ of the body) will be destroyed by God. This is not to suggest that the recipients were principled libertines; it simply means that they did not see the matter as particularly important. Use of the body was seen as trivial because bodily life was fleeting.[241]

While Paul would agree that present bodily life is fleeting, he would dispute that it is trivial. Our analysis of 1 Cor 15 demonstrated that Paul sees a deep connection between future bodily resurrection and the behavior of believers. Because of that connection, the behavior of the present body matters a great deal. He expects believers to act in a way that embodies their identity as people who will be raised from the dead, and he offered strong words of correction when he perceived that their behavior did not stand in continuity with the life of the future (15:29–34). Paul anticipates the argument of chapter 15 in the very next verse by asserting that God raised Christ from the dead and will also raise Christ-followers (6:14). He will then proceed to make the case against πορνεία by arguing that the body is a temple of God's Spirit (6:19) before concluding with an exhortation to "glorify God in your body" (6:20). That conviction is difficult to reconcile with the more indifferent attitude toward body and

---

239. May, *Body*, 105.
240. Sandnes, *Belly and Body*, 195; cf. Schrage, *Der erste Brief*, 2:20; Thiselton, *First Epistle*, 462; Collins, *First Corinthians*, 244–45.
241. May, *Body*, 95–98.

behavior in 6:13a–b. Despite the fact that body parts decompose, bodily behavior is not inconsequential. For Paul, attention must be given to the use of the body in the present precisely because the body is to be resurrected, and this is the case regardless of what happens to the body in between its death and resurrection. The present body and the future body have enough continuity that what is done in the present matters. Decomposition does not undermine or negate that continuity. The attitude that Paul articulates in 6:13a–b thus reflects a different understanding of the relationship between the body and the future than what we find elsewhere in Paul. There is no need to posit a quasi-Platonic attitude or some sort of protognostic tendency to explain the Corinthian perspective.[242] Given that there were some in the Corinthian congregation who rejected future bodily resurrection, it should not surprise us that they may have taken a lax attitude toward some matters of bodily practice.[243] The problem that Paul addresses is not simply one of bodily practice; it is aberrant bodily practice rooted in errant eschatology, and, as in 1 Cor 15, the problem could simply be denial of the resurrection.

The question remains as to why Paul introduces food and the stomach into his exhortation against πορνεία. Sandnes has convincingly demonstrated that the stomach was used as a rhetorical topos in a broad range of ancient literature where it is portrayed negatively to criticize an attitude of self-indulgence.[244] γαστήρ and κοιλία were catchwords associated with gluttony and untamed sexual appetite. Greco-Roman literature so closely relates excessive eating and drinking to sexual desire that food, wine, and sex have been called the "unholy trinity" of the ancient world.[245] Banquets were often seen as an occasion for gratifying these desires in that the meal was typically followed by sexual intercourse. Jewish writers

---

242. Thiselton raises the possibility of both; see *First Epistle*, 462. Schrage also sees gnostic tendencies underlying 6:12–20 and what is perceived as asceticism reported in 1 Cor 7:1, "A critical underlying prerequisite for libertinism and asceticism, not only in Corinth but everywhere, is a negative understanding of σῶμα, which is attacked in particular and rejected head-on in 6,12ff, even without the usually recognizable mythological background" (*Der erste Brief*, 2:15, my translation). For problems with the gnostic hypothesis, see May, *Body*, 92–98.

243. See Martin, *Corinthian Body*, 175–76.

244. Sandnes, *Belly and Body*, 24–93.

245. Alan Booth, "The Age of Reclining and Its Attendant Perils," in *Dining in a Classical Context*, ed. William J. Slater (Ann Arbor: University of Michigan Press, 1991), 105.

appropriated the belly topos to identify the life lived in service to the belly as characteristic of paganism in contrast to their own disciplined dietary practices.[246] Since dietary regulations were perceived by Jews as differentiating them from the pagan nations, attitudes toward the belly could function as a marker of social identity (see, e.g., 3 Macc 3:4–7).[247]

Paul's discussion of the belly and sexual immorality in the context of 1 Cor 6:12–20 makes a great deal of sense read against this background. Several scenarios are plausible. Paul could simply be using food and stomach figuratively for sex and sexual behavior.[248] Another scenario could be that the recipients agreed with Paul that as believers they had significant freedom with regard to food. Some of them may have utilized that liberty to justify freedom with regard to sex also.[249] Or, knowing that food and sex were closely related concepts in the Greco-Roman world, Paul may have introduced the language of the belly in order to keep the Corinthians from attempting to justify their sexual practices by appealing to their freedom at the table. Whatever the case, the key insight for our analysis is that Paul thinks their careless approach to bodily practice is substantiated by their view that bodily life is temporary.

In response to that perspective, 6:13c asserts that the present body does indeed matter and is not to be used for πορνεία, a broad term that could refer to any unlawful sexual activity including but not limited to adultery, incest, and sex with a prostitute.[250] The body is not to be used for πορνεία because "the body is for the Lord" (6:13). What Paul means will be worked out as the argument proceeds. For now, the thing to see is the authority relationship that appears to be implied. πορνεία is inappropriate because the body is the property of the Lord and is thus under the authority of the Lord. κύριος is used by Paul of Jesus commonly enough, but given that the context reflects an interest in ἐξουσία (6:12b), the significance of the title is amplified. We saw above that Paul introduced the argument with the question of lordship or mastery. Who will have authority over the believer's body? Will believers be ruled by their desires for

---

246. There is far more material than we have room here to survey; Sandnes catalogs extensive textual evidence from a variety of Second Temple period sources (*Belly and Body*, 97–107) and Philo (*Belly and Body*, 108–31).
247. See Sandnes, *Belly and Body*, 99.
248. Wright, *Resurrection*, 290.
249. Sandnes, *Belly and Body*, 195–96.
250. Thiselton, *First Epistle*, 385.

πορνεία? Or will they be ruled by the Lord? For Paul, bodies have moral significance because they are the sphere where the authority of Jesus as Lord is to be displayed.[251]

Before continuing to address the matter of πορνεία, Paul pauses to mention the topic of resurrection: "Now God raised the Lord and he will raise us by his power" (ὁ δὲ θεὸς καὶ τὸν κύριον ἤγειρεν καὶ ἡμᾶς ἐξεγερεῖ διὰ τῆς δυνάμεως αὐτοῦ, 6:14). From a rhetorical perspective, this is puzzling for two reasons. First, we have already seen that some of the recipients deny the resurrection of believers (1 Cor 15:12), and Paul will devote significant energy later in the letter to persuading them of their future resurrection. By mentioning resurrection here, he has introduced a contested topic into his argument against πορνεία. Arguing for a certain behavior on the basis of a belief that some recipients deny seems a peculiar rhetorical strategy. Second, the function of bodily resurrection in the argument of 6:12–20 is unclear. If Paul had argued that bodily behavior matters now because the body will be raised later, then the logic would be straightforward. While that may be the underlying assumption, it is not what he actually says. The argument against πορνεία would seem to work just as well, if not better, without any mention of resurrection at all.

The unarticulated assumption seems to be that the present body is significant because it stands in continuity with the resurrected body of the future. A number of commentators nuance this basic approach in various ways. Hays, for example, sees the 6:14 as an assertion of divine validation of bodily life. This is the fundamental Christian proclamation, and understanding that means understanding that bodies are not irrelevant.[252] Thiselton argues in similar fashion that Paul's view of future bodily resurrection counters Corinthian disregard for the body by showing that "resurrection destiny is precisely what gives meaning, responsibility, and significance to bodily existence in the present."[253] Wright also sees the affirmation of the believer's resurrection based on Christ's resurrection as underlying the whole argument of 6:12–20. Paul's point is to show continuity between the present body and the future body, which means bodily behavior in the present cannot be disregarded as insignificant.[254] This

---

251. See Victor Paul Furnish, *The Theology of the First Letter to the Corinthians*, New Testament Theology (Cambridge: Cambridge University Press, 1999), 57.
252. Hays, *First Corinthians*, 104.
253. Thiselton, *First Epistle*, 464–65.
254. Wright, *Resurrection*, 289–90.

2. Embracing Resurrection

approach coheres with what we have already seen in 1 Cor 15 where Paul exhorts the recipients to behave in a way that coheres with their future resurrection identity. The key thing to note is that this line of reasoning is not explicit in the text of 1 Cor 6:12–20. It remains, at this point, an unargued assumption.

After Paul's comment on the resurrection, the question of authority is played out in terms of two mutually exclusive options: membership with Christ versus membership with a πόρνη. Paul introduces the options in 6:15 by means of two rhetorical questions. The first implies that the Corinthians ought to know that "your bodies are members of Christ" (τὰ σώματα ὑμῶν μέλη Χριστοῦ ἐστιν, 6:15). The second implies that the recipients should know better than to have sex with prostitutes. We should resist any temptation to reduce σῶμα to mean something akin to personality. Paul's interest in this passage has to do with a practice (i.e., sex) performed by physical bodies. To say that the body is a limb or organ of Christ (μέλη Χριστοῦ) reflects the conviction that there is an intimately close connection between the believer's body and Christ himself.[255] Paul's portrayal of the believer's body as a limb of Christ's body substantiates the claim that the body belongs to the Lord and affirms Christ's authority over the bodies of believers. The intimacy of that relationship is evident in that Paul uses the same language to present the alternative option of becoming a "member of a prostitute" (πόρνης μέλη). Paul thus presents relationship with Christ as analogical to the sexual relationship.[256] That is, they are similar in some ways and different in others, and, as Paul will argue, the danger of this practice lies in that analogical dynamic.

The significance of the sexual act with a πόρνη is illumined with the second question in 6:15: "Shall I, therefore, remove [ἄρας] the limbs of Christ and make [ποιήσω] them members of a prostitute?" The use of αἴρω suggests more force than would have been communicated by λαμβάνω. Paul depicts a powerful taking away or wrenching off of a piece of Christ's body. ποιήσω could be a subjunctive, but the future indicative is more likely. Paul is not so much inviting deliberation, which might be communicated by the subjunctive, as he is offering a rebuke.[257] Bruce N. Fisk sees it as unclear whether "Paul believed that using a prostitute imme-

---

255. May, *Body*, 111.
256. Hays, *First Corinthians*, 104.
257. Thiselton, *First Epistle*, 465–66.

diately severed all ties to Christ."²⁵⁸ But Paul's rhetorical question brings the mutual exclusivity between union with Christ and sexual union with a πόρνη into focus. The bodies of believers are limbs on Christ's body, and Christ has authority over them. Sex with a prostitute amounts to dismembering Christ's body. It is tantamount to severing a limb from the body of Christ in order to graft it to the body of a sexual partner. For Paul, then, sex with a prostitute is detrimental to Christian identity.²⁵⁹ This may shed light on Paul's earlier mention of the believer's resurrection. I argued in the exegesis of 1 Cor 15 that future bodily resurrection functions as a possible social identity for Paul. Paul's ethical expectations in 1 Cor 15:29–34 and 58 reflected a desire for consistency between present behavior and the future identity marked by bodily resurrection. One of Paul's concerns was the recipients' bad eschatology; another concern was their resulting bad behavior. We might say that Paul assumes in 6:12–20 the future identity for which he will argue in chapter 15, and his focus in chapter 6 is on temporal somatic continuity as an aspect of that future possible identity. The present self as body will be the future self as resurrected body. Paul's problem with πόρνη-union is not simply the fact that it reflects an attitude that devalues the body and is thus discontinuous with the future identity. His problem with πόρνη-union is that it destroys that identity. One's body cannot be raised with Christ if one's body is not in union with Christ. A body cannot both belong to Christ and be severed from him at the same time.²⁶⁰ πόρνη-union separates a body from Christ and jeopardizes participation in the resurrection.

But why is it that sexual union with a prostitute is mutually exclusive to union with Christ?²⁶¹ The question brings us back to the analogy between union with Christ and union with a πόρνη, which Paul develops in 6:16–17. Rather than analogy, some interpreters are inclined to see primarily contrast between these two unions. Robert H. Gundry, for example, argues that the πόρνη-union in view is merely superficial: "To be sure, the union produces one body, or one flesh (vv. 15–16). But to what extent? Coitus with a prostitute is casual, occasional, momentary, and non-indicative of

---

258. Bruce N. Fisk, "ΠΟΡΝΕΥΕΙΝ as Body Violation: The Unique Nature of Sexual Sin in 1 Corinthians 6:18," *NTS* 42 (1996): 54.

259. May, *Body*, 113.

260. Thiselton, *First Epistle*, 466.

261. Schweitzer understood this mutual exclusivity to be a consequence of the "physical character" of union with Christ; see *Mysticism*, 128.

any other union."²⁶² In contrast, he argues, Christ-union is "fundamental, constant, and all-embracing."²⁶³ The problem with this approach is that Paul uses the same language to describe both unions, which indicates that they do indeed have something in common. In verses 16 and 17 he uses the substantive participle ὁ κολλώμενος to describe one joined to a πόρνη (v. 16) and one joined to Christ (v. 17). This repetition suggests that the πόρνη-union is more than superficial and that the two unions have something in common.²⁶⁴ Further, to substantiate the claim that πόρνη-union makes the person "one body" (ἓν σῶμα) with her, Paul cites Gen 2:24 LXX, ἔσονται οἱ δύο εἰς σάρκα μίαν. That Paul draws on this verse to substantiate the ἓν σῶμα result of πόρνη-union suggests that he is using ἓν σῶμα and σάρκα μίαν synonymously. His application of Gen 2:24 indicates that he must have seen πόρνη-union effecting the same sort of fundamental "one flesh" union as that which is accomplished through the consummation of a marriage.²⁶⁵

The contrast between πόρνη-union and Christ-union is articulated in that πόρνη-union involves becoming ἓν σῶμα with her while the Christ-union is a matter of being ἓν πνεῦμα with the Lord (vv. 16–17). Paul's use of πνεῦμα in verse 17 is illumined by verse 19, where Paul tells the recipients that "your body is a temple of the indwelling Holy Spirit" (τὸ σῶμα ὑμῶν ναὸς τοῦ ἐν ὑμῖν ἁγίου πνεύματός ἐστιν). Paul is probably thinking of the Spirit as the one who effects the union of the believer to Christ.²⁶⁶ It is because the Spirit indwells *the body* that the believer can be said to be "one spirit" with Christ. This Spirit-enabled union correlates with Christ's authority over the body. Given Paul's appeal to the resurrection of Christ and the coming resurrection of believers in 6:14, I would also suggest that Paul's language here may anticipate the language of σῶμα πνευματικόν in 15:44. Christ's resurrected body is a σῶμα πνευματικόν, and the body that believers will receive at the resurrection is also. In 1 Cor 15:44, σῶμα πνευματικόν means a body animated by the Spirit for life in the age to come. Here the presence of the Spirit *in the bodies* of believers joins them to Christ and empowers them to flee from sin in obedience to God. In this way, believers *already* have the Spirit as an empowering force in their bodies even though they

---

262. Gundry, *Sōma*, 53.
263. Gundry, *Sōma*, 53.
264. May, *Body*, 116–17.
265. May, *Body*, 115.
266. Fee, *First Epistle*, 260.

do *not yet* have bodies fully animated by the Spirit. Thus, it is the Spirit that ties Paul's attitude toward bodily practice in the present to resurrection of the body in the future. This reinforces our suggestion that πόρνη-union is at odds with Christ-union because it is discontinuous with the resurrection as a future possible identity. We found above that pneumatic language is bound up with early Christian social identity, and that the same language is associated with resurrection through the concept of a pneumatic body. If Paul's depiction of union with Christ in terms of ἕν πνεῦμα anticipates the σῶμα πνευματικόν that is raised, then it means πόρνη-union that accomplishes the ἕν σῶμα relationship with her is discontinuous with a resurrection-oriented identity. This reinforces the suggestion that Paul's reasoning in 1 Cor 6:12–20 correlates with the function of bodily resurrection as a future social identity.

Another aspect of the mutual exclusivity between Christ-union and πόρνη-union involves the issue of ἐξουσία. We observed above that Paul thinks of sexual relationships in terms of power relations. Husband and wife have ἐξουσία over one another's bodies (1 Cor 7:4). From that authority derives his instruction that husband and wife not deprive one another sexually for unnecessarily long periods of time (7:5).[267] Their bodies belong to one another. If the thing that marital union and πόρνη-union have in common is that both involve giving another authority over the body, then it helps make sense of what Paul says in the passage under consideration and why he introduced the entire argument with the question of being mastered in 6:12.[268] The believer's body belongs to Christ the Lord, to whom it has been joined by virtue of the Holy Spirit. Christ exercises authority in the sphere of the believer's body. Sexual union with a spouse is authorized and thus does not constitute a power relation that contradicts the authority of Christ. Sexual union with a prostitute is illicit and thus does constitute a power relation that contradicts the authority of Christ.

Paul's instruction to the Corinthians, then, is to stay away from πόρνη-union (Φεύγετε τὴν πορνείαν, 6:18). He distinguishes between sin done "outside the body" (ἐκτὸς τοῦ σώματος) and sin committed "into one's own

---

267. It is telling that Paul sees his advice on the conjugal rights of married persons as a concession (1 Cor 7:6). Even though the marital relationship, and the giving of authority that it entails, is sanctioned by God, Paul would rather people remain unmarried so that they can be singularly devoted to the Lord (1 Cor 7:32–35).

268. May, *Body*, 118.

body" (εἰς τὸ ἴδιον σῶμα). πόρνη-union is placed in the latter category. This distinction has been the subject of much debate.[269] Barrett sees different degrees of sin rather than a different kind of sin, and thus interprets πορνεία as a very serious act of immorality or ethical failure.[270] Others who see this as Paul's own statement affirm that he is indeed talking about two different *kinds* of sin, though this interpretation is characterized by a variety of approaches.[271] Still others see the statement, "Every sin that a person does is outside the body," as another Corinthian slogan. Taken this way, it could reflect an attitude among some recipients that deprecates the body.[272]

Paul's distinction between sin outside the body and sin into or against the body is followed by a rhetorical question implying that the body is a temple of the indwelling Holy Spirit. We discussed some aspects of that above; another implication in Paul's thinking is that the presence of the Spirit within the body means that "you are not your own" (οὐκ ἐστὲ ἑαυτῶν, 6:19). The logic is that the temple is the property of the deity who dwells in it.[273] This is further substantiated in verse 20 by the statement, "For you were purchased for a price." Both of these statements suggest that sin against the body has to do with the question: to whom does the body belong? Paul's answer is that the believer belongs to Christ. Fee is thus right to suggest that sin against or into one's own body should be understood in light of Paul's earlier statement, "the body is for the Lord" (6:13).[274] Once again, we find ourselves considering questions of lordship, authority, and power. Sexual immorality with a πόρνη is sin against one's own body because it uniquely wrenches that body away from Christ, who is its proper authority, and submits that body to the authority of the πόρνη by making it a member of her body. The Pauline imperative then is to flee from such behavior and, instead, "Glorify God, therefore, in your body" (6:20). The prepositional phrase ἐν τῷ σώματι ὑμῶν communicates location and portrays the body as the sphere where God is glorified. The imperative stands

---

269. See the useful chart of various approaches in Fisk, "ΠΟΡΝΕΥΕΙΝ," 542–43.
270. Barrett, *First Epistle*, 150–51.
271. Fisk, "ΠΟΡΝΕΥΕΙΝ," 540–58; cf., though differently, Martin, *Corinthian Body*, 176–78. Thiselton notes that "the shadings and hypotheses of this verse are almost limitless" (*First Epistle*, 472).
272. Murphy-O'Connor, "Slogans," 393; cf. Omanson, "Acknowledging Paul's Quotations," 201–13.
273. May, *Body*.
274. Fee, *First Epistle*, 262–63.

in causal relation to the preceding indicative (ἠγοράσθητε), but it should be seen as summing up the whole force of Paul's instruction, though now in positive terms. In as much as the body is a limb of Christ and is indwelt by the Spirit of God, it belongs to God. It should, therefore, be used in a way that honors God. Paul's point in this passage has been to show that πορνεία is particularly dishonoring to God. It denies God's claim on the body. It severs the believer's body from Christ. It takes what is properly submitted to Christ's authority and allows it to be mastered by another. All of this is a dishonor to God. Instead, Paul exhorts the Corinthians to use their bodies in ways that honor God's possession of their bodies.

SIT provides a framework for reflecting on the present-future dynamic that we find in 1 Cor 6:12–20. First, we may observe that the Corinthians did not seem to think that πόρνη-union carried the danger of destroying Christian identity, and this is an area where they differed from Paul. One function of 6:12–20, then, is to motivate the recipients to think about how πορνεία relates to their Christian identity with a view to persuading them that engaging in it is inconsistent with their identity. Second, why is the specific bodily practice of union with a πόρνη detrimental to Christian identity? If, as I have argued, future bodily resurrection functions in Paul's thought as a future possible social identity, then Paul will also expect believers to behave in a way that coheres with the future identity. That is, he will expect them to use their bodies in a way that coheres with bodily resurrection as a future possible identity. For Paul, πόρνη-union correlates with an attitude that sees the body as inconsequential. As a result, it is incongruous with a resurrection-oriented identity that deems bodily life in the present to have significant moral importance. Third, one challenge for Paul is that not all of the Corinthians share his vision of the group's future as characterized by bodily resurrection. He needs to persuade them to embrace bodily resurrection as a future possible identity. In this way, the effectiveness of 6:12–20 depends on the success of the argument in chapter 15. If they embrace resurrection as a future possible social identity, then they will be more likely to behave in a way that seeks to obtain not endanger that future identity.

2.1.4. Summary of 1 Corinthians

For Paul, future bodily resurrection is nonnegotiable. To deny the future resurrection of believers is to overturn the Christian faith. This illustrates its significance for Christian identity. Belief in resurrection is a hope grounded in the resurrection of Christ. What happened to Christ at his resurrection will also happen to members of the Christ-group. Belief in future bodily resurrection also serves to differentiate between group members and outsiders, and it aids in identifying subgroup members who hold errant beliefs. Paul's theology of future bodily resurrection is also deeply intertwined with his expectations for bodily practice. He believes that the body should be used in a way that correlates with its future resurrection. He also believes that some practices endanger and even destroy Christian identity. πόρνη-union falls in that category. That use of the body stands at odds with hope for resurrection. Paul's expectation is for believers to flee such behavior and pursue bodily practices that glorify God and anticipate the redemption of the body.

2.2. Second Corinthians

During the period between the writing of 1 and 2 Corinthians, Paul's relationship with the recipients deteriorated dramatically. Several factors appear to have contributed to the rising tension. Paul had intended to visit Corinth, but ultimately changed his plans (1 Cor 16:5–9; 2 Cor 1:15–17).[275] Another group, dubbed "super apostles" by Paul, has come to Corinth and questioned the credibility of his apostolic ministry (2 Cor 10:12–18; 11:4–15). There also appears to be questions with regard to Paul's handling of the collection and his refusal to accept patronage from the recipients (2 Cor 7:2; 11:7–10; 12:14–18). In response, Paul penned 2 Corinthians with the double goal of defending himself against allegations arising from these problems and facilitating reconciliation with the Corinthians.

2.2.1. Identity and the Rhetoric of Defense

Any attempt to analyze the rhetoric of 2 Corinthians is complicated by the possibility that it may be a composite document of two or more letters or fragments of letters. At one level, the question of partitions is peripheral to our analysis, because we are dealing with a single passage that falls within a section of the letter that is generally seen as a unity. So, a full analysis of the various partition theories is beyond the scope of this study, though it is

---

275. The cancelled visit would have been after what is referred to as Paul's "painful visit" (see 2 Cor 2:1).

worth noting some of the internal evidence that leads some scholars to raise questions about the letter's integrity as we prepare to discuss Paul's rhetoric in 2 Corinthians. To name only two issues, there are multiple places in 2 Corinthians where the topic changes abruptly, thus making the train of thought difficult to trace (see 2:13 and 14; cf. 7:4 and 5). Also, the very harsh tone of chapters 10–13 appears to conflict with efforts at peacemaking in 7:4–16.[276] Alternatively, a growing number of scholars now argue that 2 Corinthians is a literary unity.[277] Fredrick J. Long's recent full-length study is particularly noteworthy. He argues for the compositional unity of 2 Corinthians on the basis of substantial similarity to Greco-Roman forensic oratory in terms of exigency, arrangement, invention, and style; Paul's use of forensic topoi and idioms; and the overall coherence of the letter's rhetorical goals.[278] While the majority of scholars continue to see 2 Corinthians as a composite letter, increasing substantial arguments for the unity of the letter suggest the matter remains unsettled.

A variety of attempts have been made to analyze 2 Corinthians in light of the three species of Greco-Roman rhetoric. Those who see it as a composite document sometimes apply different genres to different parts

---

276. For a detailed analysis of the partition theories, see Margaret Thrall, *A Critical and Exegetical Commentary on the Second Epistle to the Corinthians*, 2 vols., ICC (Edinburgh: T&T Clark, 1994–2000), 3–48. Bieringer groups the partition theories into four major hypotheses; see his "Teilungshypothesen zum 2. Korintherbrief," in *Studies on 2 Corinthians*, ed. Reinmund Bieringer and Jan Lambrecht, BETL 112 (Leuven: Leuven University Press, 1994), 67–105. He provides a useful chart on pp. 96–97 that lists the scholars associated with each theory.

277. Francis Young and D. F. Ford, *Meaning and Truth in Second Corinthians*, BFT (Grand Rapids: Eerdmans, 1987), 27–59; cf. F. W. Danker, "Paul's Debt to the *De Corona* of Demosthenes: A Study of Rhetorical Techniques in Second Corinthians," in *Persuasive Artistry: Studies in New Testament Rhetoric in Honor of G. A. Kennedy*, ed. Duane F. Watson, JSNTSup 50 (Sheffield: Sheffield Academic, 1991), 268–80; Witherington, *Conflict and Community*, 333–39; Paul Barnett, *The Second Epistle to the Corinthians*, NICNT (Grand Rapids: Eerdmans, 1997), 17–25; J. D. H. Amador, "Revisting 2 Corinthians: Rhetoric and the Case for Unity," *NTS* 46 (2000): 92–111; Scott J. Hafeman, *2 Corinthians*, NIVAC (Grand Rapids: Zondervan, 2000), 31–33; Frank J. Matera, *II Corinthians: A Commentary*, NTL (Louisville: Westminster John Knox, 2003), 29–32; Fredrick J. Long, *Ancient Rhetoric and Paul's Apology: The Compositional Unity of 2 Corinthians*, SNTSMS 131 (Cambridge: Cambridge University Press, 2004); Mark A. Seifrid, *The Second Letter to the Corinthians*, Pillar New Testament Commentary (Grand Rapids: Eerdmans, 2014), xxix–xxxi.

278. Long, *Paul's Apology*, 1–14.

of the letter based on their reconstruction.[279] I am in large agreement with Long and others that 2 Corinthians bears more in common overall with forensic or judicial rhetoric than it does deliberative or epideictic.[280] Paul certainly takes a deliberative approach at times (6:14–7:1, chapters 8 and 9), but those moves support the overall apologetic aims of the letter. Forensic rhetoric was concerned with "accusation and defense" (κατηγορίας καὶ ἀπολογίας) (Aristotle, *Rhet.* 1.3.3; cf. 1.3.9; 1.10.1), which gave it an orientation toward the past (Aristotle, *Rhet.* 1.3.4). It was a matter of convention for the speaker to formally recognize that he was engaging in either accusation or defense.[281] In 2 Cor 12:19, Paul explicitly describes his efforts as a defense: "All along you think that I am defending myself [ἀπολογούμεθα] to you." Moreover, much of the letter is oriented toward justifying his actions and experiences in the past (e.g., modifying travel plans, his experience of suffering). Paul describes the allegations against him as the cancellation of his travel plans and as making decisions "according to the flesh" (2 Cor 1:15–17; cf. 10:2), which, Long argues, involved using worldly rhetoric and financial mismanagement (2 Cor 8:20–21).[282] The judicial tone is reinforced by appeal to witnesses (2 Cor 1:12, 23; 13:1) and the insistence that all must stand before Christ for judgment (2 Cor 5:10).[283] One strategy in forensic discourse was to show the general integrity of the defendant's life (Rhet. Her. 2.3.5), and such a strategy emerges in several places as part of Paul's defense (2 Cor 1:12; 2:17; 11:7–12).

This raises a variety of questions for us with regard to Paul's attitude toward the body and how that figures into his apology. In particular, how does Paul's defense of his apostolic suffering in the past and present relate to his hope for future bodily resurrection? What social dynamics can be discerned in Paul's discussion of the body in relation to the future? Also, given our findings above that resurrection functions in Paul's thought as a future social identity, we will be attentive to how he portrays his bodily

---

279. See the survey of various approaches in Duane F. Watson, "The Three Species of Rhetoric and the Study of the Pauline Epistles," in *Paul and Rhetoric*, ed. J. Paul Sampley and Peter Lampe (New York: T&T Clark, 2010), 33.

280. Long, *Paul's Apology*, 117–229; cf. Young and Ford, *Meaning*, 27–28; Witherington, *Conflict and Community*, 333–36.

281. See the many examples listed in Long, *Paul's Apology*, 39–40.

282. Long, *Paul's Apology*, 125–35.

283. Long, *Paul's Apology*, 137–41.

behavior in general and his apostolic suffering in particular in relation to that possible social identity. Is there evidence that he maintains that future identity? How does that future identity relate to the questions raised about his apostolic identity?

2.2.2. Resurrection and Paul's Apostolic Body in 2 Corinthians 4:7–5:10

This passage gives evidence throughout that Paul is evaluating his present bodily life as a suffering apostle in light of his hope for bodily resurrection from the dead. It moves from reflection on the body as a location and instrument for manifesting the death and resurrection life of Jesus (2 Cor 4:10–12) to a reaffirmation of the major argument in 1 Cor 15 that believers will be raised with Jesus (2 Cor 4:14). All of this forms the context for Paul's further reflection on what happens to believers upon the death of the body and how that relates to life in the present (2 Cor 5:6–10). As the exegesis of the passage proceeds, it will become increasingly clear that Paul's resurrection-oriented identity plays a role in his strategy to justify his apostolic vocation to the recipients.

The first major block of thought comes in 4:7–15, which is occupied with explaining why Paul's ministry is characterized by suffering instead of glory, if he has indeed received a revelation of glory (4:6).[284] Paul's answer is that his suffering is as an embodiment of the death and resurrection of Jesus.[285] The passage comes in the context of an extended defense of his apostolic ministry (3:1–6:13). Up to this point, he has been arguing that the glory of his ministry exceeds the ministry of Moses whose glory was veiled (3:7–4:6). Paul says in 4:7, however, that this great glory is contained in a clay vessel (ὀστρακίνοις σκεύεσιν), a metaphor that suggests frailty, inferiority, or ignobility. The point is to establish a contrast that he will continue to develop between the glory of the treasure and the vessel that holds it.[286] It may seem counterintuitive that the magnificent glory of God revealed in Christ would be contained and spread through a humble vessel like Paul; nevertheless, the text goes on to say, this paradoxical state of affairs exists for the purpose (ἵνα) of showing clearly that the power on display has its source in God and not in Paul.

---

284. Thrall, *Second Epistle*, 321; cf. Beker, *Paul the Apostle*, 295.
285. Wright, *Resurrection*.
286. Matera, *II Corinthians*, 108.

2. Embracing Resurrection

Despite his fragility, Paul wants the recipients to know that he has not yet been broken.[287] To that end he provides a list of eight participles which include four hardships (afflicted, perplexed, persecuted, struck down) that are each paired with a depiction of deliverance from hardship (not crushed, not in despair, not abandoned, not destroyed). The list resonates with Paul's description of the affliction (θλῖψις) he experienced in Asia (2 Cor 1:8–9; cf. 7:5), and seems to increase in intensity as it proceeds. Barnett adds that Paul's insistence that he is "not forsaken" resonates with the Old Testament theme of Yahweh's unwillingness to abandon his people (see Gen 28:15; Deut 31:6; Josh 5:1).[288] Paul thus implies that God will be faithful to him even though there are those who suggest that his afflictions do not befit an apostle of God. Paul wants to show that his sufferings do not detract from God's glory; rather, they magnify God's faithfulness.

The sentence continues in 4:10 with the addition that Paul is "always carrying the death of Jesus in the body, in order that the life of Jesus might also be manifest in our bodies" (πάντοτε τὴν νέκρωσιν τοῦ Ἰησοῦ ἐν τῷ σώματι περιφέροντες, ἵνα καὶ ἡ ζωὴ τοῦ Ἰησοῦ ἐν τῷ σώματι ἡμῶν φανερωθῇ). "Death" is thus added to the list of hardships and "life" to the list of deliverances. In particular, it is Jesus's own death and life that Paul describes, thus connecting his own suffering to Christ's death and resurrection.[289] θάνατος, not νέκρωσις, is Paul's usual word for describing Christ's death (see Rom 5:10; 6:3–5; Phil 3:10).[290] Nevertheless, νέκρωσις is used here and could refer to the process of dying or to the state of being dead.[291] That ζωή comes second in the movement from death to life indicates that it refers to the resurrection life of Jesus and not primarily to his life of ministry prior to crucifixion.[292] Margaret Thrall proposes three possible interpretations for the link between Paul's sufferings and the death of Christ: (1) Paul's suffering is in imitation of Christ; (2) Paul's suffering comes through union with Christ in baptism, or (3) Paul's sufferings reveal the crucified Christ.[293] Paul's use of φανερόω would seem to indicate that the third option is most likely.

---

287. Matera, *II Corinthians*, 108.
288. Barnett, *Second Epistle*, 234.
289. Barnett, *Second Epistle*, 235.
290. Victor Paul Furnish, *II Corinthians*, AB 32A (New York: Doubleday, 1984), 255.
291. Dunn, *Theology of Paul*, 485.
292. Furnish, *II Corinthians*, 256.
293. Thrall, *Second Epistle*, 332–34.

Barnett raises the concern, however, that this view does not adequately hold together the unity of Christ's death and resurrection.²⁹⁴ Two observations suggest he is right. First, ἵνα indicates that the revelation of Christ's life is the specific purpose of carrying his death. The carrying of death is not an end in itself; rather, it is a means to the end of revealing Christ's resurrection life. Death and life thus work closely together here. Second, the repetition of ἐν τῷ σώματι as the location where Jesus's death is carried and his life manifest suggests that the two should be interpreted as a unity.

Jean-François Collange suggests that the language of "manifested" gets at the heart of Paul's dispute with those who question his vocation: "It is the verb φανερωθῇ that is the focus of the verse. For we know that this was the question over which the Corinthians quarreled: where is the true φανέρωσις?"²⁹⁵ Several commentators note the likelihood that Paul's opponents appealed to "signs and wonders" as manifestations of divine power (cf. 2 Cor 12:2).²⁹⁶ Collange likewise suggests the possibility that Paul's opponents expect miraculous and "pneumatique" manifestations of glory, but Paul responds that any revelation that has its source in God is revealed in weakness identified with the cross of Christ.²⁹⁷ That God is the one working through Paul is reinforced by the divine passive φανερωθῇ. Thus, Paul considers his suffering to be a valid expression of apostolic ministry because it embodies the same power of God that was at work in the death and resurrection of Christ.

All of this sheds light on Paul's attitude toward his body in relation to his apostolic vocation. The repetition of the phrase ἐν τῷ σώματι emphasizes the significant role played by the body. More specifically, the phrase carries the double sense that Paul sees his body (1) as the *location* where God manifests the life of Christ and (2) the *means* through which God manifests the life of Christ.²⁹⁸ And this is the case not in spite of Paul's suffering but because of it.²⁹⁹ His bodily life, like a clay pot, is meager and

---

294. Barnett, *Second Epistle*, 236.
295. Jean-François Collange, *Énigmes de la deuxième épitre aux Corinthiens: Étude exégétique de 2 Cor. 2:14–7:4*, SNTSMS 18 (Cambridge: Cambridge University Press, 1972), 157, my translation.
296. Beker, *Paul the Apostle*, 295; cf. Ralph P. Martin, *2 Corinthians*, WBC 40 (Dallas: Word, 1986), 88; Barnett, *Second Epistle*, 235.
297. Collange, *Énigmes*, 157.
298. Martin, *2 Corinthians*, 87.
299. Matera, *II Corinthians*, 110.

2. Embracing Resurrection

fragile; nevertheless, it is filled with the treasure of Christ's resurrection life. In this way, his body *as a suffering body* is essential to his apostolic vocation. It is indispensable because it corresponds to and magnifies the dying and rising body of Jesus.

He substantiates (γάρ) and develops the theme of God's work through suffering by saying, "For we who are living are always being given over to death for Jesus's sake, in order that the life of Jesus may be manifest in our mortal flesh" (ἀεὶ γὰρ ἡμεῖς οἱ ζῶντες εἰς θάνατον παραδιδόμεθα διὰ Ἰησοῦν, ἵνα καὶ ἡ ζωὴ τοῦ Ἰησοῦ φανερωθῇ ἐν τῇ θνητῇ σαρκὶ ἡμῶν, 4:11). This verse is strikingly similar to the previous verse, yet it develops a key point in the argument with the change from the active voice to the passive voice. In verse 10, Paul spoke of carrying the death of Christ, but he now speaks of "being given over to death." The change in voice once again highlights that God is the one bringing suffering on Paul for the purpose (ἵνα) of manifesting the death and resurrection of Jesus. The paradoxical nature of this manifestation is apparent in that death is revealed in "we who are living" (ἡμεῖς οἱ ζῶντες). The personal pronoun ἡμεῖς is grammatically unnecessary, and its presence adds further emphasis on Paul and the apostles as the object of God's action to hand them over to death. Suffering is essential to apostolic life. Another change is the movement from σῶμα (4:10) to σάρξ (4:11), but they seem here virtually synonymous.[300] If the change adds anything to the argument it should probably be seen as highlighting the paradoxical way that life is revealed in mortal bodies.[301] Mark A. Seifrid adds that the repeated subjunctive φανερωθῇ adds an eschatological dimension to Paul's argument. The present display of life remains a matter of anticipation and will not be complete until the body is raised from the dead.[302] Dunn, too, sees the tension of Paul's already/not yet eschatology present in the theme of divine power revealed in human weakness.[303] The cruciform life of Christ is being manifest in Paul's suffering in the present, even though the full manifestation of life awaits the resurrection.

The language of "death" and "life" carries into verse 12, but this time there is a twist, "Thus, death works in us, but life works in you" (ὥστε ὁ θάνατος ἐν ἡμῖν ἐνεργεῖται, ἡ δὲ ζωὴ ἐν ὑμῖν). ὥστε indicates that what follows is a logical inference from what has just been said. θάνατος refers to

---

300. Martin, *2 Corinthians*, 88.
301. Wright, *Resurrection*, 362–63.
302. Seifrid, *Second Letter*, 208–9.
303. Dunn, *Theology of Paul*, 482, 485.

the way Paul's sufferings portray the death of Christ. This time, however, he does not speak of life with regard to himself as he has in the last two verses. Instead, he says that life is at work in the Corinthians. As Scott J. Hafeman recognizes, the relationship Paul describes is not reciprocal; he suffers for them, but they do not suffer for him.[304] Instead, they are beneficiaries of his suffering,[305] and the benefit they receive is an experience of Jesus's resurrection life. The suffering Paul endures as part of his apostolic ministry functions to some extent as a means of grace that those under his apostolic care might experience life (cf. 2 Cor 1:6).[306] This brings the rhetorical function of 4:7–12 into view: the recipients should not assume that suffering invalidates Paul's apostolic vocation; to the contrary, the suffering of this apostle is the very instrument by which God is at work in them. J. Christiaan Beker notes that Paul's interpretation of his sufferings distinguishes him from some less hopeful Jewish understandings of tribulation.[307] For example, 4 Ezra 6:17–25 portrays suffering as something to be endured, and those who persevere through the period of great tribulation are said to see salvation (cf. 4 Ezra 5.1–9; 9.1–12; 13.29–31; 2 Bar. 25.2–4; 1 En. 90.13–19; 91.12). Elsewhere, however, the sufferings of the martyrs are depicted as having a redemptive value on behalf of the people of God (2 Macc 7:32–38; 4 Macc 6:27–29; 17:20–22).[308] The more hopeful tone of this attitude toward suffering resonates to some degree with Paul's attitude. Nevertheless, Paul's understanding of his sufferings is to be distinguished from the sufferings of the Jewish martyrs in that his are not portrayed as having any sort of atoning value. Paul is not reenacting the redemptive work of Christ. Rather, the suffering entailed in his apostolic ministry derives from and mediates the unique life-giving power of Christ's death and resurrection to the recipients.[309]

Verse 13 moves the focus from God's work through Paul to his own work as an apostle.[310] The quote from Ps 115:1 LXX (116:10 MT) reflects a situation that bears some similarity to Paul's. The psalmist had been

---

304. Hafeman, *2 Corinthians*, 186.
305. Martin, *2 Corinthians*, 89.
306. See Barnett, *Second Epistle*, 238.
307. Beker, *Paul the Apostle*, 302; cf. Michael J. Gorman, *Cruciformity: Paul's Narrative Spirituality of the Cross* (Grand Rapids: Eerdmans, 2001), 328–29.
308. See further Wright, *The New Testament and the People of God*, 275–79.
309. Hafeman, *2 Corinthians*, 186.
310. Seifrid, *Second Letter*, 209.

2. Embracing Resurrection

ill to the point of death and called upon Yahweh to save his life. In the midst of suffering his trust in his God did not waver; thus he writes, "I believed; therefore, I spoke" (ἐπίστευσα διὸ ἐλάλησα). Convinced of Yahweh's faithfulness, he was motivated to speak about it. Paul perceives his experience in similar terms. Having suffered greatly, apparently to the point of anticipating death (2 Cor 1:9–10), he asserts that God rescued him, and he is hopeful that God will continue to rescue him (2 Cor 1:10). Like the psalmist, Paul is motivated by God's faithfulness to speak, "We believe; therefore, we speak" (ἡμεῖς πιστεύομεν, διὸ καὶ λαλοῦμεν). In light of these parallel circumstances, Paul sees "the same Spirit of faith" (τὸ αὐτὸ πνεῦμα τῆς πίστεως) at work in both instances. Philip E. Hughes interprets πνεῦμα anthropologically to mean "a spirit of meekness."[311] It is more likely a reference to the Holy Spirit.[312] The present argument is a development of Paul's earlier argument that the Spirit is at work in his ministry (2 Cor 3:6; cf. 3:3), and in 3:6, the Spirit's specific action as one who "gives life" is in view. Similarly, both in the psalm and in Paul's appropriation of it, the topic is rescue from apparently certain death to a continued experience of life.

Paul fills in the content of his belief in 4:14, "Knowing that the one who raised [the Lord] Jesus will also raise us with Jesus and present us with you" (εἰδότες ὅτι ὁ ἐγείρας [τὸν κύριον] Ἰησοῦν καὶ ἡμᾶς σὺν Ἰησοῦ ἐγερεῖ καὶ παραστήσει σὺν ὑμῖν).[313] εἰδότες ὅτι may signal the introduction of a traditional creedal formulation.[314] While God is the subject of all three verbal actions, the change in verb tense should be noted. The substantive aorist participle portrays the resurrection of Jesus in its entirety and locates it in the past (cf. the present tense in 2 Cor 1:9). In contrast, the resurrection of believers is a future event. That the future resurrection depends in principle on the resurrection of Jesus is indicated by σὺν Ἰησοῦ.[315] Paul goes on to say that God "will present us with you." The

---

311. Philip E. Hughes, *Paul's Second Epistle to the Corinthians*, NICNT (Grand Rapids: Eerdmans, 1961), 147; cf. A. Plummer, *A Critical and Exegetical Commentary on the Second Epistle of Paul to the Corinthians*, ICC (Edinburgh: T&T Clark, 1915), 133.

312. Fee, *God's Empowering Presence*, 323–24; cf. Barnett, *Second Epistle*, 240; Matera, *II Corinthians*, 112.

313. The shorter reading is probably original; see Metzger, *Textual Commentary*, 510–11.

314. Furnish, *II Corinthians*, 258.

315. Barnett, *Second Epistle*, 242.

only other use of παρίστημι in this letter comes in 2 Cor 11:2, where the context is the eschatological presentation of the recipients to Christ. The presentation is presumably also to Christ in 4:14. Paul Barnett thinks it is a presentation to Christ for judgment (cf. 5:10).[316] Seifrid disagrees and suggests rather that this "signifies arrival in the presence of God that constitutes salvation."[317] Given the overall hopeful tone of the argument at this point, I am inclined to agree with Seifrid. And judgment is surely not in view when the same verb is used in 11:3.

The two prepositional phrases, σὺν Ἰησοῦ and σὺν ὑμῖν, highlight the social nature of bodily resurrection in Paul's thought. Resurrection is not merely a matter of individual salvation. It is received through the agency of God by virtue of participation in the resurrection of Jesus together with the larger group of Christ-followers. This resonates with our reading of 1 Cor 15 above and suggests that future bodily resurrection continues to function in Paul's reasoning as a future possible social identity. When a future possible social identity is salient, group members are often motivated to reinterpret and portray the past and the present in a way that coheres with the future. The advantage is a perceived sense of temporal continuity, which is typically considered desirable.[318] This suggests we should be attentive to the ways Paul portrays his experience over time in relation to the group as a whole and in light of resurrection as a future social identity.

When 2 Cor 4:7–15 is considered from this perspective, several features of the text come to the fore. First, it is Paul's apostolic identity in relation to the Corinthians that has been challenged because the character of his ministry is off-putting to them. His attractiveness has diminished because the super apostles have influenced the recipients to evaluate him through a framework marked by different values, attitudes, and beliefs from those embraced by Paul. This resulted in the validity of his ministry being undermined among the recipients.[319] His troubles do not conform to the belief that apostles ought to manifest a ministry of glory and not anguish. That is to say, the super apostles have undermined his credibility

---

316. Barnett, *Second Epistle*, 242.
317. Seifrid, *Second Letter*, 211–12.
318. Cinnirella, "Exploring Temporal Aspects," 235–36.
319. Individual attractiveness varies depending on the group providing the frame of reference; see Turner et al., *Rediscovering*, 61–62.

2. Embracing Resurrection

as a leader *in relation to the group* by instigating a situation where Paul was perceived to have violated group norms.[320]

Second, his response to this challenge frames the conflict in light of the future resurrection-oriented identity. That is to say, Paul's present afflictions anticipate his resurrection union with Christ (σὺν Ἰησοῦ, 4:14). Paul's future resurrection is only guaranteed by a social relationship with Christ. Given that anticipated future, he is willing in the present to participate in the death to life movement that characterized Jesus's own death and resurrection in the past. Thus, Paul interprets his present bodily suffering as standing in diachronic continuity with the resurrection-oriented future identity (4:14) and participation with Christ's past death and resurrection (4:10–11). In this way, Paul portrays his present experience as part of a single temporally coherent representation. His apostolic sufferings are justified because they validate the future possible identity.

Third, Paul also portrays his sufferings in a way that highlights shared categories. At times, intergroup bias can be reduced by introducing new factors like goals and benefits that reinforce the common in-group identity.[321] By explicitly describing future bodily resurrection in terms of the group (σὺν ὑμῖν, 4:14), Paul has framed himself and the recipients as sharing a common future possible in-group identity. If Paul's sufferings have caused the recipients to question the category they share with him, then the perception of a common future that is diachronically continuous with Paul's sufferings may reinforce the shared category that has been called into question and help them to embrace him once again. The shared category that has been undermined by Paul's circumstances may also be reinforced by the way he construes his suffering as a benefit to the recipients, a new factor they may not have considered. Paul's willingness to be given over to death is a means of God's grace to work resurrection life in the Corinthians (4:12). And immediately after stating the shared hope of resurrection, Paul again emphasizes the benefit of his sufferings to the recipients (4:15). If they embrace and support his cruciform ministry, which anticipates the future identity, then they also share the fruit and benefit of that ministry. If they do not embrace him, perhaps they lose further benefit. This has potential to reduce their bias against him by cultivating the perception

---

320. See the discussion of norms in Hogg and Abrams, *Social Identifications*, 158–60.

321. Gaertner and Dovidio, *Reducing Intergroup Bias*, 7, 77–82.

of a shared category.³²² Altogether these aspects of his reasoning provide occasion for the Corinthians to reevaluate their attitude toward Paul and reconsider the validity of his suffering.

A great deal of scholarly interest in 2 Cor 4:16–5:5 has been concerned with whether it represents a development of Paul's eschatology from a more Jewish-oriented concern with resurrection of the body to a more Greek influenced interest in the immortality of the soul.³²³ We will consider below the series of contrasts between the inner person and the outer person (4:16–18), the earthly dwelling and the heavenly dwelling (5:1–4), and being found naked as opposed to being further clothed. In preparation for that discussion, it should be understood that Paul's language has led some to argue that, since writing 1 Corinthians, he has abandoned his Jewish eschatology focused on bodily resurrection for a more Platonic view of the future focused on the immortality of the soul. One proponent of this approach is Marie-Emile Boismard, who argues that the change is based on theological reasons but also suggests that it was a good tactical move since Paul "knows from experience that the Greeks are allergic to any notion of resurrection."³²⁴ To be fair, Boismard sees Paul's view in 2 Corinthians to be a modification of Plato's thought to account for the language of a body to be received in heaven. Nevertheless, Paul is seen in general as having adopted a Platonic anthropology and cosmology.

Boismard appeals to 1 Cor 15:45 as evidence of Paul's earlier Semitic anthropology which gave way to a Hellenistic attitude characterized by body-soul dualism. The "inner person" corresponds to the soul that is found "naked" when the body dies (2 Cor 4:16; 5:3). The problem is that 1 Cor 15:45 provides remarkably scant evidence for constructing a Pauline anthropology. And the mere fact that Paul did not use the language of "inner person" and "earthly dwelling" in the earlier material is an appeal to silence. He does not have to say everything he believes each time he writes.

---

322. Gaertner and Dovidio (*Reducing Intergroup Bias*, 77–78) also note the potential for shared labor to reduce bias and increase the perception of a common ingroup identity, which may shed light on the extended exhortation in 2 Cor 8 and 9 inviting the recipients to participate in the collection.

323. Richard N. Longenecker, "Is There Development in Paul's Resurrection Thought?," in *Life in the Face of Death: The Resurrection Message of the New Testament*, ed. Richard N. Longenecker (Grand Rapids: Eerdmans, 1998), 171–202; cf. Thrall, *Second Epistle*, 398–400.

324. Marie-Emile Boismard, *Our Victory Over Death: Resurrection?*, trans. Madeleine Beaumont (Collegeville, MN: Liturgical Press, 1999), 82.

Further, the rhetorical situation of 1 Cor 15 involved responding to denial of future bodily resurrection. If Paul believed in an intermediate period of consciousness between the death of the body and its resurrection, it is not clear how mentioning that would have helped the carefully constructed argument in 1 Cor 15. Why introduce an issue that is beside the point? The context of 2 Cor 4:16–5:5 involves an altogether different rhetorical situation. Paul is here evaluating his suffering in light of the future. He has come face-to-face with the real possibility of his own death. It does not seem strange that he might reflect on his understanding of the intermediate state in such a setting (cf. Phil 1:20–23).

Boismard writes of 2 Cor 5:2–4, "it is noteworthy that Paul no longer speaks of resurrection since, as we have seen, he has adopted the Greek theme of immortality."[325] But what Paul says in these verses comes on the heels of a clear and straightforward affirmation of future bodily resurrection in 4:14 (cf. 1:9–10), a verse we considered in detail above. Therefore, and the exegesis below will bear this out, everything said in 4:16–5:5 must be read in light of that resurrection-oriented context. And if Paul has abandoned future bodily resurrection for "the Greek theme of immortality," then what are we to make of the later material in Romans which speaks only of future bodily resurrection with no mention of disembodied postmortem existence?[326] In chapter 4 of this study, we will consider the evidence in Phil 1:20–23 for Paul's belief in a disembodied postmortem conscious experience of being in Christ's presence. Should that later language be interpreted to suggest Paul's theology has developed again? It seems more likely that Paul's writings over the course of his ministry reflect a belief in a disembodied intermediate state that gives way to the resurrection of the body at the time of the parousia. Let me be clear that I am not saying Paul's thinking about resurrection never underwent any sort of development. I am rather raising questions about the specific interpretation that sees him abandoning hope for bodily resurrection in favor of immortality of the soul. In the rest of this section, we will consider how Paul's continued reasoning maintains his earlier affirmation of future bodily resurrection.

Following the doxological climax in 4:15, Paul begins a new line of thought in which he evaluates his experience of suffering in relation to his future hope (4:16–5:10). In short, the apostle is not discouraged by his suf-

---

325. Boismard, *Our Victory*, 94.
326. Wright, *Resurrection*, 365.

ferings because they have a renewing function that is preparing him for the future. From the standpoint of Paul's defense, if he is not discouraged, the Corinthians should not be ashamed of him.[327] He explains the function of his sufferings through a contrast between "our outer person" (ὁ ἔξω ἡμῶν ἄνθρωπος) and "our inner person" (ὁ ἔσω ἡμῶν). This is the only time Paul speaks of the "outer person," which creates some challenge in getting at his meaning. This is not his only use of "inner person," which also appears in Rom 7:22. Some of the recipients may have been familiar with that language, since the similar term ὁ ἐντὸς ἄνθρωπος was used by Plato (*Resp.* 9.588–589; cf. Philo, *Fug.* 68.1–72.3; 4 Macc 7:11–15).[328] However, there is no evidence of a direct line from Plato's use to Paul's.[329]

That the outer person is being destroyed or decaying (διαφθείρω) resonates with the fragility of the earthen vessel image from 4:7 and the hardships of 4:8-9. The outer person is the visible, afflicted, and persecuted person.[330] It involves carrying in the body the death of Jesus (4:10) and being given over to death for Jesus's sake (4:11). The outer self is associated with the present body in that the body is the means and location for carrying the death of Jesus. The outer self is not to be confused with "the old self" (ὁ παλαιὸς ἄνθρωπος) in Rom 6:6, which is a negative reference to human life under the power of sin.[331] There are no such negative connotations with the outer person. If the outer person is associated with Paul's hardships, then the contrast running through 4:7–11 sheds light on his use of "inner person." This is the whole person viewed from the experience of God's delivering and renewing power. It portrays the work of God to bring the life of Jesus to bear in a person (4:10, 11). Thus, the inner person should not be considered distinct or separate from the bodily experience.[332] Paul associated embodiment with both sides of the contrast in 4:10-11. This also helps frame Paul's language of "seen" and "unseen." The visible human body is decaying and is yet the sphere of God's invisible redemp-

---

327. Wright, *Resurrection*, 365.

328. See further T. K. Heckel, *Der innere Mensch: Die paulinishe Verarbeitung eines platonischen Motivs*, WUNT 2/53 (Tübingen: Mohr Siebeck, 1993), 11–79.

329. Hans Dieter Betz, "The Concept of the 'Inner Human Being' (ὁ ἔσω ἄνθρωπος) in the Anthropology of Paul," *NTS* 46 (2000): 19.

330. Matera, *II Corinthians*, 115; Seifrid, *Second Letter*, 216.

331. Matera, *II Corinthians*, 115.

332. Matera, *II Corinthians*, 115.

tive work.³³³ The Corinthians look at Paul and see weakness; in as much as he is embodying the death and resurrection of Christ, Paul insists he is being renewed. The contrast then is not anthropological but eschatological. The outer person is associated with the present age that is coming to a close; the inner person is the self being renewed for eschatological glory in the new age.³³⁴ Lincoln puts it well:

> The heavenly powers of the new age are at work but not in a way that alters that part of a person visible to others, the external bodily form. This is decaying. But in the heart (4:6; 5:12), in the centre of a person's being, in the 'inward man' not accessible to sight, the renovating powers of the age to come are in operation. Though the terminology Paul adopts may well come from the framework of a dualistic anthropology, his concept does not, for he is describing the one personality of the Christian believer, who lives in the period of the overlap of the ages, as seen now from the perspective of this age and now from that of the age to come.³³⁵

That Paul would speak of affliction leading to glory should come as no surprise to us. He also draws the language of suffering together with hope for glory in Rom 8:17, and there the former is portrayed as preparation for the latter, which is the specific glory of bodily resurrection (cf. Phil 3:21).³³⁶ Paul's use of glory in 2 Cor 4:17 answers the questions that suggest his apostolic standing is invalid because it is not characterized by glory. In the present, his ministry is characterized by weakness and pain, but that bodily suffering is the instrument of God's work to renew him for the eschatological glory of bodily resurrection. Paul is thus offering an evaluation of his bodily suffering in light of his hope for future bodily resurrection. In the process, he is inviting the recipients to engage in their own reevaluation of his ministry and find that his sufferings are not only justified but something to be embraced for their role in preparing him for glory.

The language in 4:18 of temporary things that can be seen and eternal things that cannot leads directly into the discussion in 5:1 of "our earthly tent-dwelling" (ἡ ἐπίγειος ἡμῶν οἰκία τοῦ σκήνους) and the "dwelling not made by hands, eternal in the heavens" (οἰκίαν ἀχειροποίητον αἰώνιον ἐν

---

333. So Lincoln: "this glory of the heavenly realm is to be lived out in and through mortal bodies" (*Paradise*, 60).
334. Barnett, *Second Epistle*, 246.
335. Lincoln, *Paradise*, 60.
336. See the discussion in chapter 3 below.

τοῖς οὐρανοῖς). If we follow the contrast that Paul has been developing, then the earthly οἰκία is associated with present embodied life and the heavenly οἰκία with the resurrection body as the climax of God's redemption of the inner person.[337] By considering the possibility that the earthly dwelling might be destroyed in 5:1, Paul entertains the possibility of death prior to the parousia. This may mark some development in his thought given that in earlier letters he seemed to locate himself among those who would be alive at the time of that event (1 Thess 4:15; 1 Cor 15:51–52). Any reevaluation is likely to have been the result of his profound experience of suffering. In the event of his death, Paul is certain that God has for him a resurrection body. This certainty is indicated by the present tense of ἔχομεν, which could be taken to mean (1) that a new body exists presently in heaven, (2) that a new body will be received immediately upon death, or (3) that the resurrection body is assured at the parousia. One difficulty with the first approach is that ἐν τοῖς οὐρανοῖς modifies οἰκίαν not ἔχομεν and may reflect quality more than location.[338] The second approach is problematic because Paul elsewhere places the timing of the resurrection at the parousia (1 Thess 4:15–16; 1 Cor 15:23; Phil 3:21). Thus, the third option is to be preferred. The present tense highlights the present certainty of the future reception of a resurrection body.[339]

The present dwelling place is said to be the place where "we groan" (στενάζομεν) in 5:2. This groaning resonates with the hardship and troubles that Paul has endured. The result is that he longs for the heavenly dwelling (τὸ ἐξ οὐρανοῦ) that is a resurrected body. Paul is not one to shy away from mixing metaphors, and he here introduces the image of being clothed (5:2, 4) in contrast to being naked (5:3–4). ἐνδυσάμενοι is better attested than ἐκδυσάμενοι, and it makes sense in context, even if it is tautological.[340] Thus, when the resurrection body is received, the believer will not be found naked. In light of this approach, γυμνός must be understood as a metaphor for the period of time between the death of the present earthly

---

337. Lincoln, *Paradise*, 61; Barnett, *Second Epistle*, 258. Shantz suggests that the contrast between dwellings reflects Paul's struggle to articulate an experience that exceeds the images he must use to express it (*Paul in Ecstasy*, 126).

338. Lincoln, *Paradise*, 63.

339. Lincoln, *Paradise*, 64; cf. Barnett, *Second Epistle*, 258–59.

340. Metzger suggests that ἐκδυσάμενοι was probably used to avoid the tautology (*Textual Commentary*, 511).

body and the reception of the heavenly resurrection body.³⁴¹ Nakedness was sometimes used in the Greco-Roman world to refer to the escape of the soul from the body (see, e.g., Plato, *Gorg.* 524d; *Crat.* 403b). This makes sense of and corresponds to the notion of being "away from the body" (ἐκδημῆσαι ἐκ τοῦ σώματος) in 2 Cor 5:7 (cf. Phil 1:20–23).³⁴² It is particularly important to see that Paul portrays this intermediate state of nakedness or being unclothed in negative light (5:4), because this distinguishes him from Platonic desire for the soul to be free from the body. Thus, while he affirms what would seem to be a conscious disembodied state in the presence of Christ, he does not see this as ultimately desirable. It is good in that it means an end to suffering, but he would rather be further clothed with the life of the resurrection body.³⁴³

The confidence he puts in the future identity is noteworthy and is expressed in the certainty of receiving a resurrected body conceived of as a heavenly dwelling (5:1). Paul restates this confidence in 5:6, and substantiates it (γάρ) with an appeal to faith over sight. Even though his status within the group has been called into question, his confidence in his future group membership remains active and sure. That confidence is evidence of the extent to which Paul himself behaves in a way that he perceives as continuous with his future identity. He is willing to allow his body to suffer and even die, because he is confident that his present bodily life will give way to new embodied life. He is even willing to endure the less than desirable experience of a disembodied state as a step toward the resurrection of his body.

Throughout 2 Cor 4:16–5:5, Paul continues to evaluate his present bodily life in light of the future resurrection-oriented identity, and his evaluation contributes to his defense by implying that the recipients should reassess their negative evaluation of his ministry. This dynamic can be seen in Paul's contrast between the outer person and the inner person and between what is visible and what is not. Paul is concerned with what is inner and invisible; the recipients are focused on what is outer and visible, namely Paul's sufferings and apparent lack of apostolic glory. This series of contrasts orients the conflict toward the future and invites the recipients to reconsider their assessment of Paul based on the way his circumstances are preparing him for the glory associated with the future identity. This alternative method of assessment is also at work in 5:7 when the value of

---

341. Lincoln, *Paradise*, 66–67; cf. Wright, *Resurrection*, 367.
342. Wright, *Resurrection*, 367.
343. See Witherington, *Conflict and Community*, 391.

judging by sight is called into question. Faith discerns the unseen work of God and is thus the preferred method of judgment. The implied invitation to reevaluate is also apparent in Paul's discussion of the earthly dwelling and the heavenly dwelling. Paul's sufferings may indeed have the destruction of his body as earthly tent-dwelling as their end; nevertheless, he perseveres in hope of realizing the future identity. Throughout the passage, Paul's recurring use of the first-person plural reinforces the sense that these values are held in common and characteristic of the group, thus inviting the recipients to embrace values and methods of judgment defined by the future possible identity.

The implied need for the recipients to reassess their judgment of Paul is capped by the reminder that all must stand before Christ for judgment (5:10). The basis of this judgment is what is done "through the body" (διὰ τοῦ σώματος), which brings the relationship between the body and the future into focus. Bodily behavior plays a significant role for Paul in that he anticipates his future status to correspond to his use of the body. From a social perspective, Paul is rejecting the group's role as judge over him and appealing to the judgment of Christ. His present bodily life is motivated not by a desire to conform to group norms articulated by the recipients or the super apostles. Rather, he aims to please Christ. Again, the implication is that the Corinthians should reconsider their judgment of Paul. If Christ is pleased with Paul's bodily life, then they should be, too.

We have noted at various places in the discussion that future social identities have potential to influence present behavior in a way that relates to social identity maintenance. In the effort to obtain a future identity, individuals will sometimes attempt to recruit others to embrace that future identity. If they do embrace it, that validation helps to maintain the future identity of the recruiter.[344] Some of these elements may be discernible in Paul's reasoning. By inviting the Corinthians to reassess his bodily behavior and sufferings, he invites them to look favorably on him *in light of his future social identity* characterized by bodily resurrection. If they are persuaded, then their judgment in his favor means they approve of behavior motivated by a hope for bodily resurrection. To that extent, they also implicitly validate the future identity, because the present and the future are portrayed as a coherent representation. If he successfully recruits them to share his perspective on the relationship between his bodily practice in

---

344. Cinnirella, "Exploring Temporal Aspects," 237.

the present and his hope for resurrection in the future, then Paul's apology for his apostolic ministry functions in part to maintain his resurrection-oriented future social identity.

2.3. Conclusion

Our analysis in this chapter has brought into focus the social dimension of Paul's attitude toward bodily resurrection. While he expects individual bodies to be raised, Paul also thinks of the future resurrection of believers in terms of the social group, not least in that the resurrection of group members is derived from their relationship to Christ whose own resurrection constitutes him as the first fruits of those who will be raised. The importance of resurrection as a future social identity is evident in that Paul portrays its denial as having disastrous consequences for the group. To deny future bodily resurrection overturns the faith and undermines the identity of the group. Additionally, that some deny future resurrection while others affirm it only exacerbates the problem of factionalism in Corinth. Thus, if Paul can persuade the resurrection deniers to embrace resurrection, then it contributes to the overall unity of the group. We have also been able to discern Paul's interest in seeing the behavior of the group stand in continuity with the anticipated future identity. This brings present bodily practice into view. Paul expects believers to use their bodies in the present in a way that coheres with the future bodily identity. This is articulated more generally in the argument of 1 Cor 15 (esp. vv. 29–34 and 58) and more specifically in 1 Cor 6:12–20, where the resurrection-oriented identity stood in conflict with πόρνη-union. In 2 Cor 4:7–5:10, the resurrection-oriented identity provided an occasion for Paul to justify his apostolic sufferings to the recipients. Despite appearances, his present bodily hardship anticipates and stands in continuity with the death and resurrection of Jesus on the one hand and Paul's own hope for resurrection on the other. This portrayal of temporal coherence between past, present, and future reinforces the future identity and invites the recipients to reassess their judgment of Paul's troubles. If they do indeed change their judgment and find in his favor, their acceptance of his explanation would validate his understanding of the present in relation to the future and thus contribute to the maintenance of his resurrection-oriented future social identity.

3
From Mortal Body to Redeemed Body: The Letter to the Romans

"Romans is suffused with resurrection," says N. T. Wright. "Squeeze this letter at any point," he adds, "and resurrection spills out; hold it up to the light, and you can see Easter sparkling all the way through."[1] Wright's perspective, however, is not representative of Pauline scholarship in the modern period. In fact, when taken beside other topics, questions related to bodily resurrection have been somewhat muted in studies of Romans. This may be due in part to the prominent role that Romans has played in post-Reformation debates over atonement and justification by faith, not to mention the well-known issues related to the meaning of πίστις Χριστοῦ and the variety of proposals regarding the purpose and occasion of the letter.[2] Some are beginning to recognize, however, that resurrection in Romans deserves a more prominent place than it has received. For example, J. R. Daniel Kirk has argued recently that resurrection is not only "the

---

1. Wright, *Resurrection*, 241.
2. For post-Reformation debates over atonement and justification by faith, see Peter M. Head, "Jesus' Resurrection in Pauline Thought: A Study in the Epistle to the Romans," in *Proclaiming the Resurrection*, ed. Peter M. Head (Carlisle: Paternoster, 1998), 59. See also Wright, "If Romans had not been hailed as the great epistle of justification by faith, it might easily have come to be known as the chief letter of resurrection" (*Resurrection*, 241). For the πίστις Χριστοῦ debate, see Michael F. Bird and Preston M. Sprinkle, eds., *The Faith of Jesus Christ: Exegetical, Biblical, and Theological Studies* (Peabody, MA: Hendrickson, 2009). Regarding the debates about the purpose and occasion of the letter, Donfried stated: "Current research concerning the purpose of Romans is in a state of confusion. Almost every recent article or monograph on the subject proposes a different solution." For this quote and a representative list of those solutions, see Karl P. Donfried, "False Presuppositions in the Study of Romans," in *The Romans Debate*, ed. Karl P. Donfried, rev. and exp. ed. (Peabody, MA: Hendrickson, 1991), 102–3.

most pervasive theme" in Romans but also the key that unlocks the letter as a whole.[3] The question of the letter's primary theme is likely to remain a matter of debate; nevertheless, the need for further investigation into the role of resurrection in Romans is warranted.[4]

Given the need for further consideration of resurrection in Romans, this chapter will investigate the role of Paul's rhetoric of future bodily resurrection as it relates to his expectations for bodily practice in the present. The analysis begins with an account of the conflict among the believers in Rome. We then turn to the rhetoric of Romans in general before looking in detail at chapters 6 and 8, which reflect a concern for the relationship between bodily resurrection in the future and bodily behavior in the present. In the course of the analysis, we will pay special attention to the function of Paul's resurrection language as it relates to the formation and maintenance of social identity, not least with regard to diachronic aspects of such an identity. It will become clear that bodily resurrection can be described as a future possible social identity, and I will argue that the conflict over table fellowship addressed in Rom 14:1–15:13 should be understood in terms of bodily practice and interpreted in light of the relationship between the future resurrection of the body and the present use of the body.

3.1. Intragroup Conflict in Rome

We begin with the situation on the ground in Rome in the middle of the first century and Paul's efforts to bring two groups, called by him the "strong" (15:1) and the "weak" (15:1; cf. 14:1), to the same table and together in worship. R. J. Karris has set forth the most well-known critique of drawing on chapters 14 and 15 to hypothesize the presence of subgroups in Rome. He argues that 14:1–15:13 are general paraenesis and not polemic directed at particular parties whose disagreement occasioned the letter.[5] Through an analysis of parallels between 1 Cor 8–10 and Rom 14:1–15:13, Karris argues that the Romans passage is an adaptation of the position Paul worked out earlier in relation to the known situation

---

3. Kirk, *Unlocking Romans*, 8.

4. The topic of resurrection has received some attention from apocalyptic interpreters also; see Beker, *Paul the Apostle*; de Boer, *Defeat of Death*.

5. R. J. Karris, "Romans 14:1–15:13 and the Occassion of Romans," in *The Romans Debate*, ed. Karl P. Donfried, rev. and exp. ed. (Peabody, MA: Hendrickson, 1991), 66.

in Corinth.⁶ Despite the parallels with 1 Cor 8–10, there remains weighty evidence that Rom 14 and 15 were written to deal with conflict between two distinct subgroups which Paul refers to as the strong and the weak. The case has been made in detail in a variety of places, and I share the view of those who identify the weak as Christ-followers who observe torah and the strong as Christ-followers who do not observe torah. For the most part, the weak would be Jewish believers and the strong gentile believers, and we can refer to them as such, if we keep in mind that the strong apparently included some Jews, like Paul (cf. 15:1), and the weak may have included some gentile proselytes.⁷

The most significant objection to identifying the weak with Jewish Christ-followers is that they are said to "eat only vegetables" (14:2), which suggests they avoid meat altogether rather than only abstaining from pork, meat that was improperly slaughtered, and meat offered to idols. Paul also suggests that they avoid drinking wine (14:21), which further complicates the problem, since refraining from all meat and wine was not included in the Jewish dietary laws.⁸ That problem is significantly mitigated, however, when it is noted that Jewish abstention from both meat and wine appears in other texts.⁹ Take, for example, the case of Daniel, who sought permission to fast from meat and wine on the grounds that he would be defiled if he ate the king's food (Dan 1:8–16). In Jud 12:1–4, Judith insists she that will not eat and drink the food and wine given to her by Holofernes. Esther

---

6. Karris, "Romans 14:1–15:13," 71–81.
7. Francis Watson, *Paul, Judaism, and the Gentiles: Beyond the New Perspective* (Grand Rapids: Eerdmans, 2007), 175–82; cf. James D. G. Dunn, *Romans 9–16*, WBC 38B (Dallas: Word, 1988), 799–802, 810–15; Douglas J. Moo, *The Epistle to the Romans*, NICNT (Grand Rapids: Eerdmans, 1996), 829–33; Esler, *Conflict*, 348; Kirk, *Unlocking Romans*, 199–200; John M. G. Barclay, *Paul and the Gift* (Grand Rapids: Eerdmans, 2015), 511–12. For the view that the recipients of Romans were exclusively gentile and that the "strong" and the "weak" are not parties but "dispositions of character," see Stanley K. Stowers, *A Rereading of Romans: Justice, Jews, and Gentiles* (New Haven: Yale University Press, 1994), 21–33, 44, 320–23, here 21; cf. Matthew Thiessen, *Paul and the Gentile Problem* (New York: Oxford University Press, 2016), 43–72; Rafael Rodríguez and Matthew Thiessen, eds., *The So-Called Jew in Paul's Letter to the Romans* (Minneapolis: Fortress, 2016).
8. Ernst Käsemann, *Commentary on Romans*, trans. Geoffrey William Bromiley (Grand Rapids: Eerdmans, 1980), 367.
9. I am here following Watson, *Paul, Judaism, and the Gentiles*, 175–76, emphasis original. For further reasons to interpret the weak as Jewish Christ-followers, see his discussion on pp. 176–77.

is said not to have eaten at Haman's table, nor did she drink wine that had been used as a drink offering (4:17^x LXX).[10] Additionally, Josephus tells of some priests who had been arrested and sent to Rome to plead their case before the emperor; Josephus praised them because "even in affliction, they had not forgotten the pious practices of religion and supported themselves on figs and nuts" (*Vita* 3). In each instance, we find Jews in a context where ritually pure meat and wine are unavailable. The result is that they abstain from meat and wine. As Francis Watson concludes, "This suggests a plausible interpretation of references to 'the weak' in Romans 14: abstention from meat and from wine was practiced by Roman Jewish Christians (or Christian Jews) *in the context of a predominantly Gentile environment*."[11] Paul's primary concern in 14:1–15:13 appears to be with table fellowship (14:2-4, 6b, 14-23), but he also mentions holy days (14:5-6) and concludes the passage with an exhortation to "welcome one another" in common worship (15:5-13). It may, therefore, be the case that the problems associated with table fellowship surfaced at communal meals when the believers met for worship. Without ruling out other reasons for writing Romans, I suggest that Paul wrote in part to mitigate division and foster unity among the recipients of the letter.[12]

3.2. Romans as Deliberative Rhetoric

There is significant debate over the literary and rhetorical genre of Romans.[13] Kennedy sees Romans as epideictic and argues that it is intended to explain Paul's understanding of the Christian faith. In contrast to what I have argued above, Kennedy does not see Paul directly addressing the problem of faction among the Roman Christ-followers. Instead, the letter

---

10. Greek Esther contains six additions not found in the Hebrew text of Esther. The versification of these additions employs the verse after which the addition follows plus consecutive superscript letters (e.g., 4:17^a, 4:17^b, 4:17^c). Thus, 4:17^x is part of the additional material found at the end of Greek Esth 4. English translations of these additions may be found in editions of the NRSV that are published with the Apocrypha. Greek Esth 4:17^x corresponds to Addition C 14:18 in Esther with Additions (NRSV).

11. Watson, *Paul, Judaism, and the Gentiles*, 176, emphasis original.

12. Moo, *Romans*, 826-33.

13. For a survey of the debate, see Christopher Bryan, *A Preface to Romans: Notes on the Epistle in Its Literary and Cultural Setting* (New York: Oxford University Press, 2000), 18-29.

functions to introduce Paul to the Romans and to anticipate the possibility of hostility to aspects of his message.[14] Robert Jewett agrees that Romans is epideictic but argues in particular that the letter fuses several subtypes of the epideictic genre: ambassadorial letter, paraenetic letter, hortatory letter, and philosophical diatribe.[15] Paul thus writes as God's ambassador with a view to unifying the Roman congregations to build support for his mission to Spain. Duane Watson urges caution, however, and suggests that Jewett relies too much on genre classifications which were not carefully distinguished in ancient practice.[16]

Since Paul is writing to people who already believe the gospel, David E. Aune argues that Romans would have functioned as epideictic rhetoric. However, he also argues that the literary form is deliberative and that the letter is a *logos protreptikos*, or a speech of exhortation, intended to persuade the recipients to embody a particular way of life.[17] The case that Romans is an example of judicial rhetoric has been made by François Vouga: "The letter to the Romans is constructed on the model of an ancient apology."[18] It is a defense both of Paul's apostleship and of his gospel. One difficulty with this view, however, is the point just raised. Paul is not writing to persuade unbelievers of the truth of the gospel. To the contrary, he affirms their shared faith (Rom 1:12; cf. 11:20). Paul's discussion of the gospel in Romans should be understood in terms of its application to the situation and behavior of the recipients. If we take what Paul says about the gospel as part of his strategy for influencing the behavior of the recipients, then the overall deliberative character of the letter is clearer. The instructions given in Rom 12–15 come to a climax with the imperative to "welcome one another" (Rom 15:7). This mutual

---

14. Kennedy, *New Testament Interpretation*, 152–53; cf. Wilhelm Wuellner, "Paul's Rhetoric of Argumentation in Romans: An Alternative to the Donfried-Karris Debate," in *The Romans Debate*, ed. Karl P. Donfried, rev. and exp. ed. (Peabody, MA: Hendrickson, 1991), 128–46.

15. Robert Jewett, *Romans: A Commentary*, Hermeneia (Minneapolis: Fortress, 2006), 44.

16. Watson, "Three Species of Rhetoric," 34.

17. David E. Aune, *The New Testament in Its Literary Environment*, LEC 8 (Philadelphia: Westminster, 1987), 219–21; cf. Anthony Guerra, *Romans and the Apologetic Tradition: The Purpose, Genre and Audience of Paul's Letter*, SNTSMS 81 (Cambridge: Cambridge University Press, 1995), 1–22.

18. François Vouga, "Römer 1,18—3,20 als narratio," *TGl* 77 (1987): 25, my translation.

hospitality is grounded in Christ's own hospitality in welcoming the recipients; they are to "welcome one another ... *as Christ has welcomed you*" (Rom 15:7, emphasis added).[19] If Christ has made peace between them and God (Rom 5:1), then they should resolve to be at peace with each other in general, and they should sit down together at the same table in particular. Paul's explanation of the gospel in Romans serves the overall deliberative aims of the letter to mitigate discord and facilitate unity among the Roman Christ-followers.[20] As this chapter proceeds, I will argue that the relationship in Romans between bodily resurrection and bodily practice functions to support that deliberative aim. Paul's desire is that the Romans would be persuaded to embody the gospel they believe and in which they hope.

3.3. Resurrection and the Rhetoric of Interrogation

The relationship between Paul's hope for resurrection and his expectations for bodily practice is as prominent in Rom 6 as it is anywhere in the letter. His understanding of that relationship is set forth through a series of rhetorical questions that focus the argument on the question of sin in the lives of believers (6:1–3, 15, 16, 21). These questions provide the occasion for Paul to provide a vision of the believer's present life that is characterized by holiness rather than sin, and that vision is grounded in his hope of participating in the bodily resurrection of Jesus.

Quintilian classified rhetorical questions as figures of thought and distinguished between simple questions intended to gain information (*percontatio*) and figured questions intended to make a point (*interrogatio*), though he acknowledged the terms are often used interchangeably (*Inst.* 9.2.6).[21] By raising questions and then answering them, Quintilian thought an orator could add a certain amount of attractive variety to a discourse (*Inst.* 9.2.14). Similarly, the author of Rhetorica ad Herennium considered reasoning by question and answer (*ratiocinatio*) useful for maintaining a conversational tone and capturing the attention of the hearer by increasing the level of anticipation for the answers to follow (Rhet. Her.

---

19. Bryan, *Preface to Romans*, 20–21.

20. Ben Witherington and Darlene Hyatt, *Paul's Letter to the Romans: A Sociorhetorical Commentary* (Grand Rapids: Eerdmans, 2004), 16–17.

21. *Interrogatio* as a rhetorical figure is distinguished from *interrogatio* as the questioning of a witness (see 5.7.27).

4.16.24; cf. Cicero, *Inv.* 1.57). The technique could also be used to anticipate and deal with possible objections or misunderstandings of what has been argued before (Quintilian, *Inst.*, 9.2.16–17).[22] As Chaïm Perelman and L. Olbrechts-Tyteca point out, the conversational tone created by the use of questions enables the speaker or author to deal with challenging or controversial topics more easily by inviting the hearer or reader to "yield to the self-evidence of truth."[23]

The series of questions in Rom 6:1–3 and 6:15–16 follow a similar pattern and divide the chapter into two sections.[24] Both series begin by raising a question with regard to what has just been said (Τί οὖν ἐροῦμεν in 6:1; and Τί οὖν in 6:15). This is followed in 6:1 and 6:15 by a question as to whether believers should sin. The emphatic answer in both cases is μὴ γένοιτο (6:2, 15). In both series the pattern concludes with another question that begins, "Do you not know that…?" (ἢ ἀγνοεῖτε ὅτι in 6:3; οὐκ οἴδατε ὅτι in 6:16). This final question in each series raises the possibility that there may be evidence that the recipients should recall or have not yet considered and prepares them to anticipate the forthcoming argument. All of these questions are undoubtedly included for their rhetorical value in moving the argument along and are clearly not included only for the sake of information gathering. The questions invite the recipients to consider the character of their lives in the present and how their lives might be different in the future. The strategy of *interrogatio* thus contributes to the deliberative tone of Paul's rhetoric.[25] He is preparing to set forth a vision of life in Christ that is characterized not by sin but by holiness, which, as I shall argue, serves to ground the expectations for table fellowship that he will articulate later in the letter.[26] That vision is challenging, to say the least, and by raising these questions Paul prepares the recipients to hear evidence refuting potential objections or misunderstandings of what he

---

22. See Witherington and Hyatt, *Romans*, 155.
23. Perelman and Olbrechts-Tyteca, *The New Rhetoric*, 37.
24. Michael J. Gorman, *Apostle of the Crucified Lord: A Theological Introduction to Paul and His Letters* (Grand Rapids: Eerdmans, 2004), 368.
25. Richard N. Longenecker, *The Epistle to the Romans*, NIGTC (Grand Rapids: Eerdmans, 2016), 610; cf. Neil Elliott, *The Rhetoric of Romans: Argumentative Constraint and Strategy and Paul's Dialogue with Judaism* (Minneapolis: Fortress, 2007), 236; Witherington and Hyatt, *Romans*, 155.
26. See C. E. B. Cranfield: "The word ἁγιασμός may be taken as the key-word of the section, though it does not occur till v. 19" (*The Epistle to the Romans*, 2 vols., ICC [Edinburgh: T&T Clark, 1975], 295).

has said thus far and explains further his expectations for holiness in their bodily life.[27]

The section that runs from 6:1–14 substantiates Paul's negative answer to the question: "Should we continue in sin in order that grace may abound?" (ἐπιμένωμεν τῇ ἁμαρτίᾳ, ἵνα ἡ χάρις πλεονάσῃ;). The question is raised to correct a potential misunderstanding of the argument in the previous chapter that the multiplication of trespass is met with the superabundance of grace (5:21).[28] Paul earlier dismissed those who falsely report him saying, "Let us do evil so that good may come" (Rom 3:8), and he here takes up the task of refuting that charge more fully.[29] The extended attention given to refuting this charge suggests that he does not presuppose consensus among recipient group members.[30] Paul's strong opposition (μὴ γένοιτο) to the notion that Christ-followers should continue in sin is substantiated by an appeal to baptism as a ritual that marks the event of union with Christ in his death.[31] This union with or incorporation into Christ means, for Paul, that what is true of Christ is also true of those whom he represents.[32] The concept is expressed through the phrase εἰς Χριστὸν Ἰησοῦν (6:3; cf. Gal 3:27).[33] The notion of union is strengthened by Paul's use of two terms prefixed with the preposition σύν.[34] The baptized are said to be "buried with" (συνετάφημεν, 6:4) Christ, and their old selves are said to be "crucified with" (συνεσταυρώθη, 6:6) him (cf. Gal 2:20). In each case, believers are identified as participating in and experiencing Christ's own death and burial.

---

27. Kirk, *Unlocking Romans*, 107.

28. James D. G. Dunn, *Romans 1–8*, WBC 38A (Dallas: Word, 1988), 306.

29. Longenecker, *Romans*, 610–11; cf. Thomas H. Tobin, *Paul's Rhetoric in Its Contexts: The Argument of Romans* (Peabody, MA: Hendrickson, 2004), 192–93.

30. Esler, *Conflict*, 203.

31. For baptism as a ritual of initiation, see Meeks, *The First Urban Christians*, 150–57; cf. Neyrey, *Paul, in Other Words*, 87–88; for baptism in relation to social identity, see Esler, *Conflict*, 209–17.

32. N. T. Wright, "The Letter to the Romans: Introduction, Commentary, and Reflections," *NIB* 10:538; cf. Kirk, *Unlocking Romans*, 114–15; Moo, *Romans*, 360.

33. For a comprehensive study of union with Christ in Paul, see Constantine R. Campbell, *Paul and Union with Christ: An Exegetical and Theological Study* (Grand Rapids: Zondervan, 2012).

34. The terms *union*, *incorporation*, and *participation* are used interchangeably in this discussion.

3. From Mortal Body to Redeemed Body

Paul does not go into detail with regard to *how* baptism unites a person to Christ. He turns instead to the implications of that union for bodily practice in the present and the hope for resurrected bodily life in the future. Richard N. Longenecker sees baptism as summing up union with Christ both in death and resurrection. To be precise, he writes that Paul urged "Christians at Rome to view their Christian baptism as representing their union with Jesus in both his death and resurrection."[35] But Paul's account of the relationship between union with Christ and the hope for resurrection requires more nuance. Paul does speak explicitly of group members having been baptized into Christ's death (6:3). He then infers that those who were baptized into Christ's death have also been buried with Christ (6:4). Crucially, however, Paul does not go on to say that baptism involves being raised with Christ. Instead, the resurrection of Jesus in 6:4 is compared to the believer's new potential to "walk in newness of life" (ἡμεῖς ἐν καινότητι ζωῆς περιπατήσωμεν). Paul often uses περιπατέω to describe the present character of a person's life.[36] The subjunctive form highlights the potential for believers to manifest this "newness of life" from the present going forward.[37] What Paul does not say is that believers have *already* been joined to Christ in his resurrection, nor does he say that believers have already been raised bodily from the dead.[38] In fact, union with Christ in the resurrection is here a matter of future expectation. This point is made explicit in 6:5, "For if we have been united with him in the likeness of his death, so shall we be united with him in the likeness of his resurrection" (εἰ γὰρ σύμφυτοι γεγόναμεν τῷ ὁμοιώματι τοῦ θανάτου αὐτοῦ, ἀλλὰ καὶ τῆς ἀναστάσεως ἐσόμεθα). Careful attention must be given to the verb tenses. When Paul spoke in the previous verse of being "buried with" Christ, he used the aorist συνετάφημεν. His introduction of the perfect γεγόναμεν in 6:5 is thus noteworthy and indicates that he has the continuing implications of past

---

35. Longenecker, *Romans*, 613.

36. Rom 8:4; 13:13; 14:15; 1 Cor 3:3; 7:17; 2 Cor 4:2; 5:7; 10:2, 3; 12:18; Gal 5:16; Phil 3:17, 18; 1 Thess 2:12; 4:1, 12.

37. For a survey of the Semitic and Hellenistic attitudes toward change and newness, see T. Michael W. Halcomb, *Paul the Change Agent: The Context, Aims, and Implications of an Apostolic Innovator*, GlossaHouse Dissertation Series 2 (Wilmore, KY: GlossaHouse, 2015), 16–22, 28–34.

38. The concept of the believer's present resurrection with Christ appears in Eph 2:5–6 and Col 2:12–23; 3:1.

union with Christ in mind.³⁹ In contrast, Paul introduces the future tense (ἐσόμεθα) to depict the as yet unrealized experience of union with Christ in his resurrection. Ulrich Wilckens and Douglas J. Moo note the possibility that ἐσόμεθα could be read naturally as a logical future (*logisches Futurum*); that is, being joined to Christ's resurrection follows logically from being joined to his death.⁴⁰ Taken this way, union with Christ in his resurrection would refer to the present life of the believer, not the future resurrection of the believer's body. Wilckens notes, however, that the present experience of the believer is communicated by the perfect γεγόναμεν, leaving ἐσόμεθα to be understood as an *eschatologisches Futurum* which describes the believer's future resurrection of the body. The parallel between 6:5 and 6:8, which Wilckens takes to be a clear reference to future bodily resurrection, lends further support to this interpretation.⁴¹ Union with Christ in his death does not mean the believer is already joined to Christ in his resurrection, but the former does point forward to the latter.⁴²

What then does the past event of incorporation into Christ mean for the believer's life in the present? Why does Paul compare the resurrection of Christ to the believer's present capacity for "newness of life"? How does that relate to the hope for resurrection in the future? The expectation of present "newness of life" in 6:4 is substantiated in 6:5 by appeal to the past reality of incorporation into Christ's death and the future hope of participation in his resurrection. The significance of the past event is further explained by 6:6, in which Paul says the "old self" (ὁ παλαιὸς ἡμῶν ἄνθρωπος) was cocrucified with Christ with the double result of the destruction of "the body of sin" (τὸ σῶμα τῆς ἁμαρτίας, 6:6) and the liberation of the believer from slavery to sin. The reign of sin was introduced in Rom 5:21 as characteristic of the old Adamic aeon, and the obedience of Christ expressed particularly in his death was portrayed as the crucial point of transition from the old age to the new age (5:12-17). If the death of the "old self" results in liberation from the power of sin, then the "old self" should be understood in terms of the Adamic self or the self as a

---

39. Dunn, *Romans 1-8*, 316.

40. Ulrich Wilckens, *Der Brief an die Römer*, 3 vols., EKKNT (Zurich: Benziger, 1978-1982), 2:15; Moo, *Romans*, 370-71. For a defense of the logical future, see Wright, "Romans," 539-40.

41. Wilckens, *Der Brief an die Römer*, 2.15; cf. Moo, *Romans*, 371.

42. Kirk, *Unlocking Romans*, 110.

participant in the old aeon (5:12-21) under the power of sin and death and subject to condemnation.[43] Union with Christ in his death liberates the believer from that power. As E. P. Sanders put it, "by *sharing* in Christ's death, one dies to the *power* of sin or to the old aeon."[44]

The other result (ἵνα) of the death of the "old self" is the destruction (καταργέω) of the body of sin (τὸ σῶμα τῆς ἁμαρτίας, 6:6). C. E. B. Cranfield takes this occurrence of σῶμα as a reference to the whole person and suggests that τὸ σῶμα τῆς ἁμαρτίας has the same meaning as ὁ παλαιὸς ἡμῶν ἄνθρωπος.[45] Wilckens, likewise, sees the later phrase as clarifying the former and referring to the whole person, "In this respect, 'our old person' is clarified by 'the body of sin'.... Rather, the body of sin is ourselves, we as 'old person,' as long as we translate what we are into action."[46] Gundry cautions against the tendency to read Paul's somatic language as referring to the whole person and argues alternatively that Paul has in mind the physical body under the power of sin.[47] His emphasis on physicality should not be disregarded given that the present argument about the abolition of τὸ σῶμα τῆς ἁμαρτίας forms part of the theological basis for the coming imperative that believers should not allow sin to exercise its reign τῷ θνητῷ ὑμῶν σώματι (6:12). More recently, Barclay has argued against readings that minimize the corporeality of τὸ σῶμα τῆς ἁμαρτίας by rendering the phrase along the lines of "the sinful person." Instead, he suggests that Paul is thinking of "the body commandeered by sin, such that its dispositions, emotions, speech-patterns, and habitual gestures are bound to systems of honor, self-aggrandizement, and license that are fundamentally at odds with the will of God."[48] In the following verse, the parts (τὰ μέλη) of the body are portrayed as objects which will be submitted by the believer either to sin or to God.[49] The question of what believers will do with their bodies is of deep concern to Paul, and it is somatic language in particular

---

43. Gorman, *Cruciformity*, 126-31. Cf. Wright, "Romans," 539.
44. E. P. Sanders, *Paul and Palestinian Judaism* (Minneapolis: Fortress, 1977), 467-68, emphasis original.
45. Cranfield, *Romans*, 309.
46. Wilckens, *Der Brief an die Römer*, 2:16-17, my translation; cf. Wright, "Romans," 539-40.
47. Gundry, *Sōma*, 58.
48. Barclay, *Paul and the Gift*, 508.
49. So Barclay: "the fact that 'yourselves' is embedded here in statements about the body suggests that the self can be 'ruled' or 'presented' only as the body is 'ruled' or 'presented'" (*Paul and the Gift*, 504).

that connects the theology of chapter 6 with the ethical material beginning in chapter 12 (σῶμα, 12:1) and extending to Paul's expectations for table fellowship in chapters 14 and 15. We should resist the Bultmannian temptation to minimize the corporeality of σῶμα by reducing it to "the self" as the object of one's attitudes, thoughts, or behaviors.[50] A mediating position is probably right.[51] Barclay captures the balance well: "The body, unambiguously identified in its physicality by this term 'organs' (μέλη), is thus the site where 'the self' is identified and designed."[52] Paul certainly sees the whole person as being liberated from sin; nevertheless, that the physical body is the place where the reign of sin is either manifest or overthrown should not be overlooked. For Paul, the body and all its parts are free for submission to God because the believer's bodily life has been liberated from the power of sin (6:6).

A further point should be made: we ought not take τὸ σῶμα τῆς ἁμαρτίας to be synonymous with ὁ παλαιὸς ἡμῶν ἄνθρωπος, as Cranfield suggests.[53] Paul's use of ἵνα in 6:6 indicates an instrumental relationship between two distinct concepts. The "old person" is crucified in union with Christ as a means to liberating the believer's bodily life from the power of sin in order that the parts of the body may then be made "instruments of righteousness" (ὅπλα ἀδικίας, 6:13) in submission to God. I suggest, then, that ὁ παλαιὸς ἡμῶν ἄνθρωπος refers to the whole person under the power of sin in the old aeon, and that τὸ σῶμα τῆς ἁμαρτίας refers to the physical body as the location where that power is manifest. "The body of sin" is bodily life characterized by sin. Dunn notes that the meaning of καταργέω can be difficult to pinpoint.[54] The term should be understood in light of the subsequent clause which further explains the purpose (ἵνα) of being crucified along with Christ: τοῦ μηκέτι δουλεύειν ἡμᾶς τῇ ἁμαρτίᾳ. That the recipients are no longer slaves to sin forms the basis of the coming imperative that they not allow sin to reign in their bodies (6:12-14). The abolition or destruction of the body of sin resulting from incorporation into the death of Christ is the decisive step that makes obedience to this command a real possibility. The powers of the old age in the sphere of the

---

50. Bultmann, *Theology of the New Testament*, 1:194-203. Cf. Barclay's critique (*Paul and the Gift*, 504-5).

51. Thomas R. Schreiner, *Romans*, BECNT (Grand Rapids: Baker, 1998), 316.

52. Barclay, *Paul and the Gift*, 504.

53. Wright, "Romans," 540.

54. For the semantic range of καταργέω, see Dunn, *Romans 1-8*, 319.

3. From Mortal Body to Redeemed Body

believer's body have been rendered ineffective. The cocrucifixion of the "old self" with Christ liberates the believer from the reign of sin and makes possible the resulting present condition in which the believer's bodily life is no longer characterized by habits and patterns of sin.

The relationship between incorporation into Christ's death and the new state of freedom is further substantiated by the statement, "For the one who has died is freed from sin" (ὁ γὰρ ἀποθανὼν δεδικαίωται ἀπὸ τῆς ἁμαρτίας, Rom 6:7). The substantive ὁ ἀποθανών could be interpreted either anthropologically or christologically. Those who take the anthropological view typically see this sentence as a general principle or maxim: "Anyone who has died has been liberated from sin." Dunn and Moo substantiate this reading by pointing to parallel proverbial statements in the rabbinic writings.[55] Taken this way, 6:7 illustrates the previous theological point with a general truth, "death severs the hold of sin on a person."[56] The chief problem with this view is that Paul does not argue that *any* death brings freedom from sin. As Wright remarks, "Paul nowhere suggests that physical death settles all accounts in God's sight."[57] To the contrary, at the climax of the argument in chapter 6, he will say that "the wages of sin is death" (6:23), which suggests that Paul sees death linked to sin as a consequence. How can a person's death free him or her from the power of sin if death is consequence or even the penalty of sin? In light of this, the christological reading is to be preferred. "The one who has died" is Christ, and it is his death that brings the reign of sin to an end. Moo rejects this reading on the grounds that it "introduces a shift in subject for which the context has not prepared us."[58] It is true that the argument of chapter 6 is largely about the believer's incorporation into Christ's death, but that line of thinking presupposes and implies the fact of Christ's death.[59] It is thus untenable to suggest that the context does not leave room for Paul to say something about the death of Christ. Paul is not merely supplying an illustration of his earlier theological point; he is articulating the crucial significance of Christ's death in relation to the believer's freedom from sin in the present. The death of Christ is the event that brings liberation from sin. Believers

---

55. Dunn, *Romans 1–8*, 320–21; Moo, *Romans*, 376–77.
56. Moo, *Romans*, 377.
57. Wright, "Romans," 540.
58. Moo, *Romans*, 377.
59. So Kirk: "In terms of what precedes, both believers and Christ are said to have died" (*Unlocking Romans*, 113).

benefit from that in so far as they are incorporated into the death of Christ, which is a key point for which Paul has argued, and one on which he will build the hope for resurrection in the very next verse.

Having established that the death of Christ brings the reign of sin to its end, Paul proceeds in verses 8–10 to develop the significance of the believer's participation in that death as grounds for the future bodily resurrection. Again, the logic of Rom 5:12–21 undergirds the argument of chapter 6. Believers can be confident in the future resurrection of their bodies because Christ has brought the dominion of death to an end (6:9). While union with Christ in the likeness of his resurrection remains unrealized in the bodies of believers, they nevertheless have been incorporated into his death (6:8). For Paul, past incorporation into the death of Christ ensures the future realization of union with Christ's resurrection (6:8). Christ has been raised, and because his death has brought the old aeon to a close, he is no longer subject to death (6:9). This is what makes his death unique (ἐφάπαξ, 6:10). As Kirk remarks, "this is Jesus' parting of ways with the old aeon, governed by sin and death, as inaugurated by Adam."[60] This introduces the new possibility for human life, pioneered by Jesus and paradigmatic for believers. The life that Jesus lives after his resurrection is a life "lived to God" (6:10). It is the life of the new aeon where sin has no power to dominate. The key point to be made, and the point that substantiates the coming imperatives concerning the use of the body, is that believers who have been cocrucified with Jesus must embody the character of the resurrection. They must live to God, even though they have not yet experienced the fullness of bodily resurrection. This is what Paul means by the imperatival form of λογίζομαι (6:11). To "reckon" themselves "dead to sin and alive to God in Christ Jesus" (6:11) is to embody the life of the age to come even though they have not yet been raised from the dead. When they are raised from the dead, they will not have to "reckon" themselves "dead to sin and alive to God." That will be the realized state of things. Until then, they must live in a way that embodies the overthrow of the old age and the inauguration of the new.

The prohibition given in Rom 6:12 depends logically (οὖν) on the whole line of reasoning in 6:1–11. Paul instructs the recipients, "Therefore, do not let sin reign in your mortal body (Μὴ οὖν βασιλευέτω ἡ ἁμαρτία ἐν τῷ θνητῷ ὑμῶν σώματι, 6:12). One problem that arises immediately is

---

60. Kirk, *Unlocking Romans*, 115–16.

the question of the believer's relationship to sin. In Rom 6:2, Paul spoke of believers as having "died to sin," yet he now instructs the recipients to resist the reign of sin in their bodies.[61] This means that, for Paul, "newness of life" is not automatic and can remain unrealized or, perhaps, be forfeited. The apostle's exhortation that the recipients resist the reign of sin recalls Rom 5:21 and, once again, locates the present behavior of the believer in the movement from the old aeon to the new.[62] The posture, then, of the one who has been incorporated into Christ's death in anticipation of sharing in the resurrection is active resistance to the continued efforts of sin to dominate. The death and resurrection of Christ have brought an end to the tyranny of sin, but Paul appears to believe that the recipients could choose to capitulate to the old age and return their loyalty to the reign of sin.

The place where the reign of sin must be resisted is "in your mortal body" (ἐν τῷ θνητῷ ὑμῶν σώματι). Dunn rejects the view that "mortal body" is to be identified with the "the physical organism."[63] He argues instead that it refers to the whole person in a state of vulnerability to the power of sin and associates the term closely with "body of sin" in Rom 6:6. Once again, however, that Paul has physicality in mind should not be deemphasized. The following prohibition makes this explicit: "Do not present your organs [τὰ μέλη] as instruments of wickedness to sin" (6:13).[64] In terms of the prohibition, τῷ θνητῷ ὑμῶν σώματι stands in parallel relationship to τὰ μέλη, which unambiguously refers to physicality[65] We should also remember that the relationship between the body in the future and the body in the present has been woven into the fabric of Paul's argument to this point in chapter 6 (see esp. Rom 6:5, 8). In Rom 7:25, Paul can speak of the "body of death." In Rom 8:10–11, he says that the "body is dead because of sin" and then goes on to describe believers' "mortal bodies" (τὰ θνητὰ σώματα) as the object of the Spirit's life-giving work. In each case, including Rom 6:12, it is the mortality of the present physical body that is emphasized in contrast to the future experience of life as bodily resurrection and freedom from mortality.[66] This is one of the differences between the present and the future. Present embodiment remains bound

---

61. Longenecker, *Romans*, 614.
62. Dunn, *Romans 1–8*, 336.
63. Dunn, *Romans 1–8*, 336.
64. For the translation of μέλη as "organs," see Barclay, *Paul and the Gift*, 504.
65. Barclay, *Paul and the Gift*, 504.
66. Barclay, *Paul and the Gift*, 501.

to death. Future embodiment will be immortal. When Paul speaks of life in the present, he is quick to qualify his terminology. In the present, believers are "*as* alive from the dead" (ὡσεὶ ἐκ νεκρῶν ζῶντας, 6:13, emphasis added). In the future, they "will be made alive with him" (6:8). In the present, believers can have "newness of life" (Rom 6:4). In the future, believers will share the likeness of the resurrection (Rom 6:5). I suggest that καινότης ζωῆς and ὡσεὶ ἐκ νεκρῶν ζῶντας are intentionally nuanced to indicate their partial and anticipatory nature. Believers experience "newness of life" now and the fullness of the resurrection later. They are *as* alive from the dead now; they will be alive from the dead later. Participation in the resurrection remains unrealized, yet it is proleptically anticipated by submitting oneself, and one's body in particular, in obedience to God. The body in bondage to mortality is the place where the character of the future bodily redemption is put on display. The key point is that the life of the future on display in the bodies of believers stands in stark contrast to the mortality of their bodies. To be clear, this newness of life is not mere behavior modification or personal reformation.[67] Transformation is only possible because they now participate in an external power located in the new age. The risen Christ is the source of this new life which enables believers to use the body as an instrument of righteousness rather than wickedness. That this newness is manifest ἐν τῷ θνητῷ ὑμῶν σώματι (6:12) "puts their lives in a state of permanent incongruity."[68] On the one hand, they continue to exist in bodies that are bound to the mortality that remains from their Adamic existence; on the other hand, they are now alive to God and enabled to live in a way that pleases God. Even though believers continue to live in dying bodies, the resurrection of Christ defines the character of their living.[69] If the character of this new life is incongruous with the present mortality of the body, it nevertheless stands in congruity with their anticipated experience of bodily resurrection. Paul clearly sees resurrection as remaining firmly in the future, and he indicates in 8:23 that this future resurrection means the redemption of the body (τὴν ἀπολύτρωσιν τοῦ σώματος ἡμῶν). As with Paul's somatic language in Rom 6, the redemption of the body should be understood in terms of corporeal redemption and not merely in vague terms of personality or self. The believer's life in the present thus

---

67. Barclay, *Paul and the Gift*, 501.

68. Barclay, *Paul and the Gift*, 501. This incongruity will surface again in Rom 8:10–11.

69. See Wright, "Romans," 538.

portrays the movement from the mortal body to the redeemed body by submitting the body and its parts to God as instruments of righteousness.[70] By submitting the parts of their bodies to God, the body itself becomes the place where hope for resurrection is made visible.[71]

The argument that runs from 6:1–14 began with the question of whether believers might legitimately commit sin given the superabundance of grace as described in Rom 5:20. Paul's emphatic rejection of that notion depends on the fact that Christ's death overthrows the power of sin associated with the old aeon and inaugurates a new aeon characterized by life and righteousness. By virtue of being incorporated into Christ, believers are transferred from the old aeon to the new. There is tension here, because the bodies of believers have not yet been raised from the dead. Nevertheless, through their union with Christ, they are enabled to embody the holy character of Christ's resurrection life as a manifestation of their participation in the new age. Paul rejects the notion that they should continue in sin because that would be to regress from the rule of God in the new aeon to the rule of sin in the old. Instead, as those under grace, the character of their embodied life should manifest the character of the new age in which they share by virtue of their union with Christ. Their present character stands in a state of incongruity with their dying bodies, but it is thoroughly consistent with their anticipated future.

The segment that runs from 6:15–23 does not give further detail about the future resurrection of the body, but it does fill in the picture of Paul's attitude toward bodily practice, the believer's freedom from sin, and the expectation for obedience to God. The question that begins this segment picks up the final assertion from 6:14 and asks whether believers should sin because they are "not under law but under grace" (Τί οὖν; ἁμαρτήσωμεν, ὅτι οὐκ ἐσμὲν ὑπὸ νόμον ἀλλ' ὑπὸ χάριν; 6:15). Paul's mention of the law recalls Rom 5:20 where the entrance of the law results in the exacerbation of transgression (cf. Rom 3:19–20).[72] The law is then associated with the reign of sin in 5:21, and thus with the old Adamic aeon, which is then overthrown by the reign of grace (ἡ χάρις βασιλεύσῃ) and the life of the new age (ζωὴν αἰώνιον, 5:21).[73] Paul thus maps νόμος and χάρις

---

70. So Käsemann: "bodily obedience is necessary as an anticipation of bodily resurrection" (*Romans*, 177).
71. Barclay, *Paul and the Gift*, 505.
72. Wright, "Romans," 530.
73. See Kirk, *Unlocking Romans*, 118.

on the aeonic divide. To be ὑπὸ νόμον is to be aligned with the old age; to be ὑπὸ χάριν is to be aligned with the new. Given that Paul has already argued believers are participants in the new age by virtue of their union with Christ, he once again answers his own question with the emphatic: μὴ γένοιτο (6:15). Nevertheless, that believers are united to Christ in the new aeon does not remove the potential for living in sin under the power of the old age. This point is made in Rom 6:16: "Do you not know that if you submit yourselves to someone as slaves for obedience, you are slaves to the one you obey?" Paul's point is that the recipients reveal which age they belong to by the character of their conduct, whether the old age dominated by sin or the new dominated by righteousness. Obedience to sin is associated with death in 6:16, which stands in contrast to the newness of life that should characterize the life of the believer who anticipates future participation in the resurrection of Christ.

It is noteworthy that liberation from sin is not absolute self-autonomy. Instead, it involves a transfer of ownership or lordship. Everyone, for Paul, is a slave to one of two powers.[74] This is apparent in 6:18: "having been set free [ἐλευθερωθέντες] from sin, you were enslaved [ἐδουλώθητε] to righteousness." The aorist participle marks time antecedent to the finite verb, portraying a temporal movement of liberation from slavery to sin into a new slavery to righteousness. Freedom means movement from the reign of sin to the reign of righteousness. This should influence our understanding of the newness of life that is Paul's hope for his recipients. The character of the believer's life in the present should be marked by obedience to God, not sin.

Of particular importance for this study is the way Paul connects this material to bodily practice: "Just as you submitted your organs [τὰ μέλη ὑμῶν] as slaves to impurity for wickedness to wickedness, so now submit your organs [τὰ μέλη ὑμῶν] as slaves to righteousness for holiness [ἁγιασμός]" (6:19). ἁγιασμός does not here refer to ritual purity (e.g., Exod 29:1, 21, 33, 33–36, 44; 30:29–30).[75] Paul's focus on the use of one's body parts suggests that he has ethical and behavioral expectations in mind. The one who participates in the new aeon should use the body in a way that expresses that participation. This involves using the parts of the body

---

74. So Wright: "Paul's point is that all human existence takes place in slavery, to one slavemaster or the other" ("Romans," 544). Cf. Paul's use of δοῦλος to describes himself in Rom 1:1.

75. Dunn, *Romans 1–8*, 355.

3. From Mortal Body to Redeemed Body 147

in ways that are pleasing to God. Paul portrays this positively in 6:20–23. Slavery to sin has death as its end (τέλος, 6:21). Alternatively, transition from slavery under sin to slavery under righteousness manifest in holiness has the life of the new age as its τέλος (6:22). By associating holiness with the new age, Paul portrays it as congruent with the future resurrection of the body, even if that holiness is incongruent with the present mortality of the body. As elsewhere in Paul, the already/not yet tension is present. Believers remain in mortal bodies even though they are called to embody the character of the resurrection life of the age to come. Holiness functions teleologically for Paul in that it anticipates the full redemption of the human body from sin and death. If, however, believers continue to submit the members of their bodies to sin, then their practices stand in fundamental incongruity with their τέλος. They manifest the life of an age from which they have been delivered by virtue of their incorporation into the death and resurrection of Christ. This, for Paul, is unacceptable, and when the question is raised, his answer is explicit and unambiguous: μὴ γένοιτο.

We must avoid the temptation to read this material solely in terms of the individual. The concept of union with Christ means that Christ acts as a representative of all who have been joined to him. That is, he acts as representative of the social group. Kirk's language of "incorporative christology" to describe union with Christ helpfully accents the social nature of the concept.[76] Believers share the benefits of union with Christ with the other members of the community who are ritually marked by baptism, and the identity that derives from being represented by Christ is a *social* identity. As Wright remarks, "Paul believed that in baptism one entered a new reality, a new family, a new version of the human race."[77] Paul's theological reasoning with regard to the experience of new life in the present and the expectation of resurrection life in the future is strengthened by the social dimension of that experience. He expects believers not to sin precisely because submitting the parts of their bodies to sin is inconsistent with their new identity as members of the group of people who have been incorporated into the death and resurrection of Christ.[78] Additionally, Paul's emphasis on the use of the body introduces a further social dynamic into his rhetoric. The body is the means by which a human being

---

76. Kirk, *Unlocking Romans*, 114–15; see the similar language of "incorporative Messiahship" in Wright, *Paul and the Faithfulness of God*, 825–26.
77. Wright, *Paul and the Faithfulness of God*, 1103.
78. Esler, *Conflict*, 219; cf. Wright, *Paul and the Faithfulness of God*, 1113.

interacts with his or her environment. It is the body that constitutes a person as a social being. As Dunn remarks, "The body ... is what makes possible a social dimension to life, is what enables the individual to participate in human society."[79] To the extent that the recipients' treatment of one another is necessarily a bodily phenomenon and a matter of bodily practice, Paul's upcoming instructions regarding table fellowship should be read in light of his attitude toward the hope for bodily resurrection and present bodily practice.

In light of our findings in Rom 6, we are able to draw some tentative conclusions with regard to Paul's understanding of the relationship between future bodily resurrection and present bodily practice. First, the full experience of participation in Christ's bodily resurrection is thoroughly a matter of future hope. Paul is certain that believers will share in the likeness of Christ's resurrection, but he does not here assert that of their present experience. Second, that the believer's resurrection is unrealized does not mean that their present life is not impacted by the hope of sharing in Christ's resurrection. To the contrary, Paul sees holiness in the present as an embodied anticipation of the future hope for resurrection. This holiness is possible, because the power of sin has been broken by the death and resurrection of Jesus. But this holiness is not automatic; it requires believers to resist the attempts of sin to regain power over them. The third point brings us to the question of bodily practice. Paul articulates the believer's present resistance to the power of sin in terms of the use of the body. Believers enact the victory of Christ over the power of sin by refusing to submit the parts of their bodies to unrighteousness, submitting them to God for holiness instead. The body is the sphere where the transition from the old age to the new age is manifest through the life of holiness in anticipation of the future realization of bodily resurrection. Fourth, if future bodily resurrection is a future possible social identity, then the life of embodied holiness stands in temporal continuity with that future identity. If believers see future bodily resurrection as a desirable group identity, then they will behave in a way that accords with that anticipated identity. If they see the life of sin as endangering or running against the anticipated identity, then they are more likely to follow Paul's prohibition and not use their bodies for sin. Paul's rhetoric thus has potential to influence the behavior of the recipients by portraying the

---

79. Dunn, *Theology of Paul*, 61; cf. Dunn, *Romans 1–8*, 319–20.

present life of obedience to God as a way of anticipating the future possible identity.

3.4. Resurrection, the Spirit, and the Hope of Creation

Paul has argued that gentiles and Jews are both justly condemned as sinners (Rom 1 and 2). This raises a problem: if the covenant people marked by circumcision are to be condemned as sinners, how will God be found faithful to keep his covenant promises to bless and multiply Abraham's family (3:1–3)? The answer comes in the revelation of the righteousness of God by which God both deals with sin and justifies both Jews and gentiles by means of the death and resurrection of Christ (3:21–26). Justification by faith further demonstrates God's faithfulness to his promises in that it is the means by which God keeps the promises made to Abraham regarding family and land (Rom 4). Having shown that Jew and gentile are both reconciled to God by faith, he proceeds to argue that this entails a transfer from the old aeon, represented by Adam, to the new aeon, represented by Christ (Rom 5). As we saw above, those who belong to Christ are to manifest in their bodies the life of the age to come by walking in holiness (Rom 6). Having been transferred from the old age to the new age, believers are also no longer bound to the law. This transfer does not mean that the law was evil; rather, its purpose was to magnify sin (Rom 7). As we come to chapter 8, Paul argues that a life pleasing to God is not only possible, it is empowered by the Spirit and anticipates the future redemption both of the body and the cosmos. Chapter 8 forms the climax of the extended *probatio* that began in 1:18. The argument as a whole demonstrates the *propositio* in 1:16–17 that the gospel is the power of God for salvation because it reveals the righteousness of God whereby God saves both Jew and gentile alike by means of faith, not only from the penalty of their sin but also from its power which enslaves them and leaves the whole creation enslaved to corruption. The climax of the argument in chapter 8 is exuberant in tone and filled with joy.[80] The *probatio* of Rom 1–8 forms a firm theological foundation for the refutation of the idea that God has been unfaithful to the Jews (Rom 9–11), and it undergirds specific ethical matters with which Paul intends to deal, table fellowship not least (Rom 12–15).

---

80. Witherington and Hyatt, *Romans*, 207.

If Rom 6 portrayed resurrection in christological perspective, then Rom 8 adds a pneumatological dimension. Paul's first mention of future bodily resurrection in the chapter comes in 8:11 and is prefaced by discussion in 8:5–8 focused on the contrast between those who are "according to the flesh" (κατὰ σάρκα) and those who are "according to the Spirit" (κατὰ πνεῦμα). Those who are "according to the Spirit" are said to "think [φρονοῦσιν] the things of the flesh" (8:5). The mind that thinks this way is associated with death in 8:6 because it does not submit (ὑποτάσσω) to God's law (8:7). This lack of submission is grounded in the conviction that the mind of the flesh is fundamentally unable to submit (οὐδὲ γὰρ δύναται, 8:7). All of this is set in contrast to "those who are according to the Spirit" (οἱ κατὰ πνεῦμα, 8:5). The person who is κατὰ πνεῦμα thinks according to the Spirit and is associated with life (ζωή) and peace (εἰρήνη, 8:6). One question that arises often at this point is whether this contrast is between a non-Christian and a Christian, or whether it addresses the possibility that a Christ-follower might revert to a manner of life controlled by the flesh.[81] φρονέω should not be understood only in terms of intellectual activity. It describes a life that is either antagonistic toward God and results in behavior that is displeasing to God or is oriented toward God and results in a life that pleases God. It reflects both thinking and acting and is, therefore, better rendered to communicate the notion of "attitude" or "mind-set."[82] When this attitude is associated with σάρξ, it refers to human life in rebellion against God and should not be taken synonymously with σῶμα.[83] Such an attitude results in death (θάνατος), which suggests that Paul has the two-age dichotomy in mind (cf. Rom 5:12).[84] The flesh is thus an attitude that is characteristic of the Adamic age, and the lives of those who live this way exhibit behavior associated with the old aeon. Given Paul's eschatological framework, pneumatic life is associated with the new age inaugurated by Christ, and ζωή and εἰρήνη should be understood as a participation in the blessing of the eschatological age.[85] What we have is two diametrically opposed dispositions: one oriented toward God and the other opposed to God.[86]

---

81. Dunn, *Romans 1–8*, 425; cf. Longenecker, *Romans*, 697.
82. Dunn, *Romans 1–8*, 425–26.
83. Wright, "Romans," 581.
84. Dunn, *Romans 1–8*, 426.
85. Dunn, *Romans 1–8*, 426.
86. Longenecker, *Romans*, 697.

3. From Mortal Body to Redeemed Body

Is it possible then for a Christ-follower to be κατὰ σάρκα? That Paul presupposes the recipients to be on the Christ side of the Adam-Christ aeonic divide is apparent by his affirmation that they are not "in the flesh but in the Spirit" (Rom 8:9).[87] Nevertheless, in Rom 6:12–14, he found it necessary to prohibit the recipients from behaving in a way that embodies the old aeon. Similarly, in Rom 8:5–8 he warns them of the dangers of the fleshly mindset. This suggests that Paul perceives a real possibility that believers may revert and begin to live according to the flesh.[88] In the case that a believer capitulates to the flesh, the potential for negative eschatological consequences comes into the equation. Paul warns the recipients of just this scenario in Rom 8:13, "If you live according to the flesh, you will certainly die" (εἰ γὰρ κατὰ σάρκα ζῆτε, μέλλετε ἀποθνῄσκειν). Dunn notes that the use of μέλλετε followed by an infinitive adds a sense of certainty, and the second person plural ζῆτε highlights Paul's perception that this is a real danger for believers.[89]

The alternative is to be "in the Spirit" (ἐν πνεύματι), and as indicated above, this is what Paul assumes of the recipients. The evidence for this is the indwelling presence of God's Spirit (Rom 8:9). The apostle uses "the Spirit of God" and "the Spirit of Christ" here almost interchangeably, making it difficult to distinguish between the two,[90] and while he spoke previously of believers being "in Christ," he now shifts to speak of Christ being in believers. In Rom 8:10, somatic language is introduced into the argument, and we find the same incongruity from chapter 6 of newness of life manifest in mortal bodies is present again. Paul's Greek in this verse is compact, and the incongruous nature of the believer's present experience is well-captured by translating the first clause of the apodosis with concessive force: "If Christ is in you, *although* the body is dead because of sin, the Spirit is life because of righteousness" (εἰ δὲ Χριστὸς ἐν ὑμῖν, τὸ μὲν σῶμα νεκρὸν διὰ ἁμαρτίαν τὸ δὲ πνεῦμα ζωὴ διὰ δικαιοσύνην).[91] The phrase σῶμα νεκρόν should not be taken as synonymous to Paul's use of σάρξ.[92] After all, he has just stated his assumption that the recipients "are not in the flesh" (8:9). Neither should it be taken as an alternative to σῶμα

---

87. Kirk, *Unlocking Romans*, 127.
88. Longenecker, *Romans*, 697.
89. Dunn, *Romans 1–8*, 448.
90. Kirk, *Unlocking Romans*, 128.
91. Gundry, *Sōma*, 44; cf. Moo, *Romans*, 492.
92. Gundry, *Sōma*, 43.

τῆς ἁμαρτίας, which refers to the physical body under the power of sin. And Paul is intent on persuading believers that their bodily life is not to be characterized or ruled by sin. Rather, σῶμα νεκρόν should be taken as a reference to the believer's present physical body that is currently liable to death but will be made alive in the future (cf. 6:12; 8:11). The word πνεῦμα could be a reference to the human spirit.[93] If so, anthropological uses of "body" and "spirit" in one sentence would be evidence for a Pauline holistic dualism. Paul will use πνεῦμα anthropologically in 8:16; nevertheless, in 8:10 πνεῦμα is most likely a reference to the Spirit of God or the Spirit of Christ. The previous verse (8:9) insisted that those who do not have the Spirit of Christ are not in Christ, and this verse (8:10) affirms the contrasting state: those who are in Christ and have Christ in them also have the Spirit working life in them. Those who belong to Christ continue to experience life in bodies that are subject to death, while at the same time the presence of the Spirit means life-giving power is at work in them. Paul proceeds to further explain the relationship between the resurrection and the work of the Spirit in 8:11 by saying that the Spirit is also "the Spirit of the one who raised Jesus from the dead" (8:11; cf. 1:4), and the indwelling presence of that Spirit "will give life to your mortal bodies" (ὁ ἐγείρας Χριστὸν ἐκ νεκρῶν ζωοποιήσει καὶ τὰ θνητὰ σώματα ὑμῶν). Paul thus draws an analogy between the giving of life to Jesus's dead body and the giving of life to those in whom the Spirit dwells. Given the earlier explicit reference to the resurrection of Jesus, the future ζωοποιήσει should be taken as a reference to the future bodily resurrection and not to a present spiritual transformation.[94] The logic of the verse depends on the analogous work of God with regard to Jesus's resurrection and the expectation of the same for those who belong to him.[95] If God raised Christ, God will also raise those in whom the Spirit of Christ dwells.[96] Two observations should be made. First, for Paul, resurrection is accomplished by the power of God

---

93. Longenecker, *Romans*, 698–99.

94. Murray J. Harris, *Raised Immortal: Resurrection and Immortality in the New Testament* (Grand Rapids: Eerdmans, 1985), 145; cf. Moo, *Romans*, 493; Wright, "Romans," 585; Witherington and Hyatt, *Romans*, 216.

95. Gaffin, *Resurrection and Redemption*, 67.

96. Shantz sees the prevalence of pneumatic language in this passage as evidence of Paul's ecstatic experience that points to his effort to describe his own transformation (*Paul in Ecstasy*, 127–31). If the recipients had such experiences, it would contribute to the sense of shared identity between Paul and the believers in Rome.

and no other.⁹⁷ God is the one who raised Jesus from the dead, and if believers are to be raised, God is the one who will do it with the indwelling Spirit functioning as the agent of that divine action.⁹⁸ Second, the body that experiences resurrection in the future is the same body that experiences mortality in the present.⁹⁹ There is no hint that the bodies of the believers will be destroyed and replaced by an altogether new body at the resurrection. To the contrary, the present "mortal bodies" (θνητὰ σώματα, 8:11) of believers are the same bodies that will be given new somatic life at the future resurrection. Lorenzo Scornaienchi considers these two points, when held properly in balance, as an argument against Rudolf Bultmann's existentialist interpretation of σῶμα:

> The fact that σῶμα is at the center of the antithesis between existence in the present and existence in the Eschaton is not an innate quality of σῶμα. The solution offered by idealistic exegesis and Bultmann's existential interpretation stands on the view that σῶμα is a neutral term, which means "form" or "real me" and which ensures continuity between earthly and postmortem existence. However, Paul expressly emphasizes that somatic existence in the eschaton is possible solely by the work of God and is based on the physical resurrection of Jesus Christ. The σῶμα in itself is mortal.¹⁰⁰

The term σῶμα is central to Paul's anthropology both in the present and in the future, but the continuity derives from God's grace not human anthropology. As Barclay remarks, "It is crucial to Paul's theology that this new life is not in the first place an *anthropological* phenomenon."¹⁰¹ Rather, θνητὰ σώματα are acted upon by God's gracious and redemptive life-giving power in Christ and through the Spirit. This idea is reflected in the objective genitive of Rom 8:23: τὴν ἀπολύτρωσιν τοῦ σώματος ἡμῶν. The present body in bondage to death is the object of God's redemptive work. The movement is from mortal bodies to redeemed bodies. But this power is external to them and has its source in God. To be human is to have a σῶμα, but resurrection life in the future does not inhere in that σῶμα. It is a gift from God.

---

97. Wright, *Resurrection*, 256.
98. Gaffin, *Resurrection and Redemption*, 67; cf. Wright, *Resurrection*, 256.
99. Wright, *Resurrection*, 256.
100. Scornaienchi, *Sarx und Soma*, 80, my translation.
101. Barclay, *Paul and the Gift*, 501, emphasis original.

The body is thus portrayed in Rom 8:5–16 as the place that will either manifest the life of the flesh or the life of the Spirit. And it should be clear that the bodily behavior of believers matters to Paul. If the body is aligned with the flesh, it is associated with the old aeon and the result is death. In contrast, if the body is used to manifest the life of God's Spirit, then believers participate in the eschatological blessings of the new aeon, namely, life and peace. This is only possible through incorporation into Christ through the Spirit that puts the power of Christ's resurrection to work in the lives of believers. Paul envisions the possibility that believers might turn to habitual sin and walk κατὰ σάρκα, but he expects them to live in such a way that their bodily life is not characterized by the fleshly mindset. He expects them to have holy bodies.

Beginning in Rom 8:17, Paul portrays future bodily resurrection as participation in the glory of Christ. Just as those who have died with Christ expect to be raised with him, so also those who suffer with Christ may expect to be glorified with him (συνδοξασθῶμεν, 8:17). Elsewhere in Romans, glory is something that human beings seek and is the expected reward of those who do what is good (2:7). In the present, however, glory is something that human beings lack (Rom 3:23), and Paul's positive evaluation of glorification is strengthened if it means regaining something desirable that the recipients presently do not have, which is what Paul claims in 3:23, πάντες γὰρ ἥμαρτον καὶ ὑστεροῦνται τῆς δόξης τοῦ θεοῦ. Steven E. Enderlein argues that elsewhere in Paul and the New Testament ὑστερέω has the sense of being "deficient in something desirable," and that Rom 3:23 should be translated as "lacking the glory of God" rather than "falling short of the glory of God," which is the preferred rendering in multiple major translations.[102] Jewish texts sometimes associated the loss of glory with the sin of Adam, which supports an interpretation of "the glory of God" as something that human beings lack rather than an ideal toward which they should strive.[103] The repetition of the phrase πάντες ἥμαρτον from 3:23 in Rom 5:12 calls to mind the lack of glory and associates it with the transgression of Adam and thus with the Adam side of the aeonic

---

102. Steven E. Enderlein, "To Fall Short or Lack the Glory of God? The Translation and Implications of Romans 3:23," *JSPL* 1.2 (2011): 213–24. For translations that render the verse "fall short of the glory of God," see KJV, RSV, NRSV, NASB, NIV, HCSB, and ESV.

103. For the loss of glory associated with the sin of Adam, see Apoc. Mos. 20.1–2; 21.6; Tg. Ps.-J. Gen 2.25; 3 Bar. 4.16; Gen. Rab. 12:6; Apoc. Sedr. 6.5.

divide. This suggests that Paul shares the perspective that glory was lost when Adam sinned.[104] Thus, glorification in Rom 8 was likely to have been perceived, by Paul's Jewish recipients in particular, as a favorable recovery of that which all humanity has lacked since Adam's transgression.

It is also important for this investigation that Paul understands glorification in relation to the social group of the children of God who are explicitly described as heirs with Christ: εἰ δὲ τέκνα, καὶ κληρονόμοι· κληρονόμοι μὲν θεοῦ, συγκληρονόμοι δὲ Χριστοῦ (8:17). The language of inheritance arose earlier in the letter in 4:13, where Paul recounts his expanded interpretation of the land promise to Abraham and his family that they would inherit the world (τὸ κληρονόμον αὐτὸν εἶναι κόσμου). Wright argues that Paul is drawing on a tradition like that of Ps 2:7–9, in which the Messiah is promised the nations as an inheritance.[105] Similarly, an expansion of the Abrahamic promise to include the nations can be detected in Isa 55:3–5.[106] Moo suggests that the expansion summarizes the key provisions of the promise that Abraham would have a large number of descendants who would be a blessing to "many nations" and possess "the land."[107] If Paul believes that the Messiah is to inherit the nations, then it follows from his incorporative Christology discussed above that those who belong to him would be included in that inheritance. That concept appears in Rom 5:17, where Paul writes that "those who receive the abundance of grace and the gift of righteousness *will reign in life* [ἐν ζωῇ βασιλεύσουσιν] through the one, Jesus Christ" (emphasis added). Paul's focus here is, once again, on the future, and the future reign that is predicated of the recipients of grace is granted to them by the work of another, namely, Jesus. Similar language shows up in Rom 8:32, "how will (God) not also with (Christ) graciously give us *all things*" (πῶς οὐχὶ καὶ σὺν αὐτῷ τὰ πάντα ἡμῖν χαρίσεται, emphasis added). Once again, the themes of inheritance, reign, and incorporation into Christ intertwine. The close connection between inheritance and glorification should shape our interpretation of Rom 8:17–25. For Paul, to be

---

104. Enderlein, "To Fall Short," 220.
105. Wright, *Paul and the Faithfulness of God*, 488. Additionally, it is the messianic status of Jesus as "descended from David" and "Son of God" which is in part the basis of Paul's own mission to the gentile nations in Rom 1:3–5.
106. For similar language elsewhere in Jewish literature, cf. Sir 44:19–21; Jub. 22.14; 32:19; 2 Bar. 14.13; 51.13.
107. Moo, *Romans*, 274; cf. Esler, *Conflict*, 191. See Gen 12:2–3; 13:15–17; 15:5, 12–21; 17:4–8, 16–20; 17:8; 18:18; 22:17–18.

glorified with Christ is an eschatological reward in which the people of God are granted authority over the world by virtue of their participation in Christ. As we shall see, this should not be understood in isolation from bodily resurrection. Glorification consists of resurrection to new life in order to participate in the reign of Christ over the nations.[108]

That bodily component is explicit in Rom 8:23. Those who have the Spirit are said to be groaning with the creation "while awaiting adoption, the redemption of our bodies" (υἱοθεσίαν ἀπεκδεχόμενοι, τὴν ἀπολύτρωσιν τοῦ σώματος ἡμῶν, 8:23). Paul's use of υἱοθεσία here reveals some flexibility with the metaphor of adoption in his already/not yet framework. In Rom 8:15, it was used to depict the believers present possession of the Spirit; in 8:23, it depicts the future resurrection of body. Paul apparently sees no contradiction there. In both instances, adoption is associated with the work of the Spirit.[109] In terms of the *already*, adoption is associated with the reception of the Spirit. In terms of the *not yet*, the Spirit empowers believers as they empathize with the suffering of creation and anticipate in hope the resurrection of the body.[110] In this way, the believer identifies with and embodies the already/not yet tension that is true of creation as a whole, namely, the tension between the redemptive work of God inaugurated but not yet consummated. This tension is communicated by saying that believers have the "first fruits of the Spirit" (8:23). The work is in progress. It has begun, but it is not yet complete. This tension corresponds to the incongruity between the believer's present mortal body and the future redeemed body. For Paul, σῶμα is a means by which believers participate in the suffering of creation in bondage to decay, yet in that the σῶμα is indwelt by God's Spirit, it also points forward to the coming redemption. The body is the believer's point of contact with creation, and through that contact it becomes a sign of hope that all creation will experience liberation into God's new age. We found above that the hope for bodily redemption is anticipated in the present through bodily practice characterized by holiness. We can now say that, in so far as the believer embodies the sufferings of creation, holiness displayed in mortal bodies that walk according to the

---

108. So Wright: "The *reign* of human beings is what will matter in the new world. Humans are not to be passive recipients of God's mercy and grace; they are to have 'glory', in the sense that they are to be given stewardship of the world, as the creator always intended" (*Paul and the Faithfulness of God*, 488, emphasis original).

109. Dunn, *Romans 1–8*, 475.

110. See Jewett, *Romans*, 519.

Spirit embodies and anticipates the hope of the nonhuman creation to be liberated from destruction and decay. A mortal yet holy body expresses hope for all creation.

3.5. Bodily Resurrection as Future Social Identity

We saw above that Paul's concept of "incorporative Christology" in Rom 6 contributed a social dimension to the apostle's understanding of resurrection. It should be apparent that the social nature of resurrection is also apparent in Rom 8. This is particularly prominent in the use of familial language to describe the future resurrection in 8:9–25. He addresses the recipients as "brothers" (ἀδελφοί, 8:9). Those "who are led by the Spirit of God are *children of God*" (8:14, emphasis added). The spirit they have received is also the "Spirit of adoption" that enables believers to address God as "Abba, Father" (8:15), and the Spirit testifies to their status as "children of God" (8:16), which also makes them "heirs of God and heirs together with Christ" (8:17). In 8:24, Paul explicitly connects the familial language with bodily resurrection by describing the awaited adoption as "the redemption of our bodies." The impact of this familial language is reinforced by the introduction of first-person plural pronouns in verse 12, which adds to the sense of shared identity. In short, the presence in individual believers of the Spirit of the one who raised Jesus from the dead constitutes them as a family whose destiny is bodily resurrection. Thus, in Paul's thinking, resurrection is a social category. It is something that happens to the group of people who are members of the family of God. In both cases, the Spirit acts instrumentally as the agent of resurrection. We have seen already that resurrection of the body is a fully future expectation for Paul. Therefore, in so much as Paul and other believers can perceive themselves as members of the group that will be raised bodily from the dead, we can describe resurrection as a future social identity. The question is how Paul's language of resurrection functions to form and maintain a temporally consistent social identity. To that end, and since individuals tend to embrace positively valued future possible social identities, we need to consider the extent to which Paul attributes positive value to the future bodily resurrection.[111]

First, as was the case in 1 Corinthians, Paul evaluates his vision of the future resurrection using categories from the Greco-Roman honor system,

---

111. Cinnirella, "Exploring Temporal Aspects," 235.

δόξα in particular.¹¹² The significance of attaining honor in the Roman world is difficult to overstate. As J. E. Lendon observes, "life was lived under the constant, withering gaze of opinion, everyone constantly reckoning up the honor of others."¹¹³ It was presupposed that the desire for honor was the primary motivation to act in almost any case, even and perhaps especially in cases of danger, labor, or self-sacrifice.¹¹⁴ Greater honor also meant greater power to exert influence over others. To have honor was to have social authority; those with less honor were expected to defer to those with more.¹¹⁵ The insatiable desire for honor among the Romans is well illustrated by Cicero: "Nature has made us, as I have said before—it must often be repeated—enthusiastic seekers after honor, and once we have caught, as it were, some glimpse of its radiance, there is nothing we are not prepared to bear and go through in order to secure it" (*Tusc.* 2.24.58 [King]).¹¹⁶ Given the unparalleled importance of glory and honor in the Roman Empire, if Paul were able to persuade his audience that bodily resurrection is a way of receiving honor as a gift from the divine benefactor, then it would carry significant potential to bring a social identity characterized by future resurrection to salience. We are not suggesting that Paul adopts the values of the Greco-Roman honor system as a whole, especially with regard to competitive efforts to attain glory and honor. To the contrary, he "counters the competitive quest for honor" by exhorting the recipients to avoid "rivalry and jealousy" (ἔρις καί ζῆλος, Rom 13:13).¹¹⁷ If they receive glory, it will not be because they have competed for and attained it through their own resources; glory will be granted from God to the members of the community.¹¹⁸

Given the preoccupation for gaining honor that saturated the city of Rome in the first century, the prospect of elevated status through participation in the reign of Christ over the world is overwhelmingly positive. Paul

---

112. For a survey of proposals for interpreting Paul's "glory" language, see Ben C. Blackwell, "Immortal Glory and the Problem of Death in Romans 3.23," *JSNT* 32 (2010): 286–93.

113. J. E. Lendon, *Empire of Honour: The Art of Government in the Roman World* (Oxford: Oxford University Press, 1997), 36.

114. Lendon, *Empire of Honour*, 35.

115. Lendon, *Empire of Honour*, 55–73.

116. See Joseph H. Hellerman, *Reconstructing Honor in Roman Philippi: Carmen Christi as Cursus Pudorum*, SNTSMS 132 (Cambridge: Cambridge University Press, 2005), 34.

117. Barclay, *Paul and the Gift*, 509.

118. Barclay, *Paul and the Gift*, 510.

has associated bodily resurrection with one of the most important social values of the Greco-Roman world, and that impact would have been felt on both Jewish and gentile recipients alike. To be sure, Paul has filled those values with christological content; nevertheless, the appeal of receiving glory and honor would have resonated with the deepest sensibilities of his original hearers. For Jewish hearers in particular, Paul's favorable evaluation of future glory is strengthened by its association with the Abrahamic inheritance. From the perspective of SIT, Paul's positive evaluation of bodily resurrection functions to strengthen a resurrection-oriented future possible social identity. What is particularly important is that none of the ethnically diverse recipients are asked to abandon their distinct subgroup identities. By associating resurrection with the receipt of glory and honor, Paul has tapped into a system of highly desired societal values without encouraging the aspects of that system that would undermine the cohesion of the group.

The second aspect of Paul's positive evaluation has to do with the liberation of the nonhuman creation from bondage to decay. This is particularly noteworthy since Paul nowhere else considers humanity in relation to the nonhuman creation.[119] We noted above that future glory is set in contrast to present sufferings in Rom 8:18. In 8:19, creation is said to be "eagerly awaiting the revelation [ἀποκάλυψις] of the children of God." The use of ἀποκάλυψις in 8:19 ties the expectation of creation together with the glorification of believers described in 8:18, where Paul says that glory will be "revealed [ἀποκαλύπτω] in us." If glorification involves resurrection and reign, as I have argued above, then Paul means that creation is awaiting human beings to be given their proper place of authority.[120] When this happens creation "will be set free from bondage to decay" and will itself be transferred from that bondage to freedom received through the agency of glorified human beings (8:21).[121] In short, Paul has boldly asserted that the hope of the whole world depends on the relatively small movement of Christ-followers.[122] Esler's comments on the significance of this SIT reading are worth quoting at length:

---

119. Brendan J. Byrne, *Reckoning with Romans: A Contemporary Reading of Paul's Gospel*, GNS 18 (Wilmington, DE: Glazier, 1986), 165.

120. See Jewett: "The sons and daughters of God demonstrate their status by exercising the kind of dominion that heals rather than destroys" (*Romans*, 519).

121. See Wright, "Romans," 597.

122. Esler, *Conflict*, 261. Cf. Dunn: "For the spokesman of a small movement still in its infancy, the vision is audacious" (*Romans 1–8*, 489).

> Social identity theory helps us to appreciate the momentous nature of its relevance to the status of Paul's addressees in Rome. He is boldly personifying the whole of creation and then aligning its unhappy experience and expectation with the existence and destiny of a small band of Christ-followers. The effect of this is to magnify the various elements of their group identity. The cognitive dimension, the sheer fact of belonging to a group like this, is enhanced by the incorporation, as it were, of creation itself as an associate member. Of all the millions of people alive in the known world, creation was aligned with, and supportive of, the tiny minority constituting the Christ-movement. From this it necessarily followed that the emotional and evaluative dimensions (how they felt about belonging to a group like this and how they rated themselves in comparison with other groups) were also greatly augmented.[123]

Building on the foundation established by Esler, the point to add, given the questions of this study, is that Paul has made the destiny of creation dependent on the future resurrection of believers. The redemption of creation follows from and is patterned after the bodily redemption of those in Christ. As they move from mortality to resurrection, creation moves from bondage to liberty. As they enter the glory of reigning in eternal resurrection life, creation escapes subjection to futility. The groaning creation is waiting specifically for the redemption of human bodies (8:22–24).

If the believer's resurrection can be described as a future social identity, then we should also ask whether and to what extent Paul portrays the past to cohere with his positive evaluation of the group's future. That question leads us to Paul's portrayal of Abraham's faith as faith in the God who raises the dead. No small amount of literature has been produced with the goal of explaining the role of Abraham in Rom 4. The patriarch has been interpreted as a useful example or prooftext for justification by faith from Israel's Scriptures.[124] Abraham has been understood as a "test case" to show that a person can be justified by faith and not works of the law.[125] His faith has been taken as a "typological foreshadowing" or "prefiguration" of the

---

123. Esler, *Conflict*, 262.
124. Sanders, *Paul and Palestinian Judaism*, 483, 87; cf. E. P. Sanders, *Paul, the Law, and the Jewish People* (Philadelphia: Fortress, 1983), 21; Richard N. Longenecker, *Introducing Romans: Critical Issues in Paul's Most Famous Letter* (Grand Rapids: Eerdmans, 2011), 367.
125. Dunn, *Romans 1–8*, 194, 226.

faithfulness of Christ.[126] Another account finds in Rom 4 evidence that justification by faith is a liberating, generative, and transformational divine act instead of the traditional view that it is a forensic or juridical declaration.[127] The argument is also made that Paul in Rom 4 is interpreting Gen 15 to demonstrate that the promise to Abraham is fulfilled in the revelation of the righteousness of God in the gospel.[128] The present discussion comes from a somewhat different angle given the SIT lens through which we are reading, though there will be points of contact with some of these interpretations. We will find that Paul's portrayal of Abraham in Rom 4 functions in part to establish a point of continuity between the recipients and the patriarch in that both have the God who raises the dead as the object of their faith.[129]

Esler has argued that Abraham functioned as a prototype of the new identity in Christ for the recipients of Paul's letter to Rome. The use of *prototype* by social psychologists should be distinguished from its use elsewhere. By prototype Esler means "a summary representation that is considered to capture the central tendency of the category and derives from multiple experiences with category members."[130] A prototype is an ideal person who embodies the group's positive perception of itself. An actual person who embodies the identity of the group is called an *exemplar* by social psychologists.[131] Esler argues that the use of Abraham facilitates Paul's goal of recategorizing the ethnically diverse Christ-followers in Rome into a new identity in Christ. By showing that Judean and non-Judean believers could claim Abraham as their ancestor by appealing to the reckoning of righteousness through faith, Paul portrayed Abraham as a prototype of the new identity. The discussion of a prototype highlights the diachronic nature of social identity formation, and by giving an account of Abraham's role as idealizing the new identity in Christ, Esler shows that temporal continuity was an important component of Paul's attempt to persuade his recipients to embrace their new identity. The remainder of this section aims to develop that key insight by arguing that for Paul the faith

---

126. Hays, *The Conversion of the Imagination*, 84; cf. Campbell, *The Deliverance of God*, 753–54.
127. Campbell, *The Deliverance of God*, 749–50.
128. N. T. Wright, *Pauline Perspectives: Essays on Paul, 1978–2013* (Minneapolis: Fortress, 2013), 555–56.
129. See Cinnirella, "Exploring Temporal Aspects," 235.
130. Esler, *Conflict*, 172.
131. Esler, *Conflict*, 172–73.

by which Abraham was reckoned righteous, and the faith that defines the identity of the family of God through time, is faith in the resurrecting God.

Before proceeding to consider the specific nature of Abraham's faith in the resurrecting God, we should note that Paul's telling of the Abraham story plays a key role in his argument that Jewish believers and gentile believers are equal and unified members of the people of God in Christ. Paul's argument in Rom 4:9–12 that Abraham is the common ancestor of all who have faith regardless of their ethnicity follows from the conviction expressed in Rom 3:29–30 that unity among believers derives from the unity of God.[132] However, the basic concept that God accepts both Jews and gentiles on the basis of faith (Rom 3:30) is rhetorically insufficient to effect the resocialization of those two groups into a single group marked by a distinct, common, and superordinate identity. That Paul appeals to Abraham as a figure who embodies the central features of the new identity deriving from the unity of God highlights the deep interrelatedness of theology and social identity.[133] That interrelatedness is an aspect of the relationship between faith in the resurrecting God and Paul's effort at cultivating unity between the Jewish and gentile Christ-followers in Rom 14 and 15. Paul's concern for multiethnic unity among the people of God comes through most clearly in the question raised in 4:9, where he asks whether the blessing of justification and the nonreckoning of sin apart from works is for the circumcised Jew only or also for the uncircumcised gentile. To answer this question Paul appeals to the chronology of the Abraham narrative in Genesis. He observes in Rom 4:11 that Abraham's act of faith in God and the righteousness that was given to him as a result (cf. Gen 15:6) preceded his circumcision (cf. Gen 17:9–14, 23–27). In fact, Paul considers circumcision a sign (σημεῖον) that that functions to seal or confirm (σφραγίς) the righteous status that already belonged to Abraham by virtue of the faith he expressed prior to his circumcision. The sequence of events is essential for Paul's argument.[134] That Abraham's faith and righteous status stands prior to and independent of his circumcision makes his experience paradigmatic for gentile believers.[135] Paul's use of εἰς τό with

---

132. So Wright: "the unity of God himself grounds the unity of the community" (*Paul and the Faithfulness of God*, 641).

133. Esler, *Conflict*, 190–91.

134. Witherington and Hyatt, *Romans*, 126; cf. Hays, *The Conversion of the Imagination*, 75–76; Wright, *Pauline Perspectives*, 557.

135. Barclay, *Paul and the Gift*, 487.

the infinitive εἶναι indicates purpose, which means Paul is suggesting that the very purpose of the faith-followed-by-circumcision sequence was to obtain the result of a multiethnic family, "*in order that* he might be father of all who believe, despite being uncircumcised" (4:11). This, of course, does not exclude circumcised Jews from justification by faith. They are included also on the basis of faith like that of Abraham (4:12). Paul has thus chosen Abraham as one who typifies the common ingroup identity that he wants the recipients to adopt.[136] His persuasive strategy is particularly strong in that it requires neither Jew nor gentile to abandon subgroup identities in order to embrace a new shared identity in Christ.

So, Abraham's precircumcision faith opens the door to the inclusion of the gentiles among the children of Abraham, as Paul asserts in Rom 4:16, the promise is for all "who share the faith of Abraham." But this leaves open a further question: What sort of faith did Abraham have? And what is the specific characteristic of Abraham's faith that makes it paradigmatic for faith in Jesus? For Paul, the answer to this question is straightforward: Abraham's faith is faith in the God who raises the dead.

Two features of the text should be observed. First, Paul repeatedly defines faith in terms of believing in the resurrecting God, and, second, his description of Abraham's faith in that God is articulated in terms strikingly similar to those used in Rom 8 to describe the future resurrection hope. Consider Rom 4:17, where Paul specifically defines the God in whom Abraham believed as "the one who gives life to the dead" (τοῦ ζωοποιοῦντος τοὺς νεκρούς). He uses the participial form of ζωοποιέω, which is the same verb used in 8:11 to describe the future resurrection of believers. This repetition creates a point of contact between the faith of Abraham and that of the recipients. Abraham believed in the God who gives life out of death; Paul's recipients believe in the same God, who raised Jesus from the dead and who will raise them from the dead. Further in Rom 8:11, Paul's description of God as τοῦ ἐγείραντος τὸν Ἰησοῦν ἐκ νεκρῶν is nearly identical to the description of the God in whom Abraham was said to believe in 4:24, τὸν ἐγείραντα Ἰησοῦν τὸν κύριον ἡμῶν ἐκ νεκρῶν. Again, Paul portrays Abraham as having faith in the resurrecting God which stands in diachronic continuity with the faith of Paul and his recipients. Another example is Paul's interest in the way Abraham embodied faith in the God who gives life to the dead expressed through his belief that God would

---

136. Esler, *Conflict*, 189.

give him a son in his old age. Paul says in 4:19 that Abraham's body was "already dead" (κατενόησεν τὸ ἑαυτοῦ σῶμα [ἤδη] νενεκρωμένον). Nevertheless, God was able to give him a son; that is, God brought newborn life out of Abraham's dead body. Some manuscripts leave out "already," probably as an attempt to soften the difficulty of the suggestion that a living person's body could *already* be dead (MSS B, F, G, etc.). Commentators sometimes note that translations mute the difficulty and render the phrase "as good as dead" rather than simply "dead." But the deadness of Abraham's body and Sarah's womb is precisely Paul's point, and it is essential for connecting Abraham's faith with faith in Christ.[137] The God who gives life to the dead (4:17) manifests that life-giving power in Abraham's own body by keeping the promise to Abraham that he would have a son (4:18–20).

For Paul, Abraham's faith was not an amorphous belief in an undefined object; it was particular faith in the specific God who raises the dead. This is the point of connection between Abraham's faith and faith in Christ. Paul portrays Abraham's faith as resurrection faith, which is analogous to the faith of Paul and the recipients who believe in the God "who raised Jesus our Lord from the dead" (Rom 4:24).[138] Importantly, as Kirk observes, what is predicated in 4:17 is demonstrated in 4:23–34.[139] Abraham actually becomes the father of all who believe—both Jew and gentile—by means of resurrection-oriented faith.[140] Thus, by making the case that Abraham's resurrection faith makes him the father of all who believe in the God who raised Jesus from the dead, Paul constructs a coherent representation where the past and his vision of the future stand in diachronic continuity.

From the perspective of social identity theory, the advantage of this line of reasoning is straightforward. Individuals tend to find appeal in continuity of identity through time. The Abraham story functions as a "life-story" in which Paul reinterprets the past in light of the resurrection of Jesus and in light of Paul's hope in the God who raised Jesus and who will raise those who have been incorporated into Jesus.[141] Paul's reinterpretation is designed to make the case that Abraham's faith in the resurrecting

---

137. Kirk, *Unlocking Romans*, 72.

138. Campbell, *The Deliverance of God*, 738.

139. Kirk, *Unlocking Romans*, 75.

140. Kirk, *Unlocking Romans*, 74–75.

141. Cinnirella defines "life stories" as "narratives of the group which tie past, present, and predicted futures into a coherent representation ("Exploring Temporal Aspects," 235–36).

God makes him father both to uncircumcised gentiles *as uncircumcised gentiles* and to circumcised Jews *as circumcised Jews*. When considered in terms of diachronic process, the new identity available to both groups can be seen as characterized by faith in the resurrecting God. Paul wants both subgroups to see themselves as members of the same family, namely, that of Abraham, yet neither group is required to forsake its ethnically distinct identities in order to adopt the new one. Paul's resurrection language functions in part to facilitate this process of social recategorization. By portraying Abraham's faith in a way that coheres with future resurrection, a new possibility for superordinate group identity emerges that will allow the members of each subgroup to maintain their distinctive identities and thus increase the likelihood of reducing conflict between them.

3.6. Table Fellowship as Bodily Practice

We argued above that Paul wrote Romans in part to address and facilitate reconciliation of the intragroup conflict among the Christ-followers in Rome, which was expressed particularly through a reluctance to share table fellowship. In Rom 14:1–15:13, Paul makes his case for why the recipients should be reconciled and "welcome one another" (15:7). If the letter is to function in this way, it needs to facilitate the process of social recategorization by encouraging the members of each group—the strong and the weak—to think of themselves as a single group that shares a common identity.[142] Paul needs to shift the category of social identity from Roman Christ-followers, on the one hand, and Jewish Christ-followers, on the other, to the new identity in Christ. I argue that Paul's resurrection language plays a role in that recategorization. If he is successful, the members of each subgroup will prioritize their loyalty to the community of Christ-followers as a whole over their loyalty to those who share their distinct ethnic identities. The effectiveness of this process increases if the letter refrains from encouraging the members of disparate groups to abandon their sense of ethnic distinctiveness while simultaneously encouraging a superordinate ingroup identity. The goal is not to erase ethnic distinctions; it is to shift the level of inclusiveness from ethnicity to the group of Christ-followers as a whole.[143] If that goal is

---

142. Gaertner and Dovidio, *Reducing Intergroup Bias*, 33.
143. Gaertner and Dovidio, *Reducing Intergroup Bias*, 34–35.

realized, such inclusivity ought to be realized in shared table fellowship among the believers. The question for this investigation is how that table fellowship relates to Paul's understanding of future bodily resurrection in relation to the use of the body in the present.

I propose that the table fellowship Paul hopes to see is itself a bodily practice. Paul's appeal for shared table fellowship comes at the end of a larger section of the letter which began at 12:1 and which is focused primarily on matters of ethics and behavior. As Barclay observes, Paul's discussion of the "presentation" of the body in Rom 6 (vv. 12–14, 19) is directly linked to the opening of chapter 12, "I urge you, therefore, brothers and sisters, by the mercies of God, to present your bodies [παραστῆσαι τὰ σώματα ὑμῶν] as a living sacrifice, holy [ἅγιος] and pleasing to God" (12:1).[144] That the bodily life of believers should be "holy" further reinforces the connection to the earlier material (cf. ἁγιασμός in 6:22). The following verse puts the exhortation negatively and sets the instruction in the context of the believer's movement from the old aeon to the new aeon: "And do not be conformed to this age [τῷ αἰῶνι τούτῳ], but be transformed by the renewal of your mind [νοῦς] in order that you may discern what is the will of God" (12:2).[145] Together these verses constitute a general exhortation that will be applied to particular situations in the remainder of the section that runs through 15:13. As Barclay remarks, "That is why the bodily reorientation described in Romans 6 is given some exemplification in Romans 12–15, which concerns the formation of a community structured by and oriented to the good news."[146] Given the connections between the exhortation in Rom 12:1-2 to present the body in worship and Paul's earlier discussion of the body in chapters 6 and 8, the expectations set forth in 12–15 should

---

144. Barclay, *Paul and the Gift*, 494.

145. For the view that ὁ αἰὼν οὗτος implies the contrast from Jewish eschatology between "the present age" and "age to come," see Ridderbos, *Paul: An Outline of His Theology*, 52; cf. Dunn, *Romans 9–16*, 712; Schreiner, *Romans*, 647–48; Gorman, *Cruciformity*, 354; Wright, "Romans," 705; Witherington and Hyatt, *Romans*, 286; Longenecker, *Romans*, 922–23. Esler disagrees with an eschatological interpretation of ὁ αἰὼν οὗτος and argues instead that it "refers to the present period and realm inhabited by persons and powers to which the redemption offered in Christ stands in contradiction," which here includes "the realm of ethnic hostility and conflict" (*Conflict*, 310–11). For the term elsewhere in Paul, see 1 Cor 1:20; 2:6, 8; 3:18; 10:11; 2 Cor 4:4; Gal 1:4.

146. Barclay, *Paul and the Gift*, 508.

be understood as implications of Paul's theology of the body and bodily practice worked out earlier in the letter.

This is particularly the case with regard to the question of table fellowship in Rom 14:1–15:13. The evidence suggests that Jewish believers (the weak) and gentile believers (the strong) did not avoid each other completely. For one group to boast over the other (Rom 11:18) requires some contact.[147] Nevertheless, if Rom 14:1 is a clue, their gatherings were marked by dispute. The letter itself was presumably read during a meeting at which representatives from both groups were present. Welcoming one another in peace instead of passing judgment on one another (14:10, 13) is a particular expression of the general expectation of presenting their bodies to God in worship (12:1). To go a step further, to fellowship around the table is something one does with the body. As a bodily practice, table fellowship among Christ-followers will be a matter either of submitting the parts of the body to sin for death or to God as alive from the dead (cf. Rom 6:13). If the strong and the weak are unwilling to welcome one another at the table as Christ has welcomed them, then they use their bodily organs as instruments of wickedness. This would be submitting the parts of the body to sin and could be construed as reverting to the ways of the old Adamic age. Alternatively, if they use their hands to put food in their mouths as they eat together at the same table, then they are using these parts of their bodies as instruments of righteousness. They show themselves to be participants in the new age of grace and life. They embody in the present their hope of future bodily resurrection. For Paul, using the body in a way that is congruent with bodily resurrection means bringing one's body to the table with believers of other ethnicities. Further, if using the body as an instrument of righteousness also points forward to the liberation of all creation, then coming together at the table anticipates the hope of all creation to be set free from bondage to decay.

Taking these matters through the lens of social identity, Paul's expectations for bodily practice at the table in 14:1–15:13 stand in continuity with the resurrection-oriented future social identity that we inferred based on Paul's attitude toward the body and bodily practice in the earlier parts of the letter. Believers—both Jew and gentile—are part of the group "in Christ" that will be raised from the dead in the future. They are included in the family of Abraham by virtue of sharing faith in the God who raises

---

147. Esler, *Conflict*, 345.

the dead. Thus, their behavioral practices in the present expressed in their common life should embody that shared identity. Given Paul's understanding of the bodily practice in the present and bodily resurrection in the future, the recipients should engage in shared table fellowship as a present expression of their temporally coherent resurrection-oriented future identity. If they do not, they fail to embody their future possible identity.

Evidence that bodily resurrection plays a role in the relationship between identity and behavior appears also in Rom 14:7–9. Believers should not pass judgment (14:3–4, 10) on one another on matters of the Sabbath and diet (14:6) because in passing judgment they are living to themselves rather than living to the Lord (14:7–8). To substantiate this point Paul reminds the recipients, "For this reason Christ died and lived again [ἔζησεν], in order that he might be Lord of both the dead and the living" (14:9). The aorist form of ζάω should be taken as a reference to the resurrection of Christ, given its placement in the verse subsequent to his death. By appealing to the resurrection and lordship of Jesus, Paul aims to orient the life of the community around the authority of the resurrected Christ. When they pass judgment on one another's habits of eating and worship, they make value judgments that do not accord with a resurrection-oriented identity. Paul invites the recipients to reconsider their value judgments in light of the resurrection of Christ in which they hope to participate in the future. If the resurrected Christ orients their social life, then their practices ought to embody a shared identity oriented toward the future possibility of sharing in Christ's resurrection. Eating together without dispute over the menu is a characteristic of a community defined by such an identity.

That the future possible resurrection-oriented identity does not negate their ethnic distinctiveness is apparent in 15:1–13. Paul does not call upon Jewish believers to abandon their scruples with regard to food. Rather, he calls upon gentiles believers to "bear the weaknesses of the weak" (τὰ ἀσθενήματα τῶν ἀδυνάτων βαστάζειν, 15:1). That is, Paul anticipates that the Jews will continue to abstain from meat, and he wants the gentiles to accept them that way. Thus, by sitting at the same table, yet still engaging in different dietary practices, they simultaneously embody both unity and diversity. The result is a harmony that glorifies God with a single voice (15:6). That diversity in harmony is further expounded in 15:7–12. The appeal to "welcome one another" in 15:7 is substantiated by the point that "Christ has become a servant of the circumcised for the sake of the truth of God, in order to confirm the promise to the patriarchs, and in order that the gentiles might glorify God for his mercy" (15:8-9). Here again the distinctive identities of both subgroups are embraced by Paul. Christ's ministry to the Jews functions instrumentally in relation to the gentiles. In the doxological material of 15:10-11, the gentiles are exhorted to rejoice and praise God along with the people of God, once again indicating the continuance of ethnic distinction within the larger community of believers. The implication is that these distinctions are not disregarded, but neither are they determinative as markers of Christian identity. That identity is characterized by faith in the God who raised Christ and who will raise those "in Christ."

In sum, Paul has cast a vision of the people of God that embraces ethnic distinctiveness and assimilates it into a higher level of group inclusion. Jewish believers and gentile believers alike are invited to embrace a new identity in Christ which includes the future possible identity of bodily resurrection, yet neither group is required to yield their subgroup distinctiveness. One concrete and embodied expression of this identity is welcoming one another at the table. Their differences serve to glorify God all the more by displaying diversity in harmony through their embodied life in general and their table and worship practices in particular.

3.7. Conclusion

Paul's understanding of the relationship between bodily practice in the present and bodily resurrection in the future is consistently portrayed in Romans in terms of the dichotomy between the old age and the new age. Although believers have not yet been raised from the dead, they participate in the new age by virtue of their incorporation into Christ, and they anticipate their future resurrection with bodily practices characterized by holiness and not sin. This transformation is enabled by the indwelling presence of God's Spirit, who empowers believers to use the body for righteousness as members of the new age, even though their bodies are bound to mortality. The incongruity between present mortality and future resurrection depicts in the bodies of believers the tension that characterizes all of creation in that it is awaiting redemption while remaining in bondage to decay. I have emphasized throughout Paul's view that resurrection is something that will happen in the future, and it will happen to the group of people who are in Christ and in whom the Spirit dwells. To that extent, future bodily resurrection can be described as a temporally consistent future possible social identity that can be embraced by Jewish believers and gentile believers without requiring either of them to abandon their distinct ethnic identities. The key insight is that if they embrace bodily resurrection as a future possible identity, then it has potential to influence their social practices. I have argued that this sheds light on the problem of table fellowship in Rom 14 and 15. Table fellowship can be viewed as a bodily practice precisely because it involves bringing the bodies of the recipients together at the table. If table fellowship is a bodily practice, then Paul's instructions with regard to the body in Rom 6 and 8 have bearing on our reading of Rom 14 and 15. If Jewish believers and gentile believers share the same resurrection-oriented future possible identity, then they ought to use their bodies in accord with that identity. Refusing to share table fellowship runs against their shared identity and against the ethics of the new aeon. However, if they bring their diverse bodies to the same table, their practices embody their shared identity in a way that anticipates the future resurrection of the body and the redemption of all creation.

4
Resurrection or Destruction?
The Letter to the Philippians

The Letter to the Philippians is distinctive in terms of the data it provides with regard to Paul's attitude toward the body and his hope for bodily resurrection. Unlike the other letters under consideration in this study, Paul wrote Philippians while facing the real possibility that he might soon die at the hands of the Roman Empire, and evidence in the letter suggests that death and questions related to postmortem existence were very much on his mind. Thus, as Wright observes, "we should not be surprised to find here as well some of his clearest statements about Christian hope beyond death," and I would add the hope for resurrection not least.[1] As we consider the question of Paul's attitude toward resurrection in Philippians and its contribution to the function of the letter, we will find that his language about the body and the resurrection of the body carries significant potential to strengthen the shared identity of the Philippian Christ-followers. This, in turn, supports the letter's rhetorical goals to mitigate the potential for internal faction and to strengthen the community to withstand external opposition.

4.1. The Rhetorical Situation in Philippi

We begin with a look at the rhetorical situation in Philippi and the problem that Paul aimed to address. Duane Watson's early study on the rhetoric of Philippians identified the exigence as "the appearance of a rival gospel in Philippi."[2] This he infers from the warning that Paul issues in chapter 3

---

1. Wright, *Resurrection*, 225.
2. Duane F. Watson, "A Rhetorical Analysis of Philippians and its Implicatons for the Unity Question," *NovT* 30 (1988): 58.

about a group of potential opponents.³ Watson interprets the warning as an expression of Paul's concern over the ongoing influence of Judaizers, even though he admits they are not "firmly entrenched."⁴ While the possibility of a false gospel in Philippi is plausible, it is not explicit in the text and does not necessarily follow from Paul's warning about these opponents.⁵ Paul is never so harsh toward the Philippians as he was toward the Galatians when he perceived that some among their number were turning to a false gospel (Gal 1:6-9). To the contrary, the generally positive and friendly tone of Philippians is commonly recognized. Could there be a more probable problem that this letter was intended to address?

Keeping in mind that Paul's portrayal of the situation is itself part of his rhetoric, I suggest there were at least two distinct but related issues that formed the exigence of the letter and contributed to Paul's motivation for writing: (1) the Philippians were experiencing persecution or suffering of some kind from outsiders, and (2) there was some level of divisiveness present within the group, though the extent of this divisiveness remains unclear.⁶ Evidence for the first issue comes in 1:28-30, where Paul exhorts the Philippians to resist intimidation by their opponents (1:28). He then describes the presence of opposition as an opportunity to suffer for Christ (1:29) and compares it to his own ongoing struggle (1:30). That is not to suggest that members of the Philippian congregation were imprisoned or facing the possibility of imminent martyrdom as Paul was, and he does not provide detail with regard to the specific nature of their suffering; rather, the point of comparison highlights Paul's conviction that following Jesus may result in suffering of various kinds.⁷ The clearest evidence for the presence of divisiveness comes in 4:2-3. Paul here names two female leaders and instructs them "to be of the same mind" (τὸ αὐτὸ φρονεῖν). He follows this up by calling upon a third person, known only as "my loyal companion," to help the process of restoring unity. The direct appeal to these women

---

3. For a survey of possibilities regarding the opponents in Philippians, see Gordon D. Fee, *Paul's Letter to the Philippians*, NICNT (Grand Rapids: Eerdmans, 1995), 7-10; see further G. Walter Hansen, *The Letter to the Philippians*, Pillar New Testament Commentary (Grand Rapids: Eerdmans, 2009), 28-30, esp. 28 n. 106.

4. Watson, "Rhetorical Analysis," 59.

5. See the warning from John M. G. Barclay, "Mirror-Reading a Polemical Letter: Galatians as a Test Case," in *The Galatians Debate*, ed. Mark D. Nanos (Peabody, MA: Hendrickson, 2002), 367-82.

6. Sandnes, *Belly and Body*, 139.

7. Cf. Hansen, *Philippians*, 27-28.

by name and the repetition of παρακαλῶ together serve to highlight the urgency of Paul's concern for their reconciliation. Before addressing the two women by name, Paul exhorts the community in general to be unified at a variety of points in the letter (1:27; 2:1–4, 14–15; 3:15–17). The most likely explanation is that in Paul's mind the disagreement poses a threat to the overall unity of the group as a whole. There is no evidence to suggest that the factions are so far developed as those dealt with in 1 Corinthians; however, as with 1 Corinthians, the rhetorical objective here is to cultivate concord among the Philippian Christ-followers.[8]

It is worth observing that while these matters of external opposition and internal dispute are clearly distinct, they nevertheless have potential to bear upon one another. This is clear in 1:27–28, "Only live as citizens in a manner worthy of the gospel of Christ, so that … I will know you are standing firm in *one spirit*, striving side by side with *one mind* for the faith of the gospel, and are in *no way intimidated by your opponents*" (emphasis added). Group unity and strength in the face of persecution are here held together as ways of faithfully living worthily of the gospel. In order to stand firm against external opposition, the Philippians must be unified within. The stronger the social bond within the group, the more likely they are to resist and withstand suffering imposed on them by outgroupers. Whatever rhetoric Paul thus deploys must deal with this explicit double threat.[9] I suggest that this account of the exigence makes a great deal of sense in light of Paul's rhetoric. I further suggest, and the argument below will bear it out, that Paul's rhetoric as it relates to the resurrection, particularly with his use of examples and the rhetorical *synkrisis* between the respective destinies of the recipients and their opponents, functions in two ways. First, it strengthens the salience of the common in-group identity of the Philippian Christ-followers

---

8. Ben Witherington, *Paul's Letter to the Philippians* (Grand Rapids: Eerdmans, 2011), 25. There is not enough evidence to support the proposal of Davorin Peterlin, who gives a detailed reconstruction of "the church polarized around Euodia and Syntyche who were the forces of disunity"; see Peterlin, *Paul's Letter to the Philippians in the Light of Disunity in the Church*, NovTSup 79 (Leiden: Brill, 1995), 221; cf. the critiques by Fee, *Philippians*, 7 n. 24, 66 n. 41; Hansen, *Philippians*, 25–26.

9. I will add that our focus on these two matters does not rule out other issues to which Paul attends and which contributed to his motivation for writing. For example, he also writes to commend Epaphroditus (2:25–30) and to acknowledge the support given by the Philippians (4:10–20). While these aspects of the letter contribute to the occasion for the letter, from a rhetorical perspective the matters of suffering and faction form the exigence of the letter; they are the double problem in need of solution.

by constructing a temporally coherent social identity, which increases the letter's potential to mitigate discord among the Philippians. Second, it puts the recipients in a better position to remain faithful in spite of persecution. The problem is the double danger of suffering and discord, and the contrast between the two groups functions to deal with that problem.

4.2. Rhetoric and Social Identity

This is a good place to reiterate the potential of employing SIT together with rhetorical analysis. The exigence for which I have argued exists because of conflict between distinct groups, and the presence of divisiveness at least introduces the potential for growing conflict between subgroups among the Christ-followers in Philippi. Nevertheless, whatever subgroups may have arisen within the congregation, they remain a single group in contrast to the outsiders who may be the cause of their shared suffering. SIT would suggest that, in such circumstances, Paul needs to cultivate a salient superordinate identity among the members of the Christ-following in-group that is inclusive of any subgroups that are present in order to help them overcome discord, cultivate group unity, and gain a better chance of living worthily of the gospel (1:27) by standing firm and unified against suffering and opposition.[10] As we shall discover, the insights of our rhetorical analysis will be confirmed and further illumined when combined with an SIT approach to the text. As stated above, Paul's rhetoric needs to produce a salient in-group social identity among the in-group that is able to undergird the behavior he desires from the recipients, namely concord and steadfastness; the basic thesis of this chapter is that his portrayal of bodily resurrection contributes to that necessity.

Once again, careful attention to temporal dynamics in social identity is a potentially fruitful lens through which to consider Paul's interest in the resurrection of the body. Philippians has not been the subject of SIT analysis to the same extent as some of the lengthier Paulines. There is undoubtedly a variety of reasons for this, not least the significant volume of social data found in the longer letters. When SIT has been applied to the text of Philippians, the focus has been on the letter's potential to form and maintain a Christ-oriented social identity among the recipients and how

---

10. Samuel L. Gaertner et al., "The Common Ingroup Identity Model: Recategorization and the Reduction of Intergroup Bias," *ERSP* 4 (1993): 6.

such an identity might relate to the complex dynamics of social identities shaped by membership in various Greco-Roman and Jewish groups.[11] Among the limited studies that analyze Philippians through the lens of SIT, temporal dynamics in identity formation have not featured prominently. This increases the potential of the present study for taking scholarship in a fresh and hopefully fruitful direction.

A brief review will keep the theory fresh in mind before turning to our analysis of the text. Cinnirella argues for a category he calls possible social identity, which is the self's perception of present or future group memberships.[12] Cinnirella hypothesizes that in-group members will typically try to persuade other members of the group to endorse positively evaluated possible social identities, that is, to accept a desired vision of the group's future. Part of this process involves crafting "life stories" or group narratives that lend coherence to the past, present, and desired future of the group. A coherent portrayal of group identity over time carries potential to strengthen the social identity of group members and may persuade them to adopt a particular aspect of the desired future group identity. I aim to show that Paul's rhetoric of the body and bodily resurrection functions to increase the salience of the recipients' Christ-oriented identity in a way that carries significant potential for mitigating discord and building unity among the members of the Philippian Jesus group. Paul's coherent portrayal of the group's past and future in terms of bodily resurrection strengthens his efforts to persuade them to live worthily of the gospel. The implications for Paul's rhetoric should be clear. If his language about bodily resurrection increases the salience of the Philippians' Christ-oriented identity and strengthens the unity of the group as a whole, then it increases the persuasive power of his rhetoric and the call to endure together the suffering they experience.

4.3. The Deliberative Rhetoric of Philippians

As rhetorical criticism of the New Testament was gaining prominence, Kennedy suggested that Philippians was "largely epideictic" rhetoric, but

---

11. Sergio Rosell Nebreda, *Christ Identity: A Social-Scientific Reading of Philippians 2.5–11*, FRLANT 240 (Göttingen: Vandenhoeck & Ruprecht, 2011); William S. Campbell, *Unity and Diversity in Christ: Interpreting Paul in Context* (Eugene, OR: Cascade, 2013), 212–23.

12. Cinnirella, "Exploring Temporal Aspects," 227–48.

his view has not gained much of a following.[13] As an alternative, Duane F. Watson argued in 1988 that Philippians exhibits features typical of deliberative rhetoric; this view has been accepted with little dispute and only minor nuance by scholars who engage in rhetorical studies of Philippians.[14] According to Aristotle, deliberative oratory (1) functions to exhort or dissuade, (2) is primarily oriented toward the future, and (3) has the expedient as its end (*Rhet.* 1.3.3-6; cf. Quintilian, *Inst.* 3.8).[15] Quintilian follows Cicero and includes dignity and honor with expediency as central concerns of deliberative rhetoric (*Inst.* 3.8.1-2; cf. Cicero, *De or.* 2.334; *Rhet. Her.* 3.3). The author of Rhetorica ad Herennium also highlights the future-orientation of deliberative speeches by observing that they are concerned with the choice either between two courses of action or several (3.2). Moreover, Aristotle notes the importance of examples or comparisons for deliberative rhetoric, pointing out that "it is by examination of the past that we divine and judge the future" (*Rhet.* 1.9.40). We will see below that some of the rhetorical examples and comparisons deployed by Paul in Philippians would have performed an identity-forming function also.

Each feature of deliberative rhetoric identified by the classical theorists can be observed in Philippians.[16] For Quintilian, "deliberation is about doing something" (*Inst.* 3.8.23), and the thing Paul wants the Philippians to do is articulated in the *propositio* in 1:27, "Only live as citizens

---

13. Kennedy, *New Testament Interpretation*, 77; cf. Claudio Basevi and Juan Chapa, "Philippians 2.6-11: The Rhetorical Function of a Pauline Hymn," in *Rhetoric and the New Testament: Essays from the 1992 Heidelberg Conference*, ed. Stanley E. Porter and Thomas H. Olbricht, JSNTSup 90 (Sheffield: JSOT Press, 1993), 338-56, esp. 347-49.

14. Watson, "Rhetorical Analysis," 57-88; cf. Timothy Geoffrion, *The Rhetorical Purpose and the Political and Military Character of Philippians: A Call to Stand Firm* (Lewiston, NY: Mellen Biblical, 1993), 20-22; John Marshall, "Paul's Ethical Appeal in Philippians," in *Rhetoric and the New Testament: Essays from the 1992 Heidelberg Conference*, ed. Stanley E. Porter and Thomas H. Olbricht, JSNTSup 90 (Sheffield: JSOT Press, 1993), 357-74, esp. 363; L. Gregory Bloomquist, *The Function of Suffering in Philippians*, JSNTSup 78 (London: Shiffield Academic, 1992), 119-20; Ralph Brucker, *'Christushymnen' oder 'epideiktische Passagen'? Studien zum Stilwechsel im Neuen Testament und seiner Umwelt*, FRLANT 176 (Göttingen: Vandenhoeck & Ruprecht, 1997); Sandnes, *Belly and Body*, 139-41; Hansen, *Philippians*; Dean Flemming, *Philippians: A Commentary in the Wesleyan Tradition*, NBBC (Kansas City: Beacon Hill, 2009), 34; Watson, "The Three Species of Rhetoric," 28-29; Witherington, *Philippians*, 25.

15. See the earlier discussions in chapters 2 and 3 above.

16. Watson, "Rhetorical Analysis," 59.

in a manner worthy of the gospel of Christ." So, the question is: will you Philippians live in a manner worthy of the gospel of Christ or in some manner unworthy of Christ? To connect the question with the exigence discussed above, both the presence of pressure from outsiders and the presence and potential for increasing discord among insiders threaten the prospect for living in a way that reflects well on the gospel.[17] Paul's concern for the recipients' manner of life and behavior is what gives Philippians its future orientation. He is calling upon them to be further committed in the immediate and ongoing future to behavior that embodies the gospel in their life together. We will find that, for Paul, this is both expedient and a way of gaining honor, and living worthily of Christ in the face of suffering is advantageous because it ultimately leads to salvation (1:28–29). Paul portrays that salvation in terms of future bodily resurrection, which he understands as a way of gaining honor, as evidenced in his description of that expected event with the language of the Greco-Roman honor system (e.g., δόξα, 3:21). Throughout the letter Paul appeals to examples and draws comparisons to make his case for the gospel-worthy life: Paul's account of his own attitudes and behavior (1:12–26; 3:7–16), the well-known Christ story (2:5–11), and the commendation of Timothy and Epaphroditus (2:19–30) all function as examples to be followed. Our consideration of Paul's attitude toward embodiment and bodily resurrection will focus particularly on Paul's own example and the example of Christ. These features together give the letter its overall deliberative character.

After the epistolary opening (1:1–2) and the *exordium* (1:3–11), the *narratio* (1:12–26) focuses on the fruitfulness of his suffering. This paves the way for the *propositio* in 1:27–30, calling upon the recipients to live worthily of the gospel. The *probatio* then follows in 2:1–3:4 and is divided into three proofs. The initial proof calls upon the Philippians to follow the example of Christ (2:1–30).[18] The second proof follows in 3:1–4:1 and is

---

17. So Witherington: "But he is also asking them to strengthen their unity, to continue living lives worthy of the gospel, and to prepare for and deal with both internal and external problems" (*Philippians*, 97).

18. Witherington (*Philippians*, 169) identifies the end of the first appeal at 2:18 before the introduction of Timothy and Epaphroditus in 2:19–30, which he takes as the second appeal. I have included these verses in the first appeal because they function to further exemplify the same character commanded in 2:1–4 (i.e., other-oriented concern, humility) and exemplified by the self-emptying of Christ in 2:5–8. Alternatively, Watson ("Rhetorical Analysis," 60) takes 2:19–30 as a *digressio*, as does Jean-Baptiste Edart, who further classifies the passage as "discours de visite." See

characterized by rhetorical comparisons that we will look at more closely below. The third proof is an explicit appeal to resolve conflict (4:2-3).[19] The argument concludes with a *peroratio* in 4:4-9 and an *insinuatio* in 4:10-20 before the letter closes with final greetings and a benediction (4:21-23).[20] The key passages for Paul's attitude toward the body come in the *narratio* of 1:12-26 (esp. 1:20-22) and in the second proof of the *probatio* in 3:1-4:1 (esp. 3:10-11, 21). Given the priority of Paul's attitude toward bodily resurrection in this study, I begin with the material in Phil 3 in which the apostle sets forth his vision of resurrection before I work through the material related to behavior and its relationship to resurrection.

4.4. Bodily Resurrection in Philippians

Paul's hope for bodily resurrection emerges explicitly in Phil 3:10-11: τοῦ γνῶναι αὐτὸν καὶ τὴν δύναμιν τῆς ἀναστάσεως αὐτοῦ καὶ [τὴν] κοινωνίαν [τῶν] παθημάτων αὐτοῦ, συμμορφιζόμενος τῷ θανάτῳ αὐτοῦ, εἴ πως καταντήσω εἰς τὴν ἐξανάστασιν τὴν ἐκ νεκρῶν. These verses follow Paul's narrative account of his life as a Pharisee in 3:4-8, a subject to which we will return below when we consider the social function of Paul's own example. In that discussion Paul attributed surpassing value to knowing Christ (τὸ ὑπερέχον τῆς γνώσεως Χριστοῦ Ἰησοῦ, 3:8), and he reiterates that desire to know Christ and develops his meaning in 3:10-11. It is possible that the articular infinitive could be seen as taking three objects: (1) αὐτόν, (2) τὴν δύναμιν τῆς ἀναστάσεως αὐτοῦ, and (3) κοινωνίαν παθημάτων αὐτοῦ. More likely, however, is that the initial καί functions epexegetically and indicates Paul's intent to explain knowing Christ in terms both of experiencing the power

---

Edart, *L'Épître aux Philippiens: Rhétorique et Composition Stylistique* (Paris: Gabalda, 2002), 201-3.

19. Watson includes 4:2-3 in the *peroratio* ("Rhetorical Analysis," 76-77). However, Paul is not simply recapitulating issues from earlier in the letter; he is giving instructions with regard to divisive attitudes among some of the local leadership, which is an appeal in itself; see further Witherington, *Philippians*, 234.

20. In his earlier work on Philippians, Witherington identified the *peroratio* as 4:4-20; see Ben Witherington, *Friendship and Finances in Philippi: The Letter of Paul to the Philippians*, New Testament in Context (Valley Forge, PA: Trinity Press International, 1994), 19. More recently, however, he has argued that the *peroratio* is limited to 4:4-9 and that 4:10-20 is an additional argument in the form of *insinuatio* to deal with the more problematic issue of the Philippians financial gift to Paul; see Witherington, *Philippians*, 29-30.

of his resurrection and participation in his sufferings.[21] The bracketed articles are present in ℵ² D F G Ψ and 𝔐 but are absent from 𝔓⁴⁶ ℵ* and B. The shorter reading is earlier and more difficult and is thus preferred.[22] Since these two concepts of resurrection and suffering are controlled by the same article, they should be seen as two closely related aspects of the one experience of knowing Christ.[23] The order of ideas is counterintuitive. Why does Paul mention the resurrection of Christ first and then Christ's sufferings afterward?[24] Fee suggests two reasons: first, the verses that follow are largely concerned with the future, and the power of Christ's resurrection is crucial to believers living in a way that anticipates the future experience of resurrection; second, by putting resurrection in the place of emphasis, the suffering both of Paul and the Philippians is placed within a context that helps make sense of their persecution.[25] The chiastic structure of verses 10–11 strengthens the point:

A   τὴν δύναμιν **τῆς ἀναστάσεως** αὐτοῦ
   B   καὶ [τὴν] κοινωνίαν [τῶν] **παθημάτων** αὐτοῦ,
   B′ συμμορφιζόμενος **τῷ θανάτῳ** αὐτοῦ,
A′ εἴ πως καταντήσω εἰς **τὴν ἐξανάστασιν** τὴν ἐκ νεκρῶν

For Paul, it is the power of Christ's resurrection that enables perseverance through suffering; that suffering, therefore, is articulated within a context of resurrection power and hope.[26]

The meaning of "the power of his resurrection" has been contested. The phrase τὴν δύναμιν τῆς ἀναστάσεως αὐτοῦ could be taken as a genitive of source or origin, which would then be translated "the power which emanates (or proceeds from) his resurrection."[27] In this view, the power is that which the resurrected Christ himself exercises toward believers. Joseph A. Fitzmyer argues, however, that this view wrongly locates the source of

---

21. Hansen, *Philippians*, 243.
22. Fee, *Philippians*, 328.
23. Cf. Fee, *Philippians*, 331.
24. Dunn, *Theology of Paul*, 487.
25. Fee, *God's Empowering Presence*, 330.
26. So Flemming: "Paul's participation in Christ's sufferings and death is surrounded by the reality of Christ's resurrection and his experience of it" (*Philippians*, 174).
27. Harris, *Raised Immortal*, 97, 104.

this power in Christ when it should be located in God: "It emanates from the Father, raises Jesus from the dead at his resurrection, endows him with a new vitality, and finally proceeds from him as the life-giving, vitalizing force of the 'new creation' and of the new life that Christians in union with Christ experience and live."[28] The power that Paul desires to know, then, is the power of God that raised Christ from the dead and which is at work in believers in the midst of suffering. This power enables him to embody Christlike perseverance through suffering and even death in order to attain the resurrection of the body.[29]

Given the strength of Paul's hope in the power of God to raise the dead, the apparent contingency in verse 11 with regard to Paul's own participation in the future resurrection has been perceived by some as somewhat surprising. The language in question is εἴ πως καταντήσω εἰς τὴν ἐξανάστασιν τὴν ἐκ νεκρῶν ("if somehow I may attain the resurrection from the dead"). Fee makes the point in striking fashion, "But how he says it is especially puzzling ... why he should begin the sentence with 'if somehow,' which might seem to imply doubt."[30] Fee attempts to solve the puzzle by suggesting that what is uncertain is whether Paul will be resurrected or transformed (cf. 3:20–21).[31] We should remember, however, that Paul raises the possibility in 1 Cor 9:27 that he might be "disqualified" even after having preached the gospel, and in Rom 11:17–22 he warns his gentile recipients about the possibility that God might cut them off for unbelief even though they presently stand by faith. In light of passages like these it may be more accurate to say that resurrection is a certain hope for Christ-followers *who persevere*, a framework within which the sense of contingency in Phil 3:11 fits perfectly.[32]

The already/not yet tension that commonly characterizes Paul's thought is here evident,[33] and it is perhaps even highlighted by the sense of contingency. The resurrection of the body remains a fully future event,

---

28. Joseph A Fitzmyer, "'To Know Him and the Power of His Resurrection' (Phil 3:10)," in *Mélanges bibliques en hommage au R P Béda Rigaux*, ed. A. Descamps and A. de Halleux (Gembloux: Duculot, 1970), 20; cf. Flemming, *Philippians*, 174. Cf. Rom 1:4; 8:11; 1 Cor 6:14; 2 Cor 13:4; Col 2:12; Eph 1:19–20.

29. See Dunn, *Theology of Paul*, 487.

30. Fee, *Philippians*, 335.

31. Fee, *Philippians*, 335–36.

32. Flemming, *Philippians*, 176; Witherington, *Philippians*, 208.

33. Fee, *Philippians*, 332; cf. Wright, *Resurrection*, 235.

and individual participation in it is not yet guaranteed. Nevertheless, as Wright puts it, "Paul believes that God's power, unleashed in Jesus' resurrection and awaiting its full unveiling when Jesus returns, is already available through the gospel for those who believe."[34] Though he experiences the power of Christ's resurrection as he participates in Christ's sufferings, Paul still awaits the final realization of bodily resurrection.[35] Indeed, as indicated above, it is likely that Paul thinks of his present perseverance in suffering as enabled and empowered through "the power of his resurrection."[36] The present/future tension is further apparent in 3:12, where Paul emphatically insists that he has not yet obtained the resurrection. Nevertheless, his life in the present is shaped and driven by desire that manifests in striving to make Christ his own (3:12–14). This is the prize for which he strains.

Especially significant for our study is the place of the body in the midst of the tension. As with Christ, Paul's body is the locus of his suffering. This is explicit in Phil 1:20 (see below); he wants Christ to "be exalted in my body, whether through life or through death." It is Paul's body that is imprisoned (1:7, 14, 17). It his body that awaits trial. If he speaks with all boldness, he will do so with his body (1:20). If he lives, he does so ἐν σαρκί (1:22), and if he dies, he looks forward to attaining the resurrection of the body (3:11). The resurrection is *not yet* realized in Paul's body, still he strives to live as one in whom the power of Christ's resurrection is *already* on display in his bodily life.[37]

If Paul's hope for resurrection has not yet been realized, he anticipates that it will be when Christ returns from heaven (3:20–21). When this happens, Paul expects his body to be transformed, and he describes that transformation (μετασχηματίζω) of the body (σῶμα) from a state characterized by lowliness or humility (ταπείνωσις) to a state of glory (δόξα).[38] The apostle's description of somatic transformation leaves little doubt that

---

34. Wright, *Resurrection*, 234–35.
35. Lincoln, *Paradise*, 92.
36. See Dunn, *Theology of Paul*, 486–87.
37. See Sandnes: "Body and bodily behavior mattered to Paul since participation in Christ was expressed in bodily terms" (*Belly and Body*, 162).
38. Cf. Fee: "The genitive (ταπεινώσεως) is not descriptive (as the NIV, 'lowly'), but expresses 'belonging.' The 'our' and 'his' in both cases go with 'humiliation' and 'glory' respectively, not with 'body.' Thus it is not 'our lowly bodies,' but 'the body that belongs to our humiliation,' or that 'belongs to his 'glory.' Thus, the body itself is not 'lowly' but is the locus of present suffering and weakness, hence 'the body of our pres-

he, once again, has the resurrection of the body in mind.³⁹ Again, Paul's thinking exhibits characteristics of inaugurated eschatology. Believers are those who are presently able to say "our commonwealth is in heaven" (ἡμῶν γὰρ τὸ πολίτευμα ἐν οὐρανοῖς ὑπάρχει, 3:20).⁴⁰ Lincoln argues that πολίτευμα here means "state" or "commonwealth" and that the specific role of "the state as constitutive force regulating its citizens" should be kept in mind.⁴¹ It is the heavenly state, where the resurrected Christ is, that governs the behavior of its citizens. Believers are already citizens of the heavenly commonwealth, even if it is not fully and finally manifest, and that commonwealth regulates their lives in the present. This is the implication of Paul's use of the cognate πολιτεύεσθε in the *propositio* of 1:27, which is the only time that verb is used in Paul's letters. The fact that believers are citizens of the heavenly commonwealth means their lives are to be ordered by that reality, even though it is not yet fully visible.⁴² One way it will become manifest is through the resurrection of the body. When Christ comes from the heavenly commonwealth, believers will undergo bodily transformation from humility to glory, and at that time their citizenship will be fully realized. Until then, however, they must use their bodies in ways that accord with the state to which they belong, not least, as we saw above, with regard to cultivating unity among themselves and standing firm in the face of opposition (cf. 1:27-30).

It should be clear that the implications of Paul's inaugurated eschatology for his behavioral expectations are significant. In fact, scholarly treatments of Pauline ethics often take the already/not yet tension of the apostle's eschatology as the major framework for understanding his expectations for the behavior of believers, and rightly so. For Paul, the embodied

---

ent humiliation' in contrast to the body that shall be ours 'in glory' (*Philippians*, 283 n. 28).

39. See Wright, *Resurrection*, 229-36.

40. For the semantic range of πολίτευμα, see Lincoln, *Paradise*, 97-99.

41. Lincoln, *Paradise*, 99; cf. Markus Bockmuehl, *The Epistle to the Philippians*, BNTC (Peabody, MA: Hendrickson, 1998), 235; Flemming, *Philippians*, 199-200. For the view that Paul's use of πολίτευμα is intended to subvert the authority of the emperor, see Wright, 231-32; cf. Witherington: "Paul then is saying that the Christian's commonwealth and ruling principles and constitutive government come from Christ who is reigning from heaven, not the Emperor who is ruling from Rome" (*Philippians*, 217).

42. See Lincoln, *Paradise*, 101.

life of the future is anticipated in the bodily behavior of the present.[43] This study has aimed throughout to draw on the insights of SIT to consider how the eschatological dimension of Paul's ethical reasoning in general, and resurrection in particular, might have impacted his recipients cognitively and emotionally and how that impact might relate to their self-perception as members of Christ-following communities.

4.5. Future Social Identity and the Rhetoric of Contrast

Paul's description of the anticipated resurrection comes at the end of a rhetorical *synkrisis* in which he contrasts Christ-followers, who await the resurrection, with those he describes as "enemies of the cross of Christ, whose end is destruction" (τοὺς ἐχθροὺς τοῦ σταυροῦ τοῦ Χριστοῦ, ὧν τὸ τέλος ἀπώλεια, 3:18–19). Hermogenes defined *synkrisis* as "a comparison of similar or dissimilar things, or of lesser things to greater or greater things to lesser" (*Prog.* 8; cf. Aelius Theon, *Prog.* 10).[44] Rhetorical students in the classical period were taught to draw on a variety of topics when composing such a contrast, including but not limited to city and family of origin, nurture, deeds, pursuits, manner of death, and what follows death. The *synkrisis* that comprises Phil 3:17–21 is not a movement from lesser to greater but a comparison that highlights the differences between the two groups by setting the positive attributes of the Philippians and Paul against the negative qualities of the opponents.[45] This contrast is marked throughout by strong "us" versus "them" language that functions to amplify the differences between the ingroup and outgroup. No little scholarship has been written debating the possible identity of these opponents.[46] But lack of certainty with regard to their specific identity is not a major hindrance to this analysis since we are most interested in Paul's construal of the outgroup *relative to the in-group* and what light that construal might shed on

---

43. See Schrage: "we repeatedly find attempts to frame the ethical conduct of the community according to God's future and to anticipate this future in the present" (*Ethics of the New Testament*, 181, cf. 72–74); Hays, *Moral Vision*, 19–27; cf. Dunn, *Theology of Paul*, 461–72, 673.

44. All citations of the *progymnasmata* refer to the edition translated and produced by George A. Kennedy, *Progymnasmata: Greek Textbooks of Prose and Composition*. For Quintilian on *synkrisis*, see *Inst.* 2.4.21.

45. Witherington, *Philippians*, 191.

46. For a survey of proposals regarding the identity of the opponents in Philippians, see Fee, *Philippians*, 7–10.

the persuasive and identity-forming functions of the letter. Paul's positive portrayal of himself and the Philippians focuses on their heavenly citizenship and the expectation that Christ will return and endow them with glorious bodies. In contrast, he writes about the opponents whom he calls "enemies of the cross of Christ" (3:18).[47] That they are said to be "walking" (περιπατέω, 3:18) as "enemies of the cross" suggests that the critique is focused on their actions, deeds, or pursuits.[48] Paul's negative portrayal of the opponents comes in four compact and sharp statements: "whose end is destruction" (ὧν τὸ τέλος ἀπώλεια), "whose God is the belly" (ὧν ὁ θεὸς ἡ κοιλία), "who glory in their shame" (καὶ ἡ δόξα ἐν τῇ αἰσχύνῃ αὐτῶν), and "who think earthly things" (οἱ τὰ ἐπίγεια φρονοῦντες) (3:19).

The first description should be taken as a reference to eschatological destruction.[49] The wordplay between Paul's self-description as τέλειος in 3:15 and τέλος here serves to highlight the stark contrast between the in-group and the out-group. We might expect this comment to come last, but Paul mentions it first perhaps with a view to shocking the recipients.[50] The eschatological destiny of destruction stands in direct contrast with the Pauline hope for future bodily resurrection, which he has already articulated in 3:10–11 and will again in 3:21. By putting his prediction of the opponents' destruction at the top of the list, Paul has woven eschatology into the fabric of the *synkrisis*. More than its shock value, what follows substantiates his expectation of the future with regard to the fate of the opponents.

Paul's reference to the belly (κοιλία) in 3:19 is significant for this study given that the belly is an organ of the body (cf. Rom 16:8). Several propos-

---

47. Difficulty in identifying these opponents stems from the way Paul describes them. On the one hand, he "weeps" (κλαίω, 3:18) as he tells of them, which would seem to indicate that they are part of a group of Christ-followers. On the other hand, his insistence that their "end is destruction" seems to put them outside the bounds of the Christ-following community. Fee makes sense of this by saying, "They probably consider themselves to be within the household of faith, and most likely are, or were, but whom Paul now assigns to a place outside Christ, precisely because they have abandoned Christ by adopting a lifestyle that is totally opposed to the redemptive work of the cross" (*Philippians*, 371).

48. Stephen E. Fowl, *Philippians*, Two Horizons New Testament Commentary (Grand Rapids: Eerdmans, 2005), 170. Cf. Witherington: "The issue here is probably praxis, but it is a praxis grounded in theology" (*Philippians*, 215).

49. Lincoln, *Paradise*, 95; cf. Fee, *Philippians*, 370–71.

50. Bockmuehl, *Epistle to the Philippians*, 230; cf. Flemming, *Philippians*, 198.

als have been made with regard to the meaning of κοιλία. For one, the term has been taken as a reference to Jewish food laws.[51] From this perspective, the opponents are either Jews or Jewish Christ-followers who insist on strict observance of food laws. This view was held by several early church authors and is appealing because it aligns the opponents in 3:18–19 with those in 3:2.[52] However, as Markus Bockmuehl notes, Paul never aligns observance of Jewish dietary laws with idolatry.[53] Further, Sandnes has shown that when Jewish authors did use the language of belly-worship, it was often applied to those who neglected the food laws in order to obey foreign kings. That is to say, the language of belly-worship was appropriated in just the opposite manner from what is proposed by advocates of this view.[54] Second, the argument is made that Paul is here using κοιλία in a way analogous to his use of σάρξ as a description of earthly minded humanity in contrast to humanity in Christ.[55] Third, it could refer to an attitude of libertinism with regard to food and sex and, by extension, function as a metaphor for selfishness. This interpretation has wide support in Greco-Roman and Jewish literature.[56] Additionally, following Sandnes, the larger context has to do with the body and its resurrection (3:10–11, 21). If the bodies of believers are to be transformed to the body of Christ's glory, it makes sense that Paul would set that somatic glorification in contrast to a physical idolatrous stomach. In 3:14, Paul used the image of a runner racing for the finish line (σκοπός) to describe his manner of striving for knowing Christ in his death and resurrection. Again, it should not surprise us that he would set the disciplined body of the athlete in contrast to the libertinistic bodily practices of those who worship the belly. Taken in this light, the rhetorical contrast develops the previous description of eschatological destruction in terms of the present use of the body. Those who, like Paul, have the mind of Christ will use their bodies as Christ did, namely in sacrificial obedience to God (cf. Phil 2:8). And having shared in

---

51. Gerald F. Hawthorne and Ralph P. Martin, *Philippians*, rev. ed., WBC 43 (Nashville: Nelson, 2004), 224.
52. Hawthorne and Martin list Theodore of Mopsuestia, Ambrosiaster, and Pelagius (*Philippians*, 224). Fee adds Hilary, Augustine, Theodoret, and Bengel (*Philippians*, 372 n. 39).
53. Bockmuehl, *Epistle to the Philippians*, 231.
54. Sandnes, *Belly and Body*, 145–46.
55. Lincoln, *Paradise*, 96.
56. Sandnes, *Belly and Body*, 145–46.

the sufferings of Christ, they will also share in his resurrection. Alternatively, those who worship the body in general and the belly in particular, as manifest in a libertine lifestyle, demonstrate their self-oriented idolatry which ends in eschatological destruction. The contrast turns on the body. To quote Sandnes, "The body is here a distinctive mark; it is either an instrument in worshipping Christ, or it is itself turned into the object of worship; i.e., the idolatrous body."[57] For Paul and the Philippians, the body is used to glorify Christ; for the opponents, it has become an instrument of self-worship.[58]

This brings us to the third descriptor of the opponents: ἡ δόξα ἐν τῇ αἰσχύνῃ αὐτῶν. αἰσχύνη can refer to a range of disgraceful and excessive behaviors, sexual libertinism not least.[59] Paul's use of δόξα contrasts with the glory of the body of Christ to which believers will be conformed (3:21). Most scholars take it here to mean "boast" or "pride."[60] Understood this way, this descriptor continues to develop the existing contrast. Not only do the opponents worship the belly by engaging in self-oriented libertine practices, they boast and take pride in it. This stands in sharp contrast with the glory of the resurrection to which believers look forward, which depends on embodying the other-oriented and self-sacrificing mind of Christ.

The fourth and final descriptor contrasts with Paul's language of heaven in 3:20. The opponents are governed by an earthly mindset (οἱ τὰ ἐπίγεια φρονοῦντες) while Paul and other believers are governed by the heavenly πολίτευμα. Sandnes helpfully relates this contrast to the earlier suggestion that belly-worship is a metaphor for libertine bodily practices. He writes:

> There is a hidden agenda in Paul's use of the belly-*topos* here. Believers who seek their own ends, and who are unprepared to undertake a self-abnegating life according to the pattern set by Christ, have neglected their heavenly citizenship. What is true for the earthly city, goes for the heavenly *politeuma* as well; belly-devotion is a neglect of the duties of a citizen and is incompatible with true citizenship.... Since they are not prepared for a self-sacrificial life, even to death, they are not members of the heavenly *politeuma*.... Paul warns his readers against self-love, which

---

57. Sandnes, *Belly and Body*, 160.
58. Sandnes, *Belly and Body*, 164.
59. Cf. Hansen, *Philippians*, 266.
60. See, e.g., Hansen, *Philippians*, 266.

makes them unfit both for a life according to the cross of Christ, and for the final restoration of the body.[61]

The inescapable reality of bodily practice runs throughout Paul's contrast between believers and the opponents. For Paul, what is done in the body has significant implications for the future, whether for good or ill. One will either embody the mind of Christ and have hope of resurrection, or one will worship the belly and have destruction as one's destiny.

As we shall see in a moment, the contrasting anticipated futures articulated by Paul serve to define the in-group in contrast to the out-group and thus play a role in the formation of group identity. We should not overlook the role of emotion in the identity-forming process. Paul contributes the affective element by telling the Philippians of his own tears and builds on that with strikingly graphic images filled with emotional overtones: enemies of the cross, eschatological destruction, idolatrous self-worship, and earthly mindedness. Shared experiences tend to strengthen in-group solidarity. In this case, the shared experience of suffering infused with resurrection-oriented hope in contrast to a sense of sorrow or pity for the anticipated destruction of the outgroup adds an additional affective element that further defines each group and the boundary between them. Paul's language of destruction could even evoke an experience of fear if the recipients took his argument to imply they would share the destiny of the out-group if they fail to persevere through their experience of suffering. These affective elements should not be understood as an alternative strategy to logical proofs or rational argumentation. Instead, emotionality is an integral aspect of Paul's rhetoric that is woven into the persuasive form, in this case the rhetoric of contrast.[62] This combination of rational and emotional features serves to strengthen the persuasive effect of Paul's arguments, making it difficult to imagine a stronger contrast.[63]

Reading Paul's rhetoric through the lens of SIT allows us to observe that the *synkrisis* involves two very different future possible social identities, namely, destruction for the opponents and bodily resurrection for Paul and the Philippians. If, as Cinnirella hypothesizes, individuals attempt

---

61. Sandnes, *Belly and Body*, 151.
62. For the social function of emotions, see Barton, "Eschatology and Emotions," 571–91. To the present point, see his remark, "Reason and emotion are not mutually exclusive but interpenetrate each other" (589).
63. Witherington, *Philippians*, 216.

to attain positively valued social identities and avoid negatively valued social identities, then the identity forming function of the *synkrisis* turns especially on the positive evaluation of the future of the in-group and the negative evaluation of the future of the out-group. Paul's positive portrayal of the in-group as having a future social identity marked by resurrection in Christ draws on the language of the Greco-Roman honor system. The resurrection body is described as transformation to "the body of [Christ's] glory" (τῷ σώματι τῆς δόξης αὐτοῦ, 3:21, emphasis added). For the outgroup, whose τέλος is destruction, glory language is redirected toward shame. If Paul's contrast were taken by the recipients to suggest that failure to persevere on their part meant becoming endowed with shame, then his rhetoric has potential to be even more effective. In the world of Paul and his hearers, public shame was the most effective form of penalizing nonconformity to social norms. Consider Cicero's recognition of the usefulness of shame for maintaining public order:

> Nor indeed are they deterred from crime so much by the fear of the penalties ordained by law as by the sense of shame which Nature has given to man in the form of a certain fear of justified censure. The governing statesman strengthens this feeling in commonwealths by the force of public opinion and perfects it by the inculcation of principles and by systematic training, so that shame deters the citizens from crime no less effectively than fear.[64] (*Rep.* 5.6. [Keyes])

Paul's rhetoric would have likely evoked strong affective responses from the recipients inviting them to embrace one another as a means of attaining Paul's vision of their future and avoiding an alternative future characterized by the most distasteful experience of the ancient world. Future bodily resurrection is thus portrayed in Philippians as a way of receiving glory and honor while avoiding shame, which was an emotion particularly despised.

That Paul associates the outgroup with shame highlights the importance of honor for our analysis of the letter to the Christ-followers in Philippi, where some have argued that concern for public honor was exceptional in comparison to the larger empire. This is the conclusion reached by Peter Pilhofer in his study of epigraphical evidence from Philippi. In

---

64. See further Carlin A. Barton, "The Roman Blush: The Delicate Matter of Self-Control," in *Constructions of the Classical Body*, ed. James I. Porter, The Body in Theory (Ann Arbor: University of Michigan Press, 2002), 212–34, esp. 213–14.

particular, he cites the many inscriptions that identify the accomplishments of military personnel. Noting that military service creates a context in which the display of honor-meriting accomplishments is particularly suitable, he infers that the colony exhibits intense desire to showcase honorific achievements: "I take it as an indication that somone in Philippi was *particularly proud* to display his positions and posts."[65] Joseph Hellerman has further shown that this deep concern for honor ran through every level of social life in Philippi, not only among the elite but among the nonelite as well, as evidenced in numerous inscriptions of voluntary associations and cult groups. Hellerman notes that nonelite groups throughout the empire tended to replicate movement up the ladder of honor in their own contexts. Nevertheless, extensive evidence from Philippi indicates the pervasive nature of honorifics among social classes from top to bottom.[66] Given the importance of attaining honor in Mediterranean culture in general and in Philippi in particular, Paul's strategy of appealing to future resurrection as a way of receiving honor carried significant potential for maintaining a salient desired social identity perceived in terms of bodily resurrection. Add to this that honor was considered one of the main heads of advisory speeches, and the apparent strength of Paul's rhetoric becomes even more potent.[67] Here we see the mutual benefit of reading the text through the dual lens of rhetorical criticism and SIT. Scholars who read Philippians alongside the ancient oratorical handbooks recognize that the strong language of Paul's contrast throughout chapter 3 functions to draw the audience to replicate the behavior of the positive example and distance themselves from the behavior of the negative example.[68] SIT not only confirms this conclusion while employing a different methodology, it also draws our attention to the complex dynamic between group identity and individual behavior. Paul's rhetoric is not merely argument aimed at

---

65. Peter Pilhofer, *Die erste christliche Gemeinde Europas*, vol. 1 of *Philippi*, WUNT 87 (Tübingen: Mohr Siebeck, 1995), 142, my translation, emphasis original.

66. Hellerman, *Reconstructing Honor*, 88–109. See his comment: "Surviving examples of these 'outward tokens of high achievement' as Dio calls them, about in and around Philippi to a degree unparalleled elsewhere in the eastern empire" (89).

67. See Demosthenes, who appeals to the council at Athens to maintain political harmony on the basis of gaining honor not only for themselves but for all Greeks: "the present occasion, if you but chose the right course, is capable of securing for you at one stroke glory [δόξα] and salvation [σωτηρία] and freedom [ἐλευθερία]" (*Ep.* 1.2).

68. Witherington, *Philippians*, 193; cf. Carolyn Osiek, *Philippians, Philemon*, ANTC (Nashville: Abingdon, 2000), 83.

individuals; it functions in a way that strengthens group identity in which certain behaviors are both sensible, desirable, and expedient.

The function of contrasting future social identities between believers and those destined for destruction is developed with Paul's use of the language of common life as citizens in 3:20. If πολίτευμα refers to state or commonwealth, as argued above, then it also functions as part of a believer's web of social identities. If the state governs their identity, then it means they should act in a way that coheres with their civic identity. For the typical person in the city of Philippi, their πολίτευμα was Rome. Their relationship to that city and the emperor who reigned there determined their manner of life. But by attaching positive value to bodily resurrection which happens when Christ arrives from the heavenly commonwealth, Paul's rhetoric paves the way for identity salience to transfer from the Roman πολίτευμα to the heavenly one.[69] The effect would be to increase social cohesion among the Philippian believers, strengthening their potential in the present to remain unified against opposition as they await the future glory of bodily resurrection.

The strong contrast in Phil 3 between the in-group and out-group that incorporates the anticipated future of the distinct groups is to be expected. As Hogg and Abrams point out, social comparisons between an in-group and out-group have "a tendency to maximize intergroup distinctiveness—to differentiate between groups as much as possible."[70] In the case of the Letter to the Philippians, Paul's intergroup distinction depends on his vision of the future, and the apostle's language of eschatological somatic transformation functions to strengthen the positive distinctiveness of the Philippians' Christ-oriented identity relative to the anticipated future destruction of the out-group and carries the potential to endow the Philippians with a sense of honor.[71] By portraying resurrection as means of receiving glory and honor in contrast to the shameful behavior and coming destruction of the opponents, Paul has constructed an argument that reflects classical rhetorical convention and which would appeal to the deeply held cultural convictions of his Philippian audience in a way that is likely to strengthen in-group cohesion.

---

69. See Wright, *Paul and the Faithfulness of God*, 1292–93.
70. Hogg and Abrams, *Social Identifications*, 23.
71. Hogg and Abrams, *Social Identifications*, 23; cf. Michael A. Hogg et al., "Social Categorization, Intergroup Behavior and Self-Esteem: Two Experiments," *Revista de Psicología Social* 1 (1986): 23–37.

Following our temporal model and given that resurrection is a desired possible future social identity for Paul, we should also expect him to construe the past and present to cohere with his vision of the future. To explore that dynamic, we turn now to Paul's use of two examples, that of Christ and that of himself. We will begin with the example of Christ in Phil 2 and return to Phil 3 later in order to consider Paul's use of himself as an example.

4.6. Bodies, Identity, and the Rhetoric of Example

Examples in deliberative rhetoric typically had a mimetic function. They were designed to draw on the past in order to provide a reliable model on which the audience may pattern future thinking and behaving (Aristotle, *Rhet.* 1.9.40). Appeal was often made to a person that the audience held in esteem; as Aristotle recognized, people tend to deliberately do what those they admire have chosen to do (*Rhet.* 1.6.29). Of course, the presence of example does not in itself demonstrate that Philippians is deliberative; examples appear in many different types of literary works. Nevertheless, among the three species of classical rhetoric, deliberative speeches intentionally employed examples as proofs.[72] In Philippians, the example of Christ and the example of Paul function to substantiate the *propositio* that calls upon the recipients to embody a gospel-worthy life. Both examples turn on the role of suffering as it relates to living worthily of the gospel. One difference is that Christ's sufferings culminated in his death, while the outcome for Paul remained to be seen, even though he expressed commitment to imitate Christ in death. As we proceed, it will become increasingly clear that the rhetorical value of the double example—Christ and Paul—is significant. Christ is the highest example of one who embodies the life to which the Philippians are called, and Paul is their friend and coworker in mission. Even if Paul's own ability to function as an example of the gospel-worthy life depends on the extent to which he embodies the character of Christ, this is a potent combination.

Social identity theorists recognize that continuity between stories about figures from the group's past and the anticipated future of the group function to cultivate a coherent representation of ingroup identity, which in turn strengthens the persuasive appeal of the argument being made.

---

72. Mitchell, *Rhetoric of Reconciliation*, 42.

In this section, we will consider the way Paul portrays the Christ story to stand in temporal continuity with his hope for bodily resurrection. I will argue that the Christ story in Phil 2:5–11 functions as a "life story" that ties together the group's past with Paul's anticipated future. Then we will look at Paul's use of his own example as one who has in the past and continues in the present to think and live according to that vision of the future.

4.6.1. The Resurrection of Christ as Life Story

The story of Christ's self-emptying and exaltation in Phil 2:6–11 has been the subject of extensive scholarly analysis.[73] Our interest in Paul's persuasive purposes in and the social impact of Philippians will focus on the social function of Christ's role as an example for the gospel-worthy life. That Paul intends the story of Christ's suffering and exaltation as exemplary for the Philippians is plain enough in 2:5, "Have this disposition in you, which was also in Christ Jesus." This paraenetic verse implies a comparison between the behavior of Jesus and the behavior Paul expects from the Philippians. To live worthily of the gospel of Christ by persevering through persecution is to embody the disposition of the one who "was obedient to the point of death, even death on a cross" (2:8). σῶμα, of course, does not appear in this passage; nevertheless, the focus is on what Christ did, having taken a human body. This is doubly emphasized in Phil 2:7, "being born in the likeness of a human being, and being found in human form" (ἐν ὁμοιώματι ἀνθρώπων γενόμενος· καὶ σχήματι εὑρεθεὶς ὡς ἄνθρωπος). The repetition of ἄνθρωπος highlights the entrance and participation of Christ into full human life, which necessarily implies embodiment.

In classical rhetoric, the device used to praise a person's virtues or greatness was known as *encomion*. The progymnasmata instructed students of

---

73. For a discussion of Phil 2:6–11 in recent scholarship, see Witherington, *Philippians*, 132–36. For reasons that will become clear below, I refer to Phil 2:6–11 as a story even though it is commonly referred to as a hymn. For a discussion of the literary form of this passage, see Hansen, *Philippians*, 122–27. While a majority of scholars refer to this passage as a hymn, Stephen Fowl has argued that identifying 2:5–11 as a hymn is often imprecise; see his *The Story of Christ in the Ethics of Paul*, JSNTSup 36 (Sheffield: JSOT Press, 1990), 49–102; cf. Fowl, *Philippians*, 108–13. Fee also raises questions as to whether the passage is rightly understood as a hymn, insisting that the narrative character of passage should not be overlooked; see *Philippians*, 192–97. Cf. Ralph P. Martin and Brian J. Dodd, eds., *Where Christology Began: Essays on Philippians 2* (Louisville: Westminster John Knox, 1998).

rhetoric to employ *encomion* to praise national origin, family, marvelous occurrences at birth, nurture, the subject's character, the subject's pursuits, what sort of life was led, and manner of death and whether it might have been unusual (Hermogenes, *Progymnasmata* 7.15–16; cf. Aelius Theon, *Progymnasmata* 9.109). With its focus on Christ's equality with God (2:6), kenotic character (2:7), and humble obedience to the point of death (2:8), the Christ story in 2:6–11 reflects several of these concerns and comes to a crescendo of praise in verses 9–11 in describing exaltation of Jesus to the place of highest honor and cosmic authority. Paul's unrestrained praise of Christ could be considered epideictic (see Aristotle, *Rhet.* 1.33–34). It is, however, used for deliberative purposes in that Christ is being held out as an example for the Philippians to imitate.[74]

Given our interest in bodily resurrection, the careful reader may quickly raise questions about how this plays out with regard to the Christ story in Phil 2:6–11. After all, as others have noted, Paul tells the story of Christ's humiliation and exaltation, not of his resurrection.[75] The point has been made, however, that Paul's emphasis is on the fact of Jesus exaltation and not on the process by which he was exalted.[76] Additionally, the story Paul tells in 2:6–11 is clear that the exaltation of Jesus involves "transformation from the humiliation of death to the glory of resurrection."[77] So we are safe in saying that Jesus's resurrection is presupposed and implicit in the story of his exaltation in Phil 2:9–11.[78] In any case, we should not be tempted to think that Paul's language for imagining the resurrection is limited to the standard entries in the lexicon, nor that his strategy for speaking of resurrection is limited to the occurrences of the word itself. The point should not be missed: Paul's telling of the Christ story in 2:6–11

---

74. See Witherington, *Philippians*, 137.

75. So Wright: "With the famous passage 2.6–11 we meet a particular problem: that Paul here speaks, not of Jesus' death and resurrection, but of his death and *exaltation*" (*Resurrection*, 227). For the view that early Christ-followers did not distinguish between the resurrection and exaltation of Jesus, see James M. Robinson, "Jesus from Easter to Valentinus (or to the Apostles' Creed)," *JBL* 101 (1982): 5–37. For the view that Paul chose the language of exaltation instead of resurrection to subvert the emperor's claims to exalted lordship, see Wright, *Resurrection*, 227–28.

76. Bockmuehl, *Epistle to the Philippians*, 141.

77. Wright, *Resurrection*, 223.

78. So Fowl: "Although the resurrection is not explicitly mentioned in 2:9, it is clear that the power of the resurrection is the power that God displays in exalting the obedient crucified Christ" (*Philippians*, 155).

stands in temporal continuity with the vision of the group's future experience of bodily resurrection that he will set forth in 3:20–21.

Important for our purposes is the point that Paul tells the story of Jesus's resurrection in a way that emphasizes his attainment of unparalleled honor status. Indeed, the story is told not only to make the point that Jesus's death was overturned (i.e., that he was resurrected) but that his resurrection involved being endowed with honor. He is given the name above every name, a name at which every knee bows and every tongue confesses his lordship. What makes Christ's honor unique in the Roman world is the means by which he attained it. Public honor in the Roman Empire was achieved among the elite by ascending the well-defined ladder of offices of the *cursus honorum*, and Hellerman has argued that the Christ story is best understood against that background.[79] The portrayal of Christ as having highest honors conferred on him by God stands in direct contrast to the honor claims of the emperor, yet the thing that makes Christ thoroughly distinct from the emperor was his willing movement down a *cursus pudorum* set forth by Paul in Phil 2:6–8. Jesus willingly moves from equality with God to the status of a slave to the degradation of crucifixion.[80] So, Paul offers a positive evaluation of the risen Christ's unparalleled honor status, even if he rejects the imperial values to do it. The example set by Christ thus calls upon the Philippian Jesus community to reject the Roman honor system by placing the interests of one another and the community in the place of priority. This will likely result in continued opposition and suffering. Nevertheless, by following the example of Christ and living worthily of the gospel in the face of persecution, the Philippians stand to receive from God a share in the heavenly glory through their own future resurrection. By embodying the humility and suffering of Christ they are able to maintain hope of sharing in his resurrection and glory (cf. Phil 3:10–11).

I argued above that Paul's positive evaluation of a future resurrection-oriented social identity turns on the point that bodily resurrection is a way of receiving honor and glory. Thus, by construing the movement of Jesus from death to life in such a way as to emphasize the attaining of the highest possible honors, Paul has told the group's story in a way that creates a coherent representation that establishes temporal continuity between the

---

79. Hellerman, *Reconstructing Honor*.
80. Hellerman, *Reconstructing Honor*, 129–48, 162–63.

4.6.2. Paul's Body, Paul's Example

Paul's initial reflection in Philippians on embodied life is set in the context of the *narratio*, which spans the whole of 1:12–26, though his comments on the body begin explicitly in 1:20. In forensic speeches, the *narratio* was used to set forth the facts of the case on which judgment was to be pronounced (Quintilian, *Inst.* 4.2.1). In contrast, the future orientation of deliberative rhetoric did not necessitate a narration, though it was utilized often enough, as is the case in Philippians (Aristotle, *Rhet.* 3.16.1417b; Cicero, *Part. or.* 4.13).[81] When used in deliberative speeches, the *narratio* functioned to inform the hearer of circumstances relevant to the proposition under deliberation. In particular, the deliberative narration might be used to arouse or ease anger and to cultivate certain emotions in the audience like fear, desire, hatred, or pity. The *narratio* also provided the speaker an opportunity to establish goodwill with the audience and credibility as an authority on the proposition. In classical rhetorical theory, establishing the speaker's authority was considered a very important function of the deliberative narration (Quintilian, *Inst.* 3.8.11–13).

The events Paul narrates center on his suffering for Christ. He has been imprisoned, which might lead the Philippians to think that his missionary work had been halted. Somewhat counterintuitively, however, Paul reports that his imprisonment has actually functioned to advance the gospel into the ranks of the praetorian guard and to increase the evangelistic confidence of other believers (1:12–14).[82] The suffering associated with his imprisonment is compounded by certain rival preachers. Paul says little about them except that their preaching is motivated by envy (φθόνος, 1:14), rivalry (ἔρις, 1:14), and selfish ambition (ἐριθεία, 1:17). The events narrated thus set the stage for the *propositio* by highlighting antagonism

---

81. See Watson, "Rhetorical Analysis," 65; Witherington, *Philippians*, 71.

82. While Paul's use of πραιτώριον could refer to the emperor's palace, its barracks, or the permanent camp of praetorian soldiers, most scholars think it refers not to a place but to the group of men who make up the praetorian guard; see, e.g., Hansen, *Philippians*, 68–69.

from preachers from within the larger believing community and imperial persecution from without.

Two observations should be made with regard to the function of Paul's narration. First, that Paul highlights events similar to the situation in Philippi involving persecution and some level of discord has potential to increase the goodwill toward Paul among the Philippians. He identifies with their struggle. His account of his sufferings would likely arouse concern and pity on the part of the Philippians. The affective qualities of Paul's account of his circumstances function to create solidarity between author and recipients.[83] Second, Quintilian insisted that "the most important aspect of giving advice is the speaker's own authority. Anyone who wants everybody to trust his judgement on what is expedient and honorable must be, and be thought to be, both very wise and very good" (Quintilian, *Inst.* 3.8.13 [Russell]). Paul's commitment to honoring Christ in the midst of suffering for the sake of Christ establishes his credibility as an authority to call upon the Philippians to maintain unity and persevere through the suffering they were experiencing. As we shall see, Paul's focus on the similarity of his situation with that of the Philippians plays a key role in substantiating the proposition.

Before turning to the persuasive and social function of Paul's bodily suffering, we need to consider evidence that illumines Paul's attitude toward the body. The key language shows up in 1:20 with his expression of hope that, though he is suffering and faces the possibility of martyrdom, Christ will be exalted in his body (νῦν μεγαλυνθήσεται Χριστὸς ἐν τῷ σώματί μου). Paul's use of σῶμα in this instance is a matter of debate. Following Bultmann's holistic reading of Paul's anthropology, some have suggested that Paul here has in mind the whole person and not merely his physical self.[84] When it comes to commentary on Phil 1:20, however, the meaning of σῶμα is often assumed on the exegesis of other texts with little argumentation based on the context of Philippians. Gundry rejects the argument that σῶμα here refers to the self as a whole and argues instead that in this instance σῶμα describes physicality in distinction from conscious postmortem existence of the noncorporeal spirit in the

---

83. See Barton, "Eschatology and Emotions," 590.

84. Bultmann, *Theology of the New Testament*, 1:194; cf. Robinson, *The Body: A Study in Pauline Theology*, 29; Bockmuehl, *The Epistle to the Philippians*, 85; Hawthorne and Martin, *Philippians*, 53.

presence of Christ.⁸⁵ Several factors in the immediate context support this view.

First, Paul uses σῶμα to describe the sphere in which he hopes Christ will be magnified regardless of whether his trial results in life or death (εἴτε διὰ ζωῆς εἴτε διὰ θανάτου). Just as the magnification of Christ is something that happens in the sphere of Paul's bodily life, so also the outcome of the trial means that one of two things will happen with regard to Paul's σῶμα; it will remain alive or it will die. The key to Paul's meaning comes with the second option. Even if Paul's σῶμα dies at the hands of the Romans, he anticipates an experience of being in the presence of Christ. But this expectation of a better existence in which Paul is conscious of being in the presence of Christ follows after and may even require the death of the σῶμα. Thus, his expectation of subsequent entrance into the presence of Christ must, in Paul's thinking, be understood as a nonsomatic experience, and σῶμα must refer to Paul's physical body in distinction from his perception of himself in a noncorporeal state.⁸⁶ Second, in the immediate context Paul uses σῶμα interchangeably with σάρξ (1:22, 24; cf. 1 Cor 6:15–16). He develops the potential outcome of continued bodily life in terms of remaining in the flesh. Together, σῶμα and σάρξ stand in contrast to the possibility of departing to be with Christ. Once again, the strong suggestion is that Paul here thinks of σῶμα in decidedly physical terms and, in this instance, synonymous with σάρξ.⁸⁷

In light of these considerations, I agree with those who argue that Paul employs σῶμα in Phil 1:20 to refer to the physical body in distinction from a noncorporeal part of him that will exist in the presence of Christ. I should insist at the moment that this is not to downplay the importance of bodily existence for Paul or to suggest that the nonsomatic postmortem experience should be considered a full experience of human life.⁸⁸ It is not.

---

85. Gundry, *Sōma*, 37; Fee, *Philippians*, 137–38.

86. See Fee: Paul's "reason for using 'body' in this case has to do with the context; he is writing about what will happen to him 'physically,' that is, whether his trial will result in (physical) life or (bodily) death" (*Philippians*, 137–38).

87. Gundry, *Sōma*, 37.

88. So Gundry: "In the Biblical perspective, the physical body is just as essential to life which is life indeed as is the spirit.... The Biblical touchstone for truly human life is not consciousness of the spirit, let alone the material being of a physical object such as the body. Rather, man is fully himself in the unity of his body and spirit in order that the body may be animated and the spirit may express itself in obedience to God" (*Sōma*, 159–60).

Paul's rhetoric in 1:20 must be read together with 3:21, where he anticipates the resurrection of the body at the parousia. Human experience is not fully human experience unless it is embodied experience, but this does not mean that Paul does not envision the possibility of temporary noncorporeal experiences (cf., e.g., 2 Cor 12:2–3), and it must be remembered that such experiences are always seen in light of the future resurrection of the body. So, we find once again that Paul's anthropology is fundamentally holistic, even if it has room for nonbodily experiences like the intermediate state between the death of the body and its resurrection.[89]

It should be increasingly clear that Paul has used his narration of events to set forth a preliminary example of what embodied life lived worthily of the gospel looks like.[90] Paul's physical presence, his σῶμα, is the locus in which his desire to magnify Christ before the Roman tribunal is expressed. To pull back from proclaiming Christ with boldness in that setting in order to preserve his bodily life would mean shame for Paul (1:20). No amount of suffering, death included, would be worth the dishonor of betraying Christ to save himself. To the contrary, as John-Baptiste Edart recognizes, death is gain because it leads to closer union with Christ: "Death is desirable, not because it would be an escape from the pains and sufferings of this world, but because it allows one to be identified perfectly with Christ and to be united to him."[91] I agree with Edart to the extent that, for Paul, death means closer proximity to the presence of Christ. However, given what we have seen with regard to Paul's hope for resurrection, I would want to qualify that, for Paul, the climax of union with Christ and participation in his glory awaits the future resurrection of the body. Nevertheless, the point to be made here is that Paul's narration of his current situation establishes a comparison between his own attitude toward suffering and the attitude toward suffering he expects the Philippians to take and which is set forth in the *propositio* in the next section of the letter.[92] Paul

---

89. This is what John Cooper (*Body*) terms "holistic dualism."
90. Witherington, *Philippians*, 72.
91. Edart, *L'Épître aux Philippiens*, 99, my translation.
92. See Witherington: "Paul then is already in Phil. 1.12–26 through his narratio holding up for inspection once again the pattern of his life, recounting behavior under duress and house arrest … by displaying here his character and behavior as he is incarcerated and facing possible prosecution and execution, presents the audience with the most emotionally and rhetorically effective argument possible to persuade them to continue to live a life worthy of the gospel" (*Philippians*, 77–78).

himself embodies the gospel-worthy life because he is resolved to stand firm in faithfulness to Christ, even in suffering.[93] Likewise, the Philippians will live in a manner worthy of the gospel by remaining faithful in the face of the suffering inflicted on them by their opponents (Phil 1:27–28). It will be helpful to remember that, for Quintilian, comparison is at the heart of deliberation: "almost every advisory speech is nothing more than a comparison, and we need to consider what we shall gain, and by what means, so that an estimate can be made as to whether the advantage promised by our aim outweighs the disadvantage involved in the means we adopt to secure it" (Quintilian, *Inst.* 3.8.34 [Russell]). By following Paul's example, the Philippians do what is necessary to maintain the hope that they, like Paul, will gain Christ. The means by which Christ is gained is suffering like Christ for the sake of the gospel. By developing a comparison that highlights the similarity between Paul and the Philippians, the apostle fills his rhetoric with a powerful appeal to the audience's emotions. The courage and bravery that Paul embodies should arouse in the audience a desire to imitate him.

If we think about the way Paul tells his own story in terms of SIT, then we can say that his example provides a model in the present that coheres with the past as portrayed in the Christ narrative and which also coheres with the future vision of bodily resurrection. The future identity of the group is marked by the receipt of glory and honor through somatic transformation. The story of Christ's humility and exaltation to unparalleled honor stands in temporal continuity. Paul's example shows how life in the present can embody the humble suffering of Christ with a view to sharing in the glory that has been given to him. Past, present, and future, the Christian identity that emerges in Philippians is characterized by temporal coherence around the themes of movement from suffering to glory and bodily resurrection. That coherence increases the likelihood that a resurrection-oriented superordinate social identity may become salient among the Philippians.

To develop the point further, increased cohesion among the Philippians has implications for the exigence for which I argued above, that Paul is writing to strengthen the Philippians against external opposition and to

---

93. For Roman attitudes toward bodily pain and suffering, see Catherine Edwards, "The Suffering Body: Philosophy and Pain in Seneca's Letters," in *Constructions of the Classical Body*, ed. James I. Porter, The Body in Theory (Ann Arbor: University of Michigan Press, 2002), 253–68.

facilitate internal unity by guarding against factions within the group. This is precisely where Paul takes the letter after setting forth a resurrection-oriented future possible social identity which is a benefit to those who are members of the heavenly commonwealth. In 4:1, he instructs the recipients to "stand firm in the Lord" (στήκετε ἐν κυρίῳ). The verse begins with ὥστε, an inferential particle which indicates that Paul is here drawing a conclusion from what he has just said. The imperative στήκετε is a restatement of the *propositio* in 1:27, where Paul instructs them to "stand firm in one spirit" (στήκετε ἐν ἑνὶ πνεύματι) against their opponents. Paul therefore makes their eschatological hope for resurrection and their citizenship in the heavenly commonwealth the grounds for persevering against persecution from those outside their group.

In 4:2, he turns to the possibility of internal faction and instructs Euodia and Syntyche "to be of the same mind in the Lord" (τὸ αὐτὸ φρονεῖν ἐν κυρίῳ). The use of φρονεῖν ties this exhortation together with the instruction to have the mind of Christ in 2:5 which is expounded in 2:6–11. By cultivating unity and resisting faction, they will behave in a way that coheres with the life story of their community by embodying the character of Christ. Additionally, φρονεῖν also connects this instruction with Paul's exhortation in 3:15 to have a mind or disposition (φρονέω) that is striving toward the prize of eschatological union with the resurrected Christ (3:10–14), which stands in contrast to the opponents whose earthly mindedness (οἱ τὰ ἐπίγεια φρονοῦντες, 3:19) is leading them on a path to destruction instead of bodily resurrection (3:21). Reading through the lens of SIT, standing firm against opponents and maintaining group unity are portrayed in a manner that coheres with the resurrection of Jesus in the past and the future possible social identity of bodily resurrection in the future. Thus, a salient resurrection-oriented social identity has potential to facilitate perseverance and social unity.

We turn now to the part of Paul's story that begins in Phil 3:4. In particular, we will look at how Paul portrays his past social categories in relation to his hope for a future resurrection described in 3:10–11. Paul's story illustrates how a person's self-conception may be informed by many social identifications, any one of which may become salient depending on the circumstances.[94] He tells his story not in terms of chronology but as a story of his past confidence (πεποίθησις) in the flesh, which he then describes

---

94. See Hogg and Abrams, *Social Identifications*, 25.

in 3:4-6 with ethnic categories (circumcised, nation of Israel, tribe of Benjamin, Hebrew), his manner of life (Pharisaic law observance), and his achievements (zealous persecutor of the church, blameless righteousness under the law).[95] Hellerman argues that Paul has here structured his Jewish achievements to reflect the *cursus honorum*, not least in structuring the presentation with ascribed status through birth followed by acquired status through achievements.[96] This is all the more important as the story unfolds with an evaluative comparison in 3:7-8 between his Jewish experience and his experience of knowing Christ. Paul discovered that, in comparison to knowing Christ, the social identifications, manner of life, and honorific achievements that had been the basis of his confidence had become a loss to him. Indeed, he declares them to be "rubbish" (σκυβάλα). Just as Christ rejected the divine honor status that was his (2:6-8), so also Paul rejects the social values that permeated Philippi.[97] The implications of this reevaluation of his social identity are not limited to his own particular experience and practice of Judaism; he universalizes them to include all things (ἡγοῦμαι πάντα ζημίαν εἶναι, 3:8). William Campbell is thus correct to observe, "Paul did not merely contrast life as a Jew with being in Christ, but proceeded ... to include 'everything' in his comparisons."[98] That is to say, Paul narrates his Jewish experience in such a way that it can function paradigmatically for the totality of Jewish and gentile experience.

The key insight when we look at the evidence with a view to temporal processes in the formation of social identity is that Paul construes the paradigmatic story of his past in such a way that it is discontinuous with a future possible social identity characterized by bodily resurrection. He is not satisfied to say only that his experience of confidence in his practice of Judaism hindered his knowing Christ and jeopardized his status of righteousness; he insists on going further in 3:10 to say that knowing Christ is "to know him and the power of his resurrection" (ἀνάστασις). If that is not enough, he reiterates this same hope in verse 11: "if somehow I may attain to the resurrection from the dead" (τὴν ἐξανάστασιν τὴν ἐκ νεκρῶν). Paul thus construes the story of his confidence in Judaism as something that would keep him from attaining his desired future social identity.

---

95. Bruce J. Malina and John J. Pilch, *Social-Science Commentary on the Letters of Paul* (Minneapolis: Fortress, 2006), 312.
96. Hellerman, *Reconstructing Honor*, 121-23.
97. Hellerman, *Reconstructing Honor*, 127.
98. Campbell, *Unity and Diversity*, 217.

Let me be clear: I am not arguing that Judaism itself is necessarily discontinuous with bodily resurrection in Christ. I am arguing that Paul's own subjective confidence in his practice of Judaism is portrayed as discontinuous with his anticipated resurrection identity.[99] By focusing on his own subjective confidence, Paul's experience is able to function paradigmatically both for Jews who, like Paul, might be tempted to boast in their practice of Judaism, and for the Roman Philippians who may be tempted to put confidence in their honor status, a tendency that Hellerman has shown to be ubiquitous in Philippi.[100] This marks another point of agreement with Campbell that "not only Jewish values and virtues are to be revised in Christ, but also all other things, whether living as slave or freedman, including the values and the virtues of the Roman world in which his converts were immersed."[101] I am, however, wary of Campbell's suggestion that Paul is not devaluing either Hellenism or Judaism but is instead revaluing them in light of Christ.[102] Paul is certainly revaluing his experience of Judaism, but his revaluation amounts to a devaluation inasmuch as he portrays his practice of Judaism in a way that stands in temporal discontinuity with his hope in Christ for bodily resurrection. In the same way, Philippian confidence in Roman status or citizenship or anything else, for that matter, is temporally discontinuous with a future possible social identity characterized by bodily resurrection in Christ. These social categories are not obliterated, but they are subordinated to a Christ-oriented social identity, and they must be abandoned if they become a hindrance to knowing Christ in his resurrection. If these social categories can be abandoned, then they cannot be essential. For an identity category to move from a governing position in a person's identity hierarchy to nonessential seems to me a devaluation, whether it is to do with Jewish identity or gentile.

We can summarize this part of the argument by saying that, when it comes to telling stories of the past, Paul portrays the Christ story in a way that coheres with his desired future possible social identity. As bodily resurrection is a way for Paul and the Philippians to gain glory, so the

---

99. See Bockmuehl: "Paul does not here reject faithful Torah observance but rather the attitude which finds in the observance of the 'works of the Law' grounds both for self-confidence before God and the exclusion of others" (*Epistle to the Philippians*, 209).

100. Hellerman, *Reconstructing Honor*, 88–109.

101. Campbell, *Unity and Diversity*, 217.

102. Campbell, *Unity and Diversity*, 217.

resurrection of Jesus involved his being endowed with unparalleled honor. When Paul tells his own story, he construes his confidence in his Jewish identity and manner of life negatively and in such a way that it is discontinuous with the desired future possible social identity of resurrection. Additionally, he tells his story so that it functions paradigmatically for all forms of confidence other than confidence in Christ, which would include the possible temptation of the Philippians to boast in their Roman status. Such boasting is for them discontinuous with the desired future social identity of bodily resurrection and is to be avoided. Paul's construal of his own story thus strengthens a Christ-oriented in-group identity against potential competing identities (whether Jewish or gentile) that might threaten the desired future identity marked by bodily resurrection.

If I am right that Paul has here devalued his experience of Judaism in light of his experience in Christ, particularly with regard to how that experience relates to future bodily resurrection, then it is worth considering in more detail what distinguishes Paul's attitude toward resurrection from others in the same period. Such a comparison has potential to shed light on Paul's devaluation of his confidence in Judaism.

One such text is 2 Macc 7, which recounts the death of seven brothers and their mother at the hands of Antiochus Epiphanes. This passage shares with Philippians at least two similarities that make their comparison potentially fruitful.[103] First, both are written in the context of persecution. As noted above, Paul wrote Philippians while in prison (1:12–14), and he described the experience he shared with the Philippians in terms of "suffering" and as a "struggle" (1:29–30). Likewise, 2 Macc 7 describes the extreme violence of Antiochus Epiphanes against seven Jewish brothers who refuse to disobey torah and eat the flesh of swine (7:1). The brothers declare that they are prepared to die before transgressing the law (7:2). To be sure, the sense of horror is heightened in 2 Macc 7 when compared to Philippians. The seven brothers are tortured and martyred in this passage; this is to be distinguished from Paul, who faces the possibility but not the certainty of death. Both texts share a context of persecution, though the degree of urgency is far greater in 2 Maccabees than in Paul. This shared context leads us to a second key similarity between these two texts,

---

103. For parallels to 2 Macc 7, see T. Mos. 9 and 1 Macc 2:15–28, 49–68. Nickelsburg argues that each of the parallels goes back to a prominent Hasid and his seven sons who were put to death for disobeying Antiochan decrees; see Nickelsburg, *Resurrection*, 127–30.

namely, both reflect a hope for future bodily resurrection in response to the threat of death (in Paul's case) and the event of their agonizing deaths (in the case of the Maccabean martyrs). As we have seen, Paul's hope for resurrection shows up in a variety places in Philippians, not least 3:10–11 (cf. 3:21). Likewise, resurrection hope pervades 2 Macc 7. After the first brother is killed, the second brother is scalped and threatened with further bodily punishment (7:7). He responds by declaring that "the King of the cosmos will raise us up [ἀνίστημι] to an eternal renewal of life [εἰς αἰώνιον ἀναβίωσιν ζωῆς], because we have died for his laws [ὑπὲρ τῶν αὐτοῦ νόμων]" (7:9). While somatic language is here absent, the idea of being raised to eternal renewal of life likely refers to bodily resurrection. Jonathan Goldstein suggests ἀναβίωσις is included despite its redundancy to make just this point: the second brother expects to have his body brought to life again at some point after his death.[104] If there is doubt as to whether this is a return to bodily life, it is erased with the account of the third brother's death, who upon offering his hands and tongue to be severed expressed hope of receiving them back once more (7:11). The explicit mention of a receiving again a part of his body at some point after death indicates the anticipation of bodily resurrection. His specific future hope is hope for his body.[105] The fourth brother turns the hope for resurrection into an attack on his persecutors by stating his own hope to be raised and insisting that his opponents have no such hope for resurrection (ἀνάστασις, 7:14).[106] The fifth and sixth brothers also use their final breaths to taunt Antiochus before their mother summarizes their common hope by articulating the expectation that the creator would mercifully give them life and breath once again (7:23). Hope for future bodily resurrection when faced with persecution is a common theme both in Philippians and 2 Macc 7.

The sharp difference between Paul and the Maccabean martyrs comes in their differing attitudes toward the law as it relates to resurrection. The willingness of each brother to face death because they were unwilling to eat pork, and thus transgress torah, embodies the principle that death

---

104. Jonathan A. Goldstein, *Second Maccabees: A New Translation with Introduction and Commentary*, AB (New York: Doubleday, 1983), 305–6.

105. This, of course, makes a great deal of sense. If the body is damaged or even killed for obedience, it is only fitting for the body be repaired and restored.

106. This bears some resemblance to Paul's statement that persecution is evidence of the Philippians' salvation and of their opponents' destruction; see Phil 1:28.

is better than violating torah.[107] Their high level of devotion to the law of their ancestors motivates them to suffer great violence and gruesome deaths. But this raises the question of why they are so motivated. It is not a simple matter of death being better than disobedience. It has to do rather with the unjust nature of their deaths. The injustice of suffering for obedience to the creator God and his laws must, from their perspective, be vindicated, and that vindication takes the shape of bodily resurrection. In this instance, death which results from disobeying Antiochus is the same as torah obedience,[108] and because they have obeyed torah by disobeying the tyrant king, they expect the King of the cosmos to overturn their deaths. This should not be taken simply as some sort of works righteousness. They do not gain right standing before the creator God because they keep torah. They are already members of the people of the creator God. Rather, the focus here is on how their covenant membership plays out in the context of persecution. As George W. E. Nickelsburg notes, "The basis for their choice is their TRUST in God."[109] Their commitment to ancestral law is an expression of that trust. In keeping the law and refusing to eat unclean food, they are keeping their part of the covenant, and they expect their God to keep his part also. That is not to mute the connection between confidence in law keeping and hope for resurrection; as we shall see, the hope for resurrection is explicitly grounded in obedience to the law. The point is that obedience to torah finds its context in the covenant.

The dying words of the second brother make the connection between law observance and hope for resurrection explicit: God "will raise us up to eternal renewal of life, *because* we died for his laws" (ἀποθανόντας ἡμᾶς ὑπὲρ τῶν αὐτοῦ νόμων, 7:9, emphasis added). The aorist adverbial participle functions to explain the cause or reason for this resurrection hope. Obedience to torah is the cause which brings about the effect of resurrection from the dead. The same conviction can be heard in the dying words of the third brother also: "I got these (hands) from heaven, and because of his laws [διὰ τοὺς αὐτοῦ νόμους], I disregard them, and from him I hope to receive them again" (7:11). The use of διά plus the accusative indicates causation. Willingness to suffer and die, along with hope for vindication through bodily resurrection, is substantiated by confidence in torah observance. Again, the mother praises her sons and substantiates her hope that her sons will

---

107. See Goldstein, *Second Maccabees*, 303.
108. Nickelsburg, *Resurrection*, 121.
109. Nickelsburg, *Resurrection*, 120, emphasis original.

have life and breath given back to them "since [ὡς] you now disdain them because of his laws [διὰ τοὺς αὐτοῦ νόμους]" (7:23). The subordinating conjunction here has causative force and once again directly connects hope for resurrection with law observance. The seventh and final brother is also motivated by commitment to torah, though he does not mention resurrection. Like the others, he does connect his own martyrdom to his obedience to torah: "I, like my brothers, give up my body [σῶμα] and life [ψυχή] for the laws of our ancestors [περὶ τῶν πατρίων νόμων]." It is fair to assume that he shares his mother's and his brothers' hope for bodily resurrection. Four times then in 2 Macc 7, martyrdom and hope for resurrection are substantiated by expressions that reflect confidence in law observance: ὑπὲρ νόμων, διὰ νόμους, and περὶ νόμων. To adapt a sentence from Nickelsburg: God will raise them from the dead *because* they die for torah.[110]

In contrast to 2 Macc 7, Paul's former subjective confidence in the flesh, which for him includes confidence in torah observance (Phil 3:5–6, 9), is precisely that which he devalues to the point of being nonessential. He has come to consider such confidence on his part not only a loss but a hindrance to gaining Christ and thus a hindrance to participating in the bodily resurrection (Phil 3:7–11). If the "dogs" of Phil 3:2–3 are the same as the "enemies of the cross of Christ" in 3:18, then such confidence in the flesh is potentially disastrous and leads to destruction rather than resurrection. Let me be clear once again that this argument does not mean that confidence in Christ is incompatible with torah observance. One could presumably have confidence in Christ and still observe torah. The issue for Paul is not the objective practice of keeping the law but the subjective confidence in keeping the law as the cause for hope in and experience of future bodily resurrection.

Returning to the function of Paul's example in Phil 3, the apostle sets himself forth as one who puts no confidence in anything other than Christ. As confidence in law-keeping motivated the Maccabean martyrs to suffer violently with hope for bodily resurrection, so Paul's confidence in Christ motivates his willingness to suffer like Christ with hope to share in Christ's resurrection (3:10–11). His attitude functions as an example to aid the Philippians in their deliberation. This is what the gospel-worthy life looks like. Suffering for the gospel is to be embraced with the knowledge that conformity to Christ in his sufferings leads to participation in

---

110. Nickelsburg, *Resurrection*, 121.

Christ's resurrection. With regard to social identity, Paul's example contributes diachronic continuity by providing a present and living example that embodies the pattern of the Christ story in 2:5–11, namely, suffering and resurrection. The then-present example of his attitude in 3:10–11 also stands in continuity with his anticipated future identity in Christ which is characterized by resurrection from the dead. This continuity through time—past, present, and future—increases the persuasive potential of Paul's deliberative rhetoric.

4.7. Conclusion

I have argued throughout this chapter that Paul's language of resurrection in Philippians functions to establish and strengthen a common in-group identity among the Philippian believers. This identity anticipates future bodily resurrection from the dead as somatic transformation which includes the bestowal of glory on those in Christ and the realization of their citizenship in the heavenly commonwealth. The Christ story in Phil 2:5–11 ties this anticipated future together with the group's past. They exist as a group because Christ, contrary to the Roman status quo, eschewed his superior status and humbled himself to become a servant through his death on the cross. His resurrection involves the receipt of unequalled glory and honor, which stands in continuity with Paul's vision of the resurrection of believers. The possible future social identity as those who will be raised from the dead is strengthened by a rhetorical *synkrisis* with those whose end is not resurrection but destruction. Stark contrast between in-group and out-group would have increased the potential for Paul's rhetoric to produce a salient common in-group identity. Paul's own example as one willing to suffer for the sake of the gospel with hope for bodily resurrection ties the story of Christ's past resurrection and the possible future social identity characterized by resurrection together with the present experience of the Philippians. Altogether, Paul's account of bodily resurrection contributes to the deliberative aim of the letter that the Philippians would live in a manner worthy of the gospel by resisting discord to pursue unity that perseveres in the face of suffering. That bodily resurrection permeates Paul's perception of group identity in Christ sheds light on his attitude toward the body. For Paul, embodiment is essential for full human life. To be sure, he can imagine a human being existing distinct from the body for a temporary period. But there is no indication in Philippians that he takes such an experience to be fully human existence. Such an experience is, for believers, always looking forward to bodily resurrection from the dead. The body is central to Paul's understanding of human life, and resurrection of the body runs straight through his Christ-oriented identity.

5
The Body and the Future in the Letters of Paul

The body and hope for its resurrection are integral to Paul's theological thinking and pastoral purposes. That hope put him right at home among other Jewish writers from the Second Temple period who expected their God to return their bodies to them at the dawn of the new age. One thing that distinguished Paul was his view that the new age had already been inaugurated with the resurrection of Jesus. That event ensured that those who belong to Jesus would also be raised. It also carried significant implications for the use of the body by believers who live between the resurrection of Christ in the past and their own resurrection in the future. In this final chapter, we will summarize our findings with regard to Paul's expectations for bodily practice in light of his hope for bodily resurrection and point to a few possibilities for further research along the way.

5.1. Bodily Resurrection in Social Perspective

One aim of this project has been to open up more generally the social dynamics at work in Paul's hope for future bodily resurrection. Those dynamics can be discerned in a variety of ways. For one, Paul deploys the hope of future bodily resurrection to reinforce boundaries between the Christ-following ingroup and outsiders. This was evident in Phil 3:12–4:1, where the recipients were portrayed as the group that will be raised in contrast to outsiders who would face destruction. The difference between denial of future bodily resurrection and belief in it marked a boundary, though not the only boundary, between subgroups within the community of Christ-followers in Corinth (1 Cor 15:12). It is striking that, in Philippians, future bodily resurrection marks the difference between the ingroup and outgroup, but in 1 Corinthians denial and affirmation of future bodily resurrection marks the difference between subgroups within the Christ-following community. Paul is certainly willing to devote considerable energy to persuading those who reject future bodily resurrection to consider embracing it. He even argues that if the deniers are correct, then the absence of resurrection overturns the whole of the Christian faith. Nevertheless, while hope for resurrection was a key marker of group identity, its denial did not necessarily mean expulsion from the group. The question remains open, however, how Paul might have responded if the deniers of resurrection continued to hold their position after his attempt to persuade them of it? Would unrepentant rejection of future bodily resurrection warrant exclusion from the community? One wonders how long he would tolerate an error of such significant proportions.

The social aspect of future bodily resurrection can be discerned in the concept of incorporative Christology. That is to say, resurrection is a benefit of membership in the "in Christ" group. This is evident in 1 Cor 15:20–28 and in Rom 5 and 6, where Paul sorts the human race into two basic groups based on their association with Adam or Christ. Membership in the Adam-group means death. Membership in the Christ-group means participation in the resurrection. In 2 Cor 4:14, resurrection is portrayed as something that happens to the community ("with you") by virtue of union with Christ ("with Jesus"). This should not overshadow the importance of individual faith in Paul's soteriology. The individual and the corporate must be kept in balance. The key thing to remember is that the benefits of participation in Christ, resurrection included, come not in the context of an individualistic relationship to Christ but as a member of the group of which Christ is representative head. Resurrection is participatory.

If the social dimension of Paul's understanding of resurrection can be seen in his Christology, it is also apparent in his use of pneumatic language. We looked at several ways pneumatic language functioned as a tool to define early Christ-followers as those who have the Spirit in contrast to those who do not. It is our contention that Paul's use of pneumatic language, a marker of social identity, in association with future bodily resurrection fills that future hope with social significance. This is a major feature of Paul's attitude toward bodily resurrection in 1 Corinthians. The future resurrection body is distinguished from present ordinary bodies in that it is a σῶμα πνευματικόν (1 Cor 15:44), a body enlivened by the Spirit. That future experience is anticipated in the present with the notion of the body as a temple of the Spirit (1 Cor 6:19). In Romans, the indwelling presence of the Spirit enables believers to cease walking according to the flesh; that is, the Spirit enables transformation in the present in anticipation of the day when God will raise believers through the power of the Spirit (Rom 8:9–12). It might be tempting to slide into an individualistic interpretation of the role of the Spirit with regard to renewal and resurrection, and it is certainly the case that Paul sees the Holy Spirit at work in individual believers and in the raising of individual bodies. My point is that the individual work is located within a communal context. That this reflects Paul's understanding is illustrated in the close association of familial language with the work of the Spirit; having the Spirit makes one an adopted member of God's family (Rom 8:14, 23), and this is preparation for resurrection as the redemption of the body (8:11, 23). Those who have the Spirit and are led by the Spirit constitute the social group that will be raised through the Spirit and given bodies perpetually enlivened by the Spirit.

That brings us to a distinctive contribution of this study. Drawing on the work of Cinnirella, I have argued throughout that Paul's vision of future bodily resurrection is accurately described as a future possible social identity. That is to say, Paul sees future bodily resurrection fundamentally in terms of the group, and individual identity derives from that group membership. For Paul, the believer's future self is the self as a member of the group of resurrected persons. As noted above, this distinguishes the believing ingroup from outgroupers destined for destruction (Phil 3:19) and highlights again the participatory nature of future bodily resurrection. Resurrection is not merely a matter of individual soteriology; hope for resurrection defines the people of God *as a people*. The social nature of future bodily resurrection is also apparent through its association with the language of citizenship (Phil 3:20). Paul repeatedly highlights the attractiveness of the future identity by portraying it positively in terms of glory and honor, which were values of highest importance in the Greco-Roman world (1 Cor 15:43; Rom 8:17–18; Phil 3:21). It is also a means of escaping the power of death and participating in the victory of Christ (1 Cor 15:26, 50–58). Further, the future resurrection-oriented identity is evaluated favorably in that it is instrumental to the future liberation of creation from bondage to decay (Rom 8:19–23). One advantage of this approach has been its ability to shed light on the relationship between future bodily resurrection and Paul's present expectations for believers' use of their bodies. When a future possible social identity is salient, the individual is more likely to be motivated to behave in a way that anticipates that future identity, a point we will say more about below.

That future bodily resurrection functions as a possible social identity in multiple letters is significant. Given that our study was limited to passages involving expectations for the use of the body, one potential avenue for further research is to consider whether resurrection can be described as a future possible identity elsewhere in Paul's letters where hope for bodily resurrection is discussed (e.g., 1 Thess 4:13–17). If resurrection can be described as a future social identity in other contexts, then how does it function? How does Paul portray the past and the present given this particular future identity? To what extent does it create positive distinction for Paul and the recipients? How does it relate to Paul's pastoral and persuasive purposes? Another question to consider is the relationship of Paul's perspective to other New Testament authors. Do other New Testament documents show evidence that they perceive future bodily resurrection in social categories?[1] If so, to what extent does their attitude reflect Paul's view? To what extent are they distinct?

5.2. Resurrection and the Rhetoric of Reconciliation

All four of the letters under consideration in this study are addressed to situations involving conflict. In 1 Corinthians, Romans, and Philippians, there is conflict among subgroups within the congregation. The situation in Rome is distinct in that the conflict is primarily between diverse ethnic groups, and the situation of conflict within the Philippian community is compounded by additional struggle with outsiders. Second Corinthians involves conflict between Paul and the recipients, which will be reviewed below in the discussion of Paul's suffering. In 1 Corinthians, Romans, and Philippians, I argued that the future resurrection-oriented social identity functions in part to form and maintain a common ingroup identity that supports Paul's rhetorical goals of mitigating factionalism and cultivating concord. In Philippians, this relates to the apparent conflict between Eudodia and Syntyche. In 1 Corinthians, Paul portrays the factionalism in various ways, and the most we can say is that a perception of common ingroup identity with regard to the future resurrection would support, but probably not fulfill, the overall deliberative aim of producing concord among the recipients.

---

1. For attention to social dynamics in the eschatology of Hebrews, see Matthew P. O'Reilly, "Rest Now or Not Yet? Temporal Aspects of Social Identity in Hebrews 3:7–4:11," in *Listen, Understand, Obey: Essays on Hebrews in Honor of Gareth Lee Cockerill*, ed. Caleb Friedeman (Eugene, OR: Pickwick, 2017), 37–53.

Turning to Romans, it appears that the recipients divided predominantly along ethnic lines regarding the matter of table fellowship. Taking that conflict in light of the resurrection-oriented future identity, I argued that table fellowship can be interpreted as a bodily practice. For Paul, the believer's union with Christ in his death anticipates future union with Christ in his resurrection and frees the believer from the power of sin in the present. Based on this theological principle, Paul can call upon believers to resist the temptation to submit the parts of their body to unrighteousness and sin, instructing them instead to submit their bodies in holiness to God (12:1). I also argued that if the general exhortation with regard to bodily practice in 12:1 is particularized in the various instructions that follow, then the matter of table fellowship should be understood in light of Paul's theology of the body and bodily resurrection in Rom 6 and 8. For Paul, bringing ethnically diverse bodies together at the same table is a bodily practice that stands in continuity with the future resurrection-oriented identity. Of particular importance is that this future social identity does not call upon the members of either subgroup to abandon their ethnic identity or distinctiveness. This creates the perception of new shared identity without the difficulties that arise in being asked to reject an existing identity, thus increasing the likelihood that the new identity will be embraced.

5.3. Resurrection and the Suffering Body

The use of the body in situations involving suffering arose in our discussions of 2 Corinthians and Philippians. In 2 Corinthians, Paul has come through significant trouble such that he seems to have thought himself near death. Conflict arose with the Corinthians because, among other things, a group known as the super apostles portrayed Paul's suffering as a violation of the group's expectations for apostolic ministry; a true apostle should be characterized by glory, not trouble. In response to that charge, Paul portrayed his sufferings in a way that cohered with the past death and resurrection of Christ and his own future hope of bodily resurrection. That is to say, Paul justified his bodily affliction by evaluating it in light of his future resurrection-oriented social identity and as an expression of his conformity to Christ's death. As one who saw himself as a member of the people who will be raised from the dead, he sees his sufferings as a participation in the suffering and death of Christ so that in the future he will likewise share in the resurrection of Christ. We also noted that by portraying his suffering in continuity with the future identity, Paul invited the recipients to reconsider their evaluation of him in light of their shared hope for resurrection.

The question of suffering arose in Philippians also with regard to Paul and the recipients. Two major aspects of his persuasive strategy involved the example of Christ (2:5–11) and Paul's own example (1:20–21). I argued that the Christ-story in Phil 2:5–11 functioned as what Cinnirella calls a "life story" that ties the group's history together with its future into a single coherent representation. Within this story, Paul's own experience functions as an example of using the body to honor Christ even when suffering results. This strengthens one deliberative aim of the letter to motivate the Philippians to stand firm in their own experience of suffering.

The suffering Paul endured as a precursor to writing 2 Corinthians and Philippians appears to have been the occasion for him to reflect and write on the possibility of dying before the parousia. These two letters give evidence that Paul anticipated a period of conscious disembodied existence in the presence of Christ prior to the resurrection of believers at the parousia. This has prompted some scholars to suggest that Paul's view of the afterlife developed from a Jewish hope for resurrection to a more Hellenistic expectation for a disembodied soul. We found this approach unpersuasive and argued instead that Paul's earlier writing reflected an expectation of being alive at the parousia, which would make a disembodied intermediate state irrelevant. Reflecting upon the prospect of his own bodily death prior to the parousia, Paul sets forth the expectation that he will enter into the presence of Christ (2 Cor 5:8; Phil 1:23) until his body is raised from the dead. This is desirable for Paul in that it means relief from sufferings and closer proximity to Christ, but it should not be seen as a substitute for future bodily resurrection. Nor should it be seen as a full experience of human life. We took Paul's displeasure with being unclothed in preference for being further clothed in 2 Cor 5:4 this way: Paul's desire is not to cast off the body but to take up a new resurrected body. A disembodied intermediate state is thus acceptable because it is temporary and will give way to a fully human resurrected body.

5.4. The Body and the Question of Perseverance

Our study of bodily practice also carries implications for the question of perseverance in Paul's theological thinking. Are believers unquestionably assured of their final perseverance? Or is it possible, under certain circumstances, that they might lose their membership in the "in Christ" group and thus fail to persevere? The question arose in the exegesis of 1 Cor 6:12–20, where Paul argues that πόρνη-union dismembers the body of Christ. That is to say, if a believer is a member of the body of Christ, the act of sex with a πόρνη wrenches that member from the rest of the body. Paul's rationale is that union with Christ and union with a πόρνη are mutually exclusive unions. If the body is to be raised as a member of the group in union with Christ, πόρνη-union would seem to pose a threat to the hope of participating in the resurrection. Even if this act does not immediately sever the relationship with Christ, Paul's line of reasoning requires the possibility that membership in the body of Christ can be broken, and it follows that he does not see perseverance as a certainty. This resonates with our reading of Philippians, where Paul's hope of participating in the resurrection is portrayed with some level of contingency (3:11). Additionally, one of Paul's rhetorical goals was to strengthen the Philippian Christ-followers to stand firm against persecution because he was apparently concerned that they might not persevere. If the resurrection-oriented future social identity were to become salient in their case, then they would likely be more motivated to stand firm in the face of suffering in order to attain the future identity.

5.5. Resurrection and Present Transformation

The question of transformed bodily practice relates to the future possible resurrection-oriented identity in that individuals are often motivated to behave in a way that anticipates or helps to achieve a possible social identity. This sort of connection arose multiple times in our study. The ethical expectations of 1 Cor 15:29–34 were directly connected to Paul's vision for resurrected bodies and suggested that Paul intends believers to behave in a way that stands in continuity with the future resurrection-oriented identity. We took this as a framework for interpreting Paul's prohibition of πόρνη-union as a bodily practice that was inconsistent with the resurrection-oriented future identity. In Romans, the resurrection-oriented identity formed the basis for Paul's expectation that believers not use their bodies for sin and unrighteousness but for righteousness and holiness. The body is the sphere where submission to the lordship of Christ is expressed, because transformed bodily life in the present reveals the character of bodily resurrection. There is a sense of incongruity in that the present dying body portrays the life of the future resurrection. But there is also a sense in which the present life is congruous with the life to come in that embodied holiness now prefigures resurrected bodies later. In 2 Cor 4:16, Paul portrays present renewal and transformation as preparation for the glory of future bodily resurrection. In each case, he expects present bodily life to embody the future resurrection of the body. To put it in SIT terms, he expects bodily life in the present to cohere with the future resurrection-oriented identity. Further research could be conducted that relates our conclusions about bodily practice and transformation to Paul's ethics more broadly.

5.6. Conclusion

For Paul, embodiment is essential to human identity, and this is true for the future as much as the present. The apostle's attitude toward the body is not exclusively a matter of anthropology. It has bearing on his Christology and pneumatology, his ethics and eschatology. Embodiment is also fundamentally social. It is through the body that we engage one another and our environment. This is no less true when we come to Paul's understanding of future bodily resurrection. Resurrected bodies are social bodies. They act as agents in relation to one another and in relation to creation to bring liberty from bondage to decay. The future social dynamic also involves future social identity. Hope for resurrection is shared hope. In Paul's thinking, the believer's future self is the self as a member of the resurrected group, and he insists that bodily behavior in the present be appropriate to that future social identity. If the use of the body runs counter to the life of the future, then Paul expects that behavior to change. In Paul's case, attaining that future identity is so valuable that he is willing to suffer and even die to gain it. After all, that is the pattern defined by Christ with his death and resurrection. Embodied life now anticipates and finds its fulfillment in the future resurrection of the body. In this way, we might say, bodily practice in the present is practice for the full experience of human life and community that comes with the resurrection of the body.

Bibliography

Allison, Dale C. *The End of the Ages Has Come: An Early Interpretation of the Passion and Resurrection of Jesus*. Philadelphia: Fortress, 1985.
Amador, J. D. H. "Revisting 2 Corinthians: Rhetoric and the Case for Unity." *NTS* 46 (2000): 92–111.
Aristotle. *On the Heavens*. Translated by W. K. C. Guthrie. LCL. Cambridge: Harvard University Press, 1939.
———. *On the Soul; Parva Naturalia; On Breath*. Translated by W. S. Hett. LCL. Cambridge: Harvard University Press, 1957.
———. *Art of Rhetoric*. Translated by John Henry Freese. LCL. Cambridge: Harvard University Press, 2000.
Aune, David E. "Apocalypticism." Pages 27–35 in *Dictionary of Paul and His Letters*. Edited by Gerald F. Hawthorne and Ralph P. Martin. Downers Grove, IL: InterVarsity Press, 1993.
———. *The New Testament in Its Literary Environment*. LEC 8. Philadelphia: Westminster, 1987.
Avery-Peck, A. J., and J. Neusner, eds. *Death, Life-after-Death, Resurrection and the World-to-Come in the Judaisms of Antiquity*. Part 4 of *Judaism in Late Antiquity*. Leiden: Brill, 2000.
Bachmann, Philipp. *Der erste Brief des Paulus an die Korinther*. KNT 7. Leipzig: Deichert, 1910.
Bailey, Kenneth E. *Paul through Mediterranean Eyes: Cultural Studies in 1 Corinthians*. Downers Grove, IL: IVP Academic, 2011.
Barclay, John M. G. "Mirror-Reading a Polemical Letter: Galatians as a Test Case." Pages 367–82 in *The Galatians Debate*. Edited by Mark D. Nanos. Peabody, MA: Hendrickson, 2002.
———. *Paul and the Gift*. Grand Rapids: Eerdmans, 2015.
———. *Pauline Churches and Diaspora Jews*. Grand Rapids: Eerdmans, 2016.
Barnett, Paul. *The Second Epistle to the Corinthians*. NICNT. Grand Rapids: Eerdmans, 1997.

Barrett, C. K. *Commentary on the First Epistle to the Corinthians*. BNTC. London: Black, 1971.

Barton, Carlin A. "The Roman Blush: The Delicate Matter of Self-Control." Pages 212–34 in *Constructions of the Classical Body*. Edited by James I. Porter. The Body in Theory. Ann Arbor: University of Michigan Press, 2002.

Barton, Stephen C. "Eschatology and Emotions in Early Christianity." *JBL* 130 (2011): 571–91.

Basevi, Claudio, and Juan Chapa. "Philippians 2.6–11: The Rhetorical Function of a Pauline Hymn." Pages 338–56 in *Rhetoric and the New Testament: Essays from the 1992 Heidelberg Conference*. Edited by Stanley E. Porter and Thomas H. Olbricht. JSNTSup 90. Sheffield: JSOT Press, 1993.

Bauckham, Richard. "Apocalypses." Pages 136–87 in *The Complexities of Second Temple Judaism*. Vol. 1 of *Justification and Variegated Nomism*. Edited by D. A. Carson, Peter T. O'Brien, and Mark A. Seifrid. Grand Rapids: Baker, 2001.

Beker, J. Christiaan. *Paul the Apostle: The Triumph of God in Life and Thought*. Philadelphia: Fortress, 1980.

Betz, Hans Dieter. *2 Corinthians 8 and 9: A Commentary on Two Administrative Letters of the Apostle Paul*. Hermeneia. Philadelphia: Fortress, 1985.

———. "The Concept of the 'Inner Human Being' (ὁ ἔσω ἄνθρωπος) in the Anthropology of Paul." *NTS* 46 (2000): 315–41.

———. *Galatians: A Commentary on Paul's Letter to the Churches in Galatia*. Hermeneia. Philadelphia: Fortress, 1979.

Bieringer, Reinmund. "Teilungshypothesen zum 2. Korintherbrief." Pages 67–105 in *Studies on 2 Corinthians*. Edited by Reinmund Bieringer and Jan Lambrecht. BETL 112. Leuven: Leuven University Press, 1994.

Bird, Michael F., and Preston M. Sprinkle, eds. *The Faith of Jesus Christ: Exegetical, Biblical, and Theological Studies*. Peabody, MA: Hendrickson, 2009.

Blackwell, Ben C. "Immortal Glory and the Problem of Death in Romans 3.23." *JSNT* 32.3 (2010): 285–308.

Bloomquist, L. Gregory. *The Function of Suffering in Philippians*. JSNTSup 78. London: Sheffield Academic, 1992.

Bockmuehl, Markus. *The Epistle to the Philippians*. BNTC. Peabody, MA: Hendrickson, 1998.

Boer, Martinus C de. *The Defeat of Death: Apocalyptic Eschatology in 1 Corinthians 15 and Romans 5*. JSNTSup 22. Sheffield: JSOT Press, 1988.
Boismard, Marie-Emile. *Our Victory Over Death: Resurrection?* Translated by Madeleine Beaumont. Collegeville, MN: Liturgical Press, 1999.
Bolt, Peter G. "Life, Death, and the Afterlife in the Greco-Roman World." Pages 51–79 in *Life in the Face of Death: The Resurrection Message of the New Testament*. Edited by Richard N. Longenecker. Grand Rapids: Eerdmans, 1998.
Booth, Alan. "The Age of Reclining and Its Attendant Perils." Pages 105–20 in *Dining in a Classical Context*. Edited by William J. Slater. Ann Arbor: University of Michigan Press, 1991.
Brookins, Timothy A. "The (In)frequency of the Name 'Erastus' in Antiquity: A Literary, Papyrological, and Epigraphical Catalog." *NTS* 59 (2013): 496–516.
Brown, Alexandra. *The Cross and Human Transformation: Paul's Apocalyptic Word in 1 Corinthians*. Minneapolis: Fortress, 1995.
Brown, Paul J. *Bodily Resurrection and Ethics in 1 Corinthians 15: Connecting Faith and Morality in the Context of Greco-Roman Mythology*. WUNT 2/360. Tübingen: Mohr Siebeck, 2014.
Brown, Peter. *The Body and Society: Men, Women, and Sexual Renunciation in Early Christianity*. Lectures on the History of Religions 13. New York: Columbia University Press, 1988.
Bruce, F. F. *1 and 2 Corinthians*. NCB. Grand Rapids: Eerdmans, 1971.
Brucker, Ralph. *'Christushymnen' oder 'epideiktische Passagen'? Studien zum Stilwechsel im Neuen Testament und seiner Umwelt*. FRLANT 176. Göttingen: Vandenhoeck & Ruprecht, 1997.
Bryan, Christopher. *A Preface to Romans: Notes on the Epistle in Its Literary and Cultural Setting*. New York: Oxford University Press, 2000.
Bultmann, Rudolf. *Theology of the New Testament*. 2 vols. Translated by Kendrich Grobel. New York: Scribner, 1951–1955.
Bünker, Michael. *Briefformular und rhetorische Disposition im 1. Korintherbrief*. GTA 28. Göttingen: Vandenhoek & Ruprecht, 1984.
Byrne, Brendan J. *Reckoning with Romans: A Contemporary Reading of Paul's Gospel*. GNS 18. Wilmington, DE: Glazier, 1986.
Campbell, Constantine R. *Paul and Union with Christ: An Exegetical and Theological Study*. Grand Rapids: Zondervan, 2012.
Campbell, Douglas A. *The Deliverance of God: An Apocalyptic Rereading of Justification in Paul*. Grand Rapids: Eerdmans, 2009.

Campbell, William S. *Unity and Diversity in Christ: Interpreting Paul in Context*. Eugene, OR: Cascade, 2013.

Cave, David, and Rebecca Sachs Norris, eds. *Religion and the Body: Modern Science and the Construction of Religious Meaning*. Studies in the History of Religions 138. Leiden: Brill, 2012.

Chamblin, J. K. "Psychology." Pages 765–75 in *Dictionary of Paul and His Letters*. Edited by Gerald F. Hawthorne and Ralph P. Martin. Downers Grove, IL: InterVarsity Press, 1993.

Charles, R. H. *A Critical History of the Doctrine of a Future Life in Israel, in Judaism, and in Christianity*. 2nd ed. London: Black, 1913.

Chrysostom, Dio. *Discourses 1–11*. Translated by J. W. Cohoon. LCL. Cambridge: Harvard University Press, 1932.

Churchland, Patricia Smith. *Brain-Wise: Studies in Neurophilosophy*. Cambridge: MIT Press, 2002.

———. *Neurophilosophy: Toward a Unified Science of the Mind-Brain*. Cambridge: MIT Press, 1986.

Ciampa, Roy E., and Brian S. Rosner. *The First Letter to the Corinthians*. Pillar New Testament Commentary. Grand Rapids: Eerdmans, 2010.

Cicero. *On the Nature of the Gods*. Translated by H. Rackham. LCL. Cambridge: Harvard University Press, 1933.

———. *On the Orator: Book 3; On Fate; Stoic Paradoxes; Divisions of Oratory*. Translated by H. Rackham. LCL. Cambridge: Harvard University Press, 1942.

Cicero. *On the Republic; On the Laws*. Translated by Clinton W. Keyes. LCL. Cambridge: Harvard University Press, 2006.

———. *Rhetorica ad Herennium*. Translated by Harry Caplan. LCL. Cambridge: Harvard University Press, 1954.

———. *De Senectute; De Amicitia; De Divinatione*. Translated by W. A. Falconer. LCL. Cambridge: Harvard University Press, 1996.

Cinnirella, Marco. "Exploring Temporal Aspects of Social Identity: The Concept of Possible Social Identities." *EJSP* 28 (1998): 227–48.

Clarke, A. D. "Another Corinthian Erastus Inscription." *TynBul* 42 (1991): 146–51.

———. *Secular and Christian Leadership in Corinth: A Socio-historical and Exegetical Study of 1 Corinthians 1–6*. AGJU 18. Leiden: Brill, 1993.

Cohen, Shaye J. D. *From the Maccabees to the Mishnah*. LEC 7. Philadelphia: Westminter, 1987.

Collange, Jean-François. *Énigmes de la deuxième épitre aux Corinthiens: Étude exégétique de 2 Cor. 2:14–7:4.* SNTSMS 18. Cambridge: Cambridge University Press, 1972.

Collins, John J. *The Apocalyptic Imagination: An Introduction to Jewish Apocalyptic Literature.* Biblical Resource Series. Grand Rapids: Eerdmans, 1998.

———. *Daniel: A Commentary on the Book of Daniel.* Hermeneia. Minneapolis: Fortress, 1993.

Collins, Raymond F. *First Corinthians.* SP. Collegeville, MN: Liturgical Press, 1999.

Condor, Susan. "Social Identity and Time." Pages 285–315 in *Social Groups and Identities: Developing the Legacy of Henri Tajfel.* Edited by P. Robinson. Oxford: Butterworth Heinemann, 1996.

Conzelmann, Hans. *1 Corinthians: A Commentary.* Hermeneia. Philadephia: Fortress, 1975.

Cooper, John W. *Body, Soul, and Life Everlasting: Biblical Anthropology and the Monism-Dualism Debate.* Grand Rapids: Eerdmans, 1989.

Cousar, Charles B. *A Theology of the Cross: The Death of Jesus in the Pauline Letters.* Overtures to Biblical Theology 24. Minneapolis: Fortress, 1990.

Cranfield, C. E. B. *The Epistle to the Romans.* 2 vols. ICC. Edinburgh: T&T Clark, 1975.

Crick, Francis H. *The Astonishing Hypothesis: The Scientific Search for the Soul.* New York: Simon & Schuster, 1994.

Cullmann, Oscar. *Christ and Time: The Primitive Christian Conception of Time and History.* Translated by Floyd V. Filson. London: SCM, 1951.

———. *Immortality of the Soul or Resurrection of the Dead?* London: Epworth, 1958.

Dahl, M. E. *The Resurrection of the Body.* London: SCM, 1962.

Danker, F. W. "Paul's Debt to the *De Corona* of Demosthenes: A Study of Rhetorical Techniques in Second Corinthians." Pages 268–80 in *Persuasive Artistry: Studies in New Testament Rhetoric in Honor of G. A. Kennedy.* Edited by Duane F. Watson. JSNTSup 50. Sheffield: Sheffield Academic, 1991.

Deissmann, A. *Light from the Ancient East: The New Testament Illustrated by Recently Discovered Texts of the Greco-Roman World.* London: Hodder & Stoughton, 1927.

Demosthenes. *Funeral Speech; Erotic Essay; Exordia; Letters.* Translated by N. W. and N. J. DeWitt. Cambridge: Harvard University Press, 1986.

Dodd, Brian J. *Paul's Paradigmatic 'I': Personal Example as Literary Strategy.* JSNTSup 177. Sheffield: Sheffield Academic, 1999.
Dodd, C. H. *The Apostolic Preaching and Its Developments.* Repr. Grand Rapids: Baker, 1980.
———. *New Testament Studies.* New York: Scribners, 1954.
Donfried, Karl P. "False Presuppositions in the Study of Romans." Pages 102–24 in *The Romans Debate.* Edited by Karl P. Donfried. Rev. and exp. ed. Peabody, MA: Hendrickson, 1991.
Douglas, Mary. *Natural Symbols.* 2nd ed. Repr. New York: Routledge, 2010.
———. *Purity and Danger: An Analysis of Concept of Pollution and Taboo.* Repr. New York: Routledge, 2009.
Dunn, James D. G. *1 Corinthians.* T&T Clark Study Series. London: T&T Clark, 2003.
———. *Romans 1–8.* WBC 38A. Dallas: Word, 1988.
———. *Romans 9–16.* WBC 38B. Dallas: Word, 1988.
———. *The Theology of Paul the Apostle.* Grand Rapids: Eerdmans, 1998.
Edart, Jean-Baptiste. *L'Épître aux Philippiens: Rhétorique et Composition Stylistique.* Paris: Gabalda, 2002.
Edwards, Catherine. "The Suffering Body: Philosophy and Pain in Seneca's Letters." Pages 252–68 in *Constructions of the Classical Body.* Edited by James I. Porter. The Body in Theory. Ann Arbor: University of Michigan Press, 2002.
Elliot, John H. *What Is Social-Scientific Criticism?* GBS. Minneapolis: Fortress, 1993.
Elliott, Neil. *The Rhetoric of Romans: Argumentative Constraint and Strategy and Paul's Dialogue with Judaism.* Minneapolis: Fortress, 2007.
Enderlein, Steven E. "To Fall Short or Lack the Glory of God? The Translation and Implications of Romans 3:23." *JSPL* 1.2 (2011): 213–24.
Endsjø, Dag Øistein. *Greek Resurrection Beliefs and the Success of Early Christianity.* New York: Palgrave Macmillan, 2009.
Engberg-Pedersen, Troels. *Cosmology and Self in the Apostle Paul: The Material Spirit.* New York: Oxford University Press, 2010.
———. *Paul and the Stoics.* Louisville: Westminster John Knox, 2000.
———, ed. *Paul beyond the Judaism/Hellenism Divide.* Louisville: Westminster John Knox, 2001.
Epictetus. *Discourses: Books 1–2.* Translated by W. A. Oldfather. LCL. Cambridge: Harvard University Press, 1925.
———. *Discourses: Books 3–4; Fragments; The Encheiridion.* Translated by W. A. Oldfather. LCL. Cambridge: Harvard University Press, 1928.

Eriksson, A. *Traditions as Rhetorical Proof: Pauline Argumentation in 1 Corinthians*. ConBNT 29. Stockholm: Almqvist & Wiksell, 1998.
Esler, Philip F. *Conflict and Identity in Romans: The Social Setting of Paul's Letter*. Minneapolis: Fortress, 2003.
———. "An Outline of Social Identity Theory." Pages 13–39 in *T&T Clark Handbook to Social Identity in the New Testament*. Edited by J. Brian Tucker and Coleman A. Baker. London: Bloomsbury T&T Clark, 2014.
Fee, Gordon D. *The First Epistle to the Corinthians*. NICNT. Grand Rapids: Eerdmans, 1987.
———. *God's Empowering Presence: The Holy Spirit in the Letters of Paul*. Peabody, MA: Hendrickson, 1994.
———. *Paul's Letter to the Philippians*. NICNT. Grand Rapids: Eerdmans, 1995.
———. *Pauline Christology: An Exegetical-Theological Study*. Peabody, MA: Hendrickson, 2007.
Festugière, A. J. *Epicurus and His Gods*. Translated by C. W. Chilton. Cambridge: Harvard University Press, 1956.
Finney, Mark T. *Honour and Conflict in the Ancient World: 1 Corinthians in Its Greco-Roman Setting*. LNTS 460. London: Bloomsbury, 2012.
Fisk, Bruce N. "ΠΟΡΝΕΥΕΙΝ as Body Violation: The Unique Nature of Sexual Sin in 1 Corinthians 6:18." *NTS* 42 (1996): 540–58.
Fitzmyer, Joseph A. "'To Know Him and the Power of His Resurrection' (Phil 3:10)." Pages 411–25 in *Mélanges bibliques en hommage au R P Béda Rigaux*. Edited by A. Descamps and A. de Halleux. Gembloux: Duculot, 1970.
Flemming, Dean. *Philippians: A Commentary in the Wesleyan Tradition*. NBBC. Kansas City: Beacon Hill, 2009.
Fowl, Stephen E. *Philippians*. Two Horizons New Testament Commentary. Grand Rapids: Eerdmans, 2005.
———. *The Story of Christ in the Ethics of Paul*. JSNTSup 36. Sheffield: JSOT Press, 1990.
Furnish, Victor Paul. *II Corinthians*. AB 32A. New York: Doubleday, 1984.
———. *The Theology of the First Letter to the Corinthians*. New Testament Theology. Cambridge: Cambridge University Press, 1999.
Gaertner, Samuel L., and John F. Dovidio. *Reducing Intergroup Bias: The Common Ingroup Identity Model*. Essays in Social Psychology. New York: Routledge, 2000.

Gaertner, Samuel L., John F. Dovidio, Phyllis Anastasio, Betty A. Bachman, and Mary C. Rust. "The Common Ingroup Identity Model: Recategorization and the Reduction of Intergroup Bias." *ERSP* 4 (1993): 1–26.

Gaffin, Richard B. *Resurrection and Redemption: A Study in Paul's Soteriology.* Peabody, MA: Hendrickson, 1978.

Garland, David E. *1 Corinthians.* BECNT. Grand Rapids: Baker, 2003.

Gaskin, John. *The Epicurean Philosophers.* Everyman Library. London: Dent, 1995.

Gaventa, Beverly Roberts. *Our Mother Saint Paul.* Louisville: Westminster John Knox, 2007.

Geoffrion, Timothy. *The Rhetorical Purpose and the Political and Military Character of Philippians: A Call to Stand Firm.* Lewiston, NY: Mellen Biblical, 1993.

Goldingay, John E. *Daniel.* WBC 30. Dallas: Word, 1989.

Goldstein, Jonathan A. *Second Maccabees: A New Translation with Introduction and Commentary.* AB. New York: Doubleday, 1983.

Goodrich, John K. "Erastus of Corinth (Romans 16.23): Responding to Recent Proposals on His Rank, Status, and Faith." *NTS* 57 (2011): 583–93.

———. "Erastus, *Quaestor* of Corinth: The Administrative Rank of ὁ οἰκονόμος τῆς πόλεως (Rom 16.23) in an Achaean Colony." *NTS* 56 (2010): 90–115.

Gorman, Michael J. *Apostle of the Crucified Lord: A Theological Introduction to Paul and His Letters.* Grand Rapids: Eerdmans, 2004.

———. *Cruciformity: Paul's Narrative Spirituality of the Cross.* Grand Rapids: Eerdmans, 2001.

———. *Inhabiting the Cruciform God: Kenosis, Justification, and Theosis in Paul's Narrative Soteriology.* Grand Rapids: Eerdmans, 2009.

Green, Joel B., *Body, Soul, and Human Life: The Nature of Humanity in the Bible.* Studies in Theological Interpretation. Grand Rapids: Baker, 2008.

———, ed. *What about the Soul? Neuroscience and Christian Anthropology.* Nashville: Abingdon, 2004.

Guerra, Anthony. *Romans and the Apologetic Tradition: The Purpose, Genre and Audience of Paul's Letter.* SNTSMS 81. Cambridge: Cambridge University Press, 1995.

Gundry, Robert H. *Sōma in Biblical Theology: With Emphasis on Pauline Anthropology.* SNTSMS 29. Cambridge: Cambridge University Press, 1976.

Gundry Volf, Judith M. *Paul and Perseverance: Staying in and Falling Away.* Louisville: Westminster John Knox, 1990.

Hafeman, Scott J. *2 Corinthians.* NIVAC. Grand Rapids: Zondervan, 2000.

Halcomb, T. Michael W. *Paul the Change Agent: The Context, Aims, and Implications of an Apostolic Innovator.* GlossaHouse Dissertation Series 2. Wilmore, KY: GlossaHouse, 2015.

Hansen, G. Walter. *The Letter to the Philippians.* Pillar New Testament Commentary. Grand Rapids: Eerdmans, 2009.

Hanson, Paul D. *The Dawn of Apocalyptic.* Philadelphia: Fortress, 1975.

Harris, Murray J. *Raised Immortal: Resurrection and Immortality in the New Testament.* Grand Rapids: Eerdmans, 1985.

Hawthorne, Gerald F., and Ralph P. Martin. *Philippians.* Rev. ed. WBC 43. Nashville: Nelson, 2004.

Hays, Richard B. *The Conversion of the Imagination: Paul as Interpreter of Israel's Scripture.* Grand Rapids: Eerdmans, 2005.

———. *First Corinthians.* Interpretation. Louisville: Westminster John Knox, 1997.

———. *The Moral Vision of the New Testament: Community, Cross, New Creation: A Contemporary Introduction to New Testament Ethics.* San Francisco: Harper Collins, 1996.

Head, Peter M. "Jesus' Resurrection in Pauline Thought: A Study in the Epistle to the Romans." Pages 58–80 in *Proclaiming the Resurrection.* Edited by Peter M. Head. Carlisle: Paternoster, 1998.

Heckel, T. K. *Der innere Mensch: Die paulinische Verarbeitung eines platonischen Motivs.* WUNT 2/53. Tübingen: Mohr Siebeck, 1993.

Hellerman, Joseph H. *Reconstructing Honor in Roman Philippi: Carmen Christi as Cursus Pudorum.* SNTSMS 132. Cambridge: Cambridge University Press, 2005.

Hengel, Martin. *Judaism and Hellenism: Studies in Their Encounter in Palestine during the Early Hellenistic Period.* London: SCM, 1974.

Hogg, Michael A., and Dominic Abrams. *Social Identifications: A Social Psychology of Intergroup Relations and Group Processes.* New York: Routledge, 1988.

Hogg, Michael A., J. C. Turner, C. Nascimento-Schulze, and D. Spriggs. "Social Categorization, Intergroup Behavior and Self-Esteem: Two Experiments." *Revista de Psicología Social* 1 (1986): 23–37.

Hollemann, Joost. *Resurrection and Parousia: A Traditio-historical Study of Paul's Eschatology in 1 Cor 15.* NovTSup 84. Leiden: Brill, 1996.

Horrell, David G. *The Social Ethos of the Corinthian Correspondence: Interests and Ideology from 1 Corinthians to 1 Clement.* Edinburgh: T&T Clark, 1996.

———. "Whither Social-Scientific Approaches to New Testament Interpretation? Reflections on Contested Methodologies and the Future." Pages 6–20 in *After the First Urban Christians: The Social-Scientific Study of Pauline Christianity Twenty-Five Years Later.* Edited by Todd D. Still and David G. Horell. New York: T&T Clark, 2009.

Hughes, Philip E. *Paul's Second Epistle to the Corinthians.* NICNT. Grand Rapids: Eerdmans, 1961.

Jewett, Robert. *Paul's Anthropological Terms: A Study of Their Use in Conflict Settings.* Leiden: Brill, 1971.

———. *Romans: A Commentary.* Hermeneia. Minneapolis: Fortress, 2006.

Johnson, Luke Timothy. *Among the Gentiles: Greco-Roman Religion and Christianity.* AYBRL. New Haven: Yale University Press, 2009.

Johnson, Mark. *The Meaning of the Body: Aesthetics of Human Understanding.* Chicago: University of Chicago Press, 2007.

Josephus. *Works.* Translated by H. St. J. Thackeray et al. 9 vols. LCL. Cambridge: Harvard University Press, 1929–1965.

Karris, R. J. "Romans 14:1–15:13 and the Occassion of Romans." Pages 65–84 in *The Romans Debate.* Edited by Karl P. Donfried. Rev. and exp. ed. Peabody, MA: Hendrickson, 1991.

Käsemann, Ernst. *Commentary on Romans.* Translated by Geoffrey William Bromiley. Grand Rapids: Eerdmans, 1980.

———. *Leib und Leib Christi.* Tübingen: Mohr, 1933.

———. *New Testament Questions of Today.* Philadelphia: Fortress, 1969.

———. *Perspectives on Paul.* Translated by M. Kohl. Philadelphia: Fortress, 1971.

Keck, Leander E. "Paul and Apocalyptic Theology." *Int* 38 (1984): 229–41.

Keener, Craig S. *1–2 Corinthians.* New Cambridge Bible Commentary. New York: Cambridge University Press, 2005.

———. *The Gospel of Matthew: A Socio-rhetorical Commentary.* Grand Rapids: Eerdmans, 2009.

Kelsey, David H. *Eccentric Existence: A Theological Anthropology.* 2 vols. Louisville: Westminster John Knox, 2009.

Kennedy, George A. *New Testament Interpretation through Rhetorical Criticism.* Chapel Hill: University of North Carolina Press, 1984.

———, ed. *Progymnasmata: Greek Textbooks of Prose and Composition.* WGRW. Atlanta: Society of Biblical Literature, 2003.

Kent, J. H. *The Inscriptions, 1926–1950.* Vol. 8.3 of *Corinth: Results of Excavations Conducted by the American School of Classical Studies at Athens.* Princeton, NJ: American School of Classical Studies at Athens, 1966.
Kim, Yung Suk. *Christ's Body in Corinth: The Politics of Metaphor.* Paul in Critical Contexts. Minneapolis: Fortress, 2008.
Kirk, J. R. Daniel. *Unlocking Romans: Resurrection and the Justification of God.* Grand Rapids: Eerdmans, 2008.
Kümmel, W. G. *Promise and Fulfillment: The Eschatological Message of Jesus.* Naperville, IL: Allenson, 1957.
LaCoque, André. *Daniel in His Time.* Columbia: University of South Carolina Press, 1988.
Laertius, Diogenes. *Books 6–10.* Vol. 2 of *Lives of Eminent Philosophers.* Translated by R. D. Hicks. LCL. Cambridge: Harvard University Press, 1925.
Lampe, Peter. "Rhetorical Analysis of Pauline Texts-Quo Vadit? Methodological Reflections." Pages 3–21 in *Paul and Rhetoric.* Edited by J. Paul Sampley and Peter Lampe. New York: T&T Clark, 2010.
Lattimore, Richard A. *Themes in Greek and Latin Epitaphs.* Urbana: University of Illinois Press, 1942.
Lee, Michelle V. *Paul, the Stoics, and the Body of Christ.* SNTSMS 137. Cambridge: Cambridge University Press, 2006.
Lehtipuu, Outi. *Debates over the Resurrection of the Dead: Constructing Early Christian Identity.* Oxford Early Christian Studies. Oxford: Oxford University Press, 2015.
Lendon, J. E. *Empire of Honour: The Art of Government in the Roman World.* Oxford: Oxford University Press, 1997.
Levenson, Jon D. *Resurrection and the Restoration of Israel: The Ultimate Victory of the God of Life.* New Haven: Yale University Press, 2006.
Lincoln, Andrew. *Paradise Now and Not Yet: Studies in the Role of the Heavenly Dimension in Paul's Thought with Special Reference to His Eschatology.* SNTSMS 43. Cambridge: Cambridge University Press, 1981.
Litwa, M. David. *Iesus Deus: The Early Christian Depiction of Jesus as a Mediterranean God.* Minneapolis: Fortress, 2014.
Long, A. A. *Stoic Studies.* Cambridge: Cambridge University Press, 1996.
Long, Fredrick J. *Ancient Rhetoric and Paul's Apology: The Compositional Unity of 2 Corinthians.* SNTSMS 131. Cambridge: Cambridge University Press, 2004.
Longenecker, Richard N. *The Epistle to the Romans.* NIGTC. Grand Rapids: Eerdmans, 2016.

———. *Introducing Romans: Critical Issues in Paul's Most Famous Letter.* Grand Rapids: Eerdmans, 2011.

———. "Is There Development in Paul's Resurrection Thought?" Pages 171–202 in *Life in the Face of Death: The Resurrection Message of the New Testament.* Edited by Richard N. Longenecker. Grand Rapids: Eerdmans, 1998.

Longman, Tremper. *Daniel.* NIVAC. Grand Rapids: Zondervan, 1999.

Lucian. *Anacharsis or Athletics; Menippus or The Descent into Hades; On Funerals; A Professor of Public Speaking.; Alexander the False Prophet; Essays in Portraiture; Essays in Portraiture Defended; The Goddesse of Surrye.* Translated by A. M. Harmon. LCL. Cambridge: Harvard University Press, 1925.

Mack, Burton L. *Rhetoric and the New Testament.* GBS. Minneapolis: Fortress, 1990.

Malcolm, Matthew R. *Paul and the Rhetoric of Reversal in 1 Corinthians: The Impact of Paul's Gospel on His Macro-rhetoric.* SNTSMS 155. Cambridge: Cambridge University Press, 2013.

Malherbe, Abraham J. "The Beasts at Ephesus." *JBL* 87 (1968): 71–80.

Malina, Bruce J. *The New Testament World: Insights from Cultural Anthropology.* 3rd ed. Louisville: Westminster John Knox, 2001.

———. "Social-Scientific Methods in Historical Jesus Research." Pages 3–26 in *The Social Setting of Jesus and the Gospels.* Edited by Wolfgang Stegemann, Bruce J. Malina, and Gerd Theissen. Minneapolis: Fortress, 2002.

Malina, Bruce J., and John J. Pilch. *Social-Science Commentary on the Letters of Paul.* Minneapolis: Fortress, 2006.

Markus, Hazel, and Paula Nurius. "Possible Selves." *American Psychologist* 41.9 (1986): 954–69.

Marshall, John. "Paul's Ethical Appeal in Philippians." Pages 357–74 in *Rhetoric and the New Testament: Essays from the 1992 Heidelberg Conference.* Edited by Stanley E. Porter and Thomas H. Olbricht. JSNTSup 90. Sheffield: JSOT Press, 1993.

Martin, Dale B. *The Corinthian Body.* New Haven: Yale University Press, 1995.

Martin, Ralph P. *2 Corinthians.* WBC 40. Dallas: Word, 1986.

Martin, Ralph P., and Brian J. Dodd, eds. *Where Christology Began: Essays on Philippians 2.* Louisville: Westminster John Knox, 1998.

Martyn, J. Louis. *Theological Issues in the Letters of Paul.* Nashville: Abingdon, 1997.

Matera, Frank J. *II Corinthians: A Commentary*. NTL. Louisville: Westminster John Knox, 2003.
Matlock, R. Barry. *Unveiling the Apocalyptic Paul: Paul's Interpreters and the Rhetoric of Criticism*. JSNTSup 127. Sheffield: Sheffield Academic, 1996.
Mauss, Marcel. "Techniques of the Body." *Economy and Society* 2 (1973): 70–88.
May, Alistair Scott. *'The Body for the Lord': Sex and Identity in 1 Corinthians 5–7*. JSNTSup 278. London: T&T Clark, 2004.
Meeks, Wayne A. *The First Urban Christians: The Social World of the Apostle Paul*. 2nd ed. New Haven: Yale University Press, 1983.
Metzger, Bruce M. *A Textual Commentary on the Greek New Testament*. 2nd ed. New York: United Bible Societies, 1994.
Miller, Stephen R. *Daniel*. NAC 18. Nashville: B&H, 1994.
Mitchell, Margaret M. *Paul and the Rhetoric of Reconciliation: An Exegetical Investigation of the Language and Composition of 1 Corinthians*. Louisville: Westminster John Knox, 1993.
Moo, Douglas J. *The Epistle to the Romans*. NICNT. Grand Rapids: Eerdmans, 1996.
Moreland, J. P., and Scott B. Rae. *Body and Soul: Human Nature and the Crisis in Ethics*. Downers Grove, IL: InterVarsity Press, 2000.
Murphy-O'Connor, Jerome. "Corinthian Slogans in 1 Cor. 6:12–20." *CBQ* 40 (1978): 390–96.
Murphy, Nancey. *Bodies and Souls, or Spirited Bodies?* Cambridge: Cambridge University Press, 2006.
Nebreda, Sergio Rosell. *Christ Identity: A Social-Scientific Reading of Philippians 2.5–11*. FRLANT 240. Göttingen: Vandenhoeck & Ruprecht, 2011.
Neusner, J., ed. *The Babylonian Talmud*. 22 vols. Peabody, MA: Hendrickson, 2011.
Newsome, James D. *The Hebrew Prophets*. Atlanta: John Knox, 1984.
Neyrey, Jerome H. *Paul, in Other Words: A Cultural Reading of His Letters*. Louisville: Westminster John Knox, 1990.
Nickelsburg, George W. E. *Resurrection, Immortality, and Eternal Life in Intertestamental Judaism and Early Christianity*. Cambridge: Harvard University Press, 2006.
Nikkel, David H. *Radical Embodiment*. Eugene, OR: Pickwick, 2010.
O'Reilly, Matthew P. "Rest Now or Not Yet? Temporal Aspects of Social Identity in Hebrews 3:7–4:11." Pages 37–53 in *Listen, Understand,*

Obey: Essays on Hebrews in Honor of Gareth Lee Cockerill. Edited by Caleb Friedeman. Eugene, OR: Pickwick, 2017.

———. "Review of *After the First Urban Christians*, Todd D. Still and David G. Horrell (eds.)." *Reviews in Religion and Theology* 19:3 (2012): 369–72.

Omanson, Roger L. "Acknowledging Paul's Quotations." *BT* 43.2 (1992): 201–13.

Osiek, Carolyn. *Philippians, Philemon*. ANTC. Nashville: Abingdon, 2000.

Paige, Terence. "Who Believes in 'Spirit'? Πνεῦμα in Pagan Usage and Implications for Gentile Christian Mission." *HTR* 95 (2002): 417–36.

Pate, C. Marvin. *The End of the Age Has Come: The Theology of Paul*. Grand Rapids: Zondervan, 1995.

Perelman, Chaïm, and L. Olbrechts-Tyteca. *The New Rhetoric: A Treatise on Argumentation*. Translated by John Wilkinson and Purcell Weaver. Repr. Notre Dame, IN: University of Notre Dame Press, 2008.

Perkins, Pheme. *First Corinthians*. Paideia Commentaries on the New Testament. Grand Rapids: Baker, 2012.

———. *Resurrection: New Testament Witness and Contemporary Reflection*. London: Geoffrey Chapman, 1984.

Peterlin, Davorin. *Paul's Letter to the Philippians in the Light of Disunity in the Church*. NovTSup 79. Leiden: Brill, 1995.

Philo. *Works*. Translated by F. H. Colson et al. 12 vols. LCL. Cambridge: Harvard University Press, 1929–1953.

Pilhofer, Peter. *Die erste christliche Gemeinde Europas*. Vol. 1 of *Philippi*. WUNT 87. Tübingen: Mohr Siebeck, 1995.

Plato. *Euthyphro; Apology; Crito; Phaedo; Phaedrus*. Translated by Harold North Fowler. LCL. Cambridge: Harvard University Press, 1914.

———. *Laches; Protagoras; Meno; Euthydemus*. Translated by W. R. M. Lamb. LCL. Cambridge: Harvard University Press, 1924.

Pliny. *Books 1–2*. Vol. 1 of *Natural History*. Translated by H. Rackham. LCL. Cambridge: Harvard University Press, 1938.

Plummer, A. *A Critical and Exegetical Commentary on the Second Epistle of Paul to the Corinthians*. ICC. Edinburgh: T & T Clark, 1915.

Porter, James I., ed. *Constructions of the Classical Body*. Body in Theory. Ann Arbor: University of Michigan Press, 1999.

Porter, Stanley E., and Bryan R. Dyer. "Oral Texts? A Reassessment of the Oral and Rhetorical Nature of Paul's Letters in Light of Recent Studies." *JETS* 55 (2012): 323–41.

Puech, Émile. *La Croyance des Esséniens en la Vie Future: Immortalité, Résurrection, Vie Éternalle? Histoire d'une Croyance dans le Judaïsme Ancien*. 2 vols. Paris: Lecoffre, 1993.
Quintilian. *The Orator's Education*. Translated by Donald A. Russell. 5 vols. LCL. Cambridge: Harvard University Press, 2001.
Rabens, Volker. *The Holy Spirit and Ethics in Paul: Transformation and Empowering for Religious-Ethical Life*. WUNT 283. Tübingen: Mohr Siebeck, 2010.
Raphael, Simcha P. *Jewish Views of the Afterlife*. Northvale, NJ: Aronson, 1994.
Reeves, Rodney. *Spirituality according to Paul: Imitating the Apostle of Christ*. Downers Grove, IL: InterVarsity Press, 2011.
Ridderbos, Herman. *Paul: An Outline of His Theology*. Translated by John Richard Dewitt. Grand Rapids: Eerdmans, 1975.
Robbins, Vernon K. *Exploring the Texture of Texts: A Guide to Socio-rhetorical Interpretation*. Valley Forge, PA: Trinity Press International, 1996.
———. *Jesus the Teacher: A Socio-rhetorical Interpretation of Mark*. Repr. Minneapolis: Fortress, 2009.
———. *The Tapestry of Early Christian Discourse: Rhetoric, Society, and Ideology*. New York: Routledge, 1996.
Robinson, James M. "Jesus from Easter to Valentinus (or to the Apostles' Creed)." *JBL* 101 (1982): 5–37.
Robinson, John A. T. *The Body: A Study in Pauline Theology*. SBT 5. Colorado Springs: Bimillenial, 1952.
Rodríguez, Rafael, and Matthew Thiessen, eds. *The So-Called Jew in Paul's Letter to the Romans*. Minneapolis: Fortress, 2016.
Roetzel, Calvin. *Paul: The Man and the Myth*. Studies on Personalities of the New Testament. Minneapolis: Fortress, 1999.
Rowland, Christopher. *The Open Heaven: A Study of Apocalyptic in Judaism and Early Christianity*. London: SPCK, 1982.
Russell, D. S. *The Method and Message of Jewish Apocalyptic*. Philadelphia: Fortress, 1964.
Sampley, J. Paul. "The First Letter to the Corinthians: Introduction, Commentary, and Reflections." *NIB* 10:771–1003.
———. *Walking between the Times: Paul's Moral Reasoning*. Minneapolis: Fortress, 1991.
Sanders, E. P. *Judaism: Practice and Belief, 63 BCE–66 CE*. Philadelphia: Trinity Press International, 1992.
———. *Paul and Palestinian Judaism*. Minneapolis: Fortress, 1977.

———. *Paul, the Law, and the Jewish People*. Philadelphia: Fortress, 1983.
Sandnes, Karl O. *Belly and Body in the Pauline Epistles*. SNTSMS 120. Cambridge: Cambridge University Press, 2002.
Saw, Insawn. *Paul's Rhetoric in 1 Corinthians 15: An Analysis Utilizing the Theories of Classical Rhetoric*. Lewiston, NY: Mellen, 1995.
Schellenberg, Ryan S. *Rethinking Paul's Rhetorical Education: Comparative Rhetoric and 2 Corinthians 10–13*. ECL 10. Atlanta: Society of Biblical Literature, 2013.
Schmeller, Thomas. *Paulus und die "Diatribe": Eine vergleichende Stilinterpretation*. NTAbh 19. Münster: Aschendorff, 1987.
Schnabel, Eckhard J. *Der erste Brief des Paulus an die Korinther*. HTA. Wuppertal: Brockhaus, 2006.
Schrage, Wolfgang, *Der erste Brief an die Korinther*. 4 vols. EKKNT 7.1–4. Zürich: Benziger, 1991–2001.
———. *The Ethics of the New Testament*. Translated by D. E. Green. Philadelphia: Fortress, 1988.
———. *Studien zur Theologie im 1. Korintherbrief*. Neukirchen-Vluyn: Neukirchener Verlag, 2007.
Schreiner, Thomas R. *Romans*. BECNT. Grand Rapids: Baker, 1998.
Schüssler Fiorenza, Elisabeth. "Rhetorical Situation and Historical Reconstruction in 1 Corinthians." *NTS* 33 (1987): 386–403.
Schweitzer, Albert. *The Mysticism of Paul the Apostle*. Translated by William Montgomery. London: Black, 1931.
———. *Paul and His Interpreters*. Repr. New York: Macmillan, 1951.
Scornaienchi, Lorenzo. *Sarx und Soma bei Paulus: Der Mensch zwischen Destruktivität und Konstruktivität*. NTOA 67. Göttingen: Vandenhoeck & Ruprecht, 2008.
Scroggs, Robin. "Paul and the Eschatological Body." Pages 14–29 in *Theology and Ethics in Paul and His Interpreters: Essays in Honor of Victor Paul Furnish*. Edited by Eugene H. Lovering and Jerry L. Sumney. Nashville: Abingdon, 1996.
Seifrid, Mark A. *The Second Letter to the Corinthians*. Pillar New Testament Commentary. Grand Rapids: Eerdmans, 2014.
Seneca. *Epistulae Morales*. Translated by R. M. Gummere. 3 vols. LCL. Cambridge: Harvard University Press, 1917–1925.
Setzer, Claudia. *Resurrection of the Body in Early Judaism and Early Christianity: Doctrine, Community, and Self-Definition*. Boston: Brill, 2004.
———. "Resurrection of the Dead as Symbol and Strategy." *JAAR* 69.4 (2001): 65–101.

Shantz, Colleen. *Paul in Ecstasy: The Neurobiology of the Apostle's Life and Thought*. New York: Cambridge University Press, 2009.
Shilling, Chris. *The Body and Social Theory*. Theory, Culture & Society. 2nd ed. London: Sage, 2003.
Shires, H. M. *The Eschatology of Paul in Light of Modern Scholarship*. Philadelphia: Westminster, 1966.
Stacey, David. *The Pauline View of Man in Relation to Its Judaic and Hellenistic Background*. London: Macmillan, 1956.
Stambaugh, John E., and David L. Balch. *The New Testament in Its Social Environment*. LEC 2. Philadelphia: Westminster, 1986.
Stamps, D. L. "Rethinking the Rhetorical Situation: The Entextualization of the Situation in New Testament Epistles." Pages 193–210 in *Rhetoric and the New Testament: Essays from the 1992 Heidelberg Conference*. Edited by Stanley E. Porter and Thomas H. Olbricht. Sheffield: Sheffield Academic, 1993.
Stone, Michael E. *Features of the Eschatology of IV Ezra*. HSS 35. Atlanta: Scholars Press, 1989.
Stowers, Stanley K. *Letter Writing in Greco-Roman Antiquity*. LEC 5. Philadelphia: Westminster, 1986.
———. *A Rereading of Romans: Justice, Jews, and Gentiles*. New Haven: Yale University Press, 1994.
Strobel, August. *Der erste Brief an die Korinther*. ZBK NT 6.1. Zürich: Theologischer Verlag Zürich, 1989.
Tajfel, Henri. "Interindividual Behavior and Intergroup Behavior." Pages 27–60 in *Differentiations between Social Groups: Studies in the Social Psychology of Intergroup Relations*. Edited by Henri Tajfel. London: Academic, 1978.
———. "Introduction." Pages 1–11 in *Social Identity and Intergroup Relations*. Edited by Henri Tajfel. European Studies in Social Psychology. Cambridge: Cambridge University Press, 1982.
———. "Social Categorization, Social Identity and Social Comparison." *Differentiation between Social Groups*. Edited by Henri Tajfel. European Monographs in Social Psychology. London: Academic, 1978.
Talbert, Charles H. *Reading Corinthians: A Literary and Theological Commentary on 1 and 2 Corinthians*. New York: Crossroad, 1987.
Theissen, Gerd. *The Social Setting of Pauline Christianity: Essays on Corinth*. Translated by John H. Schütz. Eugene, OR: Wipf & Stock, 2004.
Thiessen, Matthew. *Paul and the Gentile Problem*. New York: Oxford University Press, 2016.

Thiselton, Anthony C. *The First Epistle to the Corinthians*. NIGTC. Grand Rapids: Eerdmans, 2000.

———. "Realized Eschatology at Corinth." *NTS* 24 (1978): 510–26.

Thrall, Margaret. *A Critical and Exegetical Commentary on the Second Epistle to the Corinthians*. 2 vols. ICC. Edinburgh: T&T Clark, 1994–2000.

Tobin, Thomas H. *Paul's Rhetoric in Its Contexts: The Argument of Romans*. Peabody, MA: Hendrickson, 2004.

Tucker, J. Brian. *"Remain in Your Calling": Paul and the Continuation of Social Identities in 1 Corinthians*. Eugene, OR: Pickwick, 2011.

———. *You Belong to Christ: Paul and the Formation of Social Identity in 1 Corinthians 1–4*. Eugene, OR: Pickwick, 2010.

Tucker, J. Brian, and Coleman A. Baker, eds. *T&T Clark Handbook to Social Identity in the New Testament*. London: Bloomsbury T&T Clark, 2014.

Tuckett, Christopher M. "The Corinthians Who Say 'There Is No Resurrection of the Dead' (1 Cor 15,12)." Pages 247–75 in *The Corinthian Correspondence*. Edited by Reinmund Bieringer. BETL 125. Leuven: Leuven University Press, 1996.

Turner, John C., Michael A. Hogg, Penelope J. Oakes, Stephen D. Reicher, and Margaret S. Wetherell. *Rediscovering the Social Group: A Self-Categorization Theory*. Oxford: Blackwell, 1987.

Vos, Geerhardus. *The Pauline Eschatology*. Princeton: Princeton University Press, 1930.

Vos, Johan S. "Argumentation und Situation in 1 Kor. 15." *NovT* 41 (1999): 313–33.

Vouga, François. "Römer 1,18—3,20 als narratio." *TGl* 77 (1987): 225–36.

Wallace, Daniel B. *Greek Grammar Beyond the Basics: An Exegetical Syntax of the New Testament*. Grand Rapids: Zondervan, 1996.

Watson, Duane F. "Paul's Rhetorical Strategy in 1 Corinthians 15." Pages 231–49 in *Rhetoric and the New Testament: Essays from the 1992 Heidelberg Conference*. Edited by Stanley E. Porter and Thomas H. Olbricht. Sheffield: Sheffield Academic Press, 1993.

———. *The Rhetoric of the New Testament: A Bibliographic Survey*. Blandford Forum: Deo, 2006.

———. "A Rhetorical Analysis of Philippians and Its Implicatons for the Unity Question." *NovT* 30 (1988): 57–88.

———. "The Three Species of Rhetoric and the Study of the Pauline Epistles." Pages 25–47 in *Paul and Rhetoric*. Edited by J. Paul Sampley and Peter Lampe. New York: T&T Clark, 2010.

Watson, Francis. *Paul, Judaism, and the Gentiles: Beyond the New Perspective.* Grand Rapids: Eerdmans, 2007.
Welborn, L. L. "On the Discord in Corinth: 1 Corinthians 1–4 and Ancient Politics." *JBL* 106 (1987): 83–113.
———. *Politics and Rhetoric in the Corinthian Epistles.* Macon, GA: Mercer University Press, 1997.
White, John L. *Light from Ancient Letters.* Philadelphia: Fortress, 1986.
White, Joel R. "Recent Challenges to the *communis opinio* on 1 Corinthians 15:29." *CurBR* 10 (2012): 379–95.
Wilckens, Ulrich. *Der Brief an die Römer.* 3 vols. EKKNT. Zurich: Benziger, 1978–1982.
Witherington, Ben. *Conflict and Community in Corinth: A Socio-rhetorical Commentary on 1 and 2 Corinthians.* Grand Rapids: Eerdmans, 1995.
———. *Friendship and Finances in Philippi: The Letter of Paul to the Philippians.* The New Testament in Context. Valley Forge, PA: Trinity Press International, 1994.
———. *Jesus, Paul, and the End of the World: A Comparative Study in New Testament Eschatology.* Downers Grove, IL: InterVarsity Press, 1992.
———. *New Testament Rhetoric: An Introductory Guide to the Art of Persuasion in and of the New Testament.* Eugene, OR: Cascade, 2009.
———. *Paul's Letter to the Philippians.* Grand Rapids: Eerdmans, 2011.
Witherington, Ben, and Darlene Hyatt. *Paul's Letter to the Romans: A Socio-rhetorical Commentary.* Grand Rapids: Eerdmans, 2004.
Wright, N. T. "The Letter to the Romans: Introduction, Commentary, and Reflections." *NIB* 10:393–770.
———. *The New Testament and the People of God.* Minneapolis: Fortress, 1992.
———. *Paul and the Faithfulness of God.* Minneapolis: Fortress, 2013.
———. *Pauline Perspectives: Essays on Paul, 1978–2013.* Minneapolis: Fortress, 2013.
———. *The Resurrection of the Son of God.* Minneapolis: Fortress, 2003.
Wuellner, Wilhelm. "Greek Rhetoric and Pauline Argumentation." Pages 177–88 in *Early Christian Literature and the Classical Tradition: In Honorem Robert M. Grant.* Edited by William R. Schoedel and Robert L. Wilken. Paris: Beauchesne, 1979.
———. "Paul's Rhetoric of Argumentation in Romans: An Alternative to the Donfried-Karris Debate." Pages 128–46 in *The Romans Debate.* Edited by Karl P. Donfried. Rev. and exp. ed. Peabody, MA: Hendrickson, 1991.

Young, Francis, and D. F. Ford. *Meaning and Truth in Second Corinthians.* BFT. Grand Rapids: Eerdmans, 1987.

Zeller, Dieter. *Der erste Brief an die Korinther.* KEK. Göttingen: Vandenhoeck & Ruprecht, 2010.

Ziesler, John. *Pauline Christianity.* Rev ed. Oxford Bible Series. Oxford: Oxford University Press, 1983.

Ancient Sources Index

Hebrew Bible/Old Testament

Genesis
- 2:7 — 87
- 2:24 — 105
- 12:2–3 — 155
- 13:15–17 — 155
- 15:5 — 155
- 15:6 — 162
- 15:12–21 — 155
- 17:4–8 — 155
- 17:8 — 155
- 17:9–14 — 162
- 17:23–27 — 162
- 18:18 — 155
- 22:17–18 — 155
- 28:15 — 113

Exodus
- 19:44 — 146
- 29:1–36 — 146
- 30:29–30 — 146

Deuteronomy
- 31:6 — 113

Joshua
- 5:1 — 113

Job
- 10 — 3

Psalms
- 2:7–9 — 155
- 8:5–8 — 70
- 8:6 — 70
- 87:5 — 60
- 87:11 — 60
- 110:1 — 69
- 115:1 — 117

Ecclesiastes
- 10:9 — 74

Isaiah
- 22:13 — 76
- 25:8 — 93
- 26:14 — 11
- 26:29 — 11
- 55:3–5 — 155

Ezekiel
- 37 — 12

Daniel
- 1:8–16 — 131
- 1:10 — 74
- 12:1–3 — 11
- 12:2–3 — 12
- 12:3 — 83
- 12:13 — 11

Hosea
- 6:2 — 12
- 13:14 — 93

Jonah
- 1:4 — 74

Deuterocanonical Books

Judith
  12:1–4 — 131

Additions to Esther
  4:17ˣ — 132

Wisdom of Solomon
  3:1–4 — 51

Sirach
  43:1–10 — 81
  44:19–21 — 155

1 Maccabees
  2:15–28 — 203
  2:49–68 — 203

2 Maccabees
  7:1 — 203
  7:2 — 13, 203
  7:7 — 13, 204
  7:9 — 13, 204, 205
  7:11 — 13, 204, 205
  7:14 — 13, 204
  7:23 — 13, 204, 206
  7:32–28 — 116

3 Maccabees
  3:4–7 — 101

4 Maccabees
  6:27–29 — 116
  7:11–15 — 122
  17:20–22 — 116
  18:23 — 11

Pseudepigrapha

Apocalypse of Moses
  13.3–5 — 16
  20.1–2 — 154
  21.6 — 154
  41.1–3 — 16
  43.2–3 — 16

Apocalypse of Sedrach
  6.5 — 155

2 Baruch
  14.13 — 155
  25.2–4 — 116
  51.10 — 83
  51.13 — 155

3 Baruch
  4.16 — 154

1 Enoch
  5.3 — 14
  38.1–6 — 14
  45.5 — 14
  47.4 — 14
  50.1–5 — 14
  51.1 — 14
  51.2–5 — 14
  62.15 — 83
  90.13–19 — 116
  91.1–9 — 14
  91.10–11 — 14
  91.12 — 116
  91.19 — 14
  102.4 — 14
  103.2–3 — 51
  103.3–8 — 11
  103.4 — 14
  104.1–4 — 14
  105.11–12 — 83
  108.11–15 — 14

4 Ezra
  5.1–9 — 116
  6.17–25 — 116
  7.32 — 15
  7.32–37 — 15
  7.79 — 15
  7.85 — 15
  7.95 — 15
  9.1–12 — 116

13.29–31	116	Philo, *De fuga et inventione*	
14.35	15	68.1–72	122

Jubilees

		Philo, *De migratione Abrahami*	
22.14	155	2	11
23.31	51		
32.19	155	Philo, *De opificio mundi*	
		46	11

Psalms of Solomon	3.11–12
15	

Philo, *Quod deterius potiori insidari soleat*
22 11

Pseudo-Phocylides
105–115 11

Philo, *De specialibus legibus*
1.295 11
4.24 11

Testament of Abraham
20:14–15 11

New Testament

Testament of Benjamin
10.6–9 16

Matthew
26:60 62
27:52 63

Testament of Judah
25.4 16

Mark
12:18 11, 59

Testament of Levi
18.3 16

John
12:24 79

Testament of Moses
9 203
10.1–10 16

Acts
7:60 63
18:2 45
18:8 45
18:24 45
19:1 45
23:8 59
23:7–9 11

Ancient Jewish Writers

Josephus, *Antiquitates judaicae*
18.16 11

Josephus, *Bellum judaicum*
2.165 11

Romans
1:3–5 155
1:4 152, 180
1:12 133
1:16–17 149
1:18 149
2:7 154
3:8 136

Philo, *De Abrahamo*
258 51

Philo, *De ebrietate*
26 11

Romans (cont.)			
3:21–26	149	6:16	135, 146
3:23	154	6:19	166
3:29–30	162	6:21	147
3:30	162	6:22	166
4:9	162	6:23	141
4:9–12	162	7:22	122
4:11	162, 163	7:25	143
4:12	163	8:4	137
4:16	163	8:5	150
4:17	163, 164	8:5–8	81, 150, 151
4:18–20	164	8:5–16	154
4:19	164	8:7	150
4:23–34	164	8:9	151, 152, 157
4:24	163, 164	8:9–12	211, 211
5:1	134	8:9–25	2, 157
5:10	113	8:10	151, 152
5:12	150, 154	8:10–11	143, 144
5:12–17	138	8:11	152, 153, 163, 211
5:12–21	139, 142	8:12	157
5:17	155	8:13	81, 151
5:20	145	8:14	157, 211
5:21	136, 138, 143, 145	8:15	157, 156
6:1–3	83, 134, 135	8:16	157
6:1–11	142	8:17	123, 154, 155, 157
6:1–14	145	8:17–18	211
6:1–23	2	8:17–25	155
6:2	135, 143	8:18	159
6:3–5	113	8:19	159
6:4	144	8:19–23	211
6:5	137, 138, 143, 144	8:21	159
6:6	122, 136, 138, 139, 140, 143	8:22–24	160
6:7	141, 142,	8:23	67, 144, 153, 156, 211
6:8	138, 142, 143, 144	8:24	157
6:8–10	142	8:32	155
6:9	142	11:16	67
6:10	142	11:17–22	180
6:11	142	11:18	167
6:12	139, 142, 143, 144, 152	12–15	133, 149, 166
6:12–14	140, 151, 166	12:1	140, 166, 167, 213
6:13	140, 167	12:1–2	166
6:14	145	12:2	166
6:15	135, 145, 146	13:13	158
6:15–16	135	14–15	41, 140, 162, 170
6:15–23	145	14:1	167
		14:1–15:13	165, 167

Ancient Sources Index 241

14:3–4	168	5:1–6:20	97
14:7–8	168	5:1–16:12	45
14:9	168	5:11	97
14:10	167, 168	6:1–3	83
14:13	167	6:1–11	45, 97
15:1	168	6:10–11	45
15:1–3	168	6:12	97, 98, 99, 100, 101, 106
15:6	168	6:12–20	2, 19, 22, 41, 43, 45, 49, 97, 100–104, 106, 108, 127, 215
15:7	165, 168		
15:7–12	168	6:13	97, 99, 180, 100, 101, 107
15:8–9	169	6:14	49, 97, 99, 102, 105
15:10–11	169	6:15	97, 103
15:13	166	6:15–16	104, 197
16:8	184	6:16	105
16:18	22	6:16–17	104, 105
16:23	46, 47	6:17	105
		6:18	97, 106
1 Corinthians		6:19	99, 105, 107, 210
1:1–3	44	6:20	97, 99, 107
1:4–9	44	7:3–4	98
1:10	44, 47, 48	7:4	106
1:10–12	49	7:5	106
1:10–4:21	44	7:6	106
1:11	47	7:32–35	106
1:11–17	45	8:1–10:22	45
1:12	47, 48, 58	8:7	45
1:14	45	9:1–10:13	44
1:16	46	9:27	180
1:18–4:21	45	10:11	70, 166
1:18–16:12	45	10:23	98
1:19–3:21	44	11:17–22	46
1:20	166	11:22	46
1:26	46	11:26–27	75
2:6	85, 166	12:2	45
2:6–8	70	13:1–3	52
2:7	70	13:1–13	44
2:8	70, 166	15:1–3	56
2:9	85	15:1–11	56, 67
2:14	86	15:3–5	56
2:14–15	85, 87	15:12	56–60, 62, 77, 102, 109
3:1–3	87	15:12–19	52, 57, 58, 65, 66, 67, 94
3:18	70, 166	15:12–28	61
4:8	50	15:12–58	2, 41, 43, 49, 95
4:18	58	15:13	57, 61, 62
5:1–13	97	15:13–19	56

1 Corinthians (cont.)			
15:14	62, 93, 102	15:46	86, 88
15:15	62, 63	15:47	88
15:16	57	15:47–49	88, 94, 94
15:17	63	15:48	87, 88, 89
15:18	63, 66	15:49	89, 90, 91
15:18–19	57	15:50	92
15:19	64	15:50–57	94
15:20	57, 67	15:50–58	19, 92, 211
15:20–28	67, 71, 78, 94, 210	15:51	92
15:21	69	15:51–52	124
15:21–22	69	15:52	92
15:21–28	57	15:53	93
15:22	63, 69	15:54–55	88
15:22–23	50	15:55–57	93
15:23	67, 68, 72, 124	15:57	93
15:24	68, 70	15:58	49, 93, 127
15:24–26	93	16:5–9	109
15:25	69	16:8–9	76
15:25–28	69	16:13–14	45
15:26	68, 69, 88, 211	16:19–24	45
15:27	50	2 Corinthians	
15:29	66, 72, 73, 76, 77	1:5–17	109, 111
15:29–34	49, 57, 72, 77, 99, 104, 127, 215	1:6	116
		1:8–9	113
15:30	74	1:9	117
15:31	75	1:9–10	121
15:32	53, 75, 76	1:10	117
15:32–34	52	1:12	111
15:33	77	1:23	111
15:33–34	90	2:1	109
15:34	77, 78, 80	2:13	109
15:35	20, 51, 78, 82, 86	2:14	109
15:35–49	57, 78, 91, 94	2:17	111
15:37	79, 80	3:1–4:6	112
15:37–41	56	3:3	117
15:39–41	80	3:6	117
15:40	81	4:4	166
15:42	82, 92–93	4:6	112, 123
15:42–43	86	4:6–5:10	121
15:42–44	84	4:7	112, 122
15:42–49	82	4:7–11	122
15:43	211	4:7–12	116
15:44	20, 21, 51, 82, 86, 87, 105, 210	4:7–15	112, 118
15:45	86, 87, 120	4:7–5:10	2, 41, 112, 127

4:8–9	122	13:4	180
4:10	75, 113, 115, 122		
4:10–11	119, 122	Galatians	
4:10–12	112	1:4	166
4:11	115, 122	1:6–9	172
4:12	115, 119	4:3–5	30
4:14	112, 117, 118, 119, 121, 210		
4:15	119, 121	Ephesians	
4:16	120, 216	1:12–20	180
4:16–18	120		
4:16–5:5	120, 121, 125	Philippians	
4:17	123	1:1–2	177
4:18	123	1:3–11	177
5:1	123, 124, 125	1:7	181
5:1–4	120	1:12–14	194, 203
5:2–4	121	1:12–26	177, 178, 195, 198
5:2	124	1:14	181, 195
5:3	120	1:17	181, 195
5:3–4	124	1:20	181, 195, 196, 197, 198
5:4	124, 125, 214	1:20–21	214
5:6	125	1:20–22	178
5:6–10	112	1:20–23	121, 125
5:7	125	1:22	181, 197
5:8	214	1:23	214
5:10	111, 118, 126	1:24	197
5:12	123	1:27	173, 174, 176, 182, 200
6:14–7:1	111	1:27–28	173, 199
7:2	109	1:27–30	177, 182
7:4–5	110	1:28	172
7:4–16	110	1:28–29	177
7:5	113	1:28–30	172
8:20–21	111	1:29–30	203
10:2	111	1:30	172
10:12–18	109	2:1–4	173, 177
11:2	118	2:1–30	
11:3	118	2:1–3:4	177
11:4–15	109	2:5	192, 200
11:7–10	109	2:5–8	177
11:7–12	111	2:5–11	177, 192, 207, 214
12:2	114	2:6	193
12:2–3	198	2:6–8	194, 201
12:2–4		2:6–11	192, 193, 200
12:14–18	109	2:7	192, 193
12:19	111	2:8	185, 192, 193
13:1	111	2:9	193

Philippians (cont.)

2:9–11	193
2:14–15	173
2:19–30	177
2:25–30	173
3:1–4:1	177, 178
3:2	185
3:2–3	206
3:4	200
3:4–6	201
3:5–6	206
3:7–8	201
3:7–11	206
3:7–16	177
3:8	178, 201
3:9	206
3:10	113, 201
3:10–11	75, 178–79, 184–85, 194, 200, 204, 206–7
3:10–14	177
3:11	180, 181, 201, 215
3:12–14	181
3:12–4:1	2, 209
3:14	185
3:15	184, 200
3:15–17	173
3:17–21	183
3:18	184, 206
3:18–19	183, 185
3:19	22, 184, 200, 211
3:20	182, 186, 190, 211
3:20–21	180, 181, 194
3:21	124, 177–78, 184–86, 188, 198, 200, 204, 211
4:1	200
4:2	200
4:2–3	172, 178
4:4–8	178
4:4–9	177, 178
4:10–20	173, 178, 179
4:21–23	178

Colossians

2:12	180

1 Thessalonians

4:13	63
4:13–17	
4:15	124
4:15–16	124
4:16	93

2 Peter

3:4	63

Rabinic Works

b. Sanhedrin

90b	11

Genesis Rabbah

12.6	154

Targum Pseudo-Jonathan

Gen 2.25	154

Greco–Roman Literature

Aristotle, *De anima*

412a	7
415b	7

Aristotle, *De caelo*

2.8	81

Aristotle, *Rhetorica*

1.3.3	111
1.3.3–6	176
1.3.4	111
1.3.5	56
1.3.9	111
1.6.29	191
1.9.40	176, 191
1.10.1	111
1.33–34	193
3.16.11	57
3.16.1417b	195
3.19	92

Ancient Sources Index

Cicero, *De invention rhetorica*		Homer, *Odyssea*	
1.57	135	11.204–222	54
Cicero, *De natura deorum*		Lucian, *Menippus* (*Necyomantia*)	
2.115–116	8	17	60
2.118	9	18	60
Cicero, *De oratore*		Plato, *Cratulus*	
2.334	176	403b	125
Cicero, *Partitiones oratoriae*		Plato, *Gorgias*	
4.13	195	524d	125
8.7	65		
15.53	65	Plato, *Phaedo*	
		69e–70a	54
Cicero, *De republica*		80–83	5
5.6	188	81e–83b	52
Cicero, *De senectute*		Plato, *Phaedrus*	
77	9	245c–247c	5
Demosthenes, *Epistulae*		Plato, *Respublica*	
1.2	189	9.588–589	122
Demonsthenes, *In Cononem*		Pliny the Elder, *Naturalis historia*	
31	62	7:51–52	9
Demosthenes, [*In Neaeram*]		Plutarch, *Romulus*	
6	62	28.7–8	51
Dio Chrysostom, *De virtue* (*Or. 8*)		Quintilian, *Institutio oratoria*	
8.20–25	76	2.4.21	183
		3.8	176
Diogenes Laertius, *Vitae philosophorum*		3.8.1–2	176
7.143	8	3.8.11	195
10	6	3.8.12	65
10.63	6	3.8.13	196
10.65	7	3.8.23	176
		3.8.34	199
Epictetus, *Diatribai* (*Dissertationes*)		3.8.35	56
2.16.13	79	3.8.38–41	61
3.13.17	79	4.2.1	195
3.22.85	79	5.8.7	61
		5.13.52–58	57
		9.2.6	134

9.2.14	134
9.2.16–17	135

Rhetorica ad Herennium
2.3.5	111
2.30.47	92
3.3	176
4.16.24	134, 135

Seneca (the Younger), *Epistulae morales*
65.16	51

Modern Authors Index

Abrams, Dominic 34–35, 119, 190
Allison, Dale C. 27
Amador, J. D. H. 110
Aune, David E. 29, 133
Avery-Peck, A. J. 10
Bachmann, Philipp 67
Bailey, Kenneth E. 51
Baker, Coleman A. 33–34
Balch, David L. 37
Barclay, John M. G. 84–87, 131, 139–40, 143–45, 153, 158, 162, 166, 172
Barnett, Paul 110, 113–14, 116–18, 123–24
Barrett, C. K. 50, 63–64, 69, 88, 97, 107, 185
Barton, Carlin A. 188
Barton, Stephen C. 59, 65–66, 187, 196
Basevi, Claudio 176
Bauckham, Richard 30
Beker, J. Christiaan 27, 29, 112, 114, 116, 130
Betz, Hans Dieter 38, 122
Bieringer, Reinmund 50, 110
Bird, Michael F. 129
Blackwell, Ben C. 158
Bloomquist, L. Gregory 176
Bockmuehl, Markus 182, 184–85, 193, 196
Boer, Martinus C de 29, 51, 61, 69, 130
Boismard, Marie-Emile 120–21
Bolt, Peter G. 6, 9
Booth, Alan 100
Brookins, Timothy A. 47
Brown, Alexandra 29
Brown, Paul J. 50–55, 58, 63, 67–68, 72, 74, 78, 80, 88–91, 93
Brown, Peter 1
Bruce, F. F. 51
Brucker, Ralph 176
Bryan, Christopher 132, 134
Bultmann, Rudolf 2, 17–18, 140, 153, 196
Bunker, Michael 44
Byrne, Brendan J. 159
Campbell, Constantine R. 136
Campbell, Douglas A. 29, 161, 164
Campbell, William S. 175, 201–2
Cave, David 3
Chamblin, J. K. 17
Chapa, Juan 176
Charles, R. H. 10
Churchland, Patricia Smith 3
Ciampa, Roy E. 73
Cinnirella, Marco 35–36, 41, 59–60, 65, 78, 94–95, 118, 126, 157, 161, 164, 175, 187, 211, 214
Clarke, Andrew D. 47
Cohen, Shaye J. D. 12
Collange, Jean-Francois 114
Collins, John J. 11, 15, 29
Collins, Raymond F. 62, 73, 76, 85, 92, 98–99
Condor, Susan 35
Conzelmann, Hans. 69, 72–73, 97
Cooper, John W. 3, 18, 198
Cousar, Charles B. 29
Cranfield, C. E. B. 135, 139–40
Crick, Francis H. 3
Cullmann, Oscar 4, 27
Dahl, M. E. 17
Danker, F. W. 110

Deissmann, A. 45
Dodd, Brian J. 98, 192
Dodd, C. H. 25–27
Donfried, Karl P. 129–30, 133
Douglas, Mary 18–19, 32, 37
Dovidio, John F. 36, 119–20, 165
Dunn, James D. G. 17, 28, 32, 51, 63, 73, 88, 95, 113, 115, 131, 136, 138, 140–41, 143, 146, 148, 150–51, 156, 159–60, 166, 179–81, 183
Dyer, Bryan R. 39
Edart, Jean-Baptiste 177–78, 198
Edwards, Catherine 199
Elliot, John H. 32
Elliot, Neil 135
Enderlein, Steven E. 154–55
Endsjo, Dag Oistein 1, 9, 53, 81, 83, 92
Engberg-Pedersen, Troels 1, 5, 20, 21, 84
Eriksson, A. 55
Esler, Philip F. 34–35, 58–59, 131, 136, 147, 155, 159–63, 166–67
Fee, Gordon D. 28–29, 45, 50, 58, 60, 62–63, 67, 70, 73, 76, 80, 83, 88, 97, 105, 107, 117, 172–73, 179–81, 183–85, 192, 197
Festugiere, A. J. 6
Finney, Mark T. 79–83, 85
Fisk, Bruce N. 103–4, 107
Fitzmyer, Joseph A. 179–80
Ford, D. F. 110, 111
Fowl, Stephen E. 184, 192–93
Furnish, Victor Paul. 102, 113, 117
Gaertner, Samuel L. 36, 119–20, 165, 174
Gaffin, Richard B. 27, 28, 152–53
Garland, David E. 51, 58, 62, 64, 68, 72–73, 75–76, 85, 88, 98
Gaskin, John 6–7
Gaventa, Beverly Roberts 29
Geoffrion, Timothy 176
Goldingay, John E. 11
Goldstein, Jonathan A. 204–5
Goodrich, John K. 47
Gorman, Michael J. 29, 116, 135, 139, 166

Green, Joel B. 3, 17–18
Guerra, Anthony 133
Gundry, Robert H. 17–18, 85, 104–5, 139, 151, 196–97
Gundry Volf, Judith M. 28
Hafeman, Scott J. 110, 116
Halcomb, T. Michael W. 137
Hansen, G. Walter 172–73, 176, 179, 186, 192, 195
Hanson, Paul D. 29
Harris, Murray J. 152, 179
Hawthorne, Gerald F. 17, 29, 185, 196
Hays, Richard B. 28, 48, 51, 73, 98, 102–3, 161–62, 183
Head, Peter M. 129
Heckel, T. K. 122
Hellerman, Joseph H. 158, 189, 194, 201–2
Hengel, Martin 12
Hogg, Michael A. 34–35, 119, 190
Hollemann, Joost 67
Horrell, David G. 37, 45–46
Hughes, Philip E. 117
Jewett, Robert 81, 133, 156, 159
Johnson, Luke Timothy 54
Johnson, Mark 65, 66
Karris, Robert J. 130–31
Kasemann, Ernst 17–18, 27, 29, 131, 145
Keck, Leander E. 29–30
Keener, Craig S. 44, 48, 79
Kelsey, David H. 1, 3–4, 95–97
Kennedy, George A. 12, 38, 44, 110, 132–33, 175–76, 183
Kent, J. H. 46
Kim, Yung Suk 17
Kirk, J. R. Daniel 12, 15–16, 28, 129–31, 136, 138, 141–42, 145, 147, 151, 164
Kummel, W. G. 27
LaCoque, Andre 11
Lampe, Peter 39, 40, 111
Lattimore, Richard A. 52
Lee, Michelle V. 8, 17
Lehtipuu, Outi 59
Lendon, J. E. 158

Levenson, Jon D.	16	O'Reilly, Matthew P.	37, 212
Lincoln, Andrew	27, 50–51, 81–83, 85, 87, 89–91, 123–25, 181–82, 184–85	Osiek, Carolyn	189
		Paige, Terence	86
Litwa, M. David	9	Pate, C. Marvin	24, 28
Long, A. A.	5, 8	Perelman, Chaim	38, 135
Long, Fredrick J.	110	Perkins, Pheme	12, 73
Longenecker, Richard N.	6, 120, 135–37, 143, 150–52, 160, 166	Peterlin, Davorin	173
		Pilch, John J.	201
Longman, Tremper	11	Pilhofer, Peter	188–89
Mack, Burton L.	56–57, 92	Plummer, A.	117
Malcolm, Matthew R.	50, 53, 55	Porter, James I.	1, 188, 199
Malherbe, Abraham J.	76	Porter, Stanley E.	39, 56, 176
Malina, Bruce J.	32, 37, 201	Puech, Émile	10
Markus, Hazel	35	Rabens, Volker	84
Marshall, John	176	Raphael, Simcha P.	10
Martin, Dale B.	1, 6, 8, 12, 19–20, 44, 48, 51–52, 60, 72, 84, 89, 100, 107	Reeves, Rodney	28
		Ridderbos, Herman	27, 166
Martin, Ralph P.	17, 29, 114–16, 185, 192, 196	Robbins, Vernon K.	30, 31
		Robinson, James M.	193
Martyn, J. Louis	29	Robinson, John A. T.	17, 196
Matera, Frank J.	110, 112–14, 117, 122	Rodríguez, Rafael	131
Matlock, R. Barry	29	Roetzel, Calvin	28
Mauss, Marcel	32	Rosner, Brian S.	73
May, Alistair Scott	48, 98–100, 103–7	Rowland, Christopher	29
Meeks, Wayne A.	1, 37, 46, 136	Russell, D. S.	29
Metzger, Bruce M.	89–90, 117, 124	Sampley, J.	28, 39, 50, 111
Miller, Stephen R.	11	Sanders, E. P.	10, 139, 160
Mitchell, Margaret M.	40, 44–45, 47, 58, 95, 97, 191	Sandnes, Karl O.	6, 22, 52–53, 72, 76–78, 98–101, 172, 176, 181, 185–87
Moo, Douglas J.	131–32, 136, 138, 141, 151–52, 155	Saw, Insawn	44, 56, 61, 63, 92–93
		Schellenberg, Ryan S.	40
Moreland, J. P.	3, 18	Schmeller, Thomas	52
Murphy-O'Connor, Jerome	97, 107	Schnabel, Eckhard J.	51, 73–75, 98
Murphy, Nancey	3	Schrage, Wolfgang	28, 50, 52, 73, 98–100, 183
Nebreda, Sergio Rosell	175		
Neusner, Jacob	10	Schreiner, Thomas R.	140, 166
Newsome, James D.	11	Schüssler Fiorenza, Elisabeth	44
Neyrey, Jerome H.	17–20, 43, 48, 136	Schweitzer, Albert	24–27, 104
Nickelsburg, George W. E.	10–11, 13, 203, 205–6	Scornaienchi, Lorenzo	22–23, 153
		Scroggs, Robin	83
Nikkel, David H.	1	Seifrid, Mark A.	30, 110, 115–16, 118, 122
Norris, Rebecca Sachs	3		
Nurius, Paula	35	Setzer, Claudia	59, 68
Olbrechts-Tyteca, L.	38, 135	Shantz, Colleen	2, 124, 152
Omanson, Roger L.	98, 107	Shilling, Chris	95

Shires, H. M.	17	Ziesler, John	27
Sprinkle, Preston M.	129		
Stacey, David	17		
Stambaugh, John E.	37		
Stamps, D. L.	56		
Stone, Michael E.	14–15		
Stowers, Stanley K.	39, 131		
Strobel, August	52		
Tajfel, Henri	33–35		
Talbert, Charles H.	73		
Theissen, Gerd	37, 46–47		
Thiessen, Matthew	131		

Thiselton, Anthony C. 21, 50, 55, 57, 60, 62–64, 67–70, 73, 75–77, 80–81, 84–85, 98–104, 107
Thrall, Margaret 110, 112–13, 120
Tobin, Thomas H. 136
Tucker, J. Brian 33–34, 48–50, 68
Tuckett, Christopher M. 50
Turner, John C. 34, 118
Vos, Geerhardus 24, 27
Vos, Johan S. 52, 60, 61
Vouga, François 133
Wallace, Daniel B. 61
Watson, Duane F. 38, 56, 67, 90, 110–11, 133, 171–72, 176–78, 195
Watson, Francis 131–32
Welborn, Larry L. 47
White, John L. 39
White, Joel R. 73
Wilckens, Ulrich 138–39
Witherington, Ben 28, 31, 38, 40, 44–48, 50, 56–57, 61–62, 68, 73, 85, 92, 97, 110–11, 125, 134–35, 149, 162, 173, 176–78, 180, 182–84, 187, 189, 192–93, 195, 198
Wright, N. T. 6, 10–12, 28–29, 51, 54, 60, 64, 69–70, 75, 77, 79, 82–85, 88, 92, 101–2, 112, 115–16, 121–22, 125, 129, 136, 138–41, 144–47, 150, 152–53, 155–56, 159, 161–62, 166, 171, 180–82, 190, 193
Wuellner, Wilhelm 43–44, 133
Young, Francis 110–11
Zeller, Dieter 53

www.ingramcontent.com/pod-product-compliance
Lightning Source LLC
Chambersburg PA
CBHW030438300426
44112CB00009B/1054